AHMANSON · MURPHY
FINE ARTS IMPRINT

THE AHMANSON FOUNDATION
has endowed this imprint
to honor the memory of
FRANKLIN D. MURPHY
who for half a century
served arts and letters,
beauty and learning, in
equal measure by shaping
with a brilliant devotion
those institutions upon
which they rely.

The publisher gratefully acknowledges the generous support of the Art Endowment Fund of the University of California Press Foundation, which was established by a major gift from the Ahmanson Foundation.

Acting in the Night

Published with the assistance of The Getty Foundation.

Acting IN THE Night

MACBETH and the Places of the Civil War

ALEXANDER NEMEROV

UNIVERSITY OF CALIFORNIA PRESS
BERKELEY LOS ANGELES LONDON

University of California Press, one of the most distinguished university presses in the United States, enriches lives around the world by advancing scholarship in the humanities, social sciences, and natural sciences. Its activities are supported by the UC Press Foundation and by philanthropic contributions from individuals and institutions. For more information, visit www.ucpress.edu.

University of California Press
Berkeley and Los Angeles, California

University of California Press, Ltd.
London, England

Library of Congress Cataloging-in-Publication Data

Nemerov, Alexander.
Acting in the night : Macbeth and the places of the Civil War / Alexander Nemerov.
p. cm.
Includes bibliographical references and index.
ISBN 978-0-520-25186-1 (cloth : alk. paper)
1. United States—History—Civil War, 1861–1865—Theater and the war. 2. United States—History—Civil War, 1861–1865—Social aspects. 3. Theater and society—Washington (D.C.)—History—19th century. 4. Theater—Washington (D.C.)—History—19th century. 5. Shakespeare, William, 1564–1616. Macbeth. 6. Shakespeare, William, 1564–1616—Stage history—United States. 7. Washington (D.C.)—History—Civil War, 1861–1865—Social aspects. 8. Virginia—History—Civil War, 1861–1865—Social aspects. 9. Washington (D.C.)—Social conditions—19th century. 10. Virginia—Social conditions—19th century. I. Title.
E468.9.N46 2010
792.0973'09034—dc22 2010008817

Manufactured in the United States of America

19 18 17 16 15 14 13 12 11 10
10 9 8 7 6 5 4 3 2 1

The paper used in this publication meets the minimum requirements of ANSI/NISO Z39.48-1992 (R 1997) (*Permanence of Paper*).

TO MY BROTHER DAVID

The weaver-god, he weaves; and by that weaving is he deafened, that he hears no mortal voice; and by that humming, we, too, who look on the loom are deafened; and only when we escape it shall we hear the thousand voices that speak through it.

HERMAN MELVILLE
Moby-Dick

CONTENTS

Introduction: A Drop That Dyes the Seas 1

1. A Stone's Throw: Charlotte Cushman 7

2. The Flame of Place: Abraham Lincoln 59

3. The Glass Case: Interior Life in Washington, D.C. 94

4. Acoustic Shadows: The Battle of Bristoe Station 137

5. Center of Echoes: Castle Murray, Fauquier County, Virginia 161

6. Ghosts: The Death of Colonel Thomas Ruffin, October 17, 1863 180

7. Sound and Fury: Nature in Virginia 200

ACKNOWLEDGMENTS 227

NOTES 229

SELECTED BIBLIOGRAPHY 267

LIST OF ILLUSTRATIONS 285

INDEX 289

Introduction

A Drop That Dyes the Seas

THIS BOOK GREW OUT OF MY WISH to study a single night's performance of *Macbeth* from sometime in the mid-nineteenth century in some American city. My plan was to understand events of that day in that place by the light, or darkness, thrown by the play, and I hoped newspapers, letters, and diaries would help me along. I wanted to see how a performance of the play might have shaped a world around it. The idea came from Wallace Stevens's poem "Anecdote of the Jar," with its famous account of the centrifugal powers of aesthetic acts, the power of even a modest local aesthetic event—the placing of a jar on a hill in Tennessee—to shape the surrounding slovenly wilderness.

Stevens's poem "The Idea of Order at Key West" was also on my mind, with its description of a singer who is "the single artificer of the world / In which she sang," a person whose voice turns the "meaningless plungings of water and the wind" into an echo of herself, so that "there never was a world for her / Except the one she sang, and, singing, made." The horizon becomes a picture of her song ("It was her voice that made / The sky acutest at its vanishing"), and even when she finishes, the tilted lights of the fishing boats seem to apportion the night just as her song has, helping bestow a "Blessed rage for order." If the singer's voice could arrange the ocean, and if a jar on a hill in Tennessee "took dominion everywhere," I wanted to see how another aesthetic gesture—the performance of a play—might also turn chaos into cosmos.[1]

I had in mind *Macbeth* because both the Macbeths have such vivid spatial imaginations. Theirs, however, differ from that described in Stevens's poetry. Macbeth feels the horror of what he has done as a world-coloring nightmare:

> Will all great Neptune's ocean wash this blood
> Clean from my hand? No, this my hand will rather
> The multitudinous seas incarnadine,
> Making the green one red (2.2.63–66).[2]

Lady Macbeth summons "murdering ministers" from the thin air around her, calling on them, seemingly from every region of the universe, to help her with the crime (1.5.47). Unlike the consecrating order of Stevens's singer, Macbeth and Lady Macbeth both envision "a cosmological emptiness," in Harold Bloom's phrase. Their tragedy is a "falling in space," as the literary critic Wilbur Sanders put it, with Macbeth especially able to become, in Bloom's words, "an involuntary seer, almost an occult medium, dreadfully open to the spirits of the air and of the night."[3]

That envisioning of emptiness appealed to me as much as the ordering voice of Stevens's singer, if not more. The human gesture in *Macbeth,* like Lady Macbeth's lone candle in the sleepwalking scene, does not illuminate the world around it but rather intensifies the darkness, gathering a gloom deep and thick. The one caught in it could be forgiven for believing that the greatest aesthetic act is one that holds its flame most clearly to the void.

In looking for guides to this aesthetic power in mid-nineteenth-century America, I turned to Herman Melville and Nathaniel Hawthorne, each a devotee of *Macbeth.* In Hawthorne's *Marble Faun* (1860), set in Rome, the characters, visiting the Roman catacombs, notice that "while their collected torches illuminated this one, small, consecrated spot, the great darkness spread all around." In that small space of light, they are surrounded also by "that immenser mystery which envelopes our little life, and into which friends vanish from us, one by one."[4] Likewise, Melville's *Moby-Dick* (1851) tells of small lights and faceless immensities. When Starbuck gives Queequeg a lantern to hold aloft one night when their whaleboat is lost amid the "driving scud, rack, and mist" of a nighttime storm, the lone light is the image of Lady Macbeth's flame: "There, then, [Queequeg] sat, holding up that imbecile candle in the heart of that almighty forlornness. There, then, he sat, the sign and symbol of a man without faith, hopelessly holding up hope in the midst of despair." Ahab, with a spatial imagination like

Macbeth's, envisions the great faceless emptiness of an alien world in which vainly, heroically, he would make a mark, searching for the "unknown but still reasoning thing" that operates behind the mask of the white whale. He would confront that vast world, "undulat[ing] there on the billows, an unearthly, formless, chance-like apparition of life," like the giant squid the *Pequod* encounters, which has "no perceptible face or front," and give the amorphous emptiness a shape.[5]

Melville's preoccupation is the *Macbeth*-drawn power of the spatial void. Certainly, on occasion he gives the opposite view. His chapter "The Castaway," about the cabin boy, Pip, tells of a joyous aesthetic act that takes dominion everywhere. When Pip is happy and laughing, even the remote stars are a jangling image-echo of his contentment: his "ha-ha! . . . turned the round horizon into one star-bellied tambourine." So "the pure-watered diamond drop will healthful glow."[6] Yet the most impressive luster of the diamond drop occurs when it is placed "against a gloomy ground. . . . Then come out those fiery effulgences, infernally superb; then the evil-blazing diamond, once the divinest symbol of the crystal skies, looks like some crown-jewel stolen from the King of Hell." For Pip, this happens when, nervous, he jumps from a whaleboat during a chase and the little boat, pulled by the whale it has harpooned, travels a mile from him in three minutes, leaving him behind in the wide expanse of sea and sky. Bobbing alone in the immense ocean, he finds that his "ringed horizon began to expand around him miserably." After his fortuitous rescue, Pip is never the same, having become an "idiot."[7]

What Pip has seen, however, is almost worth the horrible isolation, for he has been "carried down alive to wondrous depths, where strange shapes of the unwarped primal world glided to and fro before his passive eyes; and the miser-merman, Wisdom, revealed his hoarded heaps." There, "among the joyous, heartless, ever-juvenile eternities, Pip saw the multitudinous, God-omnipresent, coral insects, that out of the firmament of waters heaved the colossal orbs." His vision of the teeming ocean, like Macbeth's, has become "infernally superb," and one gets the sense that Melville, assessing the relative power of aesthetic acts, judges his own conception of darkness a more lustrous gem as well.[8]

Melville and Hawthorne drew on *Macbeth* to help them investigate the wisdom of human acts that, for once, do not conceive themselves shooting forth across mountains and lakes, that do not, as Walt Whitman would have it, "skirt sierras" and "cover continents."[9] They each imagined aesthetic gestures that would, far more somberly, yet with a gleaming excitement, settle down to the careful delineation of a profound and infinite *locality,* to the creation of an artistic place amid the emptiness. They each imagined aesthetic acts—lanterns swinging at sea, torches flaming below ground—whose intensity would be so vivid, so clear, that they would leave a mark. These flares would each be a "brilliant stain" of the kind Zenobia left in the air above the place where she drowned in Hawthorne's *Blithedale Romance* (1852).[10] What these gestures lacked in world-shaping power they would make up for in their power to mark a spot. Thinking about these matters in the era's novels is one thing, but how might an actual performance of *Macbeth* engage the same issues?

I thought that finding a performance to study would be a random process. I would discover some version of the play and, without knowing much about it, more or less arbitrarily commit all my energies to studying that production. Whatever day I found would be the day I would need to know everything about: I would be an archaeologist digging in one spot, making my history from whatever I found there—a coin, a bone, a card that I might not otherwise have thought about. When I started thinking about this book, I had in mind a staging of the play in a northeastern town like Poughkeepsie, in the 1850s. I wanted to stay away from well-studied performances such as the rival productions of Edwin Forrest and William Macready that led to the Astor Place Riots in New York City in 1849.[11] I even thought I might end up writing about a show with almost no documentary record, so intent was I on finding an obscure production. I imagined the woods outside a small-town theater, a forest beyond the reach of gaslights, dark and hostile to those fitful gleams, and I even thought, with grim pleasure, of describing the production from the point of view of the trees.

I soon discovered, however, that *Macbeth* was Abraham Lincoln's favorite play. This fact, well-known to any Lincoln scholar and probably to many scholars of Shakespeare, came as news to me, an art historian. "I think nothing equals Macbeth," Lincoln wrote to the actor James Hackett in August 1863. "It is wonderful."[12] I immediately determined to write about a performance of the play that Lincoln had seen and soon learned that one had taken place on October 17, 1863, at Grover's National Theatre in Washington, D.C.

I turned to this date with some disappointment, knowing that readers would expect me to turn the play into an allegory about Lincoln and the Civil War. What could be more obvious than to link Shakespeare's story of assassination to the story of Lincoln's life and death, especially when commentators from the time quickly perceived the connection, lamenting Lincoln's murder at Ford's Theater on April 14, 1865, during a performance of *Our American Cousin,* as the "deep damnation of his taking off"?[13] I sensed that my focus on space and place might spiral away from me under the pressure of such a plain and reasonable focus for a book about *Macbeth* and Lincoln.

Readers turning to these pages for such allegorical readings, however, will be disappointed. I have stayed fixed—some will say fixated—on my initial question, the one that led me to this study. To me, the spatial and place-making powers of art in a given time are more interesting to consider than any life, even Lincoln's (which at any rate is so well documented as hardly to need further recounting here). Lincoln has remained a topic for me, yes, and even an especially important one. Deeply sensitive to place and space, he had much to say about the aesthetic issues that interest me. But he is not the sole focus of my study. The Civil War is even more important, imparting an extra urgency to the aesthetic questions I explore. But even so, I do not treat the play as an allegory of the war any more than I see it as an allegory of Lincoln.

Instead I have aimed to treat that night's performance of *Macbeth* as a place, even as a Thing in Martin Heidegger's sense. Following Heidegger, I have wanted to see the play as a "jug," a container similar to Stevens's jar, that would hold the earth and sky. The play would be a Thing, in Heidegger's sense, and therefore much more than the proverbial object of study, because it would hold a whole world—a social world as well as a natural one. Likewise I imagined the play that night resembling Heidegger's Greek temple, standing in one place and making even the alien world around it appear: "Tree and grass, eagle and bull, snake and cricket first enter into their distinctive shapes and thus come to appear as what they are" because of the temple, which makes a clearing that causes the surrounding world, apprehensible for a first time, to rise and face this one place. Above all, I had in mind Heidegger's sense that the world thus revealed was not a wholeness made newly available to the illuminations of understanding but a more primal earth of "self-secluding" and "concealed" points, each a vivid picture of "the Nothing which we scarcely know."[14]

In 1863 the capacity of an aesthetic act to produce such an earth of self-secluding points made special sense. The play that night, I began to discover, wanted to create a uniform space, a vast level field of ideological purpose, but the war inevitably worked to splinter that space into a great disarray of bones and bullets, a heterodox field in which every death, no matter how honored in the name of a cause, became a bloody spot, a single place, resisting all grandiosities of national explanation. I came to realize that the play that night might have expressed those forlorn memorable little places, might even have conceived itself among them, just as the pressures of war turned Whitman's conceptions of space tragically centripetal, and just as it intensified Lincoln's focus on mournful locations.

The play might have done so, I speculated, not as a whole but rather as a series of fragments that I would attempt to isolate. Words, gestures, intonations, and scenery might all have become some of the "hollows and recesses" that the theater historian Marc Robinson finds "everywhere on the American stage, pockmarking its deceptively smooth and secure surfaces."[15] Each of these hollows might have been a place unto itself—a cup of shade and smoke revealing both the performance's own nothing-signifying shroud of fog and night, its particularly opaque moments of presence, and the nothingness of the concealed places around it. I would need to explore other dates, I soon realized, and I would have to move away from *Macbeth* to refer to midcentury American paintings, photographs, and sculptures, as well as to novels and poems written on both sides of the Atlantic, but always to intensify my focus on the play on October 17, 1863.

The tale I tell here about that day is finally that of the performance's power to shape, or not shape, the world; its power to reach out and define a life or its failure to do so; maybe most, its power to say something meaningful precisely when it failed to send a message as planned—when it showed us instead the world of resonant emptiness and dislocation, with here and there a shaded spark or glow that helps us see the performance, too, as a glittering fragment of that lost day.

ONE

A Stone's Throw

Charlotte Cushman

CHARLOTTE CUSHMAN ARRIVED IN WASHINGTON, D.C., on the evening of Friday, October 9, 1863, to play Lady Macbeth later that month. She had returned to the United States earlier that year from Rome, where she lived, to deliver a series of benefit performances of *Macbeth* to aid the United States Sanitary Commission. A fiercely pro-Union native of Massachusetts, age forty-seven in 1863, Cushman had already performed in Philadelphia and Boston by the time she got to Washington, and she would go on to take the stage in Baltimore and New York. Her five-city tour resulted in a donation of more than $8,000 to the commission.[1] With her outsized ego, Cushman knew people would pay to see her—the most famous American actress of her generation and the most famous Lady Macbeth—and she was right.

That first evening in Washington, she arrived at the Lafayette Square home of her good friend Secretary of State William Seward, making a vivid impression on Seward's eighteen-year-old daughter Fanny. "When the front door opened Anna and I ran down stairs & met Miss Cushman on her way up—Anna first," Fanny wrote in her diary, describing her reaction and that of her sister-in-law Anna Seward, wife of her brother Fred. "After kissing Anna she gave me also a warm kiss saying she was glad to see me here."[2]

Then Cushman stepped into the parlor, and she was larger than life. "She stood talking and taking off her hat & cloak which I received," Fanny wrote, awestruck, noting all the details of the famous actress's dress. "She wore a drab travelling 'duster,' and black Neapolitan bonnet, trimmed with purple—Her dress was alpaca with white pin stripe—made in a skirt & short loose sack, the latter worn over a striped linen shirt, & showing the collar & sleeves." Fanny then gave her impressions of Cushman's prepossessing figure, big for a woman at the time—"She is very stout, but also very tall—a good deal taller than myself I believe." And she noted other details of her appearance: "Her hair, gray and inclined to wave a little, she wore drawn back from the sides of her face, but rolled forward—A black silk net at the back."

Of Cushman's face Fanny wrote, "At all times it is *full* of soul—and it will always seem to me, what ever others may call it, beautiful, far more beautiful than youth or regularity of features alone could be. . . . It possesses sublimity from intellect, it glows with benevolence, it sparkles with humor, it wins with earnest tenderness, it is cheerful, frank, natural, grand, thrilling, awful. I love the face as that of a great, true woman. . . . She seems to live as God intended life—filling each moment." A photograph of Cushman taken a few years earlier gives some sense of the person Fanny saw that evening (fig. 1).

In the next few days Cushman made an equally vivid impression on the rival managers of Washington's two most prestigious theaters, John Ford and Leonard Grover. Meeting with each man, she considered where and when she would stage her performance and decided later that week to play at Grover's National Theatre, swayed by Grover's willingness to offer the experienced professional actors Lester Wallack, Jr., and Edward Loomis Davenport in the roles of Macbeth and Macduff. On the night of Saturday, October 17, some twenty-five hundred people crowded into the theater, located on E Street between Thirteenth and Fourteenth streets, Northwest, to see the play.[3] The theater had been open in a refurbished state for only eleven days. A slightly later photograph of the building, which existed only until 1873 (when it burned down), shows the venue where Cushman performed (fig. 2).

The Washington newspapers described the performance only in general terms, reporting that it gave "the utmost satisfaction," that "the audience was enthusiastic throughout the play," that Abraham Lincoln and his family were in attendance, and that at the end Cushman stood before the curtain and received "an elegant bouquet from the ladies in Mr. Seward's box"—Fanny, Anna, and Emma Crow Cushman, the actress's niece, who accompanied her to Washington and also stayed at the Seward house.[4] Fanny

Fig. 1. Mathew Brady, *Charlotte Cushman,* 1857. Harvard Theatre Collection, Houghton Library, Harvard University.

disappoints the historian by describing the play in one of her two diaries simply as "very interesting."[5] (Her other diary is silent about the performance.) The following week, when Cushman performed the same role at the Academy of Music in New York on October 22, playing alongside Edwin Booth as Macbeth, a review was equally general: "Miss Cushman's powerful rendering of Lady Macbeth was the great treat of the occasion."[6] Even so, the many specific accounts of Cushman's acting written over the

Fig. 2. Grover's National Theatre, 1868. The Historical Society of Washington, D.C., Kiplinger Library.

course of her long career and afterward—she first took the stage in 1836 and made her last appearance in 1875, a year before her death—make clear her stage powers that evening.

Cushman commanded space. "A wave of influence, as from a magnetic battery to a company holding hands, swept from her," swelling over and silencing "the thousands in the assembly," wrote one eulogist.[7] A print of Cushman in the role of Lady Macbeth suggests the actress's stage presence (fig. 3). No one, recalled the critic William Winter, could "escape the spell of her imperial power," and when she acted some roles, including Lady Macbeth, her eyes "seemed to shoot forth a burning torrent of light," making him "fairly shr[i]nk away to the rear of the box, overwhelmed [and] astounded."[8] Julia Ward Howe's daughter Maud remembered that as a little girl in the 1860s, she crawled under a piano, as though trying to escape a natural disaster, while listening tearfully to Cushman recite a tragic poem at a private gathering.[9] Cushman, with her outsized melodramatic gestures, her booming contralto voice, her mouth like the "Arc de Triomphe," could,

Fig. 3. *Miss Charlotte Cushman as Lady Macbeth,* ca. 1850s. Harvard Theatre Collection, Houghton Library, Harvard University.

a eulogist said, "with one comprehensive and swift-revolving glance . . . gather her audience in."[10]

No space was too big for her. "Her magnificent presence answer[ed] to the proportions of the largest buildings, [and] her cathedral voice . . . could make . . . any hall a whispering-gallery."[11] Imagining the audience response to the fictional heroine of her early short story "The Actress" (1837), Cushman described the way her own acting took hold of audiences: "As she progressed, a profound silence reigned over the spacious building."[12] So it was on her benefit tour in 1863. Performing in *Macbeth* on September 26, Cushman "retained the rapt attention of all [the] great assembly" at the Boston Theatre, holding the large crowd "from the first word to the last."[13] So it must have been that night at Grover's three weeks later, when according to Benjamin Brown French, describing the performance a day later in his diary, she "was perfect. She always is. I think her the greatest actress living. In the sleep walking scene she was great."[14]

That sleepwalking scene was Cushman's last that night (after the famous somnambulism in act 5, scene 1, Lady Macbeth does not appear again until the curtain call), but her first appearance onstage at Grover's must have been equally powerful, not just for her audience but for Cushman herself. Her reading of Macbeth's letter in act 1, scene 3, was her first opportunity to fill the theater with her presence: to make herself large to fit the wide environs. A week earlier, touring Ford's Theater, Cushman and Fanny Seward had investigated a "star dressing room, a pretty little room conveniently furnished with bureau, wash-stand . . . chairs, sofa, carpet & lights," according to Fanny.[15] Grover, who refurbished his theater to stay apace with his rival Ford (who had reopened his own renovated theater on August 27), presumably had the same type of pretty little room for Cushman to use backstage on the night of October 17. Going from there to the green room and then out onto the stage—looking out at three gaslit ampitheatrical tiers seating those twenty-five hundred people—Cushman might then have felt an expansion, a becoming-vast, befitting her star power. "The actors on stage report that the house looks splendid from where they stand," noted a reporter after the opening of Grover's on October 6.[16] Cushman probably filled the greatness of that auditorium with ease, with pleasure, that night in 1863.

To command an auditorium is one thing, but to convey this larger-than-life presence even outside the theater is another. No actor or actress could extend their presence that far—that is, out into the streets and even into the perimeter of the northern Virginia countryside. Even Charlotte Cushman would be constrained by what a *Harper's Monthly* writer called in 1862 the "pitiless limits" of the theater.[17] Or would she?

In her egotism, Cushman wanted symbolic dominion over vast areas. "The circle" of her influence "was so large," wrote one eulogist, that "it was the right line of heaven and earth." Another said that her "deep, thrilling, pitiless tones" as Lady Macbeth "comprehend[ed] earth and air."[18] When Cushman had a luxury house built for her overlooking the ocean in Newport, Rhode Island, in 1870–71, she explained that she must have a view of "my sea and my sunsets."[19] When she addressed her fellow passengers shipboard en route to the United States in 1863, having heard rumors of a Confederate victory, she seemed to comprehend not just her immediate audience but the encompassing ocean when she exclaimed that she refused to believe the news.[20] To the sculptor Harriet Hosmer, a good friend, Cushman was "one lofty peak of snow / Above grand tiers of peaks below."[21] To William Winter, Cushman was proof that "human beings sometimes appear who are intrinsically great and admirable—just as the ocean is, or the starlit midnight sky."[22]

On October 17 Cushman performed in an area of Washington intent on spreading messages far and wide. Grover's Theatre was around the corner from press row in Washington, which ran up and down Fourteenth Street: from there issued many telegraphic messages, bespeaking communication across great distances, and about sixty out-of-town newspapers maintained offices on the street. The theater was also a few doors down from Willard's Hotel, the hobnobbing political center of the city, where Cushman's acquaintance and rival Julia Ward Howe had written the far-reaching anthem "The Battle Hymn of the Republic" one early morning in 1861.[23] Near Willard's and Grover's was the White House itself, where national policies were disseminated.

In partisan terms, Virginia was a political target for these messages, an area they sought to control—never more so than in that area in Washington where the benefit took place. John Bachmann's 1862 bird's-eye map shows the Fourteenth Street Bridge extending across the Potomac not far from the site of the theater (fig. 4). The Union armies marched to and fro across this bridge throughout the war on their way into and back from enemy territory. (Walt Whitman once watched as a procession of some thirty thousand Union soldiers took "four or five hours" to cross this bridge.)[24] The map, drawn by a partisan Union cartographer, implies this patriotic command, foregrounding the bustling capital city while showing Virginia as a mostly barren land, a desolate waste, taking here and there an inchoate

Fig. 4. John Bachmann, *Bird's Eye View of the City of Washington, D.C., and the Seat of War in Virginia,* 1862. Lithograph, 26 × 37 in. (66 × 94 cm). The Historical Society of Washington, D.C., Kiplinger Library.

shape, a tentative raising to the vertical, as though it were just coming under the magnetic sway of the righteous city below it. Equally partisan, the benefit performance of *Macbeth* might imagine itself stretching out and giving shape to that wasteland.

On October 17 Cushman may well have been thinking of those Virginia spaces, summoning them into her imagination of what it would be like to play her role on that day and place. On October 11 she had boarded the *Carrie Martin,* in company with Secretary of State Seward and British ambassador Lord Lyons, among others, for a trip down the Potomac. "They were gone all day visiting (hazardous) Mount Vernon, & Fort Foote," wrote Fanny. "Pickets were thrown out 4 miles at Mt. Vernon."[25] Cushman knew the Union general Gouverneur Kemble Warren, who on October 14 won the greatest military victory of his career at Bristoe Station, a Virginia railroad depot about thirty-five miles from Washington. News of the battle was the talk of the town on October 17. Warren, recently married to Emily

Forbes Chase, daughter of one of Cushman's closest friends (was there anyone she did not know?), got word of the actress's approbation soon after the battle: "I presume Emily told you the complimentary things that Charlotte Cushman had heard about you," his brother Bill wrote him on October 27.[26] With young Emily Chase Warren likely attending the play on October 17, Cushman knew well what had been happening in Virginia.

Symbolically Cushman would yell across that heart of the rebellion, screaming the defiance of John Greenleaf Whittier's "Massachusetts to Virginia," which she regarded as one of the great poems in the English language.[27] An abolitionist screed about the refusal of Cushman's home state to return a fugitive slave, "Massachusetts to Virginia" is full of italicized passages and exclamation points, echoing across the great distance between the two states:

> The blast from Freedom's Northern
> hills, upon its Southern way,
> Bears greeting to Virginia from Massa-
> chusetts Bay. . . .
>
> . . . .
> The voice of Massachusetts! Of her free
> sons and daughters,—
> Deep calling unto deep aloud,—the
> sound of many waters!
> Against the burden of that voice what
> tyrant power shall stand?
> *No fetters in the Bay State! No slave*
> *upon her land!*
>
> Look to it well, Virginians! . . .
> *No slave-hunt in our borders,—no pirate*
> *on our strand!*
> *No fetters in the Bay State,—no slave*
> *upon our land!*[28]

Cushman's voice carried symbolically into those distant spaces, moving on tracks forged by her contemporaries' understanding of Shakespeare. The Washington *Daily National Republican,* praising Cushman's performance, quoted the Reverend Henry Giles, who had written about the vast dimensions of *Macbeth* when describing the Boston Theatre production presented three weeks earlier. Giles expounded on "the hugeness of this play," the "vastness" of *Macbeth,* calling it a "stupendous drama," "a gigantic drama" of such "magnitude" that no audience member could ever keep it all in mind during a performance and few actors could do it justice. However, Cushman had made a "deep impression" and overcome these obstacles, her greatness equal to the play's.[29] Ralph Waldo Emerson described Shakespeare's mind in 1850 as "the horizon beyond which, at present, we do not see."[30] So it was that on October 17 Cushman likely gave a performance to fill space.

She did so, moreover, in a way that emulated the far reach of the Sanitary Commission itself, the beneficiary of her performance. The commission, in its aim to supply Union troops with medical and other humanitarian supplies, impatiently overruled piecemeal local aid societies to create a national distribution network, organized via subdepots in various parts of the country and designed to overcome all local bounds and obstacles. The commission was against the influence "of local or state agencies," according to a December 1863 pamphlet, partly because this influence "tends to foster, in contributor, agent and beneficiary alike, the very spirit of sectionalism and *'state-ish-ness'* to which we owe all our troubles."[31] National scope was the key, and the commission found it just as easy "to forward cargoes of ice and anti-scorbutics to South Carolina or Texas, or to transport thousands of barrels of onions and potatoes from the distant Northwest to the Armies of General Rosecrans or General Grant, as to send a few cases of shirts and drawers, and of hospital delicacies from Washington to the Army of the Potomac," Charles J. Stillé wrote in his *History of the United States Sanitary Commission* (1866). "Relief on this vast scale was the ordinary regular work of the Commission," and Cushman, performing to benefit this cause, acted in concert with the organization's wide-ranging agency and unifying power.[32]

In this respect Cushman made a perfect pair with the Reverend Henry W. Bellows, the head of the Sanitary Commission. Each was fully American, in the broadly optimistic nineteenth-century sense. Bellows was not in Washington on October 17, but he could not have found a better emissary than this actress whose vista vision had the spread of his own. Calling himself "a child of the age," Bellows had addressed his congregation at All Souls' in New York in 1859 "as Representatives of the Nineteenth Century and of this New Country," a time and a nation committed to "the real spirit of this age," namely, "essential progress in true Humanity." It was a time that "will be always memorable for two events," each wide-ranging and philanthropic: "the discovery of vaccination and the union of the hemispheres by the Atlantic Cable" (which had first happened for three weeks in 1858).

Both were "symbols of the saving powers of transmissive influences"—the spread of goodness and clarity across the globe.[33]

For Bellows, the Sanitary Commission had a comparably beneficial scope: "Our plans have a breadth and height and depth which no similar military philanthropic organization ever had, since the world began," he wrote to Frederick Law Olmsted in 1865. Cushman had the same ambitions, and as few doubts about her range: "I know of no distinction of North, East, South, or West; it is all my country," she wrote to Bellows on October 31, two weeks after her Washington performance. Her acting would be a vaccination, a cabled message, spreading the good.[34]

What did Cushman's admirers mean, though, when they said her influence was "the right line of heaven and earth"? No matter what the message, how could she actually be in a place she was not? Maybe mountains and horizons were only rhetorical approximations, vague and general indicators of her power. But what if the spatial descriptions were literal?

In one sense the idea is preposterous. How could Cushman do anything other than command her immediate audience in the theater? But in another sense it is logical. At a time when far-flung locales became closer—when the postal service, let alone the telegraph and railroad, was adjudged a magnificent conquest of distance—a great many people, not just Cushman, felt their powers had extended far beyond the place where they stood. Imagining these powers for us now means thinking about the mid-nineteenth century's theories of technological, personal, and spiritual dissemination. Cushman was a special case of all of them.

Consider the postal service and her relation to it. "In 1820 most Americans did not engage directly in any form of interactive, long-distance communications network," the historian David Henkin notes in his book *The Postal Age,* "while by 1870 most of them did."[35] Cushman took unusual advantage of the new postal world. "In the morning Miss Cushman was very busy writing letters," Fanny Seward noted in her diary on October 10. "Her correspondence is really enormous, & every mail brings her from one to many letters." So vast was this correspondence that Cushman devised a way to keep track of letters sent and received: "She showed me a curious list," Fanny wrote, "a page of letter paper divided into all the days of a month—and opposite each day she sets down not only the letters she receives and writes but other items associated with her correspondence, traveling, etc. The most compact diary I ever saw."[36] Within a few weeks the Sewards would receive their own Cushman epistles, as the actress importuned and educated from afar, seeking preferment for friends and relatives of friends: "I want very much to ask a favor of you," Cushman wrote to Fanny's brother Fred, the assistant secretary of state, just before her departure from New York for Liverpool. "And *one* more favor . . . ," she went on, before switching to Fanny, "to whom I sent some books by Express the other day" (a two-volume set of *The Poetical Works of James R. Lowell*).[37] Back in Rome, Cushman would have resumed her correspondence from her personal command post, a custom-made desk of walnut and pine, carved with no fewer than seventeen Dionysian faces—a flamboyant nerve center allowing her to stay in touch with the world.[38]

Consider also the newspapers—another widespread phenomenon of the nineteenth century that Cushman followed. She examined the Washington papers when she was in town, sizing up the slant of each. "After dinner . . . Miss C. stopped to look at the papers in the library," wrote Fanny on October 13. "She asked me for them and as I found the Republican first I gave her that, telling her it was the sensation paper. Presently the Star turned up, & she wished to know if the Republican was the Sensation what was the Star. . . . Afterwards she mentioned the matter at the table, asking about the city papers."[39]

Cushman created some of this news, encouraging messages about herself via these Washington newspapers. On October 13, when it was not yet certain where she would perform on the upcoming Saturday, the *Daily National Republican* noted that "Miss Charlotte Cushman, the distinguished *tragedienne,* visited Ford's Theatre last night . . . and expressed her determination to present her inimitable delineation of Lady Macbeth at Ford's, for the benefit of the Sanitary Commission, some time this week. A suitable representative of Macbeth is wanted for that occasion."[40] Whether or not she sent this message to the rival theater owner Leonard Grover, challenging him to top the facilities at Ford's and to offer a professional actor to play Macbeth, Cushman liked to create some of the sensations she read about.

The telegraph was also a part of this newly vast world. Samuel Morse's invention of 1844 allowing for the quick distribution of thoughts across vast distances was faster than letters and a staple of newspaper coverage. It soon informed the arts, linking author and readers in imagined filaments of "sentimental electricity."[41] By the 1860s the telegraph was in wide use, and the Civil War was famously a telegraphic conflict, with the Lincoln administration using wires for strategic and morale-building effect. As the government supplied the Associated Press "with its bulletins and official announcements," making the wire service the "semi-official medium for the distribution of information emanating from sources in the administration," as the historian Menahem Blondheim describes it, so Cushman extended her singular voice to benefit the cause under the eyes of Lincoln himself.[42]

Like Lincoln, she also received messages from afar. The telegraph, in receptive mode, "will give you ears that can hear a whisper in New Orleans," wrote Oliver Wendell Holmes, Sr., in 1859.[43] For a specially attuned person—a person, like Cushman, who wished to know what was happening all around her—that power might even be clairvoyant. Sounds might accrue to such a person almost without benefit of wires. Cushman's friend Nathaniel Hawthorne, of whom she kept a portrait in her house, sent her his novels as gifts, and Professor Westervelt's words about the clairvoyant Veiled Lady in *The Blithedale Romance* (1852) suggest Cushman's own wish to receive signals from a distance: "Sitting in this very hall, she could hear the desert-wind sweeping over the sands, as far off as Arabia; the ice-bergs grinding one against the other, in the polar seas; the rustle of a leaf in an East Indian forest."[44] In James Russell Lowell's "Columbus" (a poem Cushman especially loved—in 1876, gravely ill, she asked that it be read to her the night before she died), the Italian explorer even as a boy hears the rustling pine forests outside his home and telepathically sees the distant lands he will find:

> I in vision clear beheld
> The sudden dark of tropic night shut down
> O'er the huge whisper of great watery wastes
> The while a pair of herons trailingly
> Flapped inland, where some league-wide river
> hurled
> The yellow spoil of unconjectured realms
> Far through a gulf's green silence, never scarred
> By any but the Northwind's hurrying keels.
> And not the pines alone; all sights and sounds
> To my world-seeking heart paid fealty,
> And catered for it as the Cretan bees
> Brought honey to the baby Jupiter.[45]

If Cushman might receive such messages, she also could spread versions of herself out into the world, in the form of photographic idol-emissaries. She traveled with photographs of herself, intending to give some away. The interviewer Mrs. J. H. Hanaford, talking to Cushman in the actress's Tremont House hotel room in Boston in 1858, noted that Cushman sat at a table displaying many daguerreotypes and that at the end of their talk "she kindly presented to me a photograph of herself." The effigy then exerted its influence: "It is before me as I write," noted Hanaford, "life-like and full of intellectual beauty."[46] On October 10 Fanny wrote, "Miss Cushman showed us a number of *cartes de visite,* one of her nice colored maid Sally" and many of Cushman and her niece Emma, also at the Seward home. "There were a great variety of postures. One vignette of Miss C—not a good likeness—was very peculiar—she made great sport of it, and she called it 'Daniel Webster after he had been translated' (the latter was, I think, the word she used). There were two cards which we liked better than the rest—both of the ladies together."[47]

Cushman gave at least one of these photographs to the Sewards, tokens of her presence just like the signatures she dispensed later in the week "in several autograph books" sent to her by admiring Union officers. That week her friends were busy collecting more such images. At Ford's Theater on October 12, Cushman accompanied Fanny, Fred, and Anna to a performance of *Fanchon,* starring the popular Maggie Mitchell, and they made sure to take home pictures of the young actress: "Photographs of [Mitchell] were brought to the box for sale," Fanny noted in her diary. "Fred took two—Anna afterwards gave me one."[48] During Cushman's performance five nights later, vendors probably hawked the actress's image: she was photographed many times during her career, including in her role as Lady Macbeth.

These images were more than keepsakes. They spread tiny pieces of a person into faraway places, in keeping with Holmes's 1859 description of photographs as "forms, effigies, membranes, or *films*" detached from their subjects.[49] Holmes referred to the ancient theory of "exuviae," the idea that each person is constantly detaching images of herself from her body. He drew on Lucretius's concept that "the idols of things . . . like films peeled off from the surface . . . fly to and fro through the air" and do so not as mere fabrications but (as the word *idol* indicates) as actual pieces of the bodies they have split from, a thin skin of shavings "like the discarded 'gossamer coats of cicadas,' " as Lucretius termed them.[50] Holmes's point is that these layers, peeled constantly from one's body one after another "like the leaves of a closed book," were ephemeral until the age of photography, which enabled people to catch and fix one of them on metallic and glass plates.

Fanny, an avid collector of *cartes de visite,* felt this living power acutely. Excitedly noting the arrival of two new cards in the mail on February 9, 1863, she decided to put one of them, of the writer and editor George William

Curtis, next to that of the women's rights advocate Lucretia Mott, based on the sympathetic power of these two persons. To her, these likenesses were nearly as lifelike as the dolls she had tended as a child: "I have put his [Curtis's card] beside that of Lucretia Mott. He is the friend of woman as well as humanity. She is the friend of charity and progress."[51] Cushman, who was also represented in the Seward *carte de visite* collection, took advantage of the new photographic format's capacity to make a person present in many places at once. After the performance of *Macbeth,* audience members likely could take away filaments of the star actress, just like the journalist Hanaford had done five years earlier. In the words of the anthropologist Alfred Gell, discussing Lucretius, hers was a "distributed personhood."[52]

But when Cushman was not being photographed—when, for example, she was onstage—could she distribute herself then? Could she literally be in all places at all times? Her fellow Civil War philanthropist Clara Barton—"a Sanitary Commission of One"—tried to be everywhere during the war (and afterward, when she lectured extensively about her experiences nursing soldiers). She became famous for her efforts, but she also spread herself thin. Tending to so many of the wounded and personally supervising the search for 63,182 of the missing after the war, Barton gave of herself until the famous sign outside her Washington office and lodging—"Missing Soldiers," "Miss. Clara Barton"—suggested the sum of a ubiquity that, symbolically speaking, made the woman herself often absent.[53]

Cushman, in theory, had the same problem. The person who was everywhere was nowhere. In world-changing aspiration, her performance was like the drop of a heavy stone in the water, sending out circle after concentric circle of radiating effect. Yet the very uniformity of applause her performance elicited was as a handful of pebbles thrown into that same water—a chaos of indiscriminate energies, everyone taking from her what they might. Throw into that same water a handful of sand and the now infinite particulars of Washington and the surrounding countryside on October 17 become visible: thousands of tiny circles spreading and shifting and dissolving in a pool where the single stone struggles and fails to make its radiance clear.

Cushman's dilemma, like Barton's, was the "problem of the one and the many, which the war had made so urgent for American culture," to use the words of the literary historian James Dawes. "One million five hundred and sixteen names on the muster-rolls, of which seven hundred and ninety-seven thousand eight hundred and seven were present": General William

Tecumseh Sherman's statistical account of the Union forces at the end of the war typifies the era's statistical sublime—the grandeur of numbers that threatened to make any action, no matter how heroic and singular, less the evidence of a bird's-eye omniscience than a bit of the scrap, stick, and straw that a bird sees from above. The site of Grover's Theatre in Bachmann's map is finally indistinguishable, and the wish of the actress to incarnate the vantage that sees everything from that theater—that makes the theater's tiered balconies just the first rings in a concentric universe radiating from the stage—becomes nothing more than wishful thinking. From far above, Cushman's performance on October 17 starts to look like a tiny part of a vastly intricate pattern she could not discern and in which she, as much as Clara Barton, got lost.

But maybe there was a way that Cushman did spread *herself,* not just emissaries of herself, out into the world. Maybe she really could be everywhere, and without Barton's self-negation. Like many people of her time, Cushman understood that even the most insignificant local act might flow into the world and change it. "We cannot break a law of eternal justice, however ignorantly, but throughout the entire universe will there be a jar of discord," she wrote to a friend. Likewise, in the copy of *The Poetical Works of James R. Lowell* that she sent to Fanny Seward, Cushman noted with a pair of *X*'s Lowell's poem "The Present Crisis" and drew a vertical line in the margin next to the poem's opening lines: "When a deed is done for Freedom, through the / broad earth's aching breast / Runs a thrill of joy prophetic, trembling on from / east to west."[54]

Now we would call such an idea a "butterfly effect," one small action in one place affecting people and places far away. "Sensitive dependence" is a hallmark of contemporary chaos theory, as the scientist Peter Smith explains: "A small blue butterfly, let's suppose, sits on a cherry tree in a remote province in China. . . . The miniscule difference in the resulting eddies of air around the butterfly eventually makes the difference between whether, two months later, a hurricane sweeps across southern England or harmlessly dies out over the Atlantic. Or so the story goes."[55]

The mid-nineteenth century knew such unpredictabilities. When we throw a stone, wrote the famous Victorian philosopher Herbert Spencer in 1864, we can see the force of our muscular action out in the world, but this force is no longer recognizable: it has taken on new forms and energies and "does not exist elsewhere under any form cognizable by us."[56] Cushman's acting colleague John Wilkes Booth, firing his derringer into the back of Lincoln's head during a performance of *Our American Cousin* at Ford's Theater on April 14, 1865, created just such a butterfly effect, unleashing a countrywide storm from the small adjustments of the muscles and tendons of his hand. *Macbeth* was and is famously about this far-spreading randomness, "the little seed of evil" planted in Macbeth's mind by the witches, that, in the words of the British theater director Peter Hall, "grows into an act or murder, a *coup d'état,* the sickness of a whole country and the sickness of all the people within it."[57]

Grover's Theatre was a place that might unleash unpredictable energies. In the photograph of the façade (see fig. 2) a sign reading Deery & Simpson Billiard Saloon appears on the box protruding from the leftmost second-story window of the theater. On April 14, 1865, Booth asked John Deery, the American billiard champion, to purchase a ticket for him to the performance at Grover's that evening, on the chance that Lincoln would be there and not at Ford's. Billiards is the unintentional but vivid metaphor of the cataclysm that followed: the cue ball, having struck, would send the pack in all directions. Billiards was likewise relevant on October 17, 1863. That day, the *Daily National Republican* ran a notice of a "Great Billiard Match" below another notice about Cushman's performance ("Charlotte Cushman's Performance at Grover's Theatre—Go Early"), detailing an epic contest of "American Caroms" two nights earlier in New York. Cushman, whose acting style "possessed in a remarkable degree the element of force," as one critic put it, had in summer 1863 ordered a large custom-made billiard table from the noted Manhattan billiards company Phelan and Collender and was busy the day she arrived in Washington, October 9, figuring out how to ship the table to Boston and then back to Italy.[58] Onstage Cushman herself was like a cue ball breaking a pack, and maybe her acting at Grover's, that place of billiards, was itself a type of American caroms.

Foremost, however, Cushman and others in the mid-nineteenth century did not strive for such randomness. On the contrary, they believed in a *controlled* butterfly effect. One action would not unleash a hurricane but a force virtually identical to the initiating impulse. Telegraphic communications, carrying sentimental and ideological messages, exemplified these predictable flows. "For mankind are one in spirit, and an instinct bears / along, / Round the earth's electric circle, the swift flash of / right or wrong," wrote Lowell in "The Present Crisis."[59] If a wrong is committed, that "jar of discord" would flow around the world. If a tear was shed or a punch was thrown, then likewise somehow out there far away, the same energy would recur in basically the same form. Cushman's friend Elizabeth Barrett Browning described the effect perfectly in her sonnet "Life," published in 1853:

Each creature holds an insular point in space:
Yet what man stirs a finger, breathes a sound,
But all the multitudinous beings round
In all the countless worlds, with time and place
For their conditions, down to the central base,
Thrill, haply, in vibration and rebound,
Life answering life across the vast profound,
In full antiphony, by a common grace!—
I think, this sudden joyaunce which illumes
A child's mouth sleeping, unaware may run
From some soul newly loosened from earth's tombs.
I think, this passionate sigh, which half-begun
I stifle back, may reach and stir the plumes
Of God's calm angel standing in the sun.[60]

In this theory, the vibration and rebound between people occupying insular points in space are clear and direct. There is no signal drift, no swaying and dissolving—or, worse, morphing of action into unexpected reaction. Instead the sleeping child's smile comes from the soul of a spirit newly raised to heaven, and the poet's own half-withheld passionate sigh—a sign of her poem itself—reaches out to fan an angel's wings. Rustling plumes and poet's breath exchange a gentle calm.

These direct communications carried political messages as well. Browning's sonnet "Hiram Powers' Greek Slave," also from 1853, commands the American sculptor's famous work to send forth its message and break up slavery all over the world:

To, so, confront man's crimes in different lands
With man's ideal sense. . . .

to "break up ere long / The serfdom of this world!" to "strike and shame the strong," and to attack "man's wrong. . . . / By thunders of white silence, overthrown." The work of art, stuck in one place, can yet send its benevolent message outward, refuting the idea that "Ideal beauty cannot enter / The house of anguish."[61] Lowell had the same idea in "The Present Crisis," when he wrote that the deed done for freedom—a deed such as the writing or reading of an abolitionist poem—would communicate electrically, traveling the globe, so that "Through the walls of hut and palace shoots the / instantaneous throe."

Cushman practiced this controlled butterfly effect only sixteen days after her *Macbeth* performance. On November 2 she was in Boston to help dedicate the city's magnificent great organ at the Music Hall. Construction of the organ, about as tall as a brownstone building, had taken more than six years, through a commission to the German firm E. F. Walcker and the American furniture makers Herter Brothers, at an eventual cost of $60,000. Installed at the Music Hall, the organ was proclaimed "among the three or four greatest instruments in the world," and though it is not anywhere near as large as it is shown in an otherwise accurate period illustration, where two foreground admirers are far too tiny (fig. 5), it was big enough that the hall seemed "only the niche or shrine for this noble work."[62]

In front of a crowd of Boston society and intelligentsia on November 2, Cushman stood before the organ to read her friend Annie Fields's "Dedication Ode"—a summa of controlled butterfly effects. A photograph of the organ *in situ* at the Boston Music Hall before a centennial celebration in 1876 suggests what that scene might have been thirteen years earlier (fig. 6). Describing the organ's extensive power—its capacity to ring out a pro-Union message of emancipation and national victory—Cushman spoke the poem's Emersonian words:

> circle into circle breaking,
> Wider circles still awaking
> Every sphere can swinging hear
> The ripples of our atmosphere,
> The growing circles of our prayer;
> Circling beyond all time, all place,
> And breaking with its finite grace
> Upon dim shores of God's illimitable space.
> The poem concludes, invoking the organist,
> Now, at his touch, unveiled are hidden things,
> Now falls oppression, now decay false kings;
> Through all the tones the voice of freedom rings
> One choral chant, one song of Praise,—a NATION'S VICTORY.[63]

The literary historian Mary Loeffelholz, describing Fields's poem and the dedication ceremony, notes the implication that the Civil War could be won "by purely aesthetic means." Triumph will come "by staying at home, vibrating with responsive sympathy, and felling slavery with song—by means of the transmission of culture." Instead of a tragic view of human nature—of a person circumscribed by human and societal limitations—Cushman

Fig. 5. Organ, Music Hall, Boston, ca. 1863–84. The Bostonian Society Library and Special Collections.

and Fields were optimists, anti-Puritans: Fields, in writing her Emersonian rebuke of the Puritan fathers' narrowness and meanness; Cushman, in standing forth in all her glory, not only spreading Fields's words but offering a contrast, as Loeffelholz notes, to Hawthorne's vivid image of Hester Prynne on the scaffold: "Standing on that miserable eminence, she saw again her native village, in Old England."[64] Instead of these fated, gloomy meditations on the past—far-seeing visions of what had been—Cushman spoke

Fig. 6. Interior of Music Hall, Boston, Centennial Year, 1876. The Bostonian Society Library and Special Collections.

with a clairvoyance of the present and future, her voice going out "on the nimble air benign" like Emerson's call to duty in his 1863 poem "Voluntaries," reproduced in the *Atlantic Monthly* the month before:

Yet on the nimble air benign
Speed nimbler messages,
That waft the breath of grace divine
To hearts in sloth and ease.[65]

Cushman, reciting Fields's "Dedication Ode," stood as a national figure. She was not just the localized expositor of a subjective viewpoint but an impersonal spokeswoman, a broadcaster almost, of a message larger than any one person. Helping create "an emergent aesthetic conception of civic space," in Loeffelholz's words, Cushman spread a message so outsized, so national, that it almost seemed to demand a recording device to spread it.[66]

Julia Ward Howe, in attendance that night and herself no stranger to a national anthem made for recitation by others, called to mind this disseminating, duplicating power when she described the organ as "a single light multiplied in a hundred mirrors."[67] Perhaps the very size of the great organ symbolized the idea of a machine that could spread a message, extending that signal even from coast to coast, as if to a culture without the actual technology of a radio it would be the sheer bulk of the sound-making object that would fantastically imply this universal audibility.[68]

In Washington some two weeks earlier, Cushman had no such grand sound-making device. But she had her formidable voice and presence, delivering Shakespeare's vast play on a gigantic scale to aid the Union cause to an audience of government notables including Lincoln himself. If some thirty miles away a cap rustled on a soldier's head, or the moon gleamed on the grease of a railroad wheel, who was to say that these were only meaningless incidents? If the world was even then being carved into a relentless rationality of timetables and other coordinates, Charlotte Cushman's brand of patriotism aimed to shape that regime of certainty, that eradication of all insignificant localities. Leonard Grover called his theater the National, and on that night it might well have lived up to its name.

Even so, Cushman had a concern. The spreading, the emanating, was ephemeral. The greatest goal was permanence—to make those angel's wings hold their transformed place forever; to freeze herself *and the world she had affected* in the transformed posture she would create. But this was impossible. Cushman noted how transient her performances were, constantly molting, as all gestures and poses, no matter how solid and striking, melted into the atmosphere. The closure of an actor's death was only a more replete version of the step-by-step evaporations of an entire career. If upon an actor's death, his roles "are buried with him, as in old times, when a hero fell, the horse was killed on which he rode to death, his slaves were slain, his armor was braced upon his form, and his sword placed in his hand," as a Cushman eulogist noted in 1876, she knew that an actor's performance dies at every moment anyway.[69]

"What is or can be the record of an actress, however famous?" Cushman asked, giving a view she expressed often and ending it, in this case, with a reference to *Macbeth:*

> They leave nothing behind them but the vaguest of memories. Ask any number of persons to give you a real picture or positive image of the effect any great actor produced in his time, and they can tell nothing more

than that it was fine, it was grand, it was overwhelming; but ask them how did he do such or such a thing, how did he render such a passage? describe his manner, his gesture, even his personal appearance, that we may have a living picture of him,—and they are at once at a loss. It is all gone; passed away. Now, other artists—poets, painters, sculptors, musicians—produce something which lives after them and enshrines their memories in positive evidences of their divine mission; but we,—we strut and fret our hour upon the stage, and then the curtain falls and all is darkness and silence.[70]

In Benjamin Brown French's appreciative diary notation of October 18 ("I think her the greatest actress living. In the sleep walking scene she was great"), Cushman's performance the previous evening was already well on the way to being forgotten. Along with a few other descriptions by journalists, only the diarist's words and a souvenir program pasted on a separate page stood between her triumph and oblivion, and these already were "but the vaguest of memories." The relentless disappearance might even have been one source of Cushman's weirdly emanating power, the witchlike supernaturalism of her presence that was stranger than any character's spoken line. The entrancing effect "magically evoked by her spell," to use Henry Bellows's words, diffused her ephemeral likeness to infinity. If Maggie Mitchell's shadow dance in *Fanchon* was "the most bewitching thing in the world," as Fanny Seward reported on October 12, "wild, weird, teasing, mimicking," the severe Cushman was herself a prolific dispenser of beguiling shadows, wantonly strewing vaporous idols of herself like a magician with a wand.[71] (Was that her face reflected in a young woman's eye? Did that owl just swoop down from its branch?) If Mitchell's character, the elfin country girl Fanchon, could inspire the lovestruck country swain Landry to say in the play that "since that evening my only thought was of you; I saw no other girl than you, and see you everywhere, even where you are not," then this rueful adulation might describe not only Mitchell's but Cushman's witchlike powers to send her image-proxies out into the world.[72] Yet if Cushman were to have a *permanent* effect, then these multiple emissaries, these sheddings, discardings, and flutterings of her distributed personhood, would also have to be controlled—to be frozen, or locked into place—even if the means of control would ultimately be a further sorcery. Photography was one way to do this for Cushman—the dispensing of *cartes de visite* and the like. Sculpture was another.

To be sculptural was the way to endure. Some of Cushman's close friends

Fig. 7. Thomas Crawford, *Freedom,* 1863. Bronze cast by Clark Mills. Reproduced courtesy of the Architect of the Capitol, Washington, D.C.

and acquaintances in Italy were sculptors—Hosmer, Emma Stebbins, Randolph Rogers—and their work offered a lesson. To be a block of stone was to be impervious to time, stuck and solid: then one could be, as Macbeth wished he was, "Whole as the marble, founded as the rock, / As broad and general as the casing air" (3.4.22–23). Sculpture was on Cushman's mind in the days leading up to the Washington performance. She accompanied Secretary of the Interior John P. Usher on a tour of the Capitol Rotunda, where she lobbied Usher to commission Stebbins to sculpt a Columbus.[73] (She asked Fred Seward to follow up on this campaign.) On her tour she likely saw the multipart sculpture *The Progress of Civilization*—conceived by Thomas Crawford (1813–57), her contemporary and fellow American expatriate in Italy—which workers were then hoisting in parts onto the northeast pediment of the Capitol. That day she must also have seen Crawford's sculpture *Freedom,* cast by Clark Mills, still on the Capitol grounds and soon to be placed atop the newly completed Capitol dome on December 2. A twentieth-century photograph shows it in that now-familiar position (fig. 7).

Freedom might have impressed Cushman that day for two reasons. One was its control of space, easily imaginable even before the massive sculpture was lifted into place. Standing twenty feet tall and weighing almost fifteen thousand pounds, *Freedom* as of October 9 was "lying dismembered on the ground, her ladyship's head, arms, legs, etc., gigantic in their way, receiving the attentive admiration of the daily throng of sight-seers at the Capitol," according to the journalist Noah Brooks.[74] Likely the castings were still in that state a few days later, when Cushman paid her visit, though perhaps Crawford's sculpture had begun to take on the completed though still ground-borne look evident in a recent photograph during a restoration (fig. 8). Either way, Cushman could readily envision the nation-commanding power of such a colossus. Here was a great example of how an artistic project might defeat a merely localized relevance. The sculpture might well have struck her as embodying her own glorious national-aesthetic visions: "She was," as William Winter said about one of her roles, "higher, broader, larger, stronger than the part."[75]

Freedom might have modeled something even more elemental to Cushman: the ability of the actress not just to command space but to arrest points within it—to make solid the vaporous flow of space and time—and to turn herself (and all she beheld) into sculpture. Onstage she made herself a first example of this petrifaction, seeking to make each performance, maybe each moment in a performance, as dense as marble, as heavy as bronze. She aimed for "massive" and "simple" effects, to use Winter's terms, and a photograph of her as Lady Macbeth gives an indication of what she was after (fig. 9).[76] The frozenness of the photographic pose suggests the monumental effect she aimed to create for an audience.

Becoming her character—readying herself for an evening's performance—was likely one of Cushman's ways of making herself solid, of girding herself in the materials of a lasting likeness. Mary Braddon, in her novel *Aurora Floyd,* advertised in *Harper's Weekly* on October 17, 1863, notes the backstage preparations of William Macready, the distinguished English actor alongside whom Cushman became famous in the 1840s: "They tell us that Mr. Macready began to be Richelieu at three o'clock in the afternoon." Braddon's heroine Miss Percival, on the contrary, "was laughing and talking in

Fig. 8. Thomas Crawford, *Freedom.* Reproduced courtesy of the Architect of the Capitol, Washington, D.C.

the white-washed little green room the very minute before she ran on to the stage to wail for her murdered kinsman and banished lover."[77] Cushman, steeling herself like Macready, formed herself into her parts, the better to make them memorable. Her niece Emma remembered that she was allowed in the actress's dressing room only if she kept absolutely quiet, "the price of this coveted privilege . . . the complete effacement of my presence."[78] As the visitor disappeared, the character took shape. Likewise, when Fanny Seward watched the rehearsal at Grover's on the afternoon of October 17, perhaps she saw Cushman's character even then hardening into the shape it would take that night.[79]

Fig. 9. Charlotte Cushman as Lady Macbeth. Harvard Theatre Collection, Houghton Library, Harvard University.

Similarly, a sculpture's intensification of form was related to lasting likeness. All the world would be forgotten so that this one aesthetic act might be remembered. A sculpture modeled the centripetal density, the world-forgetting concentration of effect, that defines aesthetic power as much as any fantasy of centrifugal domination. The art historian Gabrielle Gopinath notes the remarkably self-enclosed quality of Hosmer's *Zenobia in Chains* (1859), a sculpture very popular in the 1860s (fig. 10). Zenobia, the third-

Fig. 10. Harriet Hosmer, *Zenobia in Chains,* 1859. Marble, 88 in. (223.5 cm) high. Wadsworth Atheneum Museum of Art, Hartford, Connecticut. Gift of Mrs. Josephine M. J. (Arthur E.) Dodge.

century Palmyran warrior queen, stands vanquished, humiliated, and yet commandingly self-contained in the moment Hosmer chooses to show. Defiant in her helpless calm, the queen is nobly free in her imprisonment, sovereign while bound.[80]

Cushman, even with her outsized gestures that invoked the universe itself, aimed to be a cynosure like her friend's sculpture. "There is no world without Verona's walls," says Romeo in *Romeo and Juliet,* and Cushman, playing Romeo in the breeches part as she sometimes did, exemplified this way of banishing all else but her singular presence within the theater's charmed circle.[81] The outside world became at such moments a nothingness—in Romeo's words, "purgatory, torture, hell itself" (3.3.17–18). Like Virginia in Bachmann's map when it is read centripetally (like the famous Manhattan-centric *New Yorker* cover), the outside world fades to blankness and irrelevance, becoming just a bunch of moss-stumped crevices and hills, before the monumental power of a metropolis or, in this case, of a star performance that implodes its surroundings to an empty inconsequence. Accordingly, Cushman's Lady Macbeth was a *Zenobia*-style figure of isolation, massive and simple, queenly and doomed, aspiring to cancel the rest of the world by the memorable density of her presence in one spot.

This severe condensation did not just erase those outside worlds but also gathered them into itself. The memorable sculpture or sculpturelike performance would *collect* disparate experience into the crushed density of one immovable opaque shape, condensing into memorable form a world of flowing and otherwise forgettable extent. Rainer Maria Rilke, in his 1903 essay on Auguste Rodin, wrote of a medieval sculpture of a bird that kept "distance . . . folded on each of its feathers," so that if it were to flex its wings, it could spread that sky "and make it vast." Just so, "in the restrained, hieratic gestures of ancient religions the restlessness of living surfaces was contained like water within the walls of a vessel." The sculpture that encloses the world in this way would be ageless, like *Eternal Idol,* one of the Rodin works Rilke praises—an arrested shape of self-enclosure, carved not just from space but time.[82]

When Cushman's Lady Macbeth summoned "murdering ministers" to gather at her breast, instilling her with the volition to do the crime—a line she delivered, wrote Winter, with a power to chill a listener's blood—when she called forth, in that same fabulous speech, "you spirits / That tend on mortal thoughts," when she drew down "thick night," "the dunnest smoke of hell" (1.5.37–53), to cloak and curtain the evil deed, she probably incarnated this world-stopping power of the aesthetic to inhale the universe, to internalize it as a sculpturally dense form. Like the ingredients of the witches' brew—"Eye of newt, and toe of frog, / Wool of bat, and tongue of dog" (4.1.14–15)—the far-flung world of randomness might gather in the cauldron of the play's incantations, creating an all-but-sculptural image of memorable thickness.

Of course, oblivion awaits most everything. Glintings of light on stage-steel and stage-blood are a paltry stay to life's "walking shadow," as the play knows. But in good performances, Macbeth's and Lady Macbeth's speeches still crush attention down to just the words and the figure onstage, both absorbing and erasing the world around. And as we forget that world, we more likely remember what we behold onstage. Cushman knew, to adapt Thomas De Quincey's words, in his great 1823 essay about the knocking at the gate, that at the play's key moments "we must be made sensible that the world of ordinary life is suddenly arrested—laid asleep—tranced—racked into a dread armistice; time must be annihilated; relation to things without abolished; and all must pass, self-withdrawn, into a deep syncope and suspension of earthly passion."[83]

Cushman not only fixated herself in memorable postures. She also symbolically aimed to fixate other persons, to petrify them in ever-distant zones. The world would come to a stop, extracted from the flow of time while she performed—and so the meaningless forgettable unfolding would gain shape, sculpturally cohering, if only symbolically, as a crystal land of frozen order. Loyal subjects would be struck into postures of obeisance by a person imperious enough to believe that, for just that moment, life's random flow would cease.

This fantasy had to start with the audience in the theater. Cushman was known to stop performances dead in order to stare down unruly audience members and to refuse to continue until the offender was ejected. In doing so, as one critic put it, she could "render impotent the caprice of all observers."[84] One of her private mementoes, a miniature that is alleged to be (and does appear to be) a painting of one of her eyes, reads as a token of her freezing powers of audience command—her eyes, as William Winter said, shooting forth "a burning torrent of light" (fig. 11). Onstage at the Boston Music Hall on November 2, Cushman stood alongside Crawford's larger-than-life bronze of Beethoven, a fittingly intense alter ego to the mesmerizing artist. Her choice of roles also indicated her aim to arrest audiences. As the gypsy Meg Merrilies in the stage adaptation of Sir Walter Scott's novel *Guy Mannering,* her most famous part, Cushman came onstage with makeup that required two hours to put on, doing full justice to Scott's characterization of Meg as a gorgon (fig. 12).[85] At one moment in the play, according to a London critic, Cushman "stands immovable . . . for two or three minutes."[86] Becoming a piece of sculpture herself, she aimed to freeze her audience.

Medusa was the center of this fantasy for Cushman and her circle—the

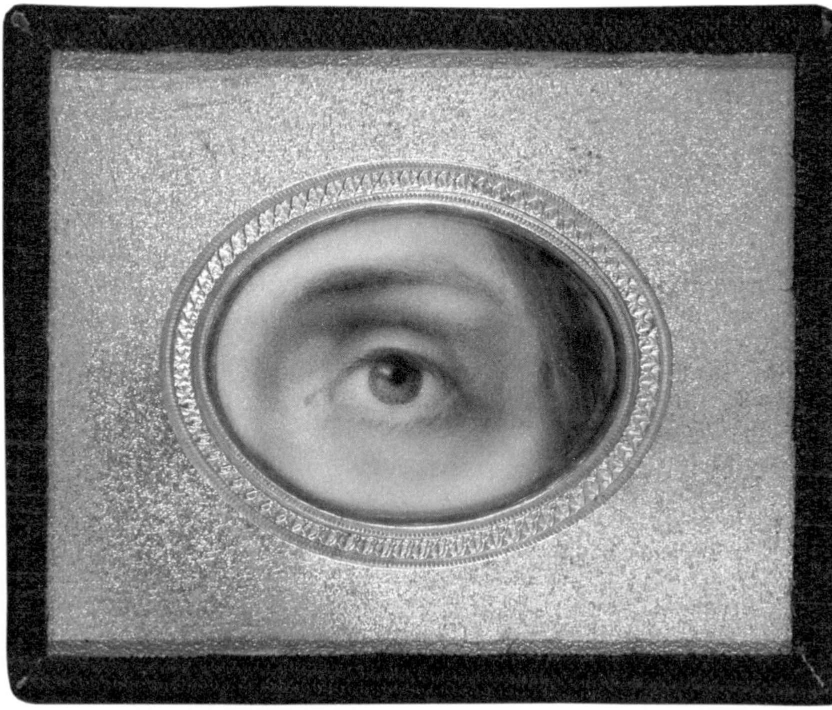

Fig. 11. Unknown artist, *Charlotte Cushman's Eye,* n.d. Watercolor with body color on ivory, ¾ × 1⅜ in (1.8 × 2.3 cm). By permission of the Folger Shakespeare Library, Washington, D.C.

exemplary figure of audience-commanding power. Hosmer's 1854 sculpture was one of many depictions of Medusa among the Cushman group (fig. 13). In 1863 her friend Adelaide Kemble Sartoris began *Medusa, and Other Tales,* a meditation like Hosmer's on the alternative myth of the tragic beautiful gorgon, here a woman named Wanda who kills her child rather than give it up, standing "as if she were made of stone," and producing the same effect in an auditor who, hearing her tale, "sat like one petrified." Sallie Bridges, another Cushman friend, published a book of poetry in 1864 called *Marble Isle,* featuring a long title poem about the fate of Sir John Franklin's crew in the Arctic, a region "cold, traceless, desolate, and still, as though / A moment's magic changed the world to stone!" That land, "like to a sculptured dream," is as still as the doomed sailors who listen to a man recite stories of murder "with air so suited to each startling tale / As thrilled

Fig. 12. Cushman as Meg Merrilies in *Guy Mannering.* Harvard Theatre Collection, Houghton Library, Harvard University.

us into statues of mute fear." A pining woman sits meanwhile on an English shore, "Transfix'd and silent, like to one who sees a / Gorgon's shield." Likewise, at the end of Hawthorne's story "The Gorgon's Head" (1851), Perseus displays the head to King Polydectes, his evil counselors, and all his fierce subjects, rendering them "all fixed, forever, in the look and attitude of that moment!"[87]

Cushman, like Hawthorne, Sartoris, and Bridges, dreamed of a Medusa-like dominion over her audience. In *Macbeth* she chose a play full of these freezing effects. "Approach the chamber and destroy your sight / With a new Gorgon" (2.3.70–71), says Macduff after he has seen the body of Duncan. So too Macbeth's head on a pike at the end of the play makes him a "male Medusa," as the critic Marjorie Garber notes.[88] The play aims at different moments for a "concentrated visual effect," in the words of critic D. J. Palmer, "a stunning sight," a "suspended, intensely charged, moment."[89] The doctor says of Lady Macbeth to the gentlewoman during the sleepwalking scene: "My mind she has mated, and amazed my sight" (5.1.77).

These moments are meant to stain the air with a permanent image. Lady

Fig. 13. Harriet Hosmer, *Medusa,* 1854. Marble, 27 × 19 × 9 in. (68.6 × 48.3 × 22.9 cm). Detroit Institute of Arts, Founders Society Purchase, R. H. Tannahill Foundation Fund. Photo: The Bridgeman Art Library.

Macbeth, even after she has departed the stage for the last time, remains. "Look after her," "still keep eyes upon her," the doctor says to the gentlewoman, also implicitly addressing the audience, who would note and never forget her even after she is gone. Cushman, in her last scene at the Grover's production, aimed perhaps not just to be massive and simple onstage but to leave an afterimage, an impression still standing in the air—an impression almost of sculptural permanence—that would freeze her beholders, amaze their sight, mate their minds, and leave them speechless.

This dream of absolute command reached ever outward. Not just the audience in the theater but whole worlds might symbolically stop before the grand actress's powers of fixation. Here Cushman had a head start: the nineteenth century was already busy turning as much as it could to stone, transforming ephemeral experience into crystal petrifactions of various kinds. The stage was a first zone, a ground zero, of this fixation. At the dedication of the great organ on November 2, Cushman stood before an instrument that transformed ethereal music into solid form. "Never did any structure so fully justify Madame de Staël's definition of architecture as frozen music," Holmes wrote. "It is as if a glorious anthem had passed into outward solid form in the very ecstasy of its grandest chorus."[90] A *Boston Daily Courier* critic wrote, following Holmes, "If one could imagine a symphony of Beethoven taking visible shape and embodying itself in forms of architecture and sculpture, the result would be the superb structure in which the pipes of the great organ are enclosed. The music seems to have made the case, as the nautilus fabricates his shell."[91] A photograph of the great organ at the Music Hall (which also shows Crawford's *Beethoven* to the left) indicates the range of frozen or petrified effects onstage that night (fig. 14). Rarely was there such an occasion when music was meant to be looked at.

Outside the Music Hall or Grover's Theatre, the world consented to be no less frozen. Social and spiritual rigidities took shape everywhere—a middle-class phenomenon. Cushman's early friend Anne Hampton Brewster published her first novel, *Spirit Sculpture,* in 1849—a Christian tale that asked its readers to "carve their own soul's statue," to portray themselves every day, sculpting themselves at each moment of their existence, so that at death the composite statue of their being would appeal to heaven. Worldly existence for Brewster remained in 1863 a portal "covered over with beautiful chiselings, sharp cut and deep laid," a chiaroscuro of sorrow and joys leading to eternal life.[92]

Within the bourgeois parlor, secular behaviors took on an equal stillness. In "Tableaux Vivans," an October 1863 story in *Harper's Monthly,* one character who "had once seen Miss Cushman" agrees to impersonate Meg Merrilies for one of these domestic tableaux, trusting "that the memory would render her own impersonation sufficiently weird and striking."[93] Beyond this imitation of a sculpturelike performance—itself a strikingly imagined case of Cushman's distributed personhood, her capacity to deliver herself, or some version of herself, into a distant space in the form of a daguerreotype, a letter, a newspaper article, or (here) an impersonation—such tableaux portrayed the bourgeois self-regulation meant to obtain at all times, game or no game. "To strike the appropriate emotional expression and pose and, in the tableau vivant, to maintain them with flawless self-discipline for half a minute: this was a frozen caricature of the genteel performance," the historian Karen Halttunen writes. "The parlor performer was thus virtually sculpted into genteel propriety."[94]

Photography kept pace with this penchant for self-freezing, adding an especially morbid dimension. By the late 1850s the new medium could make even the busiest street as eerily still as Bridges's *Marble Isle.* "It is the oriental

Fig. 14. Boston Music Hall organ, with Thomas Crawford's *Beethoven* in front on left, ca. 1863–84. From New England Conservatory of Music Archives, Boston, Massachusetts.

Fig. 15. Broadway on a rainy day, ca. 1860. Albumen print stereograph (half), 2⅞ × 2¾ in (7.4 × 6.9 cm). Courtesy of George Eastman House, International Museum of Photography and Film, Rochester, New York.

story of the petrified city made real to our eyes," marveled Holmes in 1861. "Take ten thousand instantaneous photographs of the great thoroughfare in a day," he wrote, much affected by "Mr. Anthony's miraculous instantaneous view in Broadway" (fig. 15), and "every one of them will be as still as the *tableau* in the 'Enchanted Beauty.' . . . The hurried day's life of Broadway will have been made up of just such stillnesses. Motion is as rigid as marble, if you only take a wink's worth of it at a time."[95]

No wonder Holmes focused on stereographs of Westminster Abbey ("Enough of these marbles; there is no end to them; the walls and floor of the great, many-arched, thousand-pillared, sky-lifted cavern are crusted all over with them, like stalactites and stalagmites"). No wonder that he claimed snow, ice, and stone were the stereograph's best subjects or that he examined stereographs of Pompeii. "Tread with us the streets of Pompeii for a moment: there are the ruts made by the chariots of eighteen hundred years ago."[96] When on February 5, 1863, Giorgio Sommer made stereographs of the plaster casts of the victims at Pompeii (figs. 16 and 17)—portraying the newly invented in-fill technique of the Pompeii superintendent Giovanni Fiorelli—he perfectly expressed this period kinship between sculpture, photography, and deathly stillness: a kinship that Timothy O'Sullivan would exploit, studying the same sprawl of different bodies, at the Gettysburg battlefield later that year.

Did Charlotte Cushman conceive her freezing powers in this way? Was her Medusa-like intensity a type of death ray, according to which all life around her, near and far, or at least out to a certain radius, might absolutely cease—with men, women, children, animals fixed where they were, eating, sleeping, or walking or running along, by the sheer symbolic power of her emanating performance? Perhaps she was like the musician in Henry Wadsworth Longfellow's *Tales of a Wayside Inn* (1863), "whose music had so weird a sound / The hunted stag forgot to bound."[97] Did the strength of her Lady Macbeth or her Meg Merrilies consist in her ability to make others share the characters' tragic fate, succumbing as she succumbed? When Cushman recited Charles Kingsley's "The Sands of Dee"—the poem about the fate of a lost girl, swept away so that only the echo of a voice remained, that so frightened little Maud Howe—did she succeed by making her little auditor crawl into hiding, as if sharing the fate of the girl in the poem? Did Cushman aspire to be, then, a destructive force of nature? Or, no less destructive, did she conceive herself as a camera photographing her audiences in time-bound postures of marble stillness? Did she fashion herself after a bullet or other projectile, one of the ever-more-efficient shells of different calibers and different explosions speeding across miles to stun, maim, and slaughter the distant persons who would have been safely out of harm's way in the wars of the previous generation? Was this her morbid speed, that of a person who could be the bullet and the photograph (and even the telegraph with news of the death the bullet caused) all in one devastating extension of the self? Then she would send messages with the force to petrify even remote persons.

Cushman's aim, however, was somewhat different. It was neither exactly morbid nor exactly decorous. In turning the world symbolically to stone, she did not wish to make a morgue. Neither did she wish to make spirit sculptures or tableaux of genteel deportment. Wanting to be remembered—wanting to remember—she aimed to make the world a souvenir.

Figs. 16–17. Giorgio Sommer, *Plaster Casts of Pompeii Victims, February 5, 1863*, 1863. Stereographs (two halves). Yale University Art Gallery, Gift of Mr. and Mrs. Melville Chapin.

Cushman's time was one of rapacious interest in commemorative objects, and she was a human epicenter of this souvenir culture. Signing her name for Union officers, distributing *cartes de visite,* those cardboard emissaries of herself, she also received commemorative gifts all the time, an autographed copy of *The Scarlet Letter,* for example, or a satin playbill listing the entire cast on the night of October 17, 1863.[98] Whenever she played Meg Merrilies, "the stick which she carried was always greatly in demand; and as it was one of the 'properties,' and always newly provided for each engagement, there must be many of these relics scattered about the country."[99] Cushman's repeated "final" performances starting in the 1850s, when she made the first of her retirement announcements, underscored the commemorative bent of her career. When after one of the last of these farewells, in 1875, theater personnel trundled statues onstage to help dignify the post-performance encomiums, the sculptures literalized the actress's prolific self-immortalizations, which fell from almost her every appearance, strewn by the actress to her audience like bouquets.[100]

Cushman's performance on October 17, 1863, was not exactly a retirement, but it too was a packaged effort, secure and steady down to her last line, a rendition given long after her conception of Lady Macbeth had "crystallized," in Brewster's word, when "the spontaneity of youth was gone."[101] Benjamin Brown French's words of praise—"Charlotte Cushman was perfect. She always is"—suggest the souvenir status of her performance, a keepsake no less material, no less neat and tidy, than the program he pasted in his diary. Cushman's performance was itself sculptural, as in a bust Stebbins executed of her in 1859, which appears (fittingly) in a photograph in the sculptor's scrapbook.[102] "Fame's loudest blast upon the ear of Time leaves but a dying echo," Cushman wrote in one autograph.[103] Yet with frozen testaments, personal keepsakes, idolatrous mementoes, she would outlast the moment.

Cushman's aim had its pathos and its shallowness. The souvenir suggested an intolerance of ephemeral experience—a desire to turn all fleeting events into their material embodiments, even to value events only to the extent that they produced these souvenir materializations. It also turned the artistic experience into a commodity, a scientific specimen, a historical fact—each a fossilization by which nineteenth-century middle-class culture imposed a fantastic stability and rationality on life. If for Walter Benjamin "the nineteenth century's conception of history" turned the world into "an endless series of facts congealed in the form of things . . . an inventory, point by point, of humanity's life forms and creations," the souvenir shared this definition.[104]

For Cushman as for other souvenir hunters, the key space to capture was the corner. This area of a room is most resistant to the impress of dominant forces, as Gaston Bachelard notes in *The Poetics of Space;* it is the most obscure and least functional region, where wayward experience might shelter itself.[105] The souvenir hunter, in her rapacity, would penetrate even these nooks and crannies, regarding no space as too insignificant and ephemeral to yield a solid treasure. "There is no remoteness of life and thought," Hawthorne wrote in an 1862 article about Washington, D.C., "no hermetically sealed seclusion, except, possibly, that of the grave, into which the disturbing influences of this war do not penetrate."[106] Not just the war but its souvenirs spread this way—and they did in fact extend into the grave. Even that corner of corners yielded its war mementoes. The Union hero Elmer Ellsworth, embalmed, had already become at least the temporary souvenir of himself, and the bones of the battlefield dead were fair game: Henry Bellows himself had taken from the Bull Run battlefield "a very nice *bone,* the hip bone of a loyal hero," as well as a skull.[107] Beyond the war, techniques such as Fiorelli's would soon re-create the dead in all the isolation of their ashen shrouds. For Cushman, likewise, corners and other obscure spaces were meant to be penetrated. At Grover's, according to an 1870 report, access to the third tier was via "a steep, narrow, corkscrew staircase about four feet wide."[108] Cushman, wanting to make her presence felt, regarded her performances as pointless if they did not flow and symbolically fill the nooks and crannies of the theater—if they did not in effect take a negative cast of those spaces and the people within them. She wanted to take a rubbing of the world.

The key, however—to both the artistic power of Cushman's acting and the melodramatic sculpture related to it—is that she was doomed to fail in her souvenir hunting. It was a question of gesture. Nineteenth-century melodrama, the literary critic Peter Brooks writes, tried to spread out and give meaning to the vast and newly empty postrevolutionary world through gesture. Where was cosmological order in a world without gods and kings? It would have to be searched for—in extravagant tones and movements. A critic in 1882 noted that Cushman used many melodramatic conventions: "the angular motion, the stride, the start, the labored breathing, and the stilted declamation."[109] As Brooks notes in a description of early nineteenth-century French theater, "A histrionic style of emphatic and striking proportions" did more than hold "a house in a charged emotional medium." It also indicated a presence—a return to a primal, prelinguistic way of creating meaning. The gesture conjured "forces held to be beyond the possibilities of rational apprehension and literal statement. Gesture appears as a way to make available certain occulted perceptions and relationships, to render, with the audacity of an as-if proposition, a world of significant shadows."[110] The exaggeration denoted something serious—an attempt to represent, capture, bring down out of thin air a moral universe. Cushman, striking her poses, aimed for these effects.

But the hyperbole of her gestures also admitted to a failure to find this larger significance. The melodramatic gesture was always a blind groping, even a form of stammered impatience. "Bring him to me!" Cushman once exclaimed on hearing that a friend was unexpectedly in Rome. "Bring him to me," she said, "grasping the air with 'hooked hands.' "[111] But the world, unlike Cushman's friends, did not always rise up and come near at the call of a melodramatic demand.

Of all midcentury American sculptures, Randolph Rogers's *Nydia, the Blind Flower Girl of Pompeii,* from 1854–55 (fig. 18), perfectly shows this poignancy of melodrama, and in ways that illuminate the pathos of Cushman's Lady Macbeth. Rogers (1825–92), a jealous and acerbic member of Cushman's circle in Rome, had the great hit of his career with *Nydia.* Depicting a scene from Edward Bulwer-Lytton's 1834 novel *The Last Days of Pompeii,* the sculpture shows Nydia moving through the volcanic destruction, alone accustomed to the darkness, as she listens amid the tumult for Glaucus and Ione. In the novel she survives the eruption but soon chooses to die: Rogers shows a tragic heroine.[112]

The sculpture has several odd features, all centering on its melodramatic gestures. One is the awkward way the flower girl reaches across her body to cup her left hand, palm backward, to her ear. The pose calls to mind the excessive gesture in Jean-Baptiste Carpeaux's *Young Fisherboy with a Shell* (1859), another of the midcentury's curiously numerous auditory sculptures—a gesture, in the words of a period critic, "violent and exaggerated, as if the little fisherboy were expending an awful lot of energy to lift a light seashell to his ear."[113] Rilke, in his 1903 essay on Rodin, sets Rodin apart yet uses language that makes one feel unexpectedly that the sculptor's grasping, imploring figures—*The Burghers of Calais,* for example—come out of this midcentury academic tradition in which the later master's contortions of finger and elbow were even then taking nascent shape. Rodin's gestures, Rilke writes, using terms that work well for *Nydia*'s across-the-body hand to ear, "were impatient. Like one who searches in vain for some desired object and,

Fig. 18. Randolph Rogers, *Nydia, the Blind Flower Girl of Pompeii,* ca. 1854–55. Princeton University Art Museum, Gift of Dr. J. Ackerman Coles and Emily Coles. Photograph by Bruce M. White.

not knowing where to turn, becomes more and more distracted and hasty, disturbing all about him and gathering round him a disorderly mass of things as if to compel them to join in the search."[114]

For Rilke, such importuning suggests a broad humanistic loss—a melodramatic grasping at the world akin to what Brooks would describe. "So the gestures of humanity, failing to understand their own significance, have become more impatient, more nervous, more hurried, and more abrupt," Rilke writes:

> And all the tormented questions of existence lie about them. But at the same time these movements have become more hesitating. They no longer possess the athletic and resolute directness which characterized the appropriating gestures of earlier generations. They are not like the movements preserved for us in ancient statues, of which only the beginning and the end were important. . . . The gestures of seizing, of beckoning, of relinquishing, and of holding had changed. All of them showed greater experience and, at the same time, greater ignorance; much less courage and a constant attacking of obstacles; much more mourning for what has been lost; much more calculation, judgment, reflexion, and less spontaneity.[115]

Rilke's terms for Rodin give us some insight into *Nydia,* where the heroine's arm does not corkscrew like an Aesculapian snake (as we might say of one of Rodin's gestures) but nonetheless contorts into a compellingly awkward and somehow modern pose of plaintive yearning.

What does she miss? What is she seeking? What did Cushman herself want? Nydia's gesture is about a failure to hear her friends—an unsuccessful attempt to discern their voices—and that is Rogers's lesson about melodramatic art, about its strength and limitation or, rather, the strength of its limitation. Art, this sculpture suggests, is the one thing, in 1855, in 1863, that cannot hear—that cannot discern its relation to the world. Partly this world is the trivial conversational space around it, the type of domestic environment to which realism was even then laying claim (in Flaubert's *Madame Bovary,* for example, published in book form in 1857). Nydia's hand-to-ear gesture activates these immediate domestic spaces in which copies of the sculpture knew they would find themselves. The gesture activates all the conversations, the daily gossip and other banal discourse, that the sculpture imagines to take place around it. Rogers was an expert mimic—one of the people he supremely annoyed with his powers of mimicry was Charlotte Cushman, of whose mordant poetry recitals he could do a devastating impersonation (to the lasting and indeed permanent detriment of their friendship)—and he lent to *Nydia* his own powers of cocking an ear.

Nydia also listens in vain for the technological-political-national world. At a time when, Holmes wrote, you could hear telegraphically from Boston a whisper in New Orleans or gain (on the railroad) "legs that can walk six hundred miles in a day," art was the one thing cut off.[116] It wanted nothing more than to know the larger world, as did Cushman. Melodramatic art would gladly lay claim to powers fully commensurate with the telegraph and the railroad. It would love to be a mechanistic force, petrifying and rendering the world, in even its remotest corners, a type of souvenir, frozen in thrall to its radiating power. But it did not have the power to live out this fantasy of encompassing command. The granular surface of this sculpture is so fine that nothing so uncouth as lived experience could make a disfiguring mark upon it. It is fated to irrelevance, to blind groping, in a world in which it has lost its place.

In domestic and national realms, *Nydia* is only an adornment. Unable to make contact with those worlds, it cannot find universal significances either—higher meanings, larger forces, cosmological laws. The melodramatic work of art can make only a meager and straining attempt to hear the universe but is doomed to failure. Nydia walks among explosive forces, cataclysms, that register only as energies passing across her—passing across in the sound waves of her hair and the flourishing agitation of her dress (figs. 19 and 20). The dress especially is a sign of this tumultuous cosmological life—a life that would ravish her, in the manner of cloudy Jupiter's seduction of Io—in which she yet walks unaware, even as her body courses and flutters with the divine tremors she cannot see.

The art critic John Jackson Jarves was right in 1864 when he called such sculptures "monstrous stone toys." He was right too when he wrote that *Nydia* is borrowed from the classical *Niobe* group at the Vatican, minus the pathos.[117] Emerson was right in 1850 that modern sculpture lacked "the old tragic Necessity, which lowers on the brows even of the Venuses and the Cupids of the antique" and that it was instead a "sickly beauty" of "voluptuous reveries." Emerson was right, too, to be reminded of the great gap between these works and daily life and to note that modern sculptors "reject life as prosaic, and create a death which they call poetic." And he was right to see the vast gap between these paltry marbles and the universe: "I do not wonder that Newton, with an attention habitually engaged on the paths of planets and suns, should have wondered what the Earl of Pembroke

Figs. 19–20. Randolph Rogers, *Nydia* (two details of fig. 18). Photographs by Bruce M. White.

Fig. 21. Charlotte Cushman's home, ca. 1875. Newport Historical Society, Newport, Rhode Island.

found to admire in 'stone dolls.' "[118] In *Nydia,* however, Rogers recognized this triviality and made his work's irrelevance its subject. Cushman's sleepwalking Lady Macbeth, like Nydia, cannot see. She too is cut off from daily and universal worlds, oblivious to them. But that oblivion produces a lucid self-recognition of aloneness.

Maybe this isolation is why to the last, let alone on October 17, 1863, Cushman's career can be read as a vain search for cosmic significance. Her Newport, Rhode Island, mansion, designed by Richard Morris Hunt and completed in 1871 for her permanent return to the United States, was an overelaborated dwelling even for a Victorian house (fig. 21). Known now only in a few photographs and drawings (it was destroyed in 1938), Villa

Cushman featured peaked roofs, assorted crestings and finials, high windows, sharply hooded dormers, and turrets and facetings pointing in all directions, including down to the sea a short distance away. Nicknamed the Corners, not just because of its location at the corner of Rhode Island Avenue and Catherine Street but also because of its angular, jutting profiles, the house seemed to point in all directions, as if under a requirement to multiply its contact with the world. In contrast to the Yankee merchant snug inside his perfectly built house, four-square secure in his dignity, and unconcerned with the existential void he built upon—a floating ball of matter hurtling through the universe—the Corners seemed actively to search out the cosmos.

In the photograph the mansion calls to mind an observatory, a kind of Victorian space station, bristling with antennae and other sensors. Hunt's drawing of the house's various finials, lightning rods, and other protrusions suggests the ceremonial and functional importance of these extensions into the sky, part of what the architectural historian Paul Baker calls the building's "vertical thrust" (fig. 22).[119] Expressing the personality of its owner, Villa Cushman appeared to be on the alert at all times for a sign from the vastness. The house seemed to operate under the earnest conviction that its variegated play of spike and slope, pointing in all directions at once, would increase the chance of that precious contact.

Even from the grave, Cushman sought that connection. A little more than a year before she died of pneumonia on February 18, 1876, she visited Mount Auburn Cemetery in Cambridge, Massachusetts, to select her burial site. Beset by cancer but still imperious, she "inspected a number of lots and tombs then for sale," a reporter wrote, in "very prominent portions of the cemetery." But Cushman wanted something else: "Haven't you a lot for sale where one could obtain an unobstructed view of Boston?" She was then shown the site she took, just below the cemetery's Washington Tower, which marks Mount Auburn's highest point: a plot on Palm Avenue, "strikingly beautiful, being within full view of [Boston] and overlooking the widest part of Charles River." Although trees now block that view, the visitor can still get a sense of the vista the gravesite once afforded. Cushman was so taken with the site that in the summer of 1875 "she again visited the place in company with a party of other ladies, and appeared to be greatly pleased with the selection she had made."[120]

An obelisk marks the tomb (fig. 23). Obelisks were a common enough Victorian grave marker; Mount Auburn and other period cemeteries bristle with them. Cushman's choice of the ancient Egyptian symbol of eternal

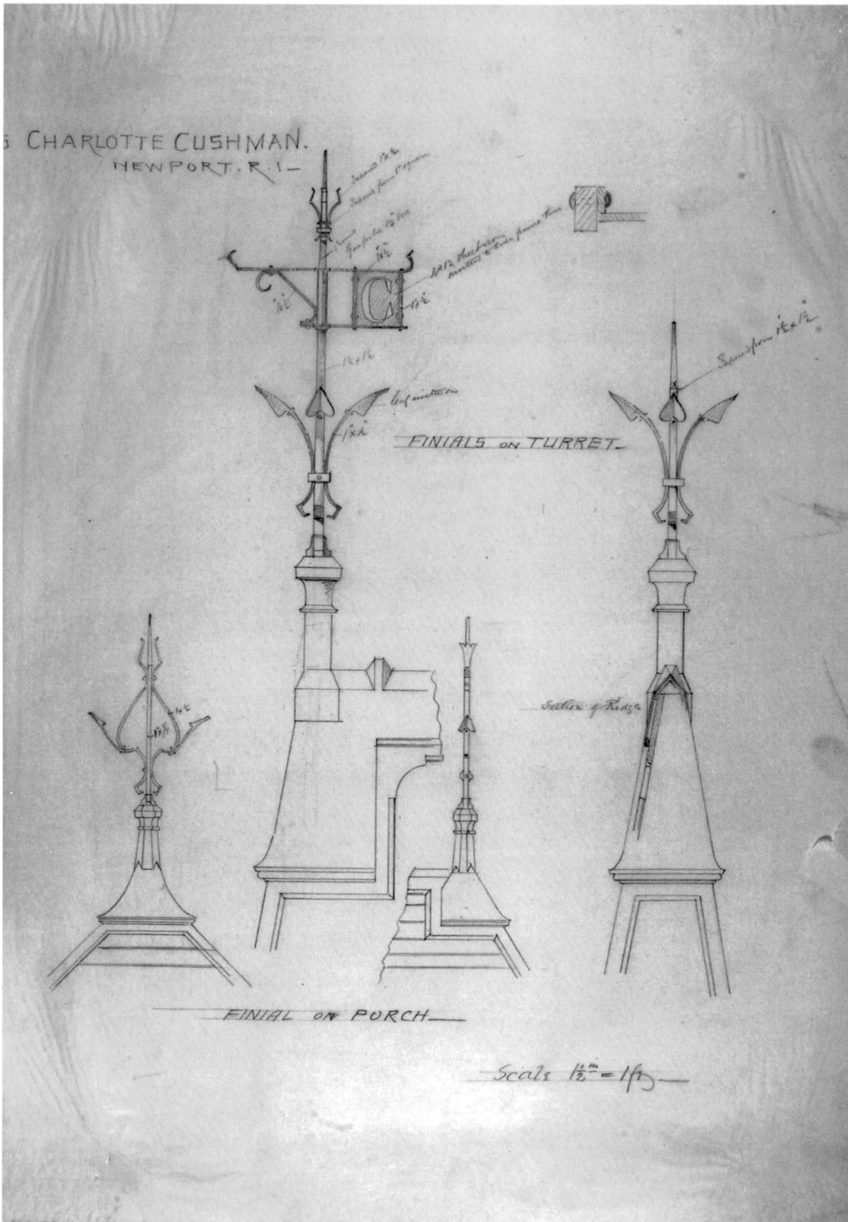

Fig. 22. Richard Morris Hunt, *Charlotte Cushman House: Details of Finials*, ca. 1870. Pencil on tracing paper, 27½ × 19 in. (69.9 × 48.3 cm). Prints and Drawings Collection, The Octagon Museum, The American Architectural Foundation, Washington, D.C.

Fig. 23. Charlotte Cushman's obelisk, 1876. Photo courtesy of Mount Auburn Cemetery, Cambridge, Massachusetts.

life is especially apt, however, telling one last time the tale of her melodramatic relation to space. The obelisk, for the philosopher Georges Bataille, was once a sign to keep out the terror of time and to drown out the chaos of space, a simple geometry that calmed the terrifying world around it. It was "the surest and most durable obstacle to the drifting away of all things," a way "for man to set the most stable limits on the deleterious movement of time," with the "mocking universe . . . slowly given over to the severe *eternity* of its almighty Father, guarantor of profound stability." Then (in Cushman's time) "moderation and platitude slowly took over the world. . . . The grim reaper went the way of all other phantoms." Satan was dead. The horizon of fear, that "Heraclitean world of rivers and flames" that the enduring obelisk had held at bay, came to be the domain only of so much "pride and glory"—the vistas of a progressive era. The obelisk stood now for human conquest of space and time, with domains of rationality extended out to the very horizon that once teemed with monsters and demons. In the emptiness of this expansion, however, there lurked a greater terror than had ever existed before—the terror of a world that had so perfectly repressed the ancient "agitation and dread," so completely persuaded itself of their abolishment, that the moment of death became a sudden explosion into realities that previous cultures had always known the presence of.[121]

In the nineteenth century, the obelisk thus marked two things, both profoundly relevant to Cushman. One was a pretentious would-be triumph over space and time. Another, more important, was a sense that this leveling of the world—completely flattening it into triumphs of rational efficiency—took away the terror that the fated person and her monument might yet heroically, blindly, gropingly, try to recover. Sheer force of gesture might summon that world of cosmological shadows and fiery demons, the world of true existential significance, gathering it round the magical monument, the talisman that draws to it the "spirits / That tend on mortal thoughts." Cushman's obelisk is melodramatic in that sense: it "aspires in its depths to the tragic deliverances of primitive Greek naiveté."[122] It is like one of her early roles, Nancy in *Oliver Twist,* which she played with a "rough but solemn tragic power" that "was like a revolting sacrifice in some rude work of early art," evoking a time "when there was the strength of genius without culture and refinement."[123] Cushman's obelisk, for all its straightness, is a gesture as bent and blind as the most limb-contorting bit of stage business. Railing against the progressive world she so loved—the world of narcissistic expansion, the self spreading out in emissaries of letter, photograph, and telegram—the obelisk, like Cushman in her lifetime, strives to summon, and knows it must fail to find, a primitively fearful universe of tragic necessity.

Consider again the photograph of Grover's Theatre (see fig. 2). The men on the street and the balcony pose for the photographer, while atop the roof, barely visible, stand the sculptures installed by Leonard Grover as testaments to the dramatic arts. The sculptures, humdrum and ordinary as they doubtless were, pose again the question of a relation between melodramatic art and the cosmos. They stand as though waiting for signs from the sky. The prospects for contact do not appear good, but there is always a chance.

The corners of the theater's façade are equally important in this quest. Interior corners are places into which an all-affecting art would dream of insinuating itself, but exterior corners like these (we see only one in the photograph) tell another story. *Macbeth* contains moments when something not quite real, not quite there, seems to appear before a character: the dagger or Banquo's ghost before Macbeth, the blood on Lady Macbeth's hands. Another such moment concerns the corners of a building—suggesting the conditions of melodramatic searching, extending, importuning that I have addressed. As Banquo looks up at the Macbeths' castle upon his arrival there in the first act, he says,

> This guest of summer,
> The temple-haunting martlet, does approve
> By his loved mansionry that the heaven's breath
> Smells wooingly here. No jutty, frieze,
> Buttress, nor coign of vantage, but this bird
> Hath made his pendent bed and procreant cradle.
> Where they most breed and haunt, I have observed,
> The air is delicate. (1.6.3–10)

This beautiful little poem figures the meeting of building and sky. The building extends outward—jutty, frieze, coign (corner) of vantage are all signs of the Macbeths' aggressive, assertive reaching out into the world. The sky, the heaven, the heaven's breath, the air, the delicate air come to meet it. The birds, the martlets, are perhaps a birth of these two opposites, stone and sky, since they are creatures that fly yet also build mansions. Appending their sexualized dwellings of testicular bed and womblike cradle, they attach to, and so seem to bestow an allegorical significance upon, the castle.

But this blending of sky and stone—this procreating of the two—is, of course, only wishful thinking. Banquo is fatally wrong in his estimation. In the end we are left with the severance of building and heaven, their incompatibility. The grand grasping gestures outward—jutty, frieze, buttress, coign of vantage—all read as failed attempts to embrace, to dig into and take a piece out of the universe.

"Mr. Bokee" of Grover's stock company played Banquo on October 17, but the words he spoke that night might as well have been Cushman's. Onstage at Grover's she wanted to make contact with life. She wanted this contact but maybe also sensed that no extension of her voice and body could provide it—that the void would only increase its silence as the vehemence of her gestures grew. The wooing breath of heaven never really caressed or impregnated or whispered to the cold stone.

TWO

The Flame of Place

Abraham Lincoln

ABRAHAM LINCOLN HAD A POWER of being in one place only. He believed in a here and now of experience, a form of presence. In such moments he would gather and crush down his sight into single places and single visions of extraordinary and lonely intensity—melancholic, ecstatic, or both. How was this sense of presence manifest as the president sat at Grover's Theatre on October 17, 1863? One can only guess, since the accounts of Lincoln at that event are limited, and since Lincoln himself provided none. But he might have watched that play as though the theater, the stage, the lines of the individual actors were the only things on earth.

The opposite was also true. If Lincoln could be so much "here," he also contemplated various "theres"—the faraway places, distant from the theater, that became subject to the force field of the play. Let us consider those places before we return to his formidable sense of the here and now.

At one point during the performance on October 17, according to the journalist Frazar Kirkland, Lincoln focused his thoughts on the distance. Malcolm spoke the line "Let us seek out some desolate shade and there / Weep our sad bosoms empty," and Edward Davenport's Macduff responded,

> Each new morn
> New widows howl, new orphans cry, new sorrows
> Strike heaven on the face. (4.3.4–6)

Hearing these lines, "Mr. Lincoln leaned back in his chair in the shade," recalled Kirkland, writing in 1866, " . . . and for a long time wore a sad, sober face, as if suddenly his thoughts had wandered from the playroom far away to where his great armies were contesting."[1] That day the *Daily National Republican* carried Lincoln's call for an additional three hundred thousand volunteers to help win the war, published widely in newspapers in the days that followed. The proclamation addressed not only "the Governors of the several States, but also the good and loyal people thereof, invoking them to lend their willing, cheerful, and effective aid."[2] Sitting in a private theater box that night, Lincoln had more reason to think of remote people and situations and had a greater ability to affect them than any other person in the country.

Macbeth that night could even make him think of specific people. At 2:45 that day Major General John Foster of Fortress Monroe, Virginia, near Norfolk, had telegraphed Lincoln to tell him that the wife of a condemned prisoner named David Wright wished to come to Washington to plead for her husband's life, encouraged by Lincoln's granting of a one-week reprieve the previous day. Lincoln telegraphed back, "It would be useless for Mrs. Dr. Wright to come here. The subject is a very painful one, but the case is settled."[3] Wright would be executed on October 23.

The Wright case was a *Macbeth*-like mix of blood, remorse, and insanity that might well have crossed Lincoln's mind as he watched the play on October 17, a few hours after pronouncing final judgment on the prisoner. On July 11, 1863, Wright had shot and killed Federal Lieutenant Anson Sanborn in Norfolk, provoked by the sight of Sanborn leading a detachment of black soldiers through the city.[4] As the column passed a dry goods store at the corner of East Main and Hill streets, Wright, standing in a doorway, called Sanborn a coward. Sanborn halted his soldiers after a few paces and turned to address Wright, responding to a provocation that was bound to happen somewhere, sometime, in that tense city. The Union had taken possession of Norfolk in May 1862 and instituted martial law after its attempts to establish a loyal city government failed, and on January 1, 1863, black residents celebrated news of emancipation by marching through the streets.[5] By June 1863 the city was no longer under martial law, but only whites who had taken an oath of allegiance to the Union could vote. So on a hot July afternoon at about four o'clock, Wright "pulled a pistol out of his right hand coat pantaloons pocket" and shot Sanborn twice. The lieutenant, according to a witness, "then slid along the store's counter and fell to the floor, blood gushing out of his mouth and nostrils."[6]

Wright immediately felt a Macbeth-like remorse for what he had done, as Lincoln knew. A prominent member of the Norfolk community, aged fifty-four in 1863, Wright "had from early youth a horror of blood; never could bring himself to the point of shooting a bird, or killing anything," according to Dr. John P. Gray, who examined the prisoner at Lincoln's request in September. Even with Sanborn dying in front of him, Wright wanted to help his victim, who until his enlistment two months earlier had been a schoolteacher in Whitford Centre, Vermont. Wright "felt the most awful agony of mind" there at the scene, according to Gray, "and thought if only those bayonets were run through him [those of the Union soldiers who had wanted to kill him], it would be a sweet death; that he would then have welcomed such a death." Wright later told Gray that he "suffered intensely for a few days, and found no relief—no tears; that at length tears came to his relief in a flood, without measure; that then he felt better—slept soundly; that the whole thing was revolting to him—to every sentiment of his nature; that it seemed to him like a horrid dream."[7]

How did Lincoln know these details? On September 10, moved by petitions from the Norfolk community, which claimed that the gentle Wright had been momentarily insane when he pulled the trigger, Lincoln had ordered Gray, superintendent of the New York State Lunatic Asylum, to conduct a special examination to determine if the doctor was out of his mind at the time of the murder. Gray visited Wright many times in his Fortress Monroe jail cell, assembling the data on which Lincoln would base his final decision on October 17 and which Gray would publish the following January in an issue of the *American Journal of Insanity.*

Gray found Wright to be a "pale, composed, gentlemanly" person who talked professional shop, giving his views of medical techniques and remedies; spoke of growing up in North Carolina and of his education in New Haven and Philadelphia; and expressed his love for his family and his special concern for his twenty-one-year-old son Minton, the second oldest of eight, whom he had not heard from since the Battle of Gettysburg, fought a few days before the shooting in Norfolk.[8] He spoke also of being a longstanding Whig and a Union man at the start of the war who only "gradually went into the current of Southern feeling," and he described his kindness toward his six slaves, three men and three women, five of them over the age of forty, who could, he had told them, "try the world for themselves; but that if they found they were not as well off as they had been with him, they might at any time return" and "receive as much kindness as before." He told Gray that his Northern education had given him a critical view of bondage but that "he afterwards changed his opinion on the subject of slavery and conscientiously believed it to be in accordance with the scriptures, and the true welfare of the negro, and that he looked upon its attempted destruction as a wrong to both races." Even so, Wright said that when Union soldiers occupied Norfolk, he told his friends to abstain from all violence and said that he had nothing against black soldiers, "though with most Southern men, he thought the arming of slaves a great wrong." On his way to make calls on July 11, Wright had happened to see Sanborn and "in an instant . . . felt the most unconquerable and desperate impulse to shoot him, and got a pistol." Gray, reviewing the case, was unmoved. He pronounced Wright sane, and on that basis Lincoln ordered the execution, denying numerous petitions to save the prisoner's life, including the appeal of Wright's wife on October 17.[9]

At the play that night, the Macbeths' guilt—"Had I but died an hour before this chance, / I had lived a blessèd time" (2.3.89–90) and "What, will these hands ne'er be clean?" (5.1.43)—resonated with Wright's. Macbeth's torment as he relived his murders was akin to the doctor's conception of the murder as a "horrid dream." Wright's horror of the blood flowing from Sanborn's nose and mouth was the horror of the Scottish couple furiously scrubbing the stain they knew would never come clean. If a relation existed between the Wright case and the play that night, however, it was not just between two sets of words and deeds but more precisely between two places: Grover's Theatre and a Fortress Monroe jail cell roughly two hundred miles away. How might Lincoln have conceived such simultaneous connections between two points in space?

The telegraph is the readiest explanation. The new device was becoming the premier metaphor for point-to-point communications, the transit of knowledge between two spots on earth, and certainly by the Civil War Lincoln was accustomed to thinking telegraphically. "During the Civil War the President spent more of his waking hours in the War Department telegraph office than in any other place, except the White House," David Homer Bates of the U.S. Military Telegraph Corps recalled in his memoir of 1907. "He visited the War Department telegraph office morning, afternoon, and evening, to receive the latest news from the armies at the front. . . . He seldom failed to come over late in the evening before retiring, and sometimes he would stay all night in the War Department." From that place Lincoln and his cabinet directed the war, commanding "widely separated armies and mov[ing] them in unison" and flashing "news of victories or defeats . . . almost instantly all over the broad land."[10]

On October 17, 1863, Lincoln's command of still-greater distances was a topic of the day. *Harper's Weekly* ran a cover story that day about the arrival of the Russian fleet in New York harbor, and in his annual message to Congress that December, Lincoln would mention his "arrangements with the Czar of Russia for the construction of a line of telegraph from our Pacific coast throughout the empire of Russia to connect with European systems," noted Bates. In that address Lincoln also urged Congress to consider "an international telegraph (cable) across the Atlantic and a cable connection between Washington and our forts and ports along the Atlantic coast and the Gulf of Mexico."[11] Not until 1866 would a transatlantic cable work consistently, and Lincoln's coastal cable never materialized, but his "far sight," as Bates called it, "is now seen to have been prophetic and his broad views . . . more comprehensive than those of others of his time."[12] For Lincoln, the connection between the play and Wright on October 17 might have been telegraphic.

Even so, a performance of *Macbeth* had no telegraphic power. Spoken words in a single location hung and dissipated in thin air, unable to shed their primitive frailty of spit and breath. To ensure the transit that they so clearly warranted in this case, given their relevance to the times (and, in Lincoln's case, their relevance to Wright), they would need to spin around themselves a fibrous sheath, a cable cocoon. In an evolution of speech, they would have to acquire this protective exoskeleton, this technological housing, to travel to the spaces they needed to reach. But even if this feat was not yet possible for speech in 1863, such national-allegorical words could perhaps, *in effect,* be conceived to travel this way. Lincoln had used the telegraph to communicate his final view of the Wright case only a few hours before the curtain went up on *Macbeth* at 8:20.[13] The play itself, bereft of actual telegraphic power, might still have figuratively traveled on wires, binding the space between Grover's Theatre and a Fortress Monroe jail cell by invisible ties. "New widows howl, new orphans cry, new sorrows / Strike heaven on the face." The words seemed to reach, to touch, people far away.

At the same time, *Macbeth* gave Lincoln a way to think of distance in a less scientific and more superstitious way. The key word for this way of thinking is "spot." During his first and only term in the U.S. House of Representatives, back in 1846–48, Lincoln gave only one memorable speech—the so-called Spot Resolutions of December 22, 1847. Criticizing President James Polk for what he believed was a reckless and deceitful war with Mexico, started on false pretenses and promoted through cynical stirrings of patriotic fervor, Lincoln spoke in lawyerly terms of here and there. If the war really began because American citizens were shot at "on our own soil," as Polk contended, then Lincoln resolved to know

> First, Whether the spot of soil on which the blood of our *citizens* was shed, as in his messages declared, was, or was not, within the territories of Spain, at least from the treaty of 1819 until the Mexican revolution.
>
> Second, Whether that spot is, or is not, within the territory which was wrested from Spain, by the Mexican revolution.
>
> Third, Whether that spot is, or is not, within a settlement of people, which settlement had existed ever since long before the Texas revolution, until its inhabitants fled from the approach of the U.S. Army.[14]

He continued with four more of these "spot resolutions" addressing the site of "bloodshed," the place "*before* the blood was shed," "the first blood so shed," the "*citizens,* whose blood was shed."[15] John Channing Briggs, in *Lincoln's Speeches Reconsidered,* notes Lincoln's clear allusions to *Macbeth* in the Mexico address, and, more importantly, its combination of bloody trauma and physical location: "The spot is the imaginative and physical space where the crime and the tainted land combine."[16] Inspiring detractors to tag him "spotty Lincoln," the speech was nonetheless a sufficient source of Whig and then Republican pride to be reprinted in full in William Dean Howells's official presidential campaign biography of 1860, a text that Lincoln read carefully and approved.[17]

The speech linked the distant location where the blood was shed with the spot on which the speaker stood. Making his only substantive speech on the floor of the House, Lincoln centered attention on himself in a presaging of the gathered intensities of his presidential declarations. Staking a position, he identified the voicing of a principle with the occupation of a single portion of ground. Moreover, he established a link between his own immovable position and the indelible stain he described. Somehow across the vast intervening space the person privileged to stand in a principled isolation could, by virtue of this placement, come to envision and maybe even feel the physicality of a far "spot of soil." Major William H. Emory, out in the Southwest on government reconnaissance in 1846–47, thought he saw "on the north side of the Gila, a perfect representation of the Capitol, with dome, wings, and portico, all complete," before the mirage "dwindled down into a distant butte."[18] Lincoln, back in Washington, envisioned an equally distant place in 1847, now imagining what the Southwest looked like from the Capitol instead of vice versa.

Lincoln's idea of the "spot" indicates a more primal, pretelegraphic conception of space—a more folkloric one that probably remained with him through the Civil War years. At the time of the Spot Resolutions, in December 1847, the telegraph was still new and hardly yet the all-purpose metaphor for point-to-point communication it would become. Not until 1857 would Lincoln thoroughly acquaint himself with the device.[19] The resolutions therefore suggest a less scientific spatial imagination for Lincoln—another way he could imagine the relation between one spot and another. He grew up in rural locales where the "superstitious settlers believed in ghosts, witches, and charms."[20] His Illinois law associate Henry C. Whitney recalled that in one county court "the doctrine of metempsychosis was discussed by the whole crowd, *i.e.,* the doctrine that when one man dies, a child is born which inherits the vital principle—the soul—of the departing one," a discussion in which Lincoln did not participate but which, according to Whitney, he understood.[21] Maybe a doctrine of this kind accounts for Lincoln's powers of bilocation that seemed to carry even into his presidential visions of here and there.

Consider further the case of Lincoln and Dr. Wright. To be in one spot was to feel the presence, out there somewhere, of some reciprocal spot that might all but hallucinate itself into one's midst. The relation between play and prisoner maybe implied a way for Lincoln to be in two places at once—to transport Wright suddenly, vividly, into the theater even as the play would lodge at Fortress Monroe. On the morning of October 23 Wright looked into the interior of his cypress coffin and gazed for some minutes at its inside walls hung with daguerreotypes of his wife and all eight of his children—Penelope, Minton, Elizabeth, Mary, John, Sallie, William, and Viola, ages twenty-three down to seven. (Minton, killed at Gettysburg, preceded his father on the journey his photograph would help assuage.) "I think there is nothing improper in that," he told a bystander. To carry images of Elsewhere—to envision an outside world that literally could not be seen, no less in the enclosure of a theater than in a casket: this too, in the traveling that could be done on one spot, was Lincoln's way of thinking.[22]

Clark Mills's cast of Lincoln's face, a tour de force of Lincoln's spatial attitudes and his much-noted admiration for *Macbeth* (fig. 24), is a key artistic reference for these views. The cast, made from life on February 11, 1865, looks eerily like a death mask. The peaceful expression, the eyes closed, makes Lincoln appear to be dead. His baldness (caused by a cap Mills placed on Lincoln's head to avoid getting plaster in his hair) adds unintentionally to the macabre effect.[23] The cast calls to mind Lincoln's morbid dreams and

Fig. 24. Clark Mills, *Life Mask of Abraham Lincoln,* ca. 1917. Plaster cast after 1865 original, 6¾ × 8 × 11¾ in. (17.1 × 20.3 × 29.8 cm). National Portrait Gallery, Smithsonian Institution, Washington, D.C.

superstitious premonitions of his death, especially one such premonition, straight from the pages of *Macbeth,* that came to him as he moved through space from one point to another.[24]

On board the presidential *River Queen* en route back to Washington from Richmond on April 9, 1865, five days before he was assassinated, Lincoln read parts of the play to other passengers. One of the president's fellow travelers, the Marquis Adolphe de Chambrun, recalled the scene many years later:

> Most of the passages he selected were from Shakespeare, especially *Macbeth.* The lines after the murder of Duncan, when the new king falls a prey to moral torment, were dramatically dwelt on. Now and then he paused to expatiate on how exact a picture Shakespeare here gives of a murderer's mind when, the dark deed achieved, its perpetrator already envies his victim's calm sleep. He read the scene over twice.[25]

The lines Lincoln spoke are Macbeth's—

> Duncan is in his grave;
> After life's fitful fever he sleeps well.
> Treason has done his worst; nor steel, nor poison,
> Malice domestic, foreign levy, nothing,
> Can touch him further. (3.2.23–27)

The shipboard recitation did more than bespeak Lincoln's identification with Duncan. In spatial terms, the flow of Lincoln's words foretold the spreading power of his death. His assassination colored the world, like Duncan's. The Scottish king's "golden blood," lacing his "silver skin . . . will the multitudinous seas incarnadine, / Making the green one red" (2.3.110, 2.2.65–66). Alchemically colored, the blood is "an enormously strong coloring agent made of perfected matter," as the Shakespeare scholar W. A. Murray has written. It spreads out as a tincture, a drop that dyes the seas, just as Lincoln's would.[26] Similarly, the president's spoken words flowing from the deck of the *River Queen* might have been conceived as spreading upon the Potomac and the Virginia air in disseminations both indelible and ephemeral. To the eye that might have discerned their effects, they would seem to be ghostly evaporations reflected in water that would take on a greater thickness, a greater substance, for having been so verbally intensified. This portentous blessing of words, overspreading the dissolving scene, was like a *realization* of the world, an invitation for it to come into its own with a sparkling and hitherto unrecognizable vivacity, for having been so spoken over.

Yet the words—"Duncan is in his grave"—also evoke the implacable presence of Mills's mask of some two months before and of Lincoln himself. The mask's predominant effect is of energy and matter all in one place: a force all the more powerful for going nowhere. In the mask Lincoln-as-Duncan is gathered down, crushed into a singular presence. It brings us back to Lincoln's power to concentrate his being only in the place where he found himself.

All comes down to a sense of hereness. The Gettysburg Address, which Lincoln delivered on November 19, 1863, a little more than a month after attending the performance of *Macbeth,* includes the word *here* seven times in its 275 or so words. In that speech Lincoln was relentlessly concerned to pinpoint the *place* of his somber words, to name not just this place but the moment of his speech, as if this underscoring of presence—here in time, here at this place—would ward off the spreading, flowing, and dissipating of this utterance, as if he not only desired but resisted the speech's telegraphic dissemination. A mere spread of words—with no attention to staining the locality—would be an aesthetic and ideological violation of the melancholy gratitude he had traveled to that one site to deliver. Here in this place all would be staked on the solemnity of speaking just for those three minutes at just that spot on the earth. Here the words would not only secrete a mechanical carapace around themselves, the better to make their fated journey around the world. They would not only have "wiring," to use Garry Wills's term, in their form and their outward-flying aim.[27] They would also hang naked in the air, distilling a magical density by their refusal to leave the scene.

"Here" is the essence of the Mills cast. Even places elsewhere come to rest within it. As in the many descriptions of Lincoln's haggard appearance by 1865, the cast seems to compress the worries of the entire Union in the president's careworn features. With the worries implanted so, the cast even suggests that by then Lincoln and the nation were becoming synonymous: the brutalized land and its citizens were all readable, supercondensed, in the face of the man in whom the entire war had come to rest. It mattered little if Lincoln's face was less an interior than a ground on which citizens then and now could project the story of his life and that of the nation, as Alan Trachtenberg notes.[28] Whether as a depth holding his thoughts or as a surface awaiting the projections of others, Lincoln's face is a gathering point in Mills's cast. The quietude of the face, in this sense, is not thought but *concentration,* as if Lincoln were not just patiently waiting for the moment when the plaster could be broken from his face, and not even taking the time to ponder the vaster world from which the making of this stony immortalization provided a few minutes' respite, but making himself properly passive for the reception of that world. Through a feat of concentration, he could allow all that was out there, all the grief and sorrow and rage, both his and others', to gather in his face.[29] The Mills cast is about the intensities of effect, of being in one place only, that were the main feature of Lincoln's conception of space.

The theater was one venue of this presence for Lincoln. At a performance of *Henry IV, Part I* at Ford's in December 1863, in which James Hackett played Falstaff, Lincoln "is studying it intensely," his private secretary William O. Stoddard noted. "He is enjoying himself. He has forgotten the war. He has forgotten Congress. . . . He is living in Prince Hal's time." When Lincoln smiled at the end of the performance, "it is absolutely the first smile you have detected during the evening upon his intensely studious, absorbed, abstracted face."[30] At a performance of *King Lear* some time during the war, Lincoln was impressed by the acting of the young John McCullough in the role of Edgar and asked McCullough to visit his box between acts. According to the journalist Noah Brooks, who attended the performance with the president, McCullough did so "still clad in his fantastic garb of rags and straw."[31] Wearing Edgar's pauper's disguise as Tom o' Bedlam, McCullough must have been a startling sight in the close confines of the box. He had crossed "that fiery frontier between fantasy and reality," in André Bazin's terms, to come directly into the presence of some of his audience. The effect must have been akin to that described by Bazin: "the disturbing atmosphere of awe which surrounds an actor still made up, like a phosphorescent light, when we visit him in his dressing room."[32]

Lincoln, having requested the intrusion, welcomed such intensities. On a ride at his Soldiers' Home rural retreat several miles from the White House, he and some visitors came close to some of the evergreen trees on the grounds. "Their branches brushed into the carriage as we passed along," recalled one of the visitors, "and left us with that pleasant, woody smell belonging to leaves." One of the riders then caught "a bit of green from one of these intruding branches."[33] Though a debate ensued about whether the needles were cedar or spruce, and though Lincoln then intervened, drawing on his backwoods experience to identify the intruding specimen and still others that he gathered to make his point, the first startling entry of the branches most comports with his sense of here and now. The branches, "brush[ing] into the carriage," were an occasion not just of taxonomy and not just of moralizing (for Lincoln went on to draw analogies between types of tree and types of men) but of a vivid presence striking into one's space, surmounting and preceding science and morals, similar to the sensuous and life-affirming hereness of McCullough's rags and straw.

Trees gave Lincoln some of his most intense apprehensions of this presence, to judge by the accounts of Chambrun, Brooks, and others. Once he "stopped to admire an exceptionally tall and beautiful tree growing by the roadside," Chambrun recalled of an incident in 1865. The tree allowed Lincoln to refer to many other trees he had seen, but always so that his audience would see "the one before us." The Indiana homestead area where the Lincoln family had moved in 1816 was "woods, woods, woods, as far as the world extends," according to a settler, but in Lincoln's later life singular trees, cut out from the world around, gave him a pure place in which to exercise his visual acuity.[34] The lone tree was an occasion for Lincoln's "extraordinary observation, mastery of descriptive language and absolute precision of mind."[35] Lincoln's Springfield, Illinois, law partner William Herndon described this faculty as his "slow, cold, clear and exact perceptions. Everything came to him in its precise shape and color. . . . He saw all things through a perfect mental lens."[36]

This tree-presence could be even more vivid. "He liked the trees when they were not in leaf," remembered Brooks, perhaps because they revealed the shape of a thing in its starkest outline. "He bade me look at the delicate yet firm outline of a leafless tree against the sky." Even when Lincoln divided his attention, the tree's presence doubled. "Pointing to the fine network of shadows cast on the snow by the branches and twigs, he said that that was the profile of the tree." And when Lincoln drew the moral, the tree did not vanish but intensified. The next day, Brooks reports, Lincoln said that "perhaps a man's character was like a tree, and his reputation like its shadow; the shadow is what we think of it; the tree is the real thing."[37] This next day, like the shadow, was a falling from the original perception, but it was not so distant, not so unrelated, that even the homespun allegory and the passing of time did not still copy the perception they fell from.

Fruit, no less than a shadow, maintained the presence of the tree. On the day he was shot, Lincoln took two women guests into the White House conservatory to see "his favorite lemon-tree," one of them recalled in 1909. "It was indeed a beauty, a perfect mass of fruit and flowers." Lincoln asked the White House gardener to gather some flowers from the tree and then picked each woman a lemon before saying good-bye. The women wore the flowers at Grover's Theatre that night, when they heard of the assassination a few blocks away at Ford's, and they kept the lemons for years. "One was finally lost; but the other, shriveled like a nut, is still treasured."[38] Falling from the man, the lemons were tokens of a presence that Lincoln found in the trees they remembered him by.

Even the twentieth-century representations that fell even farther from Lincoln, now just shadows of shadows, could still apprehend the logic of trees, perception, and presence in one place. When the Hollywood director John Ford posed Henry Fonda beneath a tree in the 1939 film *The Young Mr. Lincoln,* the gesture was perfect (fig. 25). The young Lincoln studying a law book

Fig. 25. Abraham Lincoln (Henry Fonda) reading beneath a tree. Still from *The Young Mr. Lincoln,* 1939, directed by John Ford.

reclines on his back beneath a living thing that represents not only his folksy ruggedness but his solitary precision of mind, his preternatural focus on one thing. Moreover, his unusual point of view, looking straight up at the world, allows him to see things aright, as though for the first time in all their intricacy and correct relations. Perceiving the tree, like studying the minutiae of the law, is the resolution of a seemingly infinite network into a solid and clarified whole. Another moment in Ford's movie indicates the national-telegraphic Lincoln—the moment when he casts a stone in the river and sees the circles radiate outward, auguring his widespread influence—but the scene beneath the tree captures Lincoln's equally vivid powers of being rooted in one place and one perception, so rooted that nothing can shake him from it. So do David Plowden's photographs from the 1960s, taken for the centennial of Lincoln's death (figs. 26–28).[39]

Reading and reciting Shakespeare produced such effects of hereness for Lincoln. In March 1864 he recited Richard III's opening soliloquy from memory for the painter Francis Carpenter, "rendering it with a degree of force and power," Carpenter recalled, "that made it seem like a new creation to me."[40] And at the theater, hearing actors recite lines he knew well, Lincoln could become as rapt as Carpenter. At *Macbeth* Lincoln may have been "far away," but perhaps he was also intense, his mind precisely *not* on anything else but this production of his favorite Shakespeare play. Maybe Cushman's performance produced this intensity in him, as she stood there clawing the air (as she must have done), declaiming in witchlike angularities of frozen pose, branching her limbs, a limelit presence carved from the world.

Light, more than anything else, was Lincoln's sign of presence. Lady Macbeth's candle, as Cushman brought it onstage for act 5, scene 1, was perhaps

Fig. 26. David Plowden, *Tree near Relay, Maryland,* 1964. Beinecke Rare Book and Manuscript Library, Yale University. Courtesy of David Plowden.

an aesthetic epicenter akin to Lincoln's own appreciation of lone lights. The singularity of that lone candle would not be immediately evident, however, either at the Grover's Theatre performance or in the general iconography of Lincoln's politics, both of which portrayed the president within a far-spreading illumination: as a single flame radiating an extensive national glow.

"The auditorium lights up with beautiful effect," noted a reporter perusing the newly reopened Grover's Theatre on October 7.[41] The light, of course, was gaslight. Inside the theater, according to the Washington, D.C., gaslight historian Dan Mattausch, spectators would have been treated to a rare sight, a large continuously lit space: "The general rule with nineteenth-century lighting was that you illuminated the task and not the room. The theater was one of the few places where that rule was flagrantly broken with what was often described as a dazzling blaze of light. To modern eyes, it would still have been faint, but this is actually a comment on our current penchant for turning night into day. The light-level would have been comfortable for those who wanted to read the program or spy on the latest fashions of those

Figs. 27–28. David Plowden, *Antietam,* ca. 1965, and *Aquia Creek,* ca. 1965. Both Beinecke Rare Book and Manuscript Library, Yale University. Courtesy of David Plowden.

in the audience." The lighting effects "announced urban sophistication and progress."[42]

When the play was about to begin, the house lights would dim, fading to black. Then "the footlights at the front edge of the stage would flare to life," the play would begin, and *Macbeth* would now start to contribute its own lighting effects. Cushman's script sets the play's famous first scene— "*The Open Country.—Thunder and lightning. Three WITCHES discovered.*" With the footlights probably casting a subdued glow, the audience would see the three witches, their heads together, illumined by blasts of stage lightning. A handwritten notation in the script, made by Cushman's associate R. J. Jones, underlines the initial stage directions and adds a comment: "Thunder, lightning & rain to Begin." When the witches separate to speak their lines, the audience would hear "thunder distant" at the first mention of Macbeth and "thunder loud" as the witches chant in unison, "Fair is foul, and foul is fair; / Hover through the fog and filthy air" (1.1.12–13). Still more "Thunder and lightning" would follow.[43]

Then for scene 2, at the palace at Fores, the lighting would change completely: "Put lights up full," the handwritten notation reads. Now the white-hot limelights would burn full bore, controlled by the unseen operator. There would follow many scenes of darkness punctuated by vivid flame, creating the play's intense chiaroscuro: the burning torch of Banquo and Fleance on the pitch-black night of Duncan's murder ("The moon is down," 2.1.2); the torch Fleance carries on the night Banquo is murdered ("A light, a light!" 3.3.17); Lady Macbeth's guttering candle ("Hell is murky," 5.1.36). Again the witches would appear, this time with "heavy flashes of lightning," as Jones noted in Cushman's script; the dimming of the stage lights before Macbeth's dagger speech in act 2, scene 1 ("put lights down"); the phantasmagoric parade of kings that the witches show to Macbeth ("Come like shadows, so depart," 4.1.133).[44]

Lincoln was in a place of fire. Grover's stood on the site of theaters that had burned down in 1845 and 1857, and it too would burn down in 1873 (presaging the conflagration that would destroy still another theater on the site in 1885).[45] If on that night in 1863 Lincoln "leaned back in his chair in the shade" after hearing the exchange between Malcolm and Macduff, he most likely tried to remove himself from the glare of the stage itself, which was near to where he sat and probably well lit for this scene. Along with his wife, Mary, their son Tad, and Stoddard, the private secretary, he occupied a lower box just to the right of the stage.[46] Trying to remove himself from the limelight, Lincoln was yet a part of it, and in a way that made the play

Fig. 29. *Grand Procession of Wide-Awakes at New York on the Evening of October 3, 1860,* in *Harper's Weekly,* October 13, 1860, 648–49. Beinecke Rare Book and Manuscript Library, Yale University.

for that moment inescapably national: he too was effectively on public view. If by that time many respectable theaters like Grover's dimmed the house lights during a performance—the better to allow patrons to lose themselves in the production, to have "a private, individual experience," as the theater historian Bruce McConnachie puts it—Lincoln's own experience of the play was here a matter of public inspection.[47] As the journalist Kirkland noted, "It being Mr. Lincoln's favorite play, one could not repress a certain curiosity to know . . . how certain passages would strike him."[48]

The illumination was fitting. As a sign of his national command, Lincoln was often associated with lighting effects that would symbolically radiate across the whole land. The great parade of the so-called Wide-Awakes in Manhattan on October 3, 1860, featured thousands of young torch-carrying men filing through the streets of the city, demonstrating their support for Lincoln a month before the presidential election (fig. 29). Started in Hartford, Connecticut, during a Lincoln visit earlier that year, the Wide-Awakes had come to represent a sober, dignified Republican vigilance—both peaceful and militaristic—that would extend outward, penetrating all places of darkness.[49]

In the largely Democratic city of New York, the Wide-Awake procession moved through the Bowery, "shining into every alley; glittering unexpected sheen into every dark and wretched hovel; irradiating every corner, blazing an unwelcome glare into dens that else had been ever in the darkest shadow," and then still further outward, making "the whole city luminous," as the partisan *New-York Daily Tribune* reported. "The light which flooded this central seat of Democratic power is only the forerunner of an illumination which shall include the whole land."[50]

The grand illumination in Washington near the end of the war was another Lincoln glow—a figurative bonfire so vast that it might be seen at the verge of the nation. On April 4, 1865, after news of the fall of Richmond, buildings throughout Washington displayed lamps and illuminations of various kinds. Every window of the Capitol was lit up, according to the *Washington Evening Star,* and at the top of the dome was a "brilliant light, which could have been seen a long distance."[51] Benjamin Brown French, the commissioner of public buildings who oversaw the Capitol illumination, added a special touch all his own, a gas-illuminated sign visible far up Pennsylvania Avenue featuring "the 23rd verse of the 118th Psalm printed on cloth, in enormous letters, as a transparency, and stretched on a frame the entire length of the top of the western portico, over the Library of Congress, viz. '*This is the Lord's doing; it is marvellous in our eyes.*' "[52]

Grover's on October 17 offered another marvelous display—a national radiance of dignitaries, star performers, and patriotic purpose, as French, the diary writer who noted Cushman's performance, must have sensed. More sedentary than the Wide-Awake procession, and a more genteel affair than the working-class parade through the Manhattan streets, the benefit performance nonetheless espoused "the cause of universal Freedom" that Republican radiance had symbolized on the former occasion.[53] Between the 1860 campaign and the 1865 war-ending celebration, the Grover's performance was itself a symbolic national glow.

But not necessarily for Lincoln. Universal illuminations were fine for electioneering and for other types of political theater. They even radiated a genuine gladness that was much to be admired. But his view of flames bore as little resemblance to these spectacular celebrations as an isolated fireside did to the depiction of him and running mate Hannibal Hamlin glowing beneath a dozen gaslights at a Bowery lager garden back in 1860.[54] At a rustic lodging one night in 1853 on the Illinois circuit, Lincoln's friends "left him sitting in front of the fireplace staring intently at the flames. The next morning he was still there, studying the ashes and charred logs."[55]

Outside Grover's Theatre on October 17, light only intermittently broke the darkness. A newspaper report from the Monday after the performance tells of street diggings left hazardously unmarked at night by so much as a single flare.[56] Where there was illumination, the existential effect might not have been much better. A popular theater, Canterbury Hall, "illuminated Louisiana Avenue with its powerful calcium light." Another venue, the Varieties Theatre, near the corner of Ninth and Pennsylvania, featured "a wheel of colored lights [that] revolved in kaleidoscopic brilliance above the entrance."[57] But to Lincoln these garish stimulations of happiness might only have shown the loneliness of the faces they lit.

Inside the theater, nested beneath the chandelier glitter, was the lonely fire of Lady Macbeth's single candle, the equally existential "brief candle" Macbeth speaks of. And though these fires might merely have reaffirmed the house lights, contributing to the blazing spectacle of sumptuous effect, they might just as easily have stood apart from them. To a consciousness so attuned, they might have revealed the whole theater—a spaceship of righteous semblance glowing in the declaration of national purpose—as only one flickering spot in the dark, a speck in time.

Lone-candle isolation, for Lincoln, was a light unmoored, adrift in space. So implies a poem by Herman Melville that incorporates *Macbeth,* Lincoln, and a remarkable meditation on light and dark. "The House-top," subtitled "A Night Piece (July, 1863)," describes the point of view of a solitary observer watching the New York City Draft Riots of that month. The observer, remote and lofty, is seemingly a stand-in for Melville, who moved his family back to Manhattan from the Berkshires later in summer 1863 and who seems to imagine the rioting as if he himself had witnessed it, and for Lincoln, whose war orders had precipitated the riots.[58] Alone with his night thoughts, the housetop watcher is like a tormented Macbeth:

> No sleep. The sultriness pervades the air
> And binds the brain—a dense oppression, such
> As tawny tigers feel in matted shades,
> Vexing their blood and making apt for ravage.
> Beneath the stars the roofy desert spreads
> Vacant as Libya. All is hushed near by.
> Yet fitfully from far breaks a mixed surf
> Of muffled sound, the Atheist roar of riot.

The viewer sees spots in the dark:

> Yonder, where parching Sirius set in drought,
> Balefully glares red Arson—there—and there.[59]

Each flame is distant and isolated from the man at the top of the house. Each is not here but "there—and there" to this man possessed of a Macbeth-like power of spatial imagination ("the roofy desert spreads / Vacant as Libya").[60]

Such was Lincoln's existential relation to lone candles, the kind that made the flames of *Macbeth* a statement of his own philosophy. On the night of August 24, 1864, David Bates and Major Thomas Eckert went to Lincoln's Soldiers' Home cottage to perform a signaling test for his benefit. The idea was to use "a calcium light, which could be displayed and screened at will by the use of a button, operated by hand, in the same manner as a telegraph-key . . . the alternate flashes of light, long or short, representing the dashes and dots of the Morse alphabet." Bates and Eckert sent signals to the roof of the Smithsonian castle, where their associates sent back messages in return. Lincoln, watching this exchange of blinking lights across the intervening four miles, pointed out how the system would be "of immense value to the Government."[61]

Something in the episode, however, transcends a strategic, utilitarian purpose. Two points of light communicating across a distance created a visual telegraph, but the procedure also underscored the gap across which the two points made contact, doing so in a way that a strictly telegraphic message did not. The telegraph was about continuity—the wire, the unbroken link between two points. Light signals, by contrast, emphasized the intervening darkness and hence their isolation. Lincoln, who spoke of the "mystic chords of memory, stretching from every battle-field, and patriot grave, to every living heart and hearthstone, all over this broad land," understood telegraphic communication as well as the other members of his cabinet, indeed more so.[62] Yet his conception of space and time could also be more discontinuous than theirs, more folkloric and tragic as well, and the lone light was at the center of that conception.

Consider his 1837 "Address to the Young Men's Lyceum of Springfield, Illinois." Decrying the mob violence in locations across America, he singled out one especially vivid case, a "horror-striking scene at St. Louis. A single victim was only sacrificed there," he told his audience. "His story is very short; and is, perhaps, the most highly tragic, of any thing of its length, that has ever been witnessed in real life. A mulatto man, by the name of

McIntosh, was seized in the street, dragged to the suburbs of the city, chained to a tree, and actually burned to death; and all within a single hour from the time he had been a freeman, attending his own business, and at peace with the world."[63]

The lynched mulatto stands out, as cultural historian Russ Castronovo notes: his presence in the speech is so vivid that he does not fit smoothly into a broad continuous national space. Lincoln's speech demonstrates how the attempt to portray a whole nation can vivify the particular, making it hauntingly memorable, especially when the particular is tragic. The example of McIntosh, Castronovo writes, "thwarts national narrative's compulsion toward coherence and homogeneity." Lincoln's Lyceum speech—his aim of "adding story to story"—leads, for Castronovo, "not to one larger story, but to dispersed histories that stand in uneasy relation to one another."[64]

This scattering produces discontinuous space. A patchwork dispersion of places and events, it is far different from simple pluralism. Compared to the cohesiveness of post-Revolution America—a unity based on politicians and war veterans who embodied a living history—Lincoln argued that the present day was like "a forest of giant oaks" after a hurricane has swept over it, leaving "only, here and there, a lonely trunk." If he called upon his audience to fill the places of their ancestors, to "supply their places with other pillars, hewn from the solid quarry of sober reason," creating a "*general intelligence, sound morality,* and, in particular, *a reverence for the constitution and laws,*" this sculpted scaffold of national unity still arose on a "here and there" of devastation that the melancholic Lincoln could never let his audience forget. Like the lonely trunk on which McIntosh burned, this splitting into tragic fires countered the cohesion of a national story.[65]

In pictorial terms, the question is one of illustration. By the 1860s illustrations had taken on an increasingly mass-mediated and space-traveling meaning. National news publications such as *Harper's Weekly* and *Frank Leslie's Illustrated Weekly* featured cover and center-spread illustrations and other smaller ones throughout their pages. These additions had the effect not only of illustrating specific stories but of spreading local news outward across the nation. Moreover, the many illustrations from that time that feature light—firelight, gaslight, fireworks—demonstrate the kinship between nighttime fire and black ink on white paper. Illustrating, notes the literary critic J. Hillis Miller, "means bringing to light, as a spelunker lights up a cave."[66] Even if the one would burn the other, the illustrations of fire portray the papery brightness of flame.

What was the relation of *Macbeth* on October 17, 1863, to this world of far-flowing illustration? The performance was not literally illustrated—no picture of that evening's show is known to exist—but it still might have dreamed for itself a national publication, the illustrative equivalent of the imaginary spread of voice and presence that characterized Cushman's throaty recitations. Why should not the righteousness of this benefit performance be published to the skies much as a vaporous voice might record itself on souls and spaces far away? To dream of mass communication—to see the mass media as a paradigm for the imagined centrifugal imprint of an unfortunately fugitive and all-too-local aesthetic act—would be a compelling fantasy of omnipotence for any such event with a national design. The glitter of the gaslit theater would be as one grand illustration, conjuring the newsprint, unfolding in thousands of homes, on which rocket scrawls of ink blared hallelujahs of national purpose.

Lincoln's presidential world was heavily illustrated. The *Harper's Weekly* center spread of October 13, 1860, shows the Wide-Awakes parading past the headquarters of the *New-York Daily Tribune* and the *New York Times,* perfectly stating the period relation of flame and mass-reproduced illustration (see fig. 29). That the *Tribune* offices were themselves lit up by Chinese lanterns during the Wide-Awake parade, according to the newspaper's own account, only intensified the connection.[67] The public spectacle, lamp-bearing men stretching down the streets like a Vesuvian lava flow, was a media event inviting the ink that would capture its bold visual effects. The extensiveness of the procession seemed not only to stretch symbolically into all the dark places of the city and nation, as the partisan press reported, but also to invite the Lincoln-friendly mass media that would spread the news by illustrating the event. Overseeing the procession like benevolent gods, the *Tribune* and *Times* buildings in the image glow by the light of the flames they help create. The fire of political righteousness in the 1860s was a paper crusade.

What would happen, though, if an illustration were not reproduced? If an image were one of a kind? If it had presence of that sort? Here we come closer to Lincoln's more existential and less mass-mediated conception of flame, his idea of the fire in one place, and what he might have thought of *Macbeth* on October 17. Accordingly, the work of Winslow Homer—an artist poised between illustration and one-of-a-kind painting during the war—serves as a guide to Lincoln's point of view. As an illustrator, Homer knew well the kinship between fire and page. In *Harper's Weekly* illustrations such as *Rebels Outside Their Works at Yorktown Reconnoitering with Dark Lanterns* (fig. 30), which appeared in the May 17, 1862, issue, he used light

Fig. 30. Winslow Homer, *Rebels Outside Their Works at Yorktown Reconnoitering with Dark Lanterns,* in *Harper's Weekly,* May 17, 1862. Beinecke Rare Book and Manuscript Library, Yale University, New Haven, Connecticut.

and dark to convey a moral point even as he commented on the lava spread of mass media's national illuminations. The Confederate patrol is brave in its way but also stealthy, secret like a dark-lantern political society, not out in the open like the Wide-Awakes.[68] The central Confederate, shining his light in reverse, is misguided. At the same time, *Rebels Outside Their Works* and other Homer firelight illustrations (*A Bivouac Fire on the Potomac,* December 21, 1861; *Winter Quarters of a Camp—The Inside of a Hut,* January 24, 1863) announce their power to broadcast an otherwise unseen act. To illustrate was to take a local incident and spread it across the Union, to make the Confederate's furtive lantern (or the Union man's happy campfire) gleam in thousands of homes.

Yet sometime in 1862 or 1863 the twenty-six-year-old Homer painted *In Front of Yorktown,* only the second or third stand-alone painting he had ever attempted (fig. 31).[69] Unlike his wood engravings, *In Front of Yorktown* was meant to be displayed as a singular art object, as in the exhibitions that Homer's works would soon enter. Accordingly, it focuses on the experience of a solitary figure—the pensive soldier in the center.

Wearing a poncho, his kepi drawn down over his forehead, the lone soldier stares into a fire that crackles before him, silhouetted by a stand of three denuded trees. Two other soldiers to the left drowse near the flames. To the right, between the solitary man and a stand of muskets, two other men sleep half-concealed in the crude shelter before which he sits. All of these details emphasize the central man's isolation. The stand of trees separates him from the drowsing men. His alertness contrasts with the sleep of the men by his side. Cut off from the others and from all else, he sits before the crude shelter, behind which we sense the extensive gloom of the Virginia woods at night.

The man's kinship, if he has any, is with the fire. Staring directly into the flames, he receives their light in glints on his buttons, boots, and face. Yet his is not a creaturely relation to the glow. The men to the left sit closer to the flames, receiving more of the fire's warmth. He is seated a little farther away, befitting his reflective mood, though not so far, and not perhaps so cold, as the sleeping men, mostly in the dark, who show the sprawled boots. The three sharpened stakes to the right, catching their own reflections off the fire, point like vectors to indicate the center of his attention, enforcing his uniquely meditative relation to the flames.

That he "thinks" of the flames does not quite explain his position. The flames are a little weird, a little fantastical, with their crackling sparks and plume of rising smoke. Backed by the shadowy trees that repeat their climb,

Fig. 31. Winslow Homer, *In Front of Yorktown,* ca. 1862–63. Oil on canvas, 13¼ × 19½ in. (33.7 × 49.5 cm). Yale University Art Gallery, Gift of Samuel Rossiter Betts, B.A., 1875.

the flames seem to represent a mystery that it would be vulgar to call fate or to designate by any other allegorical name. Shifting and metamorphosing, they portray the warmth of life as a mystery, a self-imploding luxuriance that generates a smoke of solid shadows. To be alone with this mystery, for Homer, is to make a light that does not illustrate.

Lincoln's fires were that way. Yes, he was a believer in illustration: he held to the belief that local events and statements could be illustrated and sent out across the land. His fast-selling *carte de visite* at the time of his Cooper Union speech in February 1860 proliferated his likeness across the land and, together with the speech, helped make him a nationally known figure. Along these lines, Lincoln might have endorsed the idea that *Macbeth* on October 17 was an illustration of some kind—a national message sent out, as though in the pages of *Harper's Weekly* and *Frank Leslie's Illustrated Weekly,* with its gaslight glow all but conjuring its publication in black and white, an illustration without the ink. But in his more darksome way Lincoln's brooding on the singular moment, the spot in time, gave him a view of a work of art, and of experience more generally, that refused the possibility that these gleaming moral-journalistic reproductions would radiate far and wide. What glowed in one place and time spent itself in that implosion, without meaning, without purpose.

The greatest flame Lincoln ever saw was Donati's Comet of 1858, one of the brightest of the nineteenth century. Increasingly discernible throughout much of Europe and North America since its detection by the Italian astronomer Giovanni Battista Donati in June, the comet reached its maximum visibility on October 5.[70] On the night of September 14 that year, Lincoln was with State Republican Committee secretary Horace White in Jonesboro, Illinois, deep in the southernmost part of the state, where he would debate Stephen Douglas the following day, the sixth of their seven famous public encounters in their race for the Senate.

White recalled years later "the splendid appearance of Donati's comet in the sky, the evening before the debate. Mr. Lincoln greatly admired this strange visitor, and he and I sat for an hour or more in front of the hotel looking at it."[71] According to another writer, Lincoln, White, and several others sat in front of the Union Hotel and "all told what they understood a comet in the heavens meant."[72] The astronomer G. P. Bond published an engraving by James Watts based on sketches of the comet made at the Harvard College observatory on September 16, giving a sense of what White, Lincoln, and the others had stared at for more than an hour two nights before (fig. 32).[73]

We don't know exactly what Lincoln thought the comet meant, but he could be forgiven for taking it as a sign. Melville's poem "The Portent (1859)" treats a celestial omen this way, describing John Brown

> Hanging from the beam,
> Slowly swaying (such the law),
> . . . . the streaming beard is shown
> (Weird John Brown),
> The meteor of the war.[74]

Moreover, there Lincoln was, in Jonesboro, farther south than Richmond, Virginia, on turf selected by Douglas precisely to pressure and embarrass him on the slavery question. Within a few miles were the slave states of Missouri and Kentucky. There he was in "Little Egypt," a small triangle of Illinois whose largest city was Cairo (pronounced KAY-ro), a region that would vote overwhelmingly against him in the presidential election of 1860.[75] Carl Sandburg, the most inclined among Lincoln's biographers to

Fig. 32. James W. Watts, *Comet of Donati 1858, September 16th,* in *Account of the Great Comet of 1858,* ed. G. P. Bond (Cambridge: Welch, Bigelow, 1862), facing p. 14.

find a sign, did not miss this one: "For Lincoln, the year of the comet was one filled with burning struggle."[76]

In another sense, however, the comet defied these meanings. Marcia Pointon, in her discussion of the British painter William Dyce's treatment of Donati's Comet in his great *Pegwell Bay, Kent—A Recollection of October 5th, 1858* (fig. 33), notes that the comet (visible at upper center) "represents a system immensely distant in space . . . and incalculable to any degree of accuracy in time." Dyce's painting, which shows a party of seashell gatherers moving about a beach surmounted by ancient limestone cliffs, presents human action as a small daily round in the face of earthly and universal immensities. Pointon quotes the British geologist Charles Lyell: "Not only the exterior of the planet but the entire earth, is but an atom in the midst of the countless worlds surveyed by the astronomer." Dyce's "simple and wise" painting, for Pointon, denies "the validity of a single human life and, even more, of a single day. Nevertheless, sea-shell gathering is—it would appear—the only reality for these people in this place on this day."[77]

The same might be said of Lincoln and this comet. This celestial event

Fig. 33. William Dyce, *Pegwell Bay, Kent—A Recollection of October 5th, 1858,* ca. 1858–60. Oil on canvas, 25 × 35 in. (63.5 × 88.9 cm). The Tate Gallery, London.

could be a political allegory. It could be personified into streaming beards or flowing veils. It could even be a sign of Lincoln himself, whom his secretary John Hay likened in 1863 to a comet. But more than any of these things, to a man accustomed to form those cold, clear, precise judgments that Herndon wrote about, to a man who "saw all things through a perfect mental lens" with "no defraction or refraction," the comet might have conjured the vastness in which a single place, the Union Hotel in Jonesboro, Illinois, for example, splinters and sways beneath one's feet, until it feels as incalculable, as curved and swooning, as the abyss this once-every-two-thousand-years light opens up. Against such an immensity, even the engraving in Bond's book underscored the existential darkness its luminous science would dispel, becoming a contradiction in terms, a black illustration. September 16, September 14, October 5—the dignity of specific days buckles, erased by the black reflections of a heavenly mirror that cancels even the observatory's commanding eye. A view, a point in time, a single place on a single day—the acumen of science, the conviviality of talk, the speculation about meanings—all this, like the gathering of seashells, is an "only reality" of being in the moment, in the place, and in that way meaningful. But the comet against the big empty backdrop is a flame whose horror is that it does not illustrate.

Far closer to earth, the moon was another such light. Walt Whitman wrote a beautiful description of the White House on February 24, 1863, describing the building under the glow of gaslights and the "soft and copious moon . . . the lustrous flooding moon." Ralph Waldo Emerson described the fast-traveling news of Lincoln's assassination as the "shadow of an uncalculated eclipse over the planet." Lincoln himself kept an eye on the moon: "The President took a look at the moon and Arcturus," wrote Hay in his diary for August 1863. One of Lincoln's most legendary law cases, his defense of family friend Duff Armstrong in 1858, hinged on whether or not a crime took place by the light of a full moon. A recent book about the Lincoln assassination by Edward Steers is called *Blood on the Moon.*[78]

Lewis Rutherfurd took a photograph of the moon on March 4, 1865, the day of Lincoln's Second Inaugural (fig. 34). The photograph is remarkable for this fact—an image of space on a momentous day in American history. As a young man, Rutherfurd had studied law in William Seward's office for two years, and he was the grandson of a senator.[79] His photograph, made from his private observatory in lower Manhattan as one of a series he created during the first days of March that year, is related to Lincoln only coincidentally, but it nonetheless identifies the president with this isolated light.

As an inadvertent portrait, an astronomical equivalent to the Mills life mask of the previous month and Gardner's photographs of the ravaged Lincoln of the later war, Rutherfurd's *Moon* teaches us to separate softened legend from grim fact, to see the difference between the diffuse glow of a widespreading folklore and the stark singularity of a mortal fate. Instead of illuminating "the White House of the land, the White House of the night," "the White House of future poems, and of dreams and dramas, there in the soft and copious moon," as Whitman had put it, Rutherfurd's photograph gives us the thing itself, so stark and gray and ugly it is a wonder it could ever shoot such beams. The photograph gives us, in other words, the light before it has spread its fanciful storytelling calm upon Lincoln—before it has become the light of a legend tragic and sentimental. Close up, almost too close up, it puts us, like astronomical pornography, into the presence of something we had seen only from afar and perhaps would prefer to see only at such a distance.

To be close up to this moon, like McCullough standing before Lincoln in his "fantastic garb of rags and straw," is to be present in a startlingly sin-

Fig. 34. Lewis Rutherfurd, *Moon, March 4, 1865,* 1865. Albumen print, 22½ × 17¼ in. (57.1 × 43.7 cm). Courtesy of George Eastman House, International Museum of Photography and Film, Rochester, New York.

gular way, maybe pleasurable, maybe not, but in either case disquietingly real. It is to experience a vivid and overwhelming star power that eclipses all else—plot, characters, meanings, and even the illustration itself, which just about cracks with the burden of showing so lifeless a thing. Starstruck, the world now very small, we see in Rutherfurd's photograph the moon, as it were, before it speaks its lines, before it gives us its well-known moods and turns of phrase. In Bazin's terms, this effect is the photograph's disturbing sense of awe—the type of isolated presence, without meaning, that so moved Lincoln and that gives us such vivid images to remember him by.

Lincoln's death was a single flame before it was anything else. In Washington on the morning of April 15, 1865, Benjamin Brown French saw such a glow. Having arrived at the Navy Yard at seven the previous evening, back from a trip to Richmond, French and his wife had reached their Capitol Hill home at eight, when they went straight to bed. At daylight the next morning, French awoke and, still in bed, "saw that the street-lamps had not been extinguished. I lay awake, perhaps ½ an hour, & seeing that they were still burning, I arose and saw a sentry pacing before my house. I thought something wrong had happened, so dressed & went down & opened the front door."[80] A soldier then told him what had happened at Ford's the previous evening. What stands out in French's account, preserved in his diary entry for the day Lincoln died, is the strange sight of the streetlamps burning still at dawn—lights that made him uneasy, that indeed told of the worst event he could imagine, that yet struck him at first as ominous but perfectly self-enclosed little fires, framed within the windows of his bedroom: flames of a single fate that yet did not illustrate.

The night before, the night Lincoln was shot, had been very illustrative. "The public buildings and many private ones were illuminated last night on the occasion of Lee's surrender," noted city resident William Owner in his diary entry for April 14, describing effects doubtless present on the evening of the fourteenth as well. Even if "there were hundreds of houses with not a single candle in their windows" (perhaps the homes of Rebel sympathizers, Owner thought), the predominant effect was brightness.[81] A few blocks from Ford's, Grover's on April 14 staged a production of *Aladdin; or, The Wonderful Lamp,* a performance that must have resonated not just with the house lights but with those around the city.[82] But the lonely glow in one place was another way to portray Lincoln, more in keeping with his own emphasis on the irreducible poetry and tragic mystery of one location.

That night flame was the twin of blood. For one thing, they both spread. The well-lit city presaged the national conflagration of Booth's shot, the fiery equivalent of seas made incarnadine by the murder. Later that month the bonfires lining parts of the Lincoln funeral train's route back to Springfield were a manifestation of this national radiance. But in a more important sense flame and blood that night of April 14, 1865, kept only one place. The Seward House on Lafayette Square, where Cushman had stayed during her visit of 1863, now became awash in the blood her performance had dramatized. Lewis Powell (alias Payne or Paine) burst into the bedroom

Fig. 35. Globe, ca. 1860. Collections of Seward House Museum, Auburn, New York.

of William Seward, who lay in bed immobilized and in deep pain from a serious carriage accident the week before, and stabbed and gashed him across the face. The blood that poured from Seward's wounds did not spread far; instead it marked only one place.

That room, soaked by blood, lit by gas, became the opposite of the wide world. Seward, as secretary of state, was a worldly man: he owned a large papier-mâché globe, some five feet high and five feet in circumference, most likely in the Lafayette Square house that night, that proclaimed his far-reaching awareness (fig. 35). Two years later, having survived Powell's attack,

Fig. 36. Emanuel Leutze, *Signing of the Alaska Treaty,* 1869. Oil on canvas, 40 × 60 in. (101.6 × 152.4 cm). Collections of Seward House Museum, Auburn, New York.

he orchestrated the purchase of Alaska for the United States, a negotiation commemorated in Emanuel Leutze's painting showing him seated next to a globe (fig. 36). "Seward's vision swept round the entire circle of the hemisphere," according to a later article. His own words in 1860 had given such a vision: "Standing here and looking far off into the northwest," Seward told an audience in St. Paul, Minnesota, "I see the Russian as he busily occupies himself in establishing seaports and towns and fortifications on the verge of this continent, as the outposts of St. Petersburg, and I say: 'Go on and build up your outposts all along the coast, up even to the Arctic ocean. They will yet become the outposts of my own country." En route to Sitka, Alaska, in 1869 to extol the virtues of the territory he had acquired, he spoke in suitably expansive terms: "I am travelling in regions grand and vast." On the night of the assassination attempt, this "imperialist before imperialism" who "looked out upon the Pacific and beheld it, if not as an American lake, at least as a means to the discovery of a new world," as one of his biographers described him, happened to be listening to his daughter Fanny read the story of Charlemagne to him. "At the height of his power, the French empire extended over what we now call France, Germany, Switzerland,

Holland, Belgium, and a great part of Italy," reads one sentence of that book.[83] Yet that night Seward's wounds were the signs of an indelible locality.

Leave it to Fanny, who witnessed the attack, to summon the requisite reference to *Macbeth.* "'I have supped full of horrors,' rang over & over in my mind," she wrote later in her diary. "Blood, blood, my thoughts seemed drenched in it—I seemed to breathe its sickening odor. My dress was stained with it—Mother's was drabbled with it—it was on everything. The bed had been covered with blood, the blankets & sheet chopped with several blows of the knife. . . . As I stood my feet slipped in a great pool of blood." Earlier on the night of April 14 Fanny and Anna had watched "a torch-light procession of employees from the Navy Yard visiting the White House" and listened to an accompanying nationalistic song ("Rally Round the Flag"). But now in the glow of the gas lamp that Fanny had turned down to let her father sleep—and probably turned back up in the commotion following the attack—she saw a face in which the gleam of blood and light seemed to express one another, to be almost the same thing, in the physical thickness of one moment and place: "Father looked so ghastly I was sure he was dead, he was white & very thin with the blood that had drained from the gashes about his face & throat."[84]

At Grover's on the night of October 17, 1863, flames abounded inside the theater. The so-called bat's-wing gas lamps were roughly the size of a human hand, thumb and pinky extended upward, middle three fingers dropped into the palm. They issued a wavering, palpitating light. Other lights, shaded, created a pulsating glow. "The shadows would dance around in some corners of the theater and in individual boxes," according to Mattausch. The theater lights may also have pulsed with fluctuations in the city's gas supply, subject to the peak-hour ebb, a wavering circulation that caused lights all over town to dip or blow.[85]

In front of the theater, a large gas lamp made a small interruption in the darkness. The lamp, visible in the photograph taken in 1868 (see fig. 2), is long gone, like the theater itself, but it was presumably much like the theater lamp that stood outside Ford's Theater, which was melted down for scrap metal during the Second World War and is now commemorated by a replica standing about thirteen feet high with a roughly four-foot glass-cased lantern box. A *Macbeth* candle come to the street, the light at Grover's on October 17 might have been a flickering sensuousness in one place. For us now, thinking of history, the lone light seems not to light the past—to be the flame whose glow would allow us to see a world we would otherwise never glimpse—but rather to *be* that past: to assert that each historical figure, each event, stands forth, if we can discern it now, not in print, not in stone, and not even exactly in "life," if by that we mean a biographical sense of what a person or situation was really like, but rather as a flame: every event, every thing, every person a flame, a city of these flames, so that there would never be for the historian, as perhaps there never was for Lincoln, a scene so vivid, so sharp and durable, that it did not also gently, strangely burn.

THREE

The Glass Case

Interior Life in Washington, D.C.

DID THE PERFORMANCE OF THE PLAY relate to other happenings in Washington that day? The readiest answer is no. Attending a play by the 1860s was an increasingly private experience, a ceremonial occasion when spectators were cut off from one another, left to lose themselves in their dreams and meditations about what they saw, and largely cut off from the world outside as well. Lincoln was not the only one to draw inward. Audiences observed "new codes of politeness," according to Bruce McConnachie. "The manners of the genteel parlor, first regularly enforced in museum theatres in the 1840s, had overtaken theatregoing by 1870."[1]

Probably the crowd at Grover's on October 17 observed such manners, though play watching that night was also a notably public experience. "Enthusiastic" throughout, according to the *Daily National Republican,* the frequently applauding crowd was a phalanx of national solidarity. But each moment of the performance would also have allowed—would even have been made for—the private consideration of viewers.[2] Cushman's friend Annie Fields, after watching the actress play Lady Macbeth in Boston on September 25, noted that the "deep-drawn breath of sleep is thrilling" in the actress's final scene. That deep-drawn breath would presumably again draw in the audience three weeks later in Washington, affording another chance for spectators to thrill privately to the action.

Only a few years before, this genteel privacy had not been so attainable.

Shakespeare in antebellum America was part of "a rich shared public culture," according to the cultural historian Lawrence Levine. The eighty-six men arrested at the Astor Place Riots of May 1849, fighting it out after rival performances of *Macbeth* in New York City, were "coopers, printers, butchers, carpenters, servants, sailmakers, machinists, clerks, masons, bakers, plumbers, laborers." In the years following Astor Place, however, "Theater no longer functioned as an expressive form that embodied all classes within a shared public space." Instead it was part of a gradual "stylistic bifurcation" into "serious" and "popular" cultures, a split that was well under way by 1863, and "serious" meant increasingly the quietude of becoming absorbed—lost—in the play.[3]

Ambitious theaters such as Grover's solidified these pretensions by actively seeking to exclude the unruliness of the outside world. In a newspaper notice on October 17 Leonard Grover encouraged those who had already purchased tickets to arrive early, lest the sight of placards reading Taken on empty seats provoke "much growling and morose feeling" when the play began. (As it was, the play that night started twenty minutes late.)[4] Once secured, these "capacious arm chairs" encouraged politeness and privacy, "so that no individual is encroached upon and every one has room enough and to spare," contributing to the theater's overall "elegance and comfort."[5] Ford's Theater, a few blocks away, aimed for the same experience. Fanny Seward noted that on her tour of Ford's with Cushman on October 10—"a very pretty theater, tasteful & convenient"—she saw on the gallery level "placards with very large letters with various hints etc, calculated to promote order."[6]

As the signs indicate, keeping everyone quiet and polite in these venues was an elusive goal. The grand opening of Grover's Theatre on October 6, a performance of *Othello,* was marred by "the heathenish conduct of boys in the gallery, who must be taught to keep still."[7] At another performance of *Othello* that fall at Niblo's Garden in New York, a "profound silence" came over the theater as Othello smothered Desdemona until, according to a *Harper's Monthly* writer who was there, "a voice proceeding from our immediate neighborhood made itself audible, as it seemed to me, to the utmost extremity of the house, perfectly calm, and clear, and resonant: 'What! Is he a-slaughtering on her?' "[8]

By contrast, a bourgeois theatergoer's exasperation at a performance was probably best expressed privately afterward. Benjamin Brown French noted in his diary on October 18 that the previous evening's performance "was well done, but, as Macbeth himself would say, 'It were well it were done quickly.' I never saw a character so 'long drawn out' as [Lester] Wallack's

Macbeth was last night. The curtain rose at about 8 & 20' and fell for the last time at 20' before 12! at least an hour longer than it should have taken." Such was "Wallack's overdoing of his part," which kept French from getting to bed until past 1:00 A.M. and caused him to remain around his Capitol Hill home and garden the next day with a severe headache.[9] At the performance itself, however, French most likely voiced his displeasure in no more than a murmur.

Theater owners and audiences had good reason to keep everything polite, neat, and orderly inside the theater. Outside was chaos. Up to the very walls of Grover's, the city was raucous and rude. Even within those walls the wild city intruded: the Deery and Simpson Billiard Saloon on the second floor was not likely a genteel place. The neighborhood was home "to the most comfortless and the groggiest of taverns," according to the English journalist George Augustus Sala.[10] Grover noted that in January 1863 many people in Washington, including army officers, reviled the recently announced Emancipation Proclamation and that "the immediate neighborhood of my theater, surrounded as it was by all kinds of saloons, was perhaps the center of such antipathy. Scenes of violence with pistol and knife were of frequent occurrence." One night outside the theater, Grover escorted the Lincolns to their presidential carriage only to discover a jeering crowd around the vehicle. The driver, while getting drunk in a nearby saloon, had entrusted the carriage to a one-armed drummer boy, who now held the reins in his one hand as the presidential party emerged onto the sidewalk. The driver, trying to remount the carriage, had twice fallen on the sidewalk and the crowd had gathered. "Any overt act, the throwing of a stone, might have resulted in catastrophe," wrote Grover, who seized the reins and himself drove the presidential party home.[11]

October 17 was an ordinary day in Washington—full of the social malfeasance and ordinary devastating unhappiness that the evening's grand performance would so earnestly try to exclude. A twenty-six-year-old woman intent on killing herself had jumped into the city's sewage-filled waterway, the Washington Canal, only to discover that the mud and water "were not deep enough to drown her while on her feet." She then lay down to submerge herself but was rescued by a passing mechanic named Alex Douglass. The woman, Rosa Bell, told officers at the Second Ward station that "her lover is 'dead and gone,' buried in the Baltimore cemetery, and she does not care to live longer." The Washington city directory turns up a widow named Sarah Bell who lived on Eighth Street and a mechanic named Alex Douglass who lived on Eleventh—close to the Tenth Street location where she jumped and not far from Grover's between Thirteenth and Fourteenth streets. "Rosa had been drinking," noted the newspaper, and she carried a letter to her sister in Baltimore. She was released to her friends at about seven in the evening on the seventeenth.[12]

Early that morning, the police arrested ten boys, aged thirteen to sixteen, for sleeping in the Centre Market at Sixth and Pennsylvania. Many of the boys were bootblacks, and their situation prompted a short opinion piece from the *Daily National Republican:* "This practice of sleeping in the markets and in wagons in the streets, demonstrates the necessity and importunes the erection of a home for the friendless, and a house of refuge in Washington." All but two of the boys were sent to the workhouse for periods of either thirty or sixty days.[13]

In the early morning of the eighteenth, long after the crowds at Grover's had dispersed, a policeman noticed a black man "mounted upon a dun colored mare, bare-backed, riding down Fourteenth street." The officer followed the man to a government stable, where the man sold the horse, and immediately arrested him on charges of horse stealing. The black man, who gave his name as John Brown, was sent to jail and the mare was impounded.[14] "The midnight streets are full of the forlorn and wretched," Charles Congdon wrote in *Harper's* in an article about the failures of theater in 1864, "and yet we go shambling and blindly blundering back to the past for the sources of tragedy!"[15]

The culture of refinement sat ensconced in splendor in the theater as the grubby outside world pressed its dirty face to the edges of the charmed circle. George Eliot's novel *Romola* (1862–63), advertised in *Harper's Weekly* on October 17, gives a superlative allegory of this state of affairs. Set in Renaissance Florence, *Romola* includes a scene of a sumptuous banquet in the Rucellai Gardens, where the city's political and cultural players gather amid luxury. The men wash their hands from a brass bowl of scented water, their ringed fingers and silver forks flashing in the candlelight of a pleasant evening outdoors, and they eat a variety of meats before coming to the grand focus of the feast—a dish so symbolic that it is understood they hardly need eat it: a peacock cooked with the feathers on and left unplucked afterward, so "that it might look as much as possible like a live peacock taking its unboiled repose."[16]

Outside, however, "in the chill obscurity that surrounded this center of warmth, and light, and savory odors," a person lurks: a "lonely disowned man was walking in gradually narrowing circuits." He is Baldassarre, the elderly mentor of Tito, one of the banqueters, who ruthlessly cast the old man out when he no longer needed him. Now Baldassarre approaches to confront his betrayer, even as "the men seated among the branching tapers and the flashing cups could know nothing of the pale fierce face that watched them from without." He penetrates the circle, his "fierce dark eyes bent on Tito's bright smiling unconsciousness." Now the others see his "sallow deep-lined face with the hatred in its eyes" that "seemed a terrible apparition across the wax-lit ease and gaiety." But Baldassarre, confused and addled, fails in his mission. He cannot remember the accusations he had carefully rehearsed, and Tito resumes his place of comfort and privilege. Baldassarre is taken away, the conversation turns to other subjects, and "something like the struggling of a man who was being dragged away" is heard outside. So the banquet—the shining circle—continues as before: "The light," notes Eliot, "can be a curtain as well as the darkness."[17]

The scene refers to *Macbeth,* with Baldassarre haunting Tito as Banquo does Macbeth, but what is most striking is Eliot's commentary on the uneasy exclusions of refined culture—not just that of fifteenth-century Florence but that of her own time and country and of mid-nineteenth-century America as well, that "isle of Cristoforo Colombo's finding," as one of the dinner guests envisions, where there will be "a popular government, in which every man is to strive for the general good."[18] In the America of October 17, the social scene at Grover's was more nearly an affair like the Rucellai supper. The play was attended by women as well as men, and not everyone was of the highest social rank, but the event was an exclusive gathering of the city's and nation's leaders, assembled in a peacock glitter of crinoline and epaulettes, savoring a rare delectation that, in a manner of speaking, they did not even need to eat to enjoy.

Did the world without—the resentment and even just the ordinary life of the city streets—penetrate the theater? A famous American painting tells us more about the neighborhood of Grover's and shows us how other cultural forms of the era—painting and the novel—portrayed a vividly dialogic social space even as theater and sculpture became more insular, more closed.

The painting is Eastman Johnson's *Negro Life at the South* (1859), which depicts a location near the theater (fig. 37). For many years the painting was known as *My Old Kentucky Home,* but the art historian John Davis in 1998 expertly identified the location Johnson shows: a block of F Street between Thirteenth and Fourteenth streets where his family lived starting in 1853. Davis even pinpoints the exact place—a lot hidden from street view "just to the east of the Johnson home" at 266 F Street, one block up from Grover's.[19] *Negro Life at the South* gives a sense of what an F Street yard looked like even

Fig. 37. Eastman Johnson, *Negro Life at the South,* 1859. Oil on canvas, 36 × 45½ in. (91.4 × 115.6 cm), acc. S-225. Collection of The New-York Historical Society.

in 1863, when the black people of Washington had been emancipated but still lived, many of them, in the same locations and the same conditions as before. Showing a banjo player at the center of a line of figures, all of them slaves except a white woman who enters the scene at far right, it evokes the socially heterodox neighborhood that the theater tried to shut out.

It is not, however, the subject of the painting but its rhetoric that most emphasizes the nearby enclosure of Grover's. We see into the space in *Negro Life at the South* as if through a magically lifted fourth wall. As a result, as Davis notes, we are privy to a scene typically hidden from view: "Close inspection of the exposed roof beams, the remnants of a perimeter foundation at the feet of the banjo player, and the plaster-coated walls, once obviously belonging to a protected interior space, leaves the impression that an entire architectural façade has been ripped away, sheared off so as better to display the activities and squalid living conditions of those who inhabit this hovel." While Southern legislators wanted to keep slavery in the capital hidden, "Johnson's painting takes on the air of muckraking journalism."[20]

Or a realist novel. Shearing off the fourth wall, *Negro Life at the South* matches the way such novels were conceived. "It is very much like playing with a dollhouse or with a toy city," writes Peter Brooks, describing an early story (from 1707) that strips away rooftops to show the private lives inside. Even in the early eighteenth century, "it is already a gesture from Honoré de Balzac or Charles Dickens, seeing through the roofs and facades of the real to the private lives behind and beneath."[21]

Eliot, in *Adam Bede* (1859), portrays the process succinctly: "Imagination is a licensed trespasser: it has no fear of dogs, but may climb over walls and peep in at windows with impunity. Put your face to one of the glass panes in the right-hand window: what do you see? . . . Let me take you into that dining-room, and show you. . . . We will enter very softly, and stand still in the open doorway."[22] Basing *Adam Bede* on the "rare, precious quality of truthfulness" in seventeenth-century Dutch paintings, Eliot is a natural parallel to Johnson, who was "moved by the great seventeenth-century genre painters" during an extended stay at The Hague in 1851–52. *Adam Bede* and *Negro Life at the South,* both of 1859, show a Dutch-inflected, genre-style realism—a lifting of the wall to create, in Eliot's phrase, "faithful pictures of a monotonous homely existence."[23]

What is revealed, moreover, is not just daily life but the operation of ideology, manifest in realist dialogic form. This type of discourse was basically unknown at the shatterproof bourgeois entertainment venue a block away. The key in *Negro Life at the South* is the friezelike arrangement of figures, an array that allows for the distribution of shocks, of reverberations, across the represented social field. The cultural critic Fredric Jameson, writing about Eliot's *Middlemarch* (1872), pinpoints the ideological differences in the realist fiction of that era and, by implication, in Johnson's painting. Novels such as *Middlemarch,* for Jameson, increasingly concern "the relationships between individuals" and, more precisely, the adjustments these individuals must make to the presence of others. In earlier novels characters had merely bumped up against one another, with the collision leaving the fundamentally static nature of each character unchanged. The new novels of the midcentury, however, portray a " 'web' of interrelationships . . . encounters, looks, demands, self-defenses," each with the capacity to change the characters. For Jameson this literature is concerned with studying "barely perceptible adjustments to the Other."[24]

Negro Life at the South fits this definition. The white woman entering at right will affect the scene. Each of the black characters, in turn, though about to be affected by her, hardly needs the white woman's presence to be conceived as already part of a synchronic network, a diverse social space. Their activities unfold in a variety of atomized yet integrated gestures for which the word "community" is too polite and the phrase "separate vignettes" is inaccurate. This is a changeable scene of separate people whose behavior—courting, dancing, singing, playing, staring—has the potential to change that of others.

This possibility might not be obvious at first. The fanning leaves of the large tree establish an easy principle of unity, an encompassing pattern of light and dark that spreads across the scene like the banjo player's plaintive song, giving the yard a static quality as though it were a pleasantly melancholy place where everyone and everything remains unchanged. But the tree, an infinite compilation of lights and darks, shifting in ever-changing patterns of wind and light, is also the icon of the reverberating social world it would control. The white woman most exemplifies this principle of change—she will alter the whole situation once all the other characters see her—but perhaps her presence is meant only to literalize the idea of "lives . . . brushing up against each other," in Jameson's phrase, that the black characters already embody.[25]

The space of Grover's on October 17 wanted to know nothing of this surrounding neighborhood. Yet in a way the private space of the theater did reach out to the Washington world around it. It connected to other interiors—other inward states and spaces as hermetic as its own. It forsook the streets and lots to connect across the city to inward places, literally to other genteel and intellectual architectural interiors. It tested whether these quarters were simply solipsistic enclosures for those who would prefer to see nothing of the world outside.[26] Reciprocally, the performance tested whether its own retreating inwardness was really cut off from everything around it. What were the dangers and the values of being separated from the world? How much or how little of the outside world might be let in? *Macbeth* that night helps us see how a history and specifics of inwardness came to be invented, imagined, and practiced by a certain class of person not just on October 17 but more broadly in wartime Washington and northeastern America.

JULIA WARD HOWE: WINDOW AND EAR

Consider the case of Julia Ward Howe. She was not in Washington on October 17 but had written the famous "Battle Hymn of the Republic" in her room at Willard's Hotel, a few doors down from Grover's, on November

19, 1861. The creation of the anthem in that spot would indeed give the nearby theater some of its radiating energy nearly two years later. Cushman's nationalistic exhortation recalled the reach of Howe, her contemporary and rival. Howe wrote the "Battle Hymn" on Sanitary Commission stationery, and she would cross paths with Cushman at the Boston Music Hall two weeks after the actress's Washington performance. More important, however, the theater's clamped-down enclosure helps us see the poem's own surprising inwardness—an interiority bound up with the space in which Howe wrote it.

Howe, in Washington with her husband, the noted reformer Samuel Gridley Howe, to inspect the sanitary conditions of the Union army camps in the area, wrote the "Battle Hymn" early one morning in her room at Willard's. Out in Virginia the day before, the Howes' party had been forced back to Washington by a Confederate attack, and on the return they sang the army marching song, "John Brown's Body" ("John Brown's body lies a-mouldering in the ground . . . "). Howe's friends asked her if she might devise less grisly lyrics for the rousing tune. The next morning, with her infant son nearby, as Howe recounts,

> I awoke in the gray of the morning twilight; and as I lay waiting for the dawn, the long lines of the desired poem began to twine themselves in my mind. Having thought out all the stanzas, I said to myself, "I must get up and write these verses down, lest I fall asleep again and forget them." So, with a sudden effort, I sprang out of bed, and found in the dimness an old stump of a pen which I remember to have used the day before. I scrawled the verses almost without looking at the paper. I had learned to do this when, on previous occasions, attacks of versification had visited me in the night, and I feared to have recourse to a light lest I should wake the baby, who slept near me.[27]

In many ways the room in which she wrote the anthem was a retreat from the world. For one, it was a departure from the relentlessly masculine parlors and hall of the hotel, the Washington epicenter of cigar smoke, where, as Nathaniel Hawthorne wrote in 1862,

> You exchange nods with governors of sovereign States; you elbow illustrious men, and tread on the toes of generals; you hear statesmen and orators speaking in their familiar tones. You are mixed up with office-seekers, wire-pullers, inventors, artists, poets, prosers (including editors, army-correspondents, *attachés* of foreign journals, and long-winded

talkers), clerks, diplomatists, mail-contractors, railway-directors. . . . You adopt the universal habit of the place, and call for a mint-julep, a whiskey-skin, a gin-cocktail, a brandy-smash, or a glass of pure Old Rye.[28]

A woman in such public spaces could be subject to scorn and ridicule. The British journalist Sala described the twenty-one-year-old abolitionist orator Anna Dickinson, sitting at breakfast at Willard's at a table next to his and wearing a "red Garibaldi jacket," her hair "cut close," and "doing considerable execution upon the buckwheat cakes and molasses." She was "a crazy Jane in a red jacket . . . utter[ing] nonsense."[29] Willard's was a man's world.

Yet in her reclusive spot in that hotel Howe found a space to make a far-reaching statement. The "Battle Hymn," as the critic Jeffrey Polizzotto points out, is about Howe's own voice, her vision: "Mine eyes have seen the glory of the coming of the Lord," "I have seen Him in the watch-fires of a hundred circling camps."[30] Howe sees further than the self-beclouded julep drinkers: she sees outward to the camps that her poetry causes to circle around her. The poem makes the dawn that lights it, and the genesis of this new world flows from the wasted remains of the previous day ("an old stump of a pen which I remember to have used the day before"). Howe praised the voice of one of her inspection party, the Reverend William Henry Channing—his sermons "rang out, clear and musical as a bell, within the walls of the Unitarian church"—and here, within another set of walls, she made her own ringing sermon, appropriating the man's authoritative voice. The day before, she had cowered inside a hospital tent rather than accept a Union colonel's request to address his troops.[31] Now, still inside, all but alone, and in a double or even triple retreat (from Virginia, from the scene at Willard's, from her husband, who wanted her to avoid becoming a public figure)—she found the extensive, hortatory words.

The window of Howe's room played a key role in this reaching outward. The gray light streaming into her room came presumably through the same Willard's window from which she had noted the scene earlier in her stay: "From my window I saw the office of the 'New York Herald,' and near it the ghastly advertisement of an agency for embalming and forwarding the bodies of those who had fallen in the fight or who had perished by fever."[32] The newspaper and the embalming office suggest the outside world the poem will connect with. They affirm the poem's aims, suggesting its own newsworthy power and its bid for permanence, insofar as embalming claims to be the opposite of the body laying "a-mouldering in the ground." In another sense, however, the sites outside the window signify the ordinary daily life of Washington that the poem aims to cancel, just as the performance of *Macbeth* on October 17 wished to do. It wants to expunge these places, which are embarrassments of loud and brutal address to the passerby, signposts to the idle gazer that beseech him so that he might recognize his mortality in the chipped paint of their quick-fading appeals.

Instead, in an atmosphere washed clean by the gray morning light, the work of art sets down a stirring biblical rhetoric beyond time. Leave it to others in town, such as the magisterial Frederick Douglass, to make their windows into proud conduits between inside and outside—to use the window, as the cultural historian Sarah Luria writes, as "the material counterpart" to calls for honest openness in society. Leave it to Douglass to add a street-fronting bay window to his Capitol Hill home, so that, as Luria notes, he could keep his eyes on the Capitol even as he invited others to see into the rectitude of his home.[33] Howe's window was less social. In her description of the morning of November 19, the world outside the window is reduced to so much context, so much meaningless background, in the midst of which the creation of the poem takes place as though within the last and littlest of a stack of nested boxes.

The world outside, however, is vital to the poem and to the concept of a meaningful interiority, as Howe herself by then was recognizing. Before the war she had liked to enclose herself in a supremely private environment to write. At the family's country retreat at Lawton's Valley, Massachusetts, she sought out one north-facing window of the house, in a tiny attic room approachable only by a narrow flight of stairs. She chose this location because she was sensitive to the stronger light of the house's south- and east-facing windows, but her choice also suggested a more thoroughgoing writerly isolation: the tiny attic "was a platform just large enough to give room for a table two feet square. The stairs were shut off from the rest of the house by a stout door. And here, through the summer heats, and in spite of many wasps," Howe wrote a play for Edwin Booth—a play that set her "dreaming of the fine emphasis [he] would give to its best passages and of the beautiful appearance he would make in classic costume." Yet nothing came of this super-enclosed interiority. The play was never performed, even when years later a ripe occasion arose to do so.[34] Dreaming—mere dreaming—was the process and endpoint of shutting oneself up.

The Willard's hotel window, by contrast, let in the outside world in just the way that Howe would note in her poem "A New Sculptor," published in the *Atlantic Monthly* in September 1862, seven months after the "Battle Hymn." Here the dreamy inwardness of a refined woman is broken by the startling and coarse entrance of a strange man:

Once to my Fancy's hall a stranger came,
    Of mien unwonted,
And its pale shapes of glory without shame
    Or speech confronted.

The woman presides over a sacrosanct gallery of sculpture—

Fair was my hall,—a gallery of Gods
    Smoothly appointed;
With Nymphs and Satyrs from the dewy sods
    Freshly anointed.[35]

Her "rude visitant" looks on all this fine whiteness without saying a word. While she waits for him to genuflect or at least pay lip service to the idea that these works of art are far above his station—and begins to think that the man's dirty clothes, hammer, and calloused hands are not so ugly after all—he startles her by smashing the marbles to pieces with the hammer and exhorting her to sweep the trash away and replace it with a sculpture of his own making. This new work is made of "our mother Earth" and is so realistic that "it breathed, it moved." It is called "To-day." Howe's narrator tries to defend her genteel works—"My marbles lived on symmetry and song," she protests—but the workman responds, "Thy Gods are gone with old-time faith and Fate; / Here is thy Neighbor." Into Fancy's hall the real world reaches its calloused hands, and if the man destroys all that is sacred, caring nothing for these lifeless symmetries, the result is an uncouth realism that breathes life into the arid emptiness of the stainless perfection.

At Willard's, what entered through the window was the newspaper office and the embalming shop, not to mention the wider life of the street—in its utter grubbiness and ordinariness. These were Howe's Neighbors; these were To-day. A popular song, the black earth and rubbed leather of its engraved rhythms, is the raw material for Howe's poem. Yes, this outside world enters her room only as a gray light that denies the very life of the street, smoothing and sifting it into a featureless clearness. And yes, this light even makes a magical pale weightless ground for words scripted as if on air (so the creation story invites us to imagine). Yet all this elaborate ground clearing too conspicuously erases the coarse clatter that must be the basis for the poem's own hammering sound.

Another interior lurks in this story of give-and-take between inside and outside: the ear. Oliver Wendell Holmes, Sr., writing about the great organ at the Music Hall, thought of the ears set to receive the organ's sounds—ears no less marvelous than the great organ itself, which he likened to private residences. These dwellings "admit Sound as a visitor" by an entrance "protected and ornamented . . . by a light movable awning." Holmes elaborates on this suite of aural rooms: sound travels through "a recess . . . at the farther end of which is the parchment-like front door . . . *(membrana tympani).*" Farther yet is an entryway leading into "the inner suite of apartments (labyrinth), which then unfolds as "an antechamber," "an arched chamber," and "a spiral chamber," and still more rooms. Sound reverberates from one end to another of this interior—this then, Holmes writes, is "the plan of the organ of hearing as an architect might describe it."[36]

Holmes's accompanying letter-coded diagram of a suite of rooms shows these refined aural apartments (fig. 38). The Brahms and Mendelssohn pieces wafting from the great organ would meet their match in these delicate chambers, entering spaces meant to receive such cultured visitants. But the diagram applies equally well to a process like Howe's, where the challenge was to transform a baser sound.

That sound had not always been so coarse for Howe. In her book *Passion-Flowers* (1854), she had described first hearing a nightingale: "A note / Fell as a star falls, trailing sound for light."[37] The goal back then was to capture an ephemeral song, bringing the bird's otherworldly music into a Fancy's hall of symmetry and song. But the wartime ear was different: it needed to welcome a ruder rhythm, a more rough-spoken guest. This coarse visitor was not just the soldiers' song but John Brown himself, who arrived at the Howe front door unannounced one day in 1859, a stranger who "came / Of mien unwonted," seeking support (which he received) from Samuel Gridley Howe and making a strong impression on Julia.

Brown came in at the Willard's window, too, while Howe strived to transform his rough moldering clay into Art. In her private room—an ear attuned to what she had heard—Howe would create an anthem that soon reverberated through the scattershot noises of the world as a unifying, singular sound. In this sense, the "Battle Hymn" is like a monument erected in the midst of disquiet, a sleek statue whose marbled surface of polished rhythm erases the scratch of other sounds. A poet like Howe might prop-

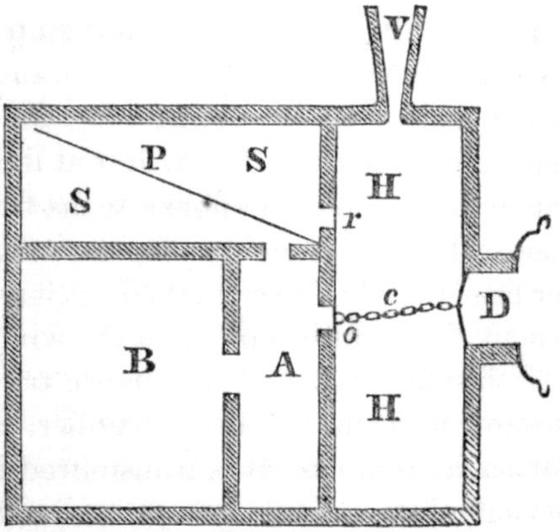

Fig. 38. "Plan of the organ of hearing as an architect might describe it." In Oliver Wendell Holmes, "The Great Instrument," *Atlantic Monthly,* November 1863, 638. Sterling Memorial Library, Yale University.

erly think of this as her aesthetic role—the unity of nation and of poem, rhyming in one sound. This might also have been the goal of *Macbeth* at Grover's on October 17—to mute the outside world, to create a clearing manifest in the respectful quiet of the audience at the right moments but, even more, in a grand ceremonial deadening of all noise, all clatter (from the whittling of a knife blade to the trundling of a carriage to the screams and sighs of a thousand citizens), so that the play might find the proper sterile blankness for its national declamations.

But Howe, near her window, allowed something else to happen. Even if her purpose was to silence the indiscriminate noise and fluster of the world, the poem could not help admitting that outside cacophony. That exterior sound is not just the army's marching song. The poem catches within itself, like a bucket does rainwater, the city noises she heard. In a letter Howe described mounted officers and orderlies galloping "to and fro" in the city and ambulances pulled by four horses through the streets and sometimes stopping at Willard's.[38] Mark Smith, in *Listening to Nineteenth-Century America,* quotes a period newspaper account to describe the ambient noise of Washington's city streets later in the war—streets resounding "with the deafening rumble of heavy wagons"; a loudly throbbing "Horseshoeing Establishment" of two hundred soot-blackened men beating on anvils, making a "deafening peal upon the ear," and "the roar of the bellows sound[ing] like the rush of a tempest sweeping upon a forest." Even back in April 1861, according to another newspaper story, in the capital "a warlike din resounds in every direction."[39] Such a diverse splatter of sounds—the noise of Washington in wartime—lurks within the poem's funneled blast.

This effect is partly because Howe admired bursts of separate sound, even as "Battle Hymn" aspired to a grand singularity. She disliked the great organ because she thought it replaced the multiple sounds of the orchestra with the false uniformity of a single all-powerful instrument. "Commend me to the strings and the brasses," she wrote. "I love the sudden zeal of the cymbals and the prudent, timely interference of the hero with the kettle drums."[40] If the visitor at the door is the element of surprise, if this entrant is the sign of the discord and shattering purpose that inspired the poem, those sounds of real life must remain within the lines that would erase them.

The "Battle Hymn" is finally a cup of national sound that holds a rich and varied noise. All the sounds it seeks to expunge remain somehow within it. In the manner of a reliquary, the poem asks us to look within its splendid shining case to the life it holds, still liquid and quivering, and not a little supernatural, within the mere jewel work we mistakenly still gaze at. The whole purpose of the poem—the reason it was created—is to hold the life outside the window.

CUT OFF: "THE CASE OF GEORGE DEDLOW" AND "THE MAN WITHOUT A COUNTRY"

Was *Macbeth,* then, out of touch on October 17? Maybe it sent out its own "Battle Hymn," but in a way that drew less on the outside world than Howe did. The bank of windows on the theater façade (see fig. 2) may have established some connection to the street, but deep in the darkened well of the theater, the performance aspired to create a private world. Was greater isolation possible from the activities outside? Not necessarily, to judge by two famous Civil War stories that described far more radical withdrawals. Each is a macabre parable about the consequences of a nearly lifeless inwardness—the kind that *Macbeth* on October 17 wanted to avoid.

One story is S. Weir Mitchell's "The Case of George Dedlow," published in the *Atlantic Monthly* in July 1866. Dedlow is a Union infantry captain shot through both arms who soon loses the right arm, amputated at the shoulder. Returning to duty after a convalescence, Dedlow is then shot through the legs, which are both amputated. His left arm soon becomes gangrenous from the old wound and it also is taken off. He is left "a useless torso, more like some strange larval creature than anything of human shape." Mitchell, a surgeon during the war, had studied the phenomenon of phantom limbs and knew how to imagine the feelings of a person like Dedlow, who narrates the story.[41] Yet "The Case of George Dedlow" goes beyond a medical context to comment on the potential nightmare of a person's extreme isolation from the culture at large.

Dedlow finds that in his physically reduced state he is capable of receiving fewer and fewer messages from the outside world. Having lost four-fifths of his bodily weight, he discovers that he needs very little food or sleep. His heartbeat slows to nearly half its former pace. His greatly reduced number of nerves also contributes to this state of "perfect quiescence." As he puts it, "About one half of the sensitive surface of my skin was gone, and thus much of relation to the outer world was destroyed. . . . Moreover, all the great central ganglia, which give rise to movements in the limbs, were also eternally at rest. Thus one half of me was functionally absent or dead." Dedlow finds, as a result, that "his sense of individual existence" is diminished.[42]

Dedlow's missing nerves make his story a parable of a person cut off from information. In the era of the telegraph, Marshall McLuhan wrote in *Understanding Media* (1964), "man had initiated that outering or extension of his central nervous system" that placed it outside the body.[43] Dedlow's quiescence is that of a person with no access to these wide worlds. Without information, his sense of individuality fades. To be human— for Dedlow, for Mitchell, for readers of the *Atlantic Monthly*—is not only a matter of having one's limbs but also of being connected to the world's flow of news.

Contrasting this story to a work of American art helps make the point. In 1872 Thomas Eakins made one of his perspective drawings for a painting he was then working on, *The Pair-Oared Shell* (fig. 39). Showing the Biglin brothers in their scull, the drawing is notable for the carefully realized perspectival grid plotting the space in which the men row the craft. The grid recedes to a vanishing point just to the right of the right-hand man, disappearing in a rectangle of dark wash along the horizon. These lines suggest the rowers' connection to the world. Like the oars themselves, they extend from the men, implying their ability to control and define the space around them. The orthogonals also zoom in on the men, nearly coinciding with their faces, implying that the world they control also comes to them.

The drawing in this sense is a parable of technological persons and, more precisely, of information-based persons. Cultural historians such as Mark Seltzer and Bill Brown have identified a logic of personal extension in American culture starting in the 1860s, an interest in the prosthetic capacity of individual bodies to extend outward in space.[44] In Eakins's drawing the prosthesis in question resembles McLuhan's outward nervous system—a web of ganglionic antennae emanating from men who would not be nearly as physically powerful, as individuated and "there," if they lacked these ex-

Fig. 39. Thomas Eakins, *Perspective Drawing for the "Pair-Oared Shell,"* 1872. Graphite, ink, and watercolor on paper, $31^{13}/_{16} \times 47^{9}/_{16}$ in. (80.8×120.9 cm). Philadelphia Museum of Art. Purchased with the Thomas Skelton Harrison Fund, 1944.

tensive filaments. The grid does more than plot a space in which the figures move. It provides attenuated feelers that shoot to and from these crisp bodies whose insular self-sufficiency would be impossible to conceive without such extensions.

Dedlow lacks this grid. His quiescence predicts the neurasthenia Mitchell would diagnose in men and women later in the century, the affliction of nerves that wore down brain workers and other thoughtful persons, including Eakins. (When Mitchell prescribed a dose of healthy activity for Eakins, who traveled to the Dakota Territory to recuperate in 1886, he was trying to reestablish the depressed man's contact with the world.) But "The Case of George Dedlow" speaks to a different isolation in the 1860s. Back then, the horrors of being out of touch were newly vivid. At the time in Washington it was still a novelty—a definition of life itself—that "on any given day, perhaps thirty specials [reporters or correspondents] made regular daily rounds of Congressional and department offices, military headquarters, nearby army camps, the railroad station, hotels, bars, and restaurants," gathering the news and then "sending their copy to New York 'in wads' by the telegraph."[45] Periodicals like the *Atlantic Monthly* were new and resplendent with their power to carry information to distant places. In the pages of that periodical, Dedlow was a curiosity to modern, educated middle-class readers: not just a medical specimen but an imagined case of some earlier, "larval" state of human connectivity: an evolutionary holdover from a time before mass communications.

The protagonist of the second wartime story has all his limbs, but he is equally remote from the present-day world. Edward Everett Hale's "The Man Without a Country," published in the *Atlantic Monthly* in December 1863, tells the story of Philip Nolan, an American officer who in 1805 is accused of treason. Asked at trial if he has always been loyal to the United States, Nolan blurts out his reply: "D__n the United States! I wish I may never hear of the United States again!" Perversely, his wish is granted. "From that moment, September 23, 1807, till the day he died, May 11, 1863," Nolan is kept prisoner on board a series of navy ships with the stipulation that no person he talks with may ever mention the United States.[46]

Nolan's curse, unlike Dedlow's, is payback for disloyalty. Hale equates Nolan with the Copperhead senator Clement Vallandigham, whose advocacy of peace with the South led to his defeat in the October 1863 congressional elections and his exile in Canada.[47] But Nolan, or No-land, evokes more tellingly a figure like Dedlow who lacks access to the wide world.

The striking fact of Nolan's isolation is not that he is removed from the United States but that he is denied all information about it. To keep up the elaborate punishment—which seems more sadistic for the pitying tone in which the narrator recounts it—Nolan's succession of jailers must scrutinize all his reading material before giving it to him, carefully excising all references to the United States in books and newspapers. "Somebody must go over them first," the narrator recounts, "and cut out any advertisement or stray paragraph that alluded to America."[48]

Nolan is like Dedlow, removed from worldly contact and correspondingly reduced as an individual, but his privation takes a different form. In his precious little bedroom aboard a ship sailing all over the world, he keeps detailed notebooks and scrapbooks. The scrapbooks, of which "he had six or eight," are divided into subjects—history, natural science, "Odds and Ends." They contain clippings from books and newspapers, "and they had bits of plants and ribbons, shells tied on, and carved scraps of bone and wood, which he had taught the men to cut for him, and they were beautifully illustrated." With so much time on his hands, Nolan knows everything about centipedes and cockroaches, and "he was the only naturalist I ever met who knew anything about the habits of the house-fly and the mosquito." He gets plenty of exercise, reads prayers beautifully, and ministers expertly to ill sailors. His room, meanwhile, contains a "great map" of the United States that he has hand drawn according to the boundaries of 1805.[49] Because of his isolation, Nolan is an eccentric, an aesthete, a connoisseur, a collector, a thinker.

He is also a dandy. His attention to aesthetic matters and his knowledge of arcane subjects qualify him as such. When the men call him "Plain-Buttons," referring to the unadorned buttons he must wear on his army uniform, without the initials or insignia of the United States, the comment on his dress suggests the stylish and unaffiliated eccentricity of the man. Even his repentant expressions of patriotism have a precious artistic flair that makes them seem somehow more than, or other than, signs of national devotion: "The stars and stripes were triced up above and around a picture of Washington, and he had painted a majestic eagle, with lightnings blazing from his beak and his foot just clasping the whole globe, with his wings overshadowed."[50]

In the deeper logic of the story, Nolan is not exactly a man punished for treason—that is, a former army officer who only subsequently develops creative skills because of his enforced privation. He is instead a man whose treason precisely *is* this form of creative isolation. With a Civil War on, there simply were more useful things for a man to do than study centipedes or cockroaches or draw beautifully.

Worthington Whittredge's little painting of 1863, *Interior of the Bedroom of Thomas Whitredge,* represents a space of aesthetic isolation akin to the one in Hale's story (fig. 40). Showing the bedroom of a well-to-do resident of Tiverton, Rhode Island, the painting depicts a creaturely indolence. A mother cat sits on the floor, basking in a patch of sunlight as her kittens come to nurse. The warmth of the sun and the sustenance of the mother cat make an equation between light and milk, each a simple life-giving pleasure. Above and to the left of the mother cat, beneath the curtained window on that side of the painting, two reddish gold slippers sit at the foot of the bed. They too indicate a life of ease in this space of well-appointed isolation whose main feature is the colonial highboy along the back wall. Whittredge shows the scene in a positive way, whereas Hale is moralistic, but both writer and painter in 1863 want to depict aesthetic isolation. At a time when James McNeill Whistler was independently starting to fashion

Fig. 40. Worthington Whittredge, *Interior of the Bedroom of Thomas Whitredge, Tiverton, Rhode Island,* ca. 1863. Oil on canvas, 24½ × 18½ in. (62.2 × 47 cm). Munson-Williams-Proctor Institute, Museum of Art, Utica, New York, 73.118.

his aesthete's persona, both Whittredge and Hale explored what aestheticism might mean in a Civil War context.[51]

Whittredge's attention to the dynamics of interiority illuminates the parallel further. Though little is known of this Thomas Whitredge (conceivably a relative of the artist, albeit one whose name was spelled differently), Whittredge makes clear that the quiet creaturely pleasure of his room is not a matter of total isolation. The world enters in the muffled, muted form of light filtering through the patterned curtains on the left. It comes in more directly on the right, where one of the curtains has been pulled back and pinned behind a chair. This window and curtain are the brightest parts of the picture. The curl of the curtain behind the chair is the painting's most sensuous painterly episode, the impasto taking on a milky thickness evoking the life-giving pleasure of the light. The outside world enters in small doses of sensuous directness. It does so, moreover, in a way that evokes Julia Ward Howe's gray dawn light, and more generally her wish that some outside force enter to break up the wan perfection of the comfortable interior. Here, however, the light from outside is not patriotic or epiphanic but a simple momentary, meaningless delight. The Marxist cultural critic Theodor Adorno would later write that the nineteenth-century bourgeois interior was the space of fantasy, of deep-grained imagination, because it blocked or filtered the outside world.[52] Whittredge's painting shows something like that. The aesthete cultivates a life of the here and now at least in part as a refusal of the networked culture of telegraphic spatial coordinates. He does not want to know about the world.

Whittredge's painting evokes Hale's story, however, for a more striking reason. It does not show Thomas Whitredge himself. It shows a country without a man. The aesthete's absence from the scene of pleasure suggests the exquisite emptiness of such a life, at least insofar as the artist was able (or was asked) to envision it. The aesthete's inwardness was so profound that even his own bodily being could hardly be suffered to disrupt it. Nolan, too, fades without a trace from all government records ("there was no such man, and never was such a man"), and his death attracts virtually no public notice. Only "in an obscure corner" of the *New York Herald* does the narrator happen to glimpse the news of this person he once knew. That the narrator does so while "devouring, to the very stubble, all the current literature I could get hold of, even down to the deaths and marriages in the 'Herald,' " suggests the extraordinary scrutiny required to perceive a man who can hardly be said to exist.[53] The aesthete simply could not be conjured in wartime. Even those who would celebrate his subjectivity could not quite envision it in patriotic times.

A novel from 1861 offers further perspective on the type of absence at the heart of Whittredge's painting and Hale's story. Theodore Winthrop's *Cecil Dreeme* tells the story of an artist, the eponymous Dreeme, a resident of the depressingly enclosed "Chrysalis College," a school cum boardinghouse with only the most narrow mullion windows so that "not too much disorganizing modern thought would penetrate." Dreeme, the most otherworldly and feminine of aesthetes, finds even this cocoon insufficiently reclusive. Only the tiniest card marks his door, and one day he does not respond to the most earnest knocks. He might be dead, for all the landlord and a fellow resident can tell: no one seems to be there. Forcing their way into the room they find him in a state of quiescence bordering on death, slumped by his easel. The landlord brings Dreeme some oysters, and the aesthete revives under these bracing infusions from the real world, delivered straight from a local tavern.[54] The reader later learns that Dreeme is really Clara Denman, a young woman who has faked her own death, donned a disguise, and gone into seclusion rather than marry Densdeth, the novel's villain. Under the brutal world's coarse shocks, the aesthete withdraws to a poetic and androgynous inconsequence. Winthrop, the author, himself came out of relative seclusion once the war began, volunteering for the Union army soon after the firing on Fort Sumter, opening "his career both as thinker and actor," his friend George William Curtis wrote, replacing the "wandering, hoping, trying, waiting" first thirty-two years of his life and satisfying his "yearning desire to be of some service in the world."[55] When Winthrop was killed less than two months later, he became a nationally known figure, visible in a way not possible by writing novels or making art, forms of feminized dreaming. Whittredge's painting, by contrast, is content to remain without a hero, or rather to make its hero the person who does not fully exist.

Disappearance in wartime, even so, might not necessarily be a treasonous aesthetic refusal or other form of dreamy retreat. The situation of Emily Dickinson in Amherst, Massachusetts, evokes the reclusiveness of Hale's story and Whittredge's painting but to a different end. Although Dickinson wrote roughly half of her more than seventeen hundred poems between 1860 and 1864, and although some of these poems do refer to the war (the Antietam-inflected "The name—of it—is Autumn," for example), she was known then, as she is now, for "the intensity of her recessiveness," as Diana Fuss puts it—namely, her reclusive life in her house and especially in her bedroom. Dickinson's profound inward turn, as Fuss notes, was part of a larger shift in bourgeois homes—in which these places became "the stage for an emerging interior life"—that this poet carried to extremes. Dickinson's poems became "miniature interiors" written on a cherry table that was itself her "bedroom's interior within an interior."[56] In wartime terms, Dickinson's dwelling in Possibility meant withdrawing from all crude cause-abiding visibility. Like Dedlow and Nolan, she was cut off, but in her case the isolation was a principled refusal of information networks (she published only a handful of her poems) and of the clear propagandistic purpose—the decipherable meanings—those public communications were supposed to convey. The purpose of that isolation, in turn, was no mere aesthetic detachment but the creation of a philosophical-poetic wisdom that, implicitly, could not exist in any other space.

Macbeth on October 17 may have invited its audience to make a comparable withdrawal, to retreat into private mental parlors full or comparatively empty of furniture. In the gas-jet glow of personal rumination, these spectators might even have forgotten they were there, each one absorbed enough in the play to forget his or her existence for a time. Yet into these reveries the performance would doubtless blast its shocks. The emptiness of aesthetic appreciation or the wisdom of a philosophy too wise to convert the performance to an allegorical message: these sensibilities lurked as the ambience the players knew they had better *fill up* with brimming demonstrations of national purpose. Only that kind of patriotism could make clear that this space was not quiescent. Only that flame and glow of extensive declamation could make clear that the play was properly networked, that it reached out with a sense of far-spreading importance, and that the audience's aesthetic enjoyment, however private, was not morbid, unpatriotic, and without apparent purpose. And if all the sound and fury signified nothing, if the play somehow railed against the existential terror of the empty room—if it was "mad" or delusional, failing to realize that half its own sensitive surface was gone and its contact with the world was greatly reduced—then it had become, as art, a very interesting case in its own right.

ADAM GUROWSKI: THINKING MAN

In wartime Washington, could a profoundly inward person be connected to the wide world? A person other than Lincoln? Adam Gurowski (1805–66), a resident of the city, had all his limbs and was able to roam as he wished, yet he was as isolated as Dedlow and Nolan were. Even so, he was perhaps the most worldly of all the capital's citizens, the one most aware of what was going on around him. A Polish count and political revolutionary in exile, Gurowski had been living in the United States since 1849, in New York, Cambridge, and then Washington.

Full of strong political opinions, he was a radical Polish patriot who had ultimately denounced and fought his fellow Polish nationalists as much as their opponents, alienating almost everyone. In Washington, fiercely loyal to the Union cause, he was no less antagonistic. His own biographer calls him "wholly obnoxious." Few, however, doubted his intellectual brilliance or his commitment to the Union, and his eccentricity could inspire devotion. On October 17, 1863, Gurowski was at the home of his friends Charles and Fanny Eames, located at the northwest corner of Fourteenth and H streets, a few blocks from Grover's. He had been living there since July, when Mrs. Eames invited him to leave his rooming house and move into her home after he had suffered an acute illness.[57]

Gurowski's room in Washington may not have been as messy as his bachelor's quarters back in Cambridge some twelve years earlier, which his friend Robert Carter described as "in dire confusion, littered with books, papers, clothing, and other articles, tossed about at random." Whether neat or dirty, however, it must have positively hummed with the volatile enclosed energy of the man. Senator Charles Sumner recalled one night in 1862 when Gurowski showed up at his residence railing about the traitorous incompetence of General George McClellan: "He became furious, and for nearly an hour stormed and stamped about the room," reminding Sumner "of the whale in Barnum's Museum, which kept going round and round in its narrow tank, blowing with all its might whenever it came to the surface."[58] (Gurowski's opinion of McClellan in his diary—"*knitted of the devil's excrements mixed with his saliva* . . . your treason is only equal to your impudence"—gives an idea of his diatribe.)[59] Ordinary rooms could barely contain this rare specimen of pent-up fervor.

Gurowski's attire further separated him. Especially when he first came to America, he enclosed himself in layers, shielding himself from the sun and protecting a ruined eye with special goggles. The count was "partly wrapped in a huge and queerly cut cloak of German material and make" the first time Carter saw him:

> On his head he wore a high, bell-shaped broad-brimmed hat from which depended a long, sky-blue veil, which he used to protect his eyes from the sunshine. His waistcoat was of bright red flannel, and as it reached to his hips and covered nearly the whole of his capacious front, it formed a startlingly conspicuous portion of his attire. In addition to the veil, his eyes were protected by enormous blue goggles, with glasses on the sides as well as in front.[60]

When he wore no clothes at all, Gurowski was equally unaware of everything except his own thoughts. Carter recalled visiting the count at his Cambridge lodgings only to find him "absolutely in a state of nature." Holding his drawers in one hand, Gurowski lectured for thirty minutes on a question of medieval history before being interrupted by the maid. With Carter imploring him to put on his clothes, he refused and stayed naked as another person knocked at the door, this time a scholar to whom, still naked, he presented still another strong opinion, this one concerning a question of natural history. When that man left, Gurowski returned to medieval history and only reluctantly, at Carter's insistence, stopped to put on his clothes.[61]

The last time Carter saw his friend, in spring 1863, Gurowski gave an ultimate picture of this exquisitely preoccupied inwardness—this time outside, a block or so from Grover's Theatre. "I was passing up Fifteenth Street, by the Treasury Department, and reached one of the cross-streets just as a large troop of cavalry came along," Carter recalled. "The street was ankle-deep with mud, only the narrow crossing being passable, and I hurried to get over before the cavalry came up. Midway on the crossing I encountered Gurowski, wrapped in a long black cloak and a huge felt hat, rather the worse for wear." The count, wrote Carter,

> threw open his arms to stop me, and, without any preliminary phrase, launched into an invective on Horace Greeley. In an instant the troop was upon us, and we were surrounded by trampling and rearing horses, and soldiers shouting to us to get out of the way. Gurowski, utterly heedless of all around him, raised his voice above the tumult, and roared that Horace Greeley was an "ass, a traitor, and a coward." It was no time to hold a parley on that question, and, breaking from him, I made for the opposite sidewalk, then, turning, saw Gurowski for the last time, enveloped in a cloud of horsemen, through which he was composedly making his way at his usual meditative pace.[62]

On the night of October 17 Gurowski's mind was far away, as it almost always was in those years, fixed on the war. Robert E. Lee's Army of Northern Virginia was somewhere not far from Washington—nobody in the city was quite sure where—and Gurowski, like others, wondered what would happen. He wrote in his diary, "*October 17: Evening.*—The knowing ones promise a battle for to-morrow. Yes, if Lee will. But if not, will Meade attack Lee? Who I am sure will continue his movement and operation whatever these may be. We are at *guessing.*"[63] The entry is striking as an indication of how close the war was that night—a rumored proximity that I treat in detail in the next chapter. But it is also striking for the image it gives of Gurowski hunkered down at his desk, absorbed in private rumination yet thinking deeply of the world around him.

In this respect he made an odd match with that other lone thinker, Lincoln—odd because Gurowski was the one man that Lincoln thought might kill him. The president was famously unconcerned about assassination, but he told his associate Ward Lamon that he did fear one man: Gurowski. "From this man Garowski *[sic]*, and from him alone, Mr. Lincoln really apprehended danger by a violent assault, although he knew not what the sense of fear was like," wrote Lamon. "Mr. Lincoln more than once said to me: 'So far as my personal safety is concerned, Garowski is the only man who has given me a serious thought of a personal nature. From the known disposition of the man, he is dangerous wherever he may be. I have sometimes thought that he might try to take my life. It would be just like him to do such a thing.' "[64]

Lincoln was not wrong to think of Gurowski in these terms. The Pole claimed to have fought more than thirty duels in Europe and to have served as second in sixty more, noting that he often used "short half round Turkish swords" as weapons. In 1832 he dueled fellow Polish nationalist Teodor Morawski at ten paces using Lepage dueling pistols that fired huge .62-caliber lead bullets, somehow surviving.[65] In New York at the Athenaeum Club in 1860 he had fought a man, the adversary using a strip of cowhide, Gurowski a carving knife.[66] In a Cambridge library one day a Harvard professor who disagreed with him on the question of Kossuth and Hungary so incensed Gurowski that, as Carter reported, the count "was foaming with rage and formally challenged the professor to settle the dispute with swords or pistols," an offer the professor declined, leaving Gurowski "dumbfounded." No person was too important for him to mock or threaten: Daniel Webster was "a humbug or an ass" for upholding the Fugitive Slave Act, and Louis Agassiz was "a mere ichthyologist."[67] In Washington, likewise, Gurowski bitterly resented William Seward, for whom he had worked until being fired for having made too many insubordinate remarks about his boss. The count wrote in his diary that Seward was a traitor and Lincoln an imbecile and that the president "ought to be shortened by the head."[68]

Gurowski's danger to Lincoln, of course, came from a political position completely opposite to that of John Wilkes Booth. For the count, Lincoln was not radical enough. Even if Gurowski was unlikely to have done harm to the president—he was too loyal to the Union and finally too respectful of Lincoln to do that—his volatile temper made him a logical enough person for Lincoln to fear, even perhaps for the president to keep in mind at a performance of *Macbeth*. (Gurowski might well have attended the play, though his diary is silent about the matter.)

Fig. 41. Thomas Crawford, *The Progress of Civilization,* ca. 1854–63. Capitol Building, Washington, D.C. Photograph courtesy of the Architect of the Capitol, Washington, D.C.

Even so, the reason we can connect the two men on the evening of October 17 is not their biographies, not their individualities, and not the themes of *Macbeth.* It is rather the idea of an interior life shaped by the outside world—of the shaping of thought itself by these outside forces. Beyond creased brows and other signs of mental engagement, this external fashioning of thought produced imagery of the mind at work and not merely in retreat from the world. The best way to see this is to look at a public sculpture of a thinker in Washington that will bring us back to Gurowski, Lincoln, and *Macbeth.*

The public sculpture is Thomas Crawford's Indian brave, second from the right on the pediment of the Senate wing of the Capitol (fig. 41). A plaster cast of the sculpture in isolation gives us a clearer view of this muscular figure (fig. 42). What do we make of the brave's thinking? Shown in the pose of melancholy, he is a grandiose version of the "vanishing race" motif starting to appear in the era's representation of Indians—a last surviving

Fig. 42. Plaster cast of Thomas Crawford's seated Indian from *The Progress of Civilization*. Photograph courtesy of the Architect of the Capitol, Washington, D.C.

warrior beset by outside forces. Perhaps for that reason, he seems the most autonomous of all the figures on the pediment—the one who stands forth most starkly from the background and the other sculptures. Although each figure on the pediment is crisply legible, the better for this public story of national destiny to read clearly, boldly, across a distance and at a height, the Indian brave's sharp angularity of bent knees and arms gives him a special, almost architectural distinctness, and his thick modeling makes him a fulsomely rounded figure of strong light and shadow—all the more still, alone, and unchangeable for having been so clearly defined.

This singularity produces a surprising imagery of thought—manifest in the figure's beautifully exaggerated outline. That outline, a meeting place between internal and external worlds, is where we might expect to find the greatest energy in a figure who thinks of the forces around him. For a figure so affected by the world, thought is manifest less in the conventional designations of tilted head and hand to the temple than in these contours where inside and outside combine. Thought is visible at—and indeed as—the junction between inner and outer worlds. The contour-as-thought suggests a period way to show an inward person affected by the world: to show a profound aloneness that is nonetheless public minded, an interiority defined by being outside, public, open to the elements—a theatrical absorption. The world is a substance coursing around the figure, shaping him, coming to rest in the intensified outline of a body that is finally only the setup, the delivery system, for that world. This outline makes the world visible as a gathering, an accretion, around the material shape that consents to be the host of this invisible outwardness—this "casing air"—of which the figure is thinking.

For Gurowski and Lincoln both, Lincoln especially, the war crushed down on them, subjecting them to huge outside pressures. "I believe I feel trouble in the air before it comes," Lincoln told his aide John Hay in September 1863 after a night in the telegraph office reading dispatches from the front.[69] Like Gurowski, he was "at *guessing,*" and both men belonged to what Marshall McLuhan calls "the Age of Anxiety," the time of that externalized central nervous system, the telegraph. Portraitists of Lincoln have shown him as a thinker, a person considering the outward world from deep within his mind. In a phenomenological history of thought, however, the mind's work is actually at the vibrant confluence of outside and inside.

There, in the eddying outline of a lone figure, the meeting of thought and world might be perceptible. For Lincoln himself to strike a cerebral pose, as he did in official representations, was to allow this process to happen, to consent for his body to be not just a center of thought emanating outward, or intensifying inward, but an impersonal shape around which thoughts of the world might collect. When Lincoln "leaned back in his chair in the shade" at the performance of *Macbeth* on October 17, thinking his faraway thoughts of distant armies, that invisible world became visible in the sharpness of a public privacy, half in shadow and half in show, that took shape for all to see. Thus did the midcentury fashion an imagery of the private thinker who was not a dreamer—whose angularities and agitations of outline would convey not the drowsy inwardness of the melancholic loner but the person whose interiority was *activated* by the world around.

We see this type of active inwardness in Crawford's sculpture, and maybe also in the performers onstage in *Macbeth,* themselves a portrayal of thought contemporaneous with the installation of Crawford's Indian brave. The sculptures for the pediment were hoisted into place between September and November 3, 1863, with the center figure ensconced first.[70] The brave took its place during the weeks or days before or after the Grover's performance on October 17. *Macbeth* onstage that night—though it doubtless aspired to be a ceremonial array of static isolated beings, striking their poses and delivering their finitudes of poetic wisdom for the ages—might also have created, from time to time, a mental energy, a limelight penumbra, a sight of something *around* the sculpted recitation of any line, any sentiment, that defined the people onstage.

What did the "outline" of Cushman or of Lester Wallack or Edward Davenport convey as these actors struck their public poses of private meditation that evening? If we accept that the outline conveyed something different from the aesthetic isolation of actress or actor, cut off from the world by the assorted splendors of a meaningless art, what outside world did it portray? Perhaps the ambient genius of Shakespeare—the way his wisdom gathered around, as if out of thin air, the shapes of the actors and actresses his words brought into being. Maybe the playwright's mind made the people onstage rather than merely being voiced by them there.

But perhaps the crowd that night was witness to a stranger outside force, barely (if at all) glimpsed but present all the same in the way that Crawford's sculpture begins to address. This force was the external pressure of the world, shaping the autonomy of these figures and crushing them down until they too gathered into shapes angular and strange, striking memorable postures of aesthetic tension for having such a weight to bear. The outside world, otherwise invisible, would appear as the shape of the person it made its host.

WALT WHITMAN'S CASES

Walt Whitman had his own view of interiors in Washington during the war. On October 17 he had just moved into a new room at 456 Sixth Street.

His lodging, as he described it, was more permeable to the outside than Howe's hotel room a few blocks away had been. Likewise, compared with what Whitman describes, the one dollop of sensuous light in Thomas Whitredge's bedroom in Rhode Island looks like an epitome of renunciation.

The room on Sixth Street was open to light and warmth, to smells and voices and presences from outside. "It is in 3d story, an addition back, . . . a very good winter room, as it is right under the roof & looks south, has low windows, is plenty big enough," Whitman wrote his mother on October 20. "Right off against my side of the house is a great old yard with grass & some trees back, & the sun shines in all day &c. & it smells sweet & good air." He hears the granddaughter of the elderly landlady, "a little girl of 4 or 5," calling *"grandma, grandma."* And he sees a twelve- or thirteen-year-old black girl, Lucy, who "comes & goes, gets water &c."[71]

The room was secluded but not shut off. Whitman liked that the front door of the house "is not locked at all at night," in pleasant contrast to his former lodging, where "the old thief the landlord had two front doors, with four locks & bolts on one, & three on the other—& a big bull-dog in the back yard—we were well fortified I tell you—sometimes I had an awful time at night getting in." Though he was mostly alone in this back part of the third story of the new house—"I am quite by myself, there is no passage up there except to my room," and though Lucy is "pretty much the only one I see"—his separation left him wide open to the world.[72]

The interior for Whitman had to do with what was outside it. This gathering world of sights and sounds, comings and goings, was active, fluttering, alive. It glittered around interior space, rescuing it from a potentially moribund isolation. The description of the room, innocent and merely informative as it may be, describes something crucial that Whitman brought to all his representations of interiors—including human interiority—during the war. No enclosed space or human case was so discrete and particular, even so doomed, that it should not also be made to glow with an excess of life. Otherwise the focus on one place, one person, would freeze it in lifeless commemoration, making one of those "cold bloodless electrotype plates of history" that he would condemn in 1876 as the war's official record.[73]

That kind of history was life turned to stone, to ice, to crystal. It was a mannequin array frozen on splendid carpets of significant moments, a statuelike finality akin to what Cushman hoped to achieve in her acting. Whitman aimed for another kind of commemoration—one that understood the fundamental fact driven home by the war: all persons die, all moments *pass,* all is gone before we know it. These passing persons and moments may each be a case study—life for the writer is a series of set pieces—yet each must be recorded in ways that avoid the coldness of tribute, the stalwart immobility of the statue that repeats the stillness of death, or the frozenness of a photograph recording a particular site.

One of Whitman's most vivid interiors embodies this conviction. On the night of February 23, 1863, he was tending to the wounded in the Patent Office, which had been converted into a temporary hospital. The beds of the wounded men in his description are arranged amid "high and ponderous glass cases" containing the various inventions, curiosities, and gifts enshrined in the building. Whitman describes the wounded as themselves "cases." He shuttles between the two types of case, the wounded man and the patented glass-enclosed invention, as in the following successive sentences: "I go sometimes at night to soothe and relieve particular cases. Two of the immense apartments are fill'd with high and ponderous glass cases."[74]

When he describes further the wounded with their "glassy eye," we are encouraged to see the poetic identity between the two kinds of case at the Patent Office. The wounded not only have the qualities of glass; they are portrayed in the glass around them. The wounded men appear outside themselves. They appear apparitionally, as if truly reflected (which no doubt they were) in the mirroring objects around them. The dying man, with his glassy eye, sees the ghost he gives up before he dies, by checking in the reflected glass his predeceased soul.

Whitman, like the inventions, stayed at the soldiers' sides. He too was a mirror in whose eyes many soldiers saw a last image of themselves, already escaped and glowing in the twinkle of this affectionate man's inventive eye. He too was there as the body, a case unto himself, into which the dying breath was blown so that it might live, escaped and safe now in this other man. Erastus Haskell's dying kiss to Whitman at the Armory Square Hospital; the many kisses between Whitman and the Confederate soldier William S. Prentiss; the kiss to Oscar F. Wilber, of the 154th New York, which Wilber "return'd fourfold"—these kisses from dying soldiers amount to an intensified breath that outlives life, a penumbra beyond the interior, around the case at hand: the air from one pair of gunshot lungs passing, as though for safekeeping, into the mouth of one still healthy and strong.[75] Like the reflections on the glass cases, kisses bloom and glow.

Likewise, Whitman animated the outside of the Patent Office, taking care to keep it from freezing, as in his description on the night of October 20, 1863. "A voluptuous half-moon slightly golden" lit the stone façade and, round about, "the sky, the planets, the constellations all so bright, so calm, so expressively silent," seemed to circulate—to "circumambiate"—around the building they illuminated. At the White House, too, on that moonlit evening of February 24 earlier that year, Whitman activated the frozen building, playing upon it "the tender and soft moonlight" and then, for good measure, "the brilliant and extra plentiful clusters of gas," and still more, around and upon it, "the forms of the trees, leafless, silent, in trunk and myriad-angles of branches, under the stars and sky." The building's stillness could not be tolerated unless around it a "soft and copious" floral crown of shadow and star were made to play.[76]

Whitman understood that his poems were interiors, rooms of verse, and that they too might become static sites, frozen spaces of commemoration, if he did not give them aureoles of radiant effect. In "Cavalry Crossing a Ford," a short poem from *Drum-Taps* (1865), the arms "flash[ing] in the sun," "the silvery river," and "splashing horses" impart a glitter, an almost gratuitous array of flash points. If Whitman had been a painter nearing completion of a canvas—a landscape, say—he would have compulsively administered daubs of white across the scene, the better, as a finishing touch, to make each leaf on each tree shine with the reflected sun. The "guidon flags" that "flutter gayly in the wind" are a sign, at the end of the poem, that Whitman must have a pennant fly from each scene he describes: all frozen moments, to avoid becoming cold and bloodless electrotypes of history, must whip in the wind.[77]

The play of light, the corona of glitter, is still more compulsive in another short poem from *Drum-Taps,* "Bivouac on a Mountain-Side." The poem describes a cessation of movement—"a traveling army halting." The scene threatens to become still, a frozen tableau, but then Whitman scatters the campfires and the stars around and above, so that here, too, we get "sparkles from the wheel," to cite the title of another of his poems (not a war poem), one that is maybe his most eloquent statement of his wish to throw sparks from the stationary scene. There Whitman describes a withered old knife grinder, at the side of the street, putting a knife to the spinning stone so that "forth issue then in copious golden jets, / Sparkles from the wheel," so that the poet, much moved, notes, "The low hoarse purr of the whirling stone, the light-press'd blade, / Diffusing, dropping, sideways-darting, in tiny showers of gold, / Sparkles from the wheel."[78]

The poet too must speak in that "low hoarse purr," and he too, "sitting down" and with "measur'd tread," must with "light-press'd" pen, moving, scribbling furiously, "diffusing, dropping, sideways-darting," distribute a copious excess of radiant effects, grinding out the campfires, the stars, the flashing sabers and fluttering guidons that must stream and proliferate from each of his verses to give the effect, as he claimed, of never producing "something finished or fixed." The rushing continuity of Whitman's words, their ceaseless flow, is itself a glittering effusion—as though the reading or (better) the speaking of a Whitman poem were to experience or enact the aureole of flying sparks.

"Vigil Strange I Kept on the Field One Night," also from *Drum-Taps,* evokes the spreading out of the stars, the fragrant night, and the moonlit battlefield. The poem speaks of the "sweet hours," the "mystic hours," the resurrecting rising sun—the panoply of immortality. The degree of Whitman's attachment to these effects, his exacting use of them, is evident in the fact that his twentieth-century emulators among battlefield writers—people such as Ernie Pyle and James Jones, with their erotic manly clasps of living and dead hands at Monte Cassino and Guadalcanal—do not bother with, do not even think of, these firmaments of eternal softness. But even more distinctive is the rushing profusion of Whitman's words—a flowing sound that amounts to a limitless poured chant, like the thrush's notes in "When Lilacs Last in the Dooryard Bloom'd," that seems to come from the bushes themselves, from the ground. The voice is a vegetal effusion that grows up protectively around the scene it describes.[79]

Yet Whitman's Civil War poetry would not be so moving if it did not acknowledge that this efflorescence always appears around a deathly stasis—a blankness—it cannot change. This center is the darkness of an imploded place. At Ford's Theater, on the night of April 14, 1865, Lincoln's assassination took place during "a pause, a hush," a moment when a scene had finished and the stage was clear. Though reactions gathered around this momentous event, "circling around it and stretching into the future for many a century, in the politics, history, art, etc., of the New World"; and though on the night in question "a deluge" of panicked action followed the single gunshot—a "mixture of horror, noises, uncertainty . . . [of] people burst[ing] through chairs and railings . . . like some horrible carnival," the audience rushing onstage, several hundred soldiers appearing suddenly in the theater, "inflamed with fury," while outside gathered "crowds of people, fill'd with frenzy"—and though Whitman bestows his wreath of sparks on the dying president, the deadly shot itself took place in a pause, a hush, a darkness, a blur.[80]

The scene of death—the deeply infolded interior of it—is hidden, gone, unknowable. The poet may strew it with effects, but the place, the moment itself, cannot be seen. The dying soldier, Whitman writes, "crawls aside to some bush-clump, or ferny tuft, on receiving his death-shot" and there dies on that "secluded spot," "unburied and unknown." When the fateful letter arrives in "Come Up from the Fields Father," we immediately read of the trees, the "leaves fluttering in the moderate wind," the "apples ripe in the orchards," "the grapes on the trellis'd vines," the "buckwheat" and the "bees . . . lately buzzing," but all this is nothing, we know, because like the letter writer's words that "*Pete will soon be better,*" these organic bursts of leaf and apple and grape can never heal the dead son.[81]

In this sense, something deathly hovers about the glowing effects Whitman conjures around each of his scenes. These effects flow out not only as emanations of ongoing, budding life but as spirits and ghosts, supernatural exuviae. When he describes the play of light and shadow on the White House façade, he writes of the moonlight "making peculiar faint languishing shades" on it—evoking the soldiers he ministered to.[82] At the Patent Office his eyes, like the glass cases, could reflect ghostly remainders as well as ongoing life.

Macbeth at Grover's on October 17 tried to present frozen individualities of actors and characters alike, each immobilized in an aura of limelight. Even if the disturbing sense of a figure's outline might disrupt the dream, making the outside world visible, each case would nonetheless ideally be clear, identical with itself, no less than the overall tableau of the stage itself: a finished picture of the world. That perfection, moreover, was dependent on the ceremonial cancellation, insofar as possible, of the random world of the Washington streets outside, with the solemnities of Art reducing it to a hush and a vapor. Whitman's war poetry, by contrast, is lit and shaded *only* by what comes from outside—by whatever breath of light and shadow happens to fall on a mirror left blank and receptive for the purpose. The poems contain a corrugated set of grooves to catch these impressions, making the chance incidents they gather seem at last indistinguishable from the poetic symmetries designed to hold them.

At Whitman's lodging, too, the forces of life and death appeared precisely not in the room by itself, not in that merely personal interior of the poet, but as a floating force around it: Lucy's comings and goings, the sweet smells of the yard outside. At 456 Sixth Street, the landlady is "old & feeble" and the granddaughter is just starting her life. They are the winter and the warmth of the place, life in phases of light and sound streaming through the windows: *Grandma, grandma.* The poet's task, for Whitman, was to summon this outside world to breathe on the glass box of art, giving it a thrall of mortal vivacity, compounded of chance, that no merely internal invention could provide.

Was *Macbeth* on October 17, in contrast to Whitman, truly just an object put on display at Grover's Theatre, nothing more than a precious artifact of Anglo-American culture, ceremoniously removed from life? Was it a "case" in this more moribund sense? Many years later Thornton Wilder would write that the Victorians made the performance of plays, even Shakespeare's, into museum pieces. The box set, the curtain, and the proscenium were the display case, an architectural framing they took seriously. According to Wilder, the Victorians "emphasized and enhanced everything that thus removed, cut off, and boxed the action, they increasingly shut the play into a museum showcase."[83]

He may have been right, but this display had its own logic and poetry. The theater-as-museum implied that the outside world was whole, complete, God given, and apprehensible as such in a designated interior, a place of culture. It implied too that a single person—such as Shakespeare or a learned member of the audience—might still keep that whole world in his or her head. And it implied that clear communication, liberated from obfuscations and distortions, would be the means to realizing this unity.

Consider the link on October 17 between Grover's Theatre and the nearby Smithsonian Institution. Alexander Dallas Bache (1806–67), a longtime member of the Smithsonian Board of Regents and vice-president of the Sanitary Commission, gives us a sense of the goals shared by the performance and the museum. On a night when Grover's "embraced within its walls a larger amount of the intellect gathered in Washington, in official circles and civic life, than is often witnessed," according to a newspaper report, Bache, as Sanitary Commission vice-president, was most likely among them.[84] One of the city's leading scientists, he was a fiercely pro-Union man who had designed and personally helped superintend the construction of defense lines around his native city of Philadelphia earlier that year.[85] For the Sanitary Commission, he had selected proper agents and streamlined methods of collecting and distributing supplies. A resident of Washington, he was in town on October 17: one of his memos for the United States Light-House Board, of which he was a member, announces a meeting to take place at noon that day.[86]

If Bache attended the performance that night, he may well have been interested in the acoustics of the theater. The clear transmission of sound was a hallmark for him of Smithsonian-style clarities of communication and the power of a local interior to encompass the whole world. These clarities could also show that this wide world could reside within the mind of a single learned person commanding that room.

Bache was a scholar of the auditorium. Together with his close friend, the Smithsonian secretary Joseph Henry, Bache had conducted many experiments to determine the optimal communication of sound in a public venue. The two men had undertaken the research back in the late 1840s to help design a fifteen-hundred-seat public lecture hall in the Smithsonian building on the National Mall. To make the clearest-sounding space they could, they had studied Captain Montgomery Meigs's plans for the new hall of the House of Representatives in the Capitol Building and, with Meigs, toured "the principal halls and churches of the cities of Philadelphia, New York, and Boston," according to Henry. They came away with "a few well-established principles of acoustics, which have been applied in the construction of the Smithsonian lecture room."[87] The first Smithsonian guidebook, published in 1857, claimed that the new auditorium was the best in the country: the "acoustic properties of the lecture-room are unsurpassed by any apartment, intended for the same purpose, in the United States."[88] The lecture room suggested the values of the whole institution: the museum would be a place where scientists could communicate their findings as clearly as possible to receptive audiences.

Establishing the speaker's singular voice—the scientist's strong authority—was vital to the design of the lecture room. The Smithsonian's original lecture hall had been conceived as more interactive, but Henry gutted that portion of the building soon after its completion to create this new auditorium, featuring "the lecturer in the center, the focus of curved, tiered seating." Henry wrote that the room would now "husband every articulation of the [speaker's] voice, and . . . transmit it unmingled with other impulses, and with as little loss as possible, to the ears of the audience."[89] The auditorium narrowed the world to a speaker whose every word was now the trumpet herald of his wisdom, the fanfare of a learning that would mute the clatter of all incidental sounds: the snores of the sleeping, the muttered rejoinders of the peevish. A picture from the 1857 guidebook shows a speaker holding forth before an attentive audience (fig. 43).

Nothing was left to chance. The walls around the speaker, the guidebook noted, "are smooth lath and plaster, giving a powerful but short resonance, which strengthens his voice." They help "send the sound out from the speaker, to increase the volume of his voice until it reaches the furthest part of the gallery. The multitude of surfaces directly in front of the speaker—gallery, pillars, stair-screens, and the seats of the audience—prevent rever-

Fig. 43. The Lecture Room. In William J. Rhees, *An Account of the Smithsonian Institution* (Washington, D.C.: Thomas McGill, 1857), 14. Smithsonian Institution Archives, Washington, D.C., image 43804-K.

beration."[90] One of Henry's early drawings for the lecture room suggests this radiating effect—which ensures that the lecturer's voice is "thrown forward upon the audience" (fig. 44). As Henry wrote in 1856, "The speaker is placed as it were in the mouth of an immense trumpet."[91]

The trumpet blast went beyond the lecture room. The Smithsonian Institution's mission would be "the increase and diffusion of knowledge among men," according to the 1829 will of the benefactor, James Smithson. Under Henry's leadership, the clear public speaking of eminent scientists was a key part of this diffusion. "Public lectures," the 1857 Smithsonian guidebook noted, had become second only to newspapers as a "means of diffusing knowledge, to influence the public mind."[92] Scientists would fill the minds of their audiences with all that they knew, and do so with ringing clarity.

The speaker's voice would travel from the lecture hall into the world at large, in a telegraphic spread addressing an age-old preoccupation. "How to communicate intelligence instantly over distances so great that the voice can-

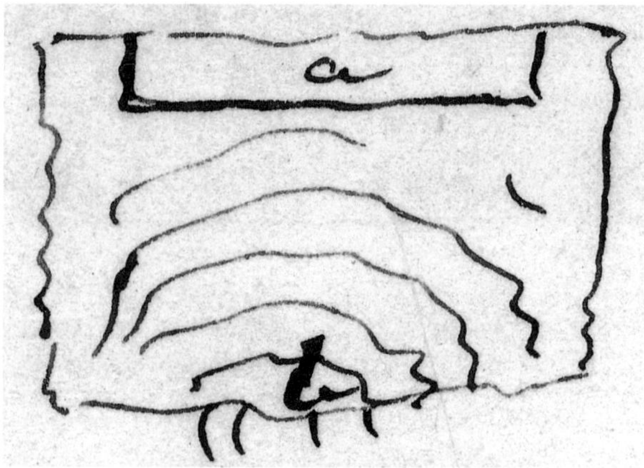

Fig. 44. Joseph Henry, drawing of new Lecture Room, from *Desk Diary of 1849,* 1849. Smithsonian Institution Archives, Washington, D.C., image 92–16513.

not be heard," as one of Henry's admirers wrote, "had been well known to organized societies from remote antiquity."[93] In his pursuit of the problem in the early 1830s, Henry had conducted experiments transmitting galvanic currents across distance through copper wires—at first 1,060 feet long and then 1.5 miles long. Now, for this man who had started his life as an aspiring actor, playing Hamlet on an Albany stage as a teenager, the speaker's voice would diffuse from the lecture hall's immense trumpet. As one of his eulogists said in 1879, "Our community, our country, the world itself, has been benefited by his existence here; and . . . as time rolls on, its course will be marked by increasing circles of appreciation, reverence, and gratitude."[94]

At the performance of *Macbeth,* Henry's friend Bache might then have considered the acoustics in Leonard Grover's Theatre, judging their relative virtues and faults. (Henry, who had been out of town and arrived back in Washington on October 17, may also have been there.)[95] Moreover, he might have been an especially good judge of the diffusive power of a localized utterance. Perhaps even better than Cushman, he could think of how a circumscribed sound within a single space might extend outward, carried forward in the minds of an educable audience, for example, who would disseminate the blasts of learning still further. But he might also have thought of how the world outside the theater came to reside within it.

Bache himself seemed to have the whole world in his head. The title of Leonard Warren's book about the Philadelphia scientist Joseph Leidy (1823–

91) might equally apply to him: *The Last Man Who Knew Everything.* "In the work of the Survey [Bache's] scientific range included everything from animal life on the ocean floor to the stars in the heavens. He measured both mountain heights and ocean depths," his biographer wrote of Bache's work for the U.S. Coast Survey. "Bache, as though with oriental magic, stretched his arms from Maine to Florida and from California to Oregon." For one of his papers, "Notice of Earthquake Waves on the Western Coast of the United States," Bache used self-registering tide gauges on the Pacific Coast to trace earthquake waves from Simoda, Japan, across the Pacific Ocean, where they achieved heights of thirty feet, to the shores of California, where they crested at six inches, enabling him to calculate the tsunami's speed.[96] Like Shakespeare in the mid-nineteenth-century imagination, Bache comprehended vastness.

Bache also kept the lights of the nation in his mind. As a longtime member of the Light-House Board, he helped oversee the construction, maintenance, and personnel of America's beacons. In 1856 he supervised the lighting of the nation's entire Pacific Coast. Then-exotic California locations appeared in his mind, as his correspondence from that time about types of lights indicates: "Pt. Bonita, 2nd order fixed; Alcatraz Island 3rd order fixed; Fort Point, 5th order fixed and Pt. Lobos 2nd & 3rd order fixed and varied by flashes." Who would man the lighthouse on the Farallon Islands off San Francisco? Bache considered such matters. Closer to home, he was preoccupied with the beacons at Cape May and Cape Henlopen, among many other places.[97] Perhaps no one in America had a more distinct vision than Bache of the nation's coasts newly lit up—newly made safe for progress—providing a network of steady and blinking sentinels.

The great burning swirl of *Macbeth* on October 17—a wavering of existential torches beneath the glitter of a thousand gaslights—might then have struck Bache more as the epitome of progress than as a swaying above the abyss. The theater interior would glow with a concentrated light as if it held the light of the entire nation on that night.

That light, too, would be clear. The legibility of light—extending from here to there, providing pathways of communication in the dark—was as important to Bache and Henry as the clear spread of sound. Henry, also on the Light-House Board, had written to Bache from Cambridge on October 3 about his latest experiments in illumination, judging whether sperm or lard oil burned brightest and longest: "I am quite absorbed in the subject of oils and have devoted every day and several nights of this week to experiments."[98] Henry, who must certainly have relayed his findings to his friend soon after he returned to Washington, pursued the clarities of fire, and so did Bache.

The display-case proscenium on October 17 might have stood out as another form of exceptional clarity to Bache. Not only was it well-lighted, blazing with limelight jets, but it was also an enclosure like the glass cases Henry had installed at the Smithsonian, which Bache must have known well. The glass of those neat and orderly cases, some of which had come from the Patent Office starting about 1857, acted like a speaker's voice, providing a clear picture of scientific objects, held up for educational purposes.[99] Shakespeare, too, might have been a scientific subject that night, an artifact put on display to show not just the poet's greatness but that of the American nation whose epic sweep his grandeur was said to envision: "As in that world of Nature all outgrown / Where Calaveras lifts his awful pines," Oliver Wendell Holmes, Sr., wrote in his 1864 poem for the tercentennial of Shakespeare's birth.[100]

God drove these clarities and unities. Bache "fully recognized the union of science and religion," according to Henry, "and held with unwavering constancy the belief that revelation, properly interpreted, and science, rightly understood, must ultimately join in perfect accord in reference to the great truths essential to the well being of man."[101] The world outside and the mind inside, the revelation and the proper interpretation, were perfectly matched.

Henry felt the same way. "The ultimate tendency of the study of Physical science," he had told his students at Princeton, is to unfold "the magnificence, the order, and the beauty of the material universe. It affords most striking proofs of the beneficence, the wisdom, and the power of the Creator."[102] In summer 1862 Titian Ramsay Peale took several photographs of the scientist's family apartments in the Smithsonian building. The blanching light coming through the window in some of these images is either an infelicity or a calculated effect by Peale, a skilled practitioner of the new medium (fig. 45).[103] Accident or not, the entering light suggests an epiphany like the one Julia Ward Howe described or the sensuous, purposeless revelation of milky light in Whittredge's painting, except here it is a more manifestly religious glow. Inspiration, the photograph implies, comes from God—the beacon that animates all interiors, illuminating the oneness of the world and the world-encompassing minds within it.

Even so, weird echoes and reverberations must also have been present amid all this clarity and singularity. One of the prized objects on display in the Smithsonian glass cases was a meteorite, the second largest in the

Fig. 45. Titian Ramsay Peale, *Interior of Joseph Henry's Apartments at the Smithsonian Building,* 1862. Smithsonian Institution Archives, Washington, D.C., record unit 95, image MAH-X3252.

country, shown here in a picture from the 1857 guidebook (fig. 46). To a person less devout than Henry or Bache, such an object might suggest a mystery—maybe even one having to do with Shakespeare—that surpassed any ready scientific explanation.

Emerson, for example, focused on such objects to address the question of Shakespeare's inspiration. How, he wanted to know, did these plays land in our midst? How did they mysteriously land even in Shakespeare's vicinity?

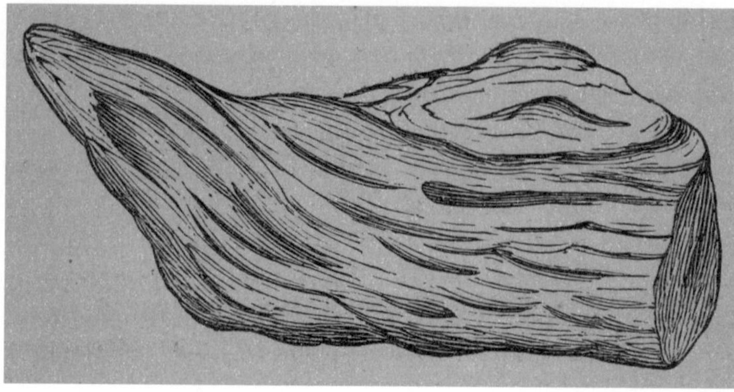

Fig. 46. Meteorite from Coahuila, Mexico. In William J. Rhees, *An Account of the Smithsonian Institution* (Washington, D.C.: Thomas McGill, 1857), 23.

Even Shakespeare, for Emerson, "cannot . . . give us anecdotes of his inspirations." A line from one of his plays is consequently "one of those skiey sentences—aerolites,—which seem to have fallen out of heaven."[104]

To a mind so attuned, the play on October 17 sat in its glass case like an aerolite, a mysterious token from elsewhere. That object, betokening a vastness impossible to comprehend, may have seemed to sit safe and tidy in its box. It may have seemed to be there only in the name of progress, to be there to edify and educate, to increase and diffuse knowledge—a fragment of outer space, a remote brilliance captured and put on display. Yet the play could still suggest an inexplicable field of mysterious forces, jettings and streamings, that mocked these shows of didactic purpose.

The outside world, as we are about to see, would press hard on the play—pushing to explode it from within. Amid such crushing forces, disintegration would be the greater splendor, and coherence a desperate falsity. The drama of the play would be how, or if, it held itself together.

FOUR

Acoustic Shadows

The Battle of Bristoe Station

THE DIARY OF WILLIAM OWNER, a resident of Washington, D.C., opens in December 1860 with a description of "Distances marked on a map of the world in the Capitol":

U States to Calcutta nautical miles	12,418 must be more
" " to Canton "	13,908
US to England	3,310
" " San Francisco via Cape Horn	16,500
Japan to San Francisco	5,200
Shanghai " " via Sandwich Is	6,100
" " Japan	420

On Saturday, October 17, 1863, Owner was thinking about a much nearer location, a few miles across the Potomac. "On Thursday there was considerable skirmishing 'all along' the front of the army which occupies in part the Old Bull Run battlefield and accounts state that the enemy are moving a force on Leesburg. The army all night were in line of battle anticipating an attack by the enemy, and rumor has it that there was fighting to day. The booming of the guns was heard on Georgetown heights."[1]

Owner describes two related echoes that coursed through Washington on October 17—the sounds of gunfire and rumor. His diary notation was itself part of this murmur of gossip and hearsay, which we can imagine as a vast sound of spoken and scribbled words. *Macbeth* that night would try to quiet these reverberations. It would take these sounds in all their wild echoing flow and consolidate them into an official discourse in which every utterance would be rehearsed and tight, singular and secure, relevant yet timeless, full of studied and official reassurance. Explosions of gunfire and explosions of words would enter the theater to reemerge as heroic diction, sculpting these shavings of scattershot slang into a sturdy would-be unity. The speaking of each line that night was a taming and shaping of heterodox sound, until rumbles and whispers alike took on the all but sculptural form of precise declaration. In place of unverifiable echoes—coming from who knows where, dropping and proliferating across the city without rhyme or reason, would be a truth, a gospel of dignified culture and patriotism.

We might call this field of sound the play would tame a world of acoustic shadows. Charles Ross, in his book on acoustic shadows during the Civil War, describes the kind that came from gunfire. On June 27, 1862, the Confederate secretary of war, George Wythe Randolph, and his staff member Robert Garlick Hill Kean observed the Battle of Gaines's Mill, northeast of Richmond. The battle was huge, involving some fifty thousand soldiers, and deafeningly loud, according to participants, who wrote of "the incessant roar of musketry and deep thunder of artillery," "the fierce firing of artillery and infantry, the crash of the shot, the bursting of shells, and the whizzing of bullets." Although the two men watched this battle from only a mile and a half away, they could hear nothing. As Kean later wrote to the British scientist John Tyndall, "*Not a single sound of the battle* was audible to General Randolph and myself. I remarked it to him at the time as astonishing." At the same time, according to newspaper accounts, the battle was heard distinctly in Staunton, Virginia, one hundred ten miles away, and in Peaks of Otter, Virginia, one hundred forty miles away.[2]

The discrepancy resulted from phenomena that Tyndall started examining in the 1870s. He surmised that differences in sound resulted from varying air temperatures and wind speeds. Joseph Henry, of the Smithsonian, was also fascinated by the question, devoting much time in the 1870s to studying the propagation of sound. Absorbed by "the abnormal phenomenon of a region of inaudibility" extending around a fog signal for a distance of two or three miles before the signal could again be heard distinctly, Henry persuaded the United States Light-House Board to lend Tyndall a giant foghorn for his studies of the same problem. Solving this "belt of silence" by analyzing "the bewildering anomalies of sound propagation," Henry "succeeded in evolving order out of apparent chaos, in reclaiming a new district, now subjected to the orderly reign of recognized law," William Taylor wrote in his 1879 memoir of the scientist. Even though Henry's conclusions were not entirely correct—there was still much to learn about acoustic shadows, in particular after the discovery of the stratosphere in 1902—his inquiry, like Tyndall's, helped roll back superstition in the name of science. During the Civil War, however, these acoustic shadows were an "insoluble mystery," as Kean wrote.[3] Or as Macbeth might say, "Can such things be, / And overcome us like a summer's cloud / Without our special wonder?" (3.4. 111–13).

The booming of the big guns heard on Georgetown Heights on October 17 may have been an acoustic shadow. About thirty miles away, near Bull Run, a seventeen-year-old Union soldier, Charles Longfellow, wrote that day to his father, Henry Wadsworth Longfellow, that "there is fighting going on today . . . we keep hearing the guns . . . heard heavy firing all day on our right."[4] Maybe that sound carried across the Potomac.

Even so, Owner's diary refers also to another acoustic shadow—the echoes of rumor. On October 14 a battle had taken place at Bristoe Station, near Bull Run and about thirty-five miles from Washington, and the capital was full of talk about another conflict soon to take place, this time still closer. "The knowing ones promise a battle for to-morrow," Adam Gurowski wrote in his diary on the evening of October 17. "And so for the second time this year, Lee shakes and disturbs our quiet in Washington."[5]

On that day the sounds of opinion and gunfire blended into one floating shadow with no identifiable source. No major fighting had taken place since Bristoe Station, and few people in Washington—and maybe even in the Union army—knew exactly what was going on. Owner, referring to General George Meade, commander of the Army of the Potomac, summarized the prevailing uncertainty a few days later: "We have to day such conflicting news from Manassas that it seems doubtful whether the situation or movement of Lee's army is known even by Meade himself." Owner added that "reports of big guns [on October 17] to the contrary . . . there was no fighting Friday or Saturday beyond some slight skirmishing."[6] Owner's diary entry for October 17 finally told of a double reverberation: he heard that others had heard the big guns.

Meanwhile, out in Virginia, another hum rose from the camps of the rival armies. On October 17, as on the two previous days, Union and Confederate soldiers wrote letters and diary entries describing the fight at Bristoe Station and much else. The journalist Noah Brooks recorded that he once came upon several thousand bivouacked Union soldiers and noted "a curious effect of whispering speech as I rode through the woods." These men, "scattered over the ground among the bushes, beguiling their time by eating, drinking, and talking in low tones," produced a "curious fluttering noise"—"the gabble of two or three thousand men, all talking at once, and producing an undulating volume of sound like the noise of birds seeking their roosts at night."[7] The letters coming out of the rival camps on the seventeenth were figuratively another such sound—a chattering and spreading to the winds. The Sanitary Commission nurse Mary Livermore wrote that in Union army camps at almost any time "you would see dozens, and sometimes hundreds, of soldiers writing letters. Some would be stretched at full length on the ground, with a book or a knapsack for a table—some sitting upright against the trunks of trees, with the paper resting on their drawn-up knees—others would stand and write."[8] If letter writing was a form of thrown speech, a transport of voice across space, then a sound akin to spoken words must have flowed from these many silent acts of composition.

Each trivial description in these letters was a voice sent forth to faraway locations. At those distant addresses the writer's voice would then be plunked down, intimately sounding where it was not. On the afternoon of October 17 the Confederate subsistence officer Thomas Claybrook Elder wrote to his wife, Anna, about the battle, which had been a disastrous Confederate defeat ("by no means a success for us") and inquired about Anna's breastfeeding: "I am sorry to hear that your breast continues to trouble you. Wont you make up your mind to wean Annie? You ought to do so." Among the Union soldiers, Charles Wellington Reed, of the Ninth Massachusetts Light Artillery Battery, wrote to his mother back in Massachusetts from Centreville, Virginia, not far from Bristoe Station, describing what he had heard of the battle (he did not participate in it), giving his sense of where Lee was now ("rumors are current that Lee is heading for Maryland again") and thanking his mother for the gift of a sketchbook that he had already begun using to make some of his drawings. From near Bristoe Station, Colonel Walter Herron Taylor of the Confederate army, Lee's adjutant, wrote to his fiancée of the carnage he had seen after the battle and, nominally switching topics, of the pleasant walk that the engaged couple had taken in Hollywood cemetery in Richmond the previous week, when he had been on leave. These communications, suddenly planting each writer's voice down in the life and locality of the person to whom he had written—in Richmond, Virginia, in Woburn, Massachusetts—were indeed "new

Fig. 47. Charles Wellington Reed, sketch of figures in tents in letter, October 2, 1863. Library of Congress, Washington, D.C.

forms of intimacy and alienation," as David Henkin suggests in *The Postal Age.* Taking part in a "remarkable cultural transformation"—the advent of a reliable and widespread postal system in America in those years—letter writers could engage more widely and frequently "in relationships with people they did not see."[9]

The letters themselves sometimes portray this strange mix of immediacy and distance. Reed's habit of illustrating his letters with pictures of men reading and writing inside tents—a logical enough subject for depictions of military life—suggests the faraway closeness of the small blue pages on which they are written (fig. 47). Like the tents, the letters are folded and creased; like them, they contain reading material; like them, they deliver a picture of army life. These little packets of tented script go far, arriving at destinations where they unfold in the hands of a person who hears the writer's voice. Letters were acoustic shadows, pockets of sound.

Is it any wonder that so many of these letter writers described gunfire? Beyond the obvious wish to report some of the fighting, their recurrent emphasis on explosions underscores something more fundamental: the symbiosis between writing and munitions, each an increasingly efficient mid-century means of affecting faraway lives. The explosive impact of a letter could be as devastating as the shot that killed.

On October 17 William W. Chamberlain of the Confederate Third Army Corps wrote to the cousin of Willie Robinson, an eighteen-year-old from Washington who had been among a regiment arrayed for battle at Bristoe Station three days before when he was struck by shell fragments during a Union artillery barrage. "The shell took off both of his arms besides wounding him in the stomach," Chamberlain wrote. "He lived but a short time afterwards."[10] Robinson, of Company G of the Sixth Virginia Infantry, was probably a member of Cooke's or Kirkland's Brigade; the two units, with some five thousand men in all, had swept across fields toward federal positions behind a railway embankment at Bristoe Station, some five hundred to seven hundred yards away, with artillery placed still further beyond, perhaps as far as twelve hundred or even two thousand yards away.[11] The explosion that killed Robinson, coming from one of the distant cannons, rushed forth from an impersonal distance. The letter, with its own devastation of personal news delivered to Robinson's cousin, replicated this burst from far away.

Such letters occupied a curious position. On the one hand, they were a benediction, a salve, a ritual to secure the writer and what he described in one place—a fixture against the whirlwind. On the other hand, they too spread the violence into the air, allowing it to come to rest far away. The Confederate Robert L. Archer, in a letter of October 19, reported that he had been in a line of five soldiers when the shell struck, killing Robinson and two other men immediately to his left. "Nothing but the interposition of a kind Providence protected me," Archer wrote, his statement itself an affirmation of that providence—declaring that there is an order in the world, a divine purpose to one's place, even when events seem most random. Archer's letter is also a consecration that helps set the dead men to rest: "A. B. Simmons, *Willie Robinson* from Washington City, and C. M. Cole of Baltimore"—as he names the dead, the letter begins to fold protectively within itself, like the petals of a flower, giving the sense of pages read and godly words spoken, all of a piece, all of a place: "A brother of Robinson's in the Company who is very pious . . . bore his loss with Christian fortitude," and "the night following the death of his brother, at the prayer meeting, (we have them nightly in the Regt.) he made a few remarks the most impressive I think I ever have heard, and he also read a Chapter from the Bible (the same he read at his brother's burial)."[12]

The letter identifies with these obsequies: reading and writing *gather* the scene and bring it to rest: "I was present at Willie Robinson's death. I assisted in carrying him from the field and at his burial the next morning—The circumstances connected with it were so impressive that I could not help shedding tears, and there were very few who did not."[13] The letter is itself a solemn ritual, a saying of last rites, a confirmation of place and person. Even so, Robinson's death is now borne in this paper and others and carried to places where his body will explode again. In the American postal age, letter writing produced a great scattering buzz of news, opinions, voices, and, here, violence.

Lifting up and away from the place, the letters coming from Bristoe Station in the days after the battle effectively scavenged the scene, taking away not only experiences but even something of the physical location itself, transporting it in a few days to places across the country and in a sense leaving the station as it was before: a transient stop along railroad tracks leading elsewhere, with barely a structure or resident to designate it as a place. By virtue of all the letter descriptions, Bristoe Station became a *bilocation:* a nonplace newly consecrated into biblical meaningfulness—saturated with a thickness it exudes still, in a litter of artifacts and ghostly actions alongside modern-day Virginia Route 619—but giving the sense also of having been largely *removed* elsewhere, scattered broadly, scavenged clean, flown and spread into warm attics of yellowy paper, so that really only a historical marker or two would tell you that anything ever happened there.

What survives here and there are not only the bilocated scenes of killing but also the quiet crystalline details of dying. Twenty-one-year-old Major Henry Abbott of the Twentieth Massachusetts, a veteran of Fredericksburg and Gettysburg, was among the Union soldiers sheltered behind the railroad embankment at Bristoe Station. As the Confederates came across the fields toward the Union line, "in their usual style, 3 lines," a close friend of Abbott's, Colonel Mallon of the Forty-Second New York, was shot and mortally wounded. In an October 17 letter to his father, Abbott described the scene: "While his eyes were glazing & he could no longer see me, he told me of his friendship. He was going towards me to speak to me when he was hit."[14]

Mallon and the Union surgeon John Perry "were lying side by side, flat on the ground, so as to be out of range of the enemy's guns," Perry wrote in his own letter, "when the colonel, who was very fond of Major Abbott, said he must take a look round and see if he were safe. I begged him not to, saying that he would surely be shot, but he answered, 'No, I cannot stand the suspense, and it will take but a moment'; whereupon he rose, and was instantly shot through the abdomen. . . . I dragged him to a little muddy stream,—the only place of safety,—where the poor fellow lay with the water almost running down his throat. He lived until the fight was almost over, and finally expired in my arms."[15] The glazed eye, the little muddy stream, the water running down the throat: each is a watery daguerreotype of the dying man's streaming life, a reversal of the wartime phenomenon of dead soldiers found clutching photographs of loved ones. Here, by letter, Mallon's own image is sent flowing away from him, so that the breath and watery glaze can reappear elsewhere, hundreds of miles distant, in precious composites of muddy glass, each containing a blurred reflection.

American poets during the war recognized the killing power of a distant scene brought home to the reader. Equating poetry with devastating effects, they built long-range power into their work. Henry Wadsworth Longfellow's "Killed at the Ford," published in the *Atlantic Monthly* in April 1866, describes a bullet that kills a son and then goes "speeding forth, / Til it reached a town in the distant North" until it struck, in letter form, "a heart that ceased to beat / Without a murmur, without a cry."[16] Emily Dickinson told the writer and Civil War veteran Thomas Wentworth Higginson, "If I feel physically as if the top of my head were taken off, I know that is poetry."[17] Herman Melville wondered, in "Shiloh," from *Battle-Pieces and Aspects of the War* (1866), "What like a bullet can undeceive!"—a question implicitly referring to poetry itself, which, for Melville, might strike like Dickinson's "Zero at the Bone," sending messages that cut to the quick.[18] "The first thing I knew, I saw a rebel shot coming bounding along," Charles Longfellow had written to his father on September 16, 1863. "It made two long jumps in front of us and then went close by my leg and hit sergeant Reed, my master sergeant, below the knee."[19] Two months later, the younger Longfellow was himself seriously wounded, by a projectile addressed to him, and the news traveled north to his father, whose "Killed at the Ford" envisions the far-spreading word of many a wound and many a death, including Lincoln's (Killed at the Ford, Killed at Ford's). Poetry, too, like projectiles, like letters, would target a reader to achieve its effects.[20]

So would the era's sensational journalism, which could produce explosive revelations, modeled on the power of ammunition and other volatile materials. In the October 17, 1863, issue of *Frank Leslie's Illustrated Weekly,* the writer of "How I Saw an Explosion" describes walking up the gangplank of a steamboat on the Mississippi and hearing "a dull, booming noise" followed suddenly by "an inability to breathe." The steamboat's boiler had burst, and the concussion knocked him off his feet and rolled him several yards up the dock. Staying within the strange world of his own perceptions, he continues, "I did not lose consciousness, and instantly sprang to my feet, though I had a sensation as if I had received a heavy blow. As I rose from the dock my eyes went directly to a row of buildings fronting the water, four story brick, with iron shutters, and I distinctly saw the body of a man falling, apparently from one of the windows. A wild, sickish feeling came over me at that instant, and I started to run, not with any intent or purpose, but much as a drunken man would run." The falling man was one of the engineers, "who was blown over sixty yards to the third story, where he struck upon one of the iron shutters and hung for a minute, in his dying struggle disengaging himself and falling to the ground."[21]

The explosion encompasses the writer. It provides his worldview, which is utterly singular, reminding him of how "soldiers have always agreed that it was impossible for them to see a battle, [that] they could only be cognizant of their own little locality." The outer rings of percussion and smoke constitute the edges of this universe, making a separate world so private that it cannot be conveyed. Yet the job of the writer, and of the journal, is to co-opt this explosiveness and this singularity and give them both the vivid impact of you-are-there journalism. The popular press, like many of the novels of the period, would distribute private sensations.

The commitment to eyewitness narrative and modes of explosive suddenness is not without feints and homage to a more respectable journalism. The two modes of reporting sometimes compete for mastery in the same publication. The center spread of the same October 17 issue of *Frank Leslie's* shows the recent Battle of Chickamauga, fought the previous month, as an affair largely of distanced, measured calibrations (fig. 48). A group of Union generals surveys the scene, the officers' position marked by a complex of sublimatory metaphors. The rising smoke and the vertical flag suggest a dignity of higher purpose and longer views that the spread-winged eagle on the flag also emphasizes. Meanwhile, however, an explosion at lower right draws the reader's eye, revealing in a jagged contrast of black and white a dead man, dead horses, and a broken carriage. Each of these explosive details indicates a more visceral, more immediate reporting that would confront the reader opening to the center spread not with the generals' measured investigation of ongoing events but with a sensational burst making even last month's battle a stunner in the reader's eyes.

Macbeth on October 17, as an official patriotic utterance, was obliged to take all this explosive rhetorical power into account. The performers could not know much about the specifics of the Bristoe soldiers' response. Nor could they know about the brewing poetic adaptation of letter writing's powers of devastation at a distance. And certainly the play, as an ambitiously high-culture production, could not try to mimic the sordid truth-telling explosions of the sensational press. But the play on that night, taking place in a city abuzz with news of Bristoe Station and of another battle purportedly soon to come—a city whose residents were not sure where General

Fig. 48. J. F. Hillers, *The War in Georgia—Battle of Chickamauga, Sept. 19 and 20.* In *Frank Leslie's Illustrated Newspaper,* October 17, 1863, 56–57. Sterling Memorial Library, Yale University.

Lee was (Gurowski's "We are at *guessing*")—would have been obliged to contain these murmurs, to frame and hold them within the reassuring spectacle of a unified production whose characters spoke words tried and true.

Likewise the performers would have felt obliged to take the muttered horror in the air—the gunshots and booming of the artillery, the torn bodies even then transiting imperceptibly in their paper tents through and around the city and to points elsewhere—and transform these into *a mere imagery* of violence. When the wounded captain appeared early in the play, reporting to King Duncan about Macbeth's fearless exploits in battle ("his brandished steel / Which smoked with bloody execution" [1.2.17–18]) and asked for help ("But I am faint; my gashes cry for help" [1.2.42]), his words gathered and held the recent Battle of Bristoe Station into a stability, a coherence, for which Shakespeare as much as the Bible would serve as a reassuring script.

Therefore to say that *Macbeth* that night was an allegory of the war is incorrect. It was not allegorical in the sense of referring *out* to the scenes around it, catching or "sticking" on those scenes. To think in this way would imply that the words spoken in the theater truly had the power to grab and hold onto the fragments of bodies and stories even then floating as acoustic shadows in the dark and the smoke and on the hills. Instead we can say that the war *came into* the theater, and that it did so almost dutifully, gathered there as though by functionaries assembled for the purpose, as an infinite set of vivid experiences, a scattering of sand. The play then took responsibility for fashioning these scattered experiences into the great, resounding, concentric circles of singular purpose it would throw back into that shot-blasted world, now ostensibly unified through the shaping power of a work of art.

When Cushman's Lady Macbeth first appeared onstage reading a letter from her husband, in act 1, scene 5, the effect was to contain the letter-bound voices spreading around the city. Cushman probably held her special letter prop—in a handwritten notation, her script mentions a "scroll not folded but rolled up with piece of floss silk attached to it" for this scene—and thereby presented a decorous image of desperate communications.[22] Even as Macbeth's letter speaks of the witches' strange prophecies, the scene most likely provided the merest general representation of the messages sounding around Washington that night: Is my husband alive or dead? Is my wife all right? And it would have wrapped those messages in an official form, for which the great actress, no less than the scroll, was an honorary and comforting case: an acceptable representation. Cushman showed Fanny Seward, on the pair's visit to Ford's Theater on October 10, "a long piece of sheet iron" suspended on the wall, explaining that "to shake this is to make stage thunder," and then shook it to give an example. "She told us how rain was represented by dried peas."[23] The sounds from the outside, even the very loud ones, were here safe, thrilling, legible. Macbeth's letter came to Lady Macbeth in a neat package of sound.

Even so, did the actress's words onstage have power, even firepower? Probably they did. Who was to deny Cushman's oratorical skill or that of actors as experienced as Lester Wallack and Edward Davenport? These performers knew how to deliver their lines. But the weaponlike impact of their oratory might have accorded more with that of political speakers than with the shattering shots, dull booms, and elemental shrieks outside. The fiery political speaker Anna Dickinson delivered a speech on one occasion that "raked the Lincoln administration fore and aft," George Augustus Sala wrote. During another speech at the House of Representatives, she "slowly paced to and fro on the platform, dropping her well-formed and compact sentences upon the people below." A Senate page recalled how before the war the Georgia senator Robert Toombs used his "ornate language . . . to strike as with a sledgehammer, blows with words of the utmost weight." A territorial delegate from Nebraska, meanwhile, was known as "a smoothbore speaker."[24] As political speakers reminded observers of famous actors, so the actors in a benefit performance might conceive themselves as political speakers. Yet each form of explosive public speaking—that of the actor, that of the politician—was finally a formal declaration that, however wide ranging it might be, aimed to be all of a piece, issuing clearly from one grand authority and, as such, producing a grand and symbolic resolution of all stray and random sounds elsewhere.

The chaos of acoustic shadows flowed into the theater, to make the point another way, only to be converted into the one-person words of an actor, to gather even in the "Arc de Triomphe" mouth of Cushman. So the perfect reading of a line, every vowel and consonant rounded and cut off, delivered with the right push of tongue on teeth and palate, might stifle a thousand cries. There and then the war could flow back out as a unity, a national picture, in which an audience was encouraged, insofar as possible, not to see, not to imagine, what still lay at Bristoe on October 17: many of the Federal dead (left during a concealed retreat on the night of the fourteenth); the graves of the Confederates (buried there on the fifteenth, after Lee's army took possession of the now-abandoned field); and a scattering of packs and other military accoutrements awaiting either theft or reuse or else starting, even then, their hundred years' slow sink into the artifactual earth.[25]

Did any utterance in Washington that week tell a profound truth about the war? If any did so, maybe it was not one spoken by a person at all. In 2006 the Prince William County Historic Preservation Division conducted a metal-detecting investigation across a small portion of the Bristoe battlefield, uncovering a few military artifacts, including a fragment of a Federal Schenkl shell, one of several types of exploding projectile in use that day (fig. 49). Fired from a rifled cannon with a three-inch bore, the shell was designed to burst in air or on contact with the ground and to send splinters and chunks of metal down or outward. David Born, the historic programs coordinator at Bristoe, guesses that this particular round contained a mix of shrapnel set in a compound of sulfur and pitch and that it would have been fitted with either a timed fuse for aerial burst or a concussion fuse that would detonate when the shell hit the ground. Because metal detectors found only these small fragments, Born guesses that this shell probably exploded in the air, noting, too, that the shards were found about at

Fig. 49. Schenkl shell fragment, 1863, Bristoe Station, Virginia. Excavated 2006. Prince William County, Virginia, Department of Public Works, Historic Preservation Division.

the place, beside present-day Virginia Route 619, where General Cooke's brigade stopped, having gone as far as it could go that day.[26]

This long-distance emissary bespeaks not only how the battle comes down to us now, as a series of rusted, almost indecipherable fragments, but how it might have come across then. Then and now, the fragment is the three-inch handheld mirror in which some vision of those events is authentically inscribed, a reddish-rust detail that does not so much glint in the sun as take on the color of the earth. Traveling far away, fragments of letters and diaries, made of paper and leather, stick a little in the ground just like the shrapnel—an effect most palpable when these writings reference the ground itself. "October 14th, 1863. . . . We . . . killed six Yanks, whom our sappers and miners buried, in a freshly seeded wheatfield, in about five minutes from the time these poor fellows were alive and walking about"; or "Oct. 16 . . . I sleep with my . . . arm upon the R.R. on a bed of iron bars by the fire"; or "Oct. 17. Lay still . . . we pluck some flowers"; or "Saturday Oct. 17th. . . . March over the land where the skirmish of the 14th occurred. Some 25 horses . . . are lying here dead."[27]

Sometimes the ground is the human body itself, pushing up beneath the writing for which it serves as a makeshift board or slab, impressing a physical urgency on the words. With "nothing to put my paper on," the Confederate Richard Henry Watkins wrote hurriedly in an awkward hand, as if pressing the paper to his palm or thigh, on October 15, 1863: "My Precious Mary. . . . The fight is to be renewed this morning near Bristoe Station and the picketts are now firing. . . . Good bye much love to all. May God preserve you & our little children my precious one and all of them who are near & dear to me—In him let us trust knowing that whatever he doeth is right lived—again good bye I love you with all my heart & think of you always and every where & long to be with you."[28]

Experience, as revealed in that rusted Schenkl fragment, is upside down, out of joint, a remnant of the split-apart world we later make whole, and that *Macbeth* on October 17 was already busy mending. The shot is the primal blow, coming from nowhere, that disorients the world—encapsulating that disorientation in the blunt stub of its fragmentary remains—and that puts to the lie all grandiloquent speech. Edward Bassett, of the First Minnesota Volunteers, was scurrying back to the Union lines under fire from Confederate skirmishers on October 14 when "a ball struck on the left side of my head, passing thru my hat. It must have glanced off, only bruizeing and making it pretty sore. It did not break the skin, altho it made me dizzy for a while." Bassett told his parents not to worry and asked that his name not be put on the wounded list. However, the injury, in the words of his son, "caused him years of intense suffering" from catalepsy and many years later led to his death in Minnesota in April 1897.[29]

Bassett's world went upside down at Bristoe Station, which would from then on stay with him. His story went out of sequence on that day. Certainly there had been life before the battle and after it: *before,* in Manhattan in August and September, helping to restore order after the draft riots with the First Minnesota and taking the twenty-hour steamboat ride aboard the *Empire City* from New York to Alexandria; *after,* life on guard duty in Nashville. Yet in another sense for Bassett there was no before and after—only a blurring, a dizzying, as the world was sent spinning by the shot that colored all else. His son wrote that in the Minnesota winter people who were caught outside in a blizzard "would very likely wander in a circle, and in all probability, become exhausted and freeze to death," a fate the elder Bassett made sure would not happen to him: he "had a rope strung between the house and the barn, so that he wouldn't lose his way in the storm." But the potential disorientation suggests the ongoing presence of Bristoe Station in his life. To walk in circles, to spin slowly around, trying to find the right line of sky and earth—to be in a blizzard or another kind of storm ("There was a sound like the rising wind. . . . The grasshoppers . . . sounded like hail as they hit the side of the building")—was to be always in the vicinity of a battle time that was neither then nor now, neither here nor there, and that linear narratives would need to control.[30]

Those controlling stories were at the ready even as the Battle of Bristoe Station was being fought. On October 14, 1863, the correspondent Alfred Waud made a drawing of the Union batteries there, a picture that would appear in the November 7 issue of *Harper's Weekly* (fig. 50). The battle for Waud unfolds according to logical coordinates of space and time. From a vantage behind the First Rhode Island Artillery, he uses the bursts from the cannon to convey excitement, but he denies these bursts the immediacy and disorientation that characterize, for example, the *Frank Leslie's* "How I Saw an Explosion" story. Instead the cannon fire unfolds with a rational simultaneity—several foreground bursts across the page—emphasizing the removed, abstract precision of gunnery.

This logical suddenness extends, moreover, to the *Harper's* publication schedule. Waud, an experienced illustrator who witnessed many battles, probably knew that his picture would not appear for several weeks and that he should emphasize immediacy—or something like delayed immediacy—to hold the interest of a reader who by early November would know many details of the battle. He produces that effect with the explosions, rhyming them with the singular frizzy-edged tree to make the scene excitingly sudden yet keeping the burst controlled and subject to a more rational temporality. The gunshots burst on October 14 and November 7, but this double-time of delayed explosion is not a recurrent nightmare of the battle's violence but a ritual ordering of it. The picture is a dutiful replay, transmitting the boom of the battle across time and place but softening the shock.

Space itself seems to make this cushion of time. The horizon in Waud's drawing implies a spread of unfolded action whose horizontality—giving the big picture, the long view—dissipates the explosive impact of any one detail. The pages of *Harper's Weekly,* spread before the reader, double this panoramic breadth where the action unfolds (though the drawing did not appear as a center spread). The implied presence of Waud's body, orienting the scene and creating the horizon, also structures the drawing, giving the battlefield the bilateral symmetry of his vision. The picture turns explosions into an official report.

Only one thing disrupts it, something that brings us back to Bassett and makes us see all the more the *Macbeth* performance's Waud-like symmetries of war. At the center left of the illustrator's Bristoe drawing is a

Fig. 50. Alfred Waud, *Battle of Bristoe Station,* 1863. Pencil on cream lined paper, 4⅜ × 14¼ in. (10.9 × 36 cm). Library of Congress, Washington, D.C.

broken-looking windmill. This must be the "dilapidated windmill . . . formerly used for pumping water" described in an October 17 *Boston Post* account of the battle.[31] Waud uses the windmill as an orientation point: the scene partly takes shape because of this fixture on the horizon, and we can imagine how welcome he must have found this point of focus as he began to make his picture. Yet in another sense the windmill, standing out starkly, recalls the landmarks that stay in the mind, oddly, stupidly, in the midst of the most profound disorientation. Carlo Rotella, in *Cut Time,* describes how a boxer stunned by a punch will focus on the most random detail—a chair, a face in the crowd—as if this object bears for him a singular, almost endless fascination.[32] As the whole world spins around him, this single object becomes a random center, making up in visual interest what it lacks in intrinsic meaning.

Bassett's experience is irrecoverable, but perhaps his moment of being spun around by a bullet produced a comparable moment of strange fixation. In that moment the one thing that ceased to twirl might signify the spinning of the entire world around it: as if the world were the blades of the windmill and the windmill itself were the one thing that did not move. The windmill is the thing in Waud's picture that most savors of particularized experience, the one thing that truly places the scene amid its generalized rhetoric of military iconography. It introduces a fragmentary fixed point at odds with the claim of Waud's picture to represent a seamless spatial and temporal clarity.

Waud's inclusion of the windmill lets us see his picture, now at the Library of Congress, as itself a dilapidated fragment—a bit of torn paper, dated October 14, 1863—as ruined as the windmill, and like it a fragment. Now it is the historian who stares with his own desperate dumb fixation, concentrating hard, stunned by the swirling temporality around this arbitrary fixed point. To study the past is to be brought before such pictures that would kindly and ignorantly take us into their putative worlds of historical generalization. Theirs is a grand review of events in which all particulars are mere details, in which the days themselves—October 14, October 17—take on the comely quality of personalities, dignitaries, grandees assembled in medaled splendor for our inspection. Insofar as these pictures dimly intuit whatever might haunt them, as the windmill haunts Waud's landscape, they cushion these fragments, building a beautiful nest of splendid soft grass to dissipate the impact—truly, the explosion—of the Particular Thing. Yet by this cushioning these pictures also protect the weird central objects they would disavow, as Waud carefully preserves his windmill for us. They make visible the motionless place-marking fragment that still makes the world spin.

What business could the polite art of the American midcentury have with such world turnings? Maybe more than we might think, more than *Macbeth* on October 17 might have wished. Take the experience of Gouverneur Kemble Warren, Cushman's friend and the Union general victorious at Bristoe Station, who later in the war received an acoustic shadow that still makes unaccountable sounds.

Warren (1830–82) was not a likely person to hear such a message. Hero of the battle, he was a logical man, a master of battlefield space. He understood how to perceive warfare abstractly, as a set of tactical possibilities and limitations, partly because he had been a military engineer. The drawings he made in the 1850s, out in the West while a member of the United States Topographical Survey, indicate his ability to conceive a landscape in direct terms, near and far, as a matter of "clear and precise information," to quote his West Point topographic textbook (figs. 51–52).[33]

Warren took that cool vision into the Civil War, where on Little Round Top at Gettysburg on July 2, 1863, as General Meade's chief of staff, he recognized that the small hill "was the key of the whole position" of the Union army and so played an important part in the victory.[34] There his young aide-de-camp was Washington Roebling, himself a master of space—the son of the famed engineer John Roebling and already the maker of several bridges, who would go on to build the Brooklyn Bridge (and who would marry Warren's sister Emily in 1865).[35] At Little Round Top, a bronze statue of Warren, unveiled in 1888, continues to assert his command over space.[36] As Gurowski coincidentally wrote in his diary as the battle began, describing Warren, "Genuine science and intelligence dawn on our muddy, dark, ignorant horizon."[37]

Warren's view of Bristoe Station was accordingly cold and clear. Under fire, he saw the embankment of the Orange and Alexandria Railroad and ordered his men to gather behind it, recognizing that this ready-made redoubt (in the vicinity of the windmill in Waud's picture) was a perfect position for withstanding the Confederate assaults.[38] Coming down the fields toward the railroad tracks, the Confederates did not stand a chance, and it is unlikely that they would even have begun had they understood that the Union soldiers lay so well protected behind this barrier. Confederate general Henry Heth defended his soldiers' conduct: "No military man who has examined the ground, or who understood the position . . . would attach blame to these two brigades" for failing in the attack.[39] Gurowski,

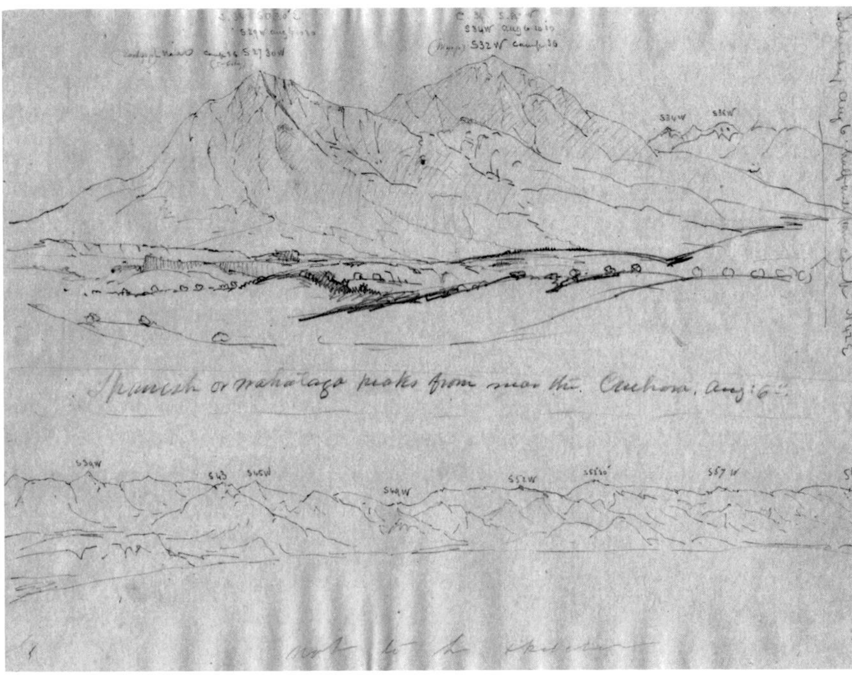

Figs. 51–52. Gouverneur Kemble Warren, *Uniontown, Karo River* and *Spanish Peaks . . . Aug. 6,* ca. 1850s. Both courtesy of the New York State Library, Manuscripts and Special Collections.

without knowing the particulars of Bristoe Station, had mocked the idea that any great general would really choose the ground on which he would fight, writing in his diary on October 17, "Who ever read that Alexander, or Cesar, or Frederic, or Napoleon, or even captains of lesser fame, selected their ground?"[40] But Warren did choose the ground and won because of it.

Warren won also because, more even than most officers, he understood the point-to-point directness of gunfire. He grew up in Cold Spring, New York, site of the largest and most productive munitions factory in the United States, the West Point Iron and Cannon Foundry, across the Hudson River from West Point. He was named after Gouverneur Kemble (1786–1875), the founder of the factory, and when he enrolled at West Point in 1846 to begin his training as an army officer, Warren already would have known more about the long-range power of artillery than many of his fellow cadets. Later, at Bristoe Station and other places, he used Parrott Guns, the muzzle-loaded rifled cannons invented by Cold Spring resident and foundry superintendent Robert Parker Parrott, introduced into military service in 1860, and built in large quantities in the hometown foundry. (John Ferguson Weir's painting *The Gun Foundry* [1864–66; Putnam County Historical Society, Cold Spring] conceivably shows Warren and his wife, Emily Chase Warren, standing beside Kemble and Mr. and Mrs. Parrott as they all watch foundry workers pour molten metal to make the guns, making Warren a solemn witness to the hellfire at his command.)[41] When Warren saw the land during the war, he saw it almost synonymously with the gunfire that would rake and traverse it.

Warren's faith in the power of effective communications was equally logical. His letters betray no special anxieties about the distance his correspondence must travel. Everything is a matter of clear transmission from sender to receiver, even when the message comes from beyond this world. On October 17, fresh from his great victory at Bristoe Station, he wrote to Emily, then his bride of four months, the good family friend of Cushman who may well have attended the performance of *Macbeth* that evening: "I have been very fortunate and if heaven ever does care for mortals like me it made me the special object of its protection in the battles on the 14th, and it must have been in answer to the prayers of your dear self, my angel. . . . Give my regards to Miss Cushman and my love to your mother."[42]

Warren was just as sure that surreptitious and wordless messages would convey a clear meaning. On October 15 he had written to Emily to say that he and his staff had stayed at the home of a rebel officer, an old friend of his, and that he had left a photograph of himself for the man's kind and lonely wife, leaving the picture "in her prayer book (lying on her shelf) at the litany. I was away before day light too early to give it to her myself."[43] Again Warren trusted in the power of a personal communication at a distance, delivered clearly if quietly from one party to another.

But then the stranger message came to him. Among his papers is a copy of the 1858 New York edition of *Sappho: A Tragedy in Five Acts,* translated by Edda Middleton from Franz Grillparzer's German original. The book is inscribed on the first page in large red-inked letters: "Chas. L. Cocke, September 16 1858 In Rebel service, leaving at home a lovely wife, and three children, December 1864." An extensive note in Warren's hand on the title page describes how the book came into his possession, given to him by a Union pillager who had ransacked the house of this Charles L. Cocke. "What did he want with anything so refined?" asks Warren in his inscription. "It was an incumbrance to him—He could not read a word of it." Warren notes that the thief found the book in a bag "where a negro servant kept blacking for his master's boots, the mark of which is still on the cover." Now it was in the general's hands, and he promised to return it if possible to Charles L. Cocke of Virginia, though he never did.[44]

What an odd communication this book was, a message from nowhere. It fell to Warren late in the war from one of "the lowest class of soldiers," who in turn found it inside a slave's boot-blacking bag—and it is a book about slavery. Melitta, one of the characters, is Sappho's slave. She tells the amorous Phaon to stay clear of her sadness and social position:

> I am a slave—
> . . . . What wouldst thou with a slave?
> Let her seek rest,
> Upon the bosom of another slave,
> Or (with emotion)
> Take her to rest in Heaven, ye Gods!

Melitta thinks of her homeland ("My father's love can never reach his child: / A broad sea intervenes 'twixt him and me"), and she describes her abduction as a child from her home "far to the East, beneath the burning sun," when one night she was

> . . . awakened by loud cries.
> My nurse, in terror, bore me from the house,
> A ruffian seized me, 'mid wild shrieks and cries,
> And then I found myself aboard a ship.[45]

What story does this copy of *Sappho* tell? A slave owner's copy of a strongly antislavery play published in New York before the war, it speaks in the voice of Melitta and in the voice of Charles L. Cocke, who wrote in the same red

Fig. 53. *Sappho,* frontispiece in Edda Middleton, *Sappho: A Tragedy in Five Acts* (New York: D. Appleton, 1858). Courtesy of the New York State Library, Manuscripts and Special Collections.

ink beneath the book's frontispiece illustration of Sappho, "Dark Sappho! Could not verse immortal save, That breast, imbued with such immortal fire" (fig. 53). The book is a series of echoes, nested one inside the other. Inscribed with the words of Cocke and Warren, it passed through the hands of nameless intermediaries, the slave and the thief. The slave kept it in the bag, safe for the master, or, if he could, perhaps to read it and furtively take pleasure in the play's sharp abolitionist rhetoric; the thief let it go as of no interest. Cocke appears to have been a doctor, the author of *An Account of the Alleghany Springs, in Montgomery County, Virginia,* a promotional pamphlet attesting to the restorative powers of certain Virginia hot springs, including the waters' skin-whitening effects.[46] The book is a fragment of improbable and unknowable sound, a picture of a vaster world—that plantation? that slave? that master?—it never lets us see.

The book, to put it another way, offers one definition of an aesthetic experience. In so doing, it says something about the improbable artistry of *Macbeth* on October 17 and suggests how that performance of the play actually might have touched life. That artistry has something to do with the power of heroines. Sappho calls to mind Warren's friend Cushman, a "Sapphic Romeo" in her performance of the breeches part in *Romeo and Juliet* and in general, as the friend and lover of many women, a fitting correlative to the poetess of Lesbos.[47] More generally, Sappho in the Middleton translation calls to mind all the tragic heroines of the 1850s—Rogers's *Nydia,* for example—who were viewed by many Americans of that time with such sentimental fascination. In his letter to Emily of October 19, Warren likened himself to Maggie Mitchell's character Cricket in *Fanchon,* the play that Fanny Seward had seen at Ford's with Cushman on October 12 and that presumably Warren and Emily had seen as well.[48] Mitchell's many *cartes de visite,* perhaps like the ones that the Sewards obtained at the theater, suggest how wide-ranging a fame the character of Cricket, like Sappho and Nydia, enjoyed in those years.

These heroines, however, did not travel "as is" to the various people who enjoyed them. They did not arrive "whole" and ready to deliver their messages, righteous or sweet. Nor was the transmission of these messages—in stories, plays, letters, books—exactly a matter of personal response, as if an awaiting audience, near or far, need only have projected its wishes and tastes onto these characters and performers to give them their most profound significance. Between the production and the reception of messages lay another realm of aesthetic possibility that was not personal at all. It was the realm of the *situation,* a chance encounter, an explosion unfolding in a small pocket of space, in which some strange and hitherto utterly unrealized view of the world might for a moment appear.

In that situation, what the far-traveling aesthetic fragment made visible and realizable was not itself and not the person who received it—not, say, the line of poetry or the vivid image of a character that had been so transported into the receiver's midst, and not the receiver him- or herself, suddenly made clear and whole in some epiphanic shock of self-awareness. Rather it made appear the place where this explosion had happened: the randomness of leaves, stone wall, and winding path (whatever the surroundings were), which became the repositories of all the mystery in this line of poetry, this unbidden image striking suddenly into a receiver's midst. At the heart of that explosion into vividness would be the aesthetic fragment itself, the sliver or shard that shaped the blankness and opacity of one's surroundings, for just that moment, into a transient yet memorable coherence.

This view—call it an artistic one—had no world-changing power. Bursting in a person's midst, it offered no perspective on events, no horizon-seeking elucidation of grand scenes and meanings. Instead it gathered down into itself an utterly small space of personal revelation, a vision closed at the edges and offering no wider view. This inward world did give a glimpse of other realms; it even contained a whole metaphysics, promising to explain a great deal. And the space it would reveal was as surely different from the space on earth as the envelope of an explosion blotting out ordinary time and space. Yet the burst revealed no grand truth precisely: for all the superb clarity it offered, it remained as dark and unknowable as the inside of the boot-blacking bag in which the copy of *Sappho* was found. Delivered into a person's midst by chance—found in pockets of smoke and dark—these sudden fragments spoke with an unforgettable and meaningless vividness.

Such was the far-ranging presence of art, casting its own acoustic shadow in the age of letters, telegraphs, and gunfire. It was a disembodied sound, discovered by chance here and there, at the side of the road, in the leaves of a tree, along the railroad tracks—never more than a quixotic but stunning momentary presence. Was any part of *Macbeth* on October 17 like that? Might we equate some of the play's utterances to the Schenkl shell fragment—such that the fragment, moldered with time, is a breathy Shakespearean epithet lodged like an aerolite where it happened to strike ground? The following chapter examines how the play sent a few of its pieces far into the Virginia countryside.

FIVE

Center of Echoes

Castle Murray, Fauquier County, Virginia

WITHIN A FEW MILES OF BRISTOE STATION is Castle Murray, a Medieval Revival home designed and built for Dr. James Murray in 1857–58. Gouverneur Kemble Warren used Murray's home as his headquarters on the night of October 13–14, 1863. At 2:00 A.M. on the fourteenth a messenger rode up to the castle with Warren's orders from General George Meade, commander of the Army of the Potomac. Warren and his staff reviewed the orders, deciding to move his men toward Confederate positions at dawn—starting the events that would culminate in the Battle of Bristoe Station late that afternoon. Timothy O'Sullivan's photograph shows what Castle Murray looked like the following month, with Union army tents pitched before it (fig. 54).

Castle Murray was a likely place for *Macbeth* to make contact. James Murray's residence is maybe a better place than most to exemplify the strange situational possibilities of a work of art touching down at a particular spot, chancing to spark a momentary realization for a person who happens to be there. "The beauty of poetry is appreciated only by those who happen to read it in the right time, place, and under the right circumstances," the Confederate infantryman Henry Kyd Douglas, who during the war read hundreds of books, wrote in 1863.[1] This power of happenstance—the chance encounter where an utterance echoes off a place, if only for a moment—even may be what Castle Murray was built for. Upon the Murray home's

Fig. 54. Timothy O'Sullivan, *Castle Murray,* 1863. Library of Congress, Washington, D.C.

sturdy walls, the play would find a receptive place to resound. Castle Murray was built to block—and yet somehow also to receive—messages from the outside. In each case the peculiar power of the building, to deny and to accept communications, had to do with slavery.

Edmund Lind, the home's architect, introduces us to the idea. Coming to America from his native England in late 1855, he settled in Baltimore and was surprised to find the virulence of the proslavery feeling there. "Niggers do not seem to be much thought of in Baltimore—the Yankee looks upon them much the same as he would his horse or dog—and treats them about as well—in many cases ten times worse," Lind wrote in his diary on January 4, 1856. "I thought when I came here that niggers enjoyed pretty good privileges—I begin to think differently—everywhere in Baltimore amongst all classes & grades, he is consid'd the animal made for the white man's use—& well the white man avails himself of the privilege. A long discussion with Granger & Barker [Lind's associates] in the evening did not tend much to the removal of this impression altho' both profess to be at enmity with slavery itself—Along a Baltimore Street a cold girl [colored? cold and colored?] could not pass without being snowball'd."[2]

Lind's personal view of slavery is unclear. He seems to deplore the treatment of blacks in Baltimore. His use of the word *niggers* may be a sardonic echo of the local parlance. Back in New York in November 1855, a few days after his arrival from England, he attended Henry Ward Beecher's Plymouth Church in Brooklyn, sitting among thousands of parishioners to hear the famous abolitionist hold forth on human accountability in a sermon based on Romans 14:12: "Every one of us will have to give an account of himself before God." Later in November, still in New York, Lind visited the "Colored Home" and the "Colored Orphan Asylum, most pleasing of all—Saw & heard the young darkies go thro' their exercises in School."[3]

Yet only the second commission Lind undertook was a country estate for a man who almost certainly owned slaves. Working in the office of Baltimore architect William Turnbull Murdoch, Lind was commissioned by Murray, a resident of Baltimore, to build a house on a large Fauquier County farm Murray had just purchased. The house Lind designed was expensive, a baronial dwelling costing $6,500.[4] It looks small in an architectural rendering that may be by Lind (fig. 55), but Castle Murray, or Melrose Castle, as Murray called it, sits imposingly on a rise called Rock Hill, several hundred yards from the Old Carolina Road (now Rogues Road). Murray must have required many slaves to run such a property. Among the papers at the Fauquier Historical Society is a recent memo about a woman who had phoned the staff wishing to learn more about Castle Murray because her great-grandmother had been a slave there and is supposed to have been buried on the property along with other slaves, in graves that were once marked.[5] James Murray, the owner, went on to serve as a doctor in the Confederate army.[6]

Castle Murray exemplifies the relation between slavery and the medieval—a relation that ultimately concerns the transmission of sound. Murray named his home "in honor of Melrose Abbey in Scotland, which he claimed as an ancestral home," and in homage to Sir Walter Scott, the Scottish expositor of knightly derring-do who set several stories at this gothic abbey near his own estate.[7] Scott, in the well-known opinion of Mark Twain, was "in great measure responsible for the war," having invented the Southern ideal of chivalry—the code of courtly refinement, brute force, and hotheaded loyalty ("Breathes there the man") that animated so many Southerners, causing them to secede from the Union.[8]

Fig. 55. *Melrose,* presentation drawing, ca. 1857–58. Watercolor and ink on paper, 9⅝ × 12⅜ in. (24.4 × 31.4 cm). Collection of E. W. Bridgeman, Jr. Courtesy of the Virginia Museum of Fine Arts, Richmond.

Such medievalism was everywhere in Virginia, lending credence to Twain's idea. Fauquier County, the location of Castle Murray, was home to one of the South's many *Ivanhoe*-style jousting tournaments.[9] In 1858 the body of former president James Madison was exhumed from Pennsylvania and reinterred in a lavish Gothic Revival tomb overlooking the James River in Richmond's Hollywood Cemetery. Our Chief, an 1876 tobacco label for the Virginia firm of William Cameron and Brothers, shows a druidical figure who resembles Robert E. Lee ordering a warrior who resembles Stonewall Jackson onward into battle as a lightninglike cascade of water electrifies the latter's shining sword (fig. 56).[10] The North had its own connections to Scotland. The Englishman James Horrocks, serving in the Union army, wrote from Washington on October 20, 1863, that he identified himself as a Scotsman to his fellow soldiers, knowing they would approve him much more than if he said he was from England.[11] The Union army included regiments, the Seventy-ninth New York and the Eighth Michigan, drawn heavily from Scottish immigrants, and at the start of the war the Seventy-ninth New York

Fig. 56. Unknown artist (for William Cameron & Brothers), *Our Chief, Lochiel,* 1876 (tobacco label). Virginia Historical Society, Richmond.

even wore Highland kilts.[12] Cushman's roles in Scott's *Guy Mannering* and as Lady Macbeth were part of her Northern righteousness, and she brought costumes for only those two roles when she sailed from Italy for her wartime benefit tour. Clearly the Scottishness of *Macbeth* on October 17 was perfectly in keeping with faith in the Union. But the South had its own special connections to Scotland. "Melrose well illustrates the impact of the 19th-century Romantic movement, more especially the Medievalism popularized by Sir Walter Scott, on Southern landed families," as a National Register of Historic Places document put it in 1981.[13]

Slavery, in turn, was never far from the South's embrace of the medieval.

The gothic revival in Great Britain began in the context of the late eighteenth-century debate about slavery, according to literary historians such as Andrea Henderson and Teresa Goddu. Important gothic writers of the time, such as Monk Lewis and William Beckford, "were either slaveowners or proslavery," Goddu notes.[14] In America the gothic became a preferred form for representing slavery, used by both proponents and the opposition. Southerners cast Nat Turner's Rebellion in gothic terms, while Frederick Douglass and Harriet Beecher Stowe also used gothic conventions to describe scenes of slavery—Douglass, for example, to portray the primal scene of Aunt Hester's whipping.[15]

Castle Murray represents a particular mix of slavery and medievalism. The home resembles a fortress against the threat of slave insurgency. In December 1856 a rumored slave uprising in Fauquier County caused the town council in Warrenton, a few miles from where Castle Murray would be built, to organize neighborhood night watches "in view of the uneasiness existing with regard to the negro population." The council also set heavy fines, from $100 to $500, for anyone selling a weapon to slaves and free blacks.[16] "The enemy is assaulting the citadel; we must concentrate our whole strength to defend it, and to repel the assault," a Southern politician warned in Washington in 1856.[17] Castle Murray was built to withstand the coming storm—an increasingly restive black population and the ever more likely physical assaults of war.

The structure was a fortress in another sense as well. It was to be an impregnable castle against the influence of far-spreading opinion—of news and newspapers, of abolitionist outcries such as Whittier's "Massachusetts to Virginia"—that alarmed Southern slaveholders. The possible meanings of the medieval revival help us see how this is so. Victor Hugo, in *Notre-Dame de Paris* (1831), describes the "mountain" of the Gothic church that before the Gutenberg Revolution had served to assemble the agreed-upon concatenation of all thought, the bedrock of all belief, into an absolute certainty at the center of a community. Then, as Hugo describes, the advent of printing turned thought "into a flock of birds . . . scattered on the four winds, occupying every point of air and space simultaneously." The whirlwind of books and other publications allowed any person, anywhere, to form an opinion, independent of a central authority. Although Hugo appreciates the new medium—"A book is so soon made, it costs so little, and it can travel so far!"—he laments that "architecture will no longer be the social, the collective, the dominant art."[18]

Castle Murray was an attempt to reimagine architecture as a vital force of unquestioned belief. Not all Medieval Revival architecture is indebted to Victor Hugo, or more especially to Hugo's point about the dichotomy between books and buildings, but Castle Murray seems to take Hugo's implied credo seriously: an imposing monument in the nineteenth century can exist only as an imaginative recovery of a time before printed books and before oratory that effectively published itself on the air. In the antebellum South this preliterary medievalism had a specific resonance. A stronghold made of stone, set on a hill, Castle Murray was meant as the opposite of paper and the opposite of spoken words coming from the outside. It wanted no indiscriminate communication from that outside world—not in an era of increasingly widespread antislavery publications, most famously Stowe's *Uncle Tom's Cabin* (1851), or far-spreading speech, like Henry Ward Beecher's booming sermons that made "the Rocky Mountains . . . his sounding board."[19] Consider Beecher's description of a chimney sweep's voice on a Brooklyn street—a voice that he says all public speakers should emulate (and that presumably Beecher himself already was embodying). The chimney sweep's voice made

> the whole air . . . full and overflowing with a sound as smooth, round, and melodious as an organ diapason. It fairly rained down for abundance and universality. The houses reflected it. The streets were channels in which the airy stream flowed. I looked in every direction for the cause. No man seemed the author. I looked up and down the street, turned around to every quarter,—for the sound came equally from everywhere,—until at length, mounted upon the chimney-top of one of the highest houses, sat the fellow like a king on his throne.[20]

Receiving such signals in Virginia, Castle Murray asserted its power to absorb and silence them. The thickness of the building's walls was a permanent rebuff to outside sound, not only swallowing and quieting these flows of words but implicitly, by material force of contrast, naming them as only so much ephemera. In this way, Castle Murray had a specific relation to writing and reading. In one sense, the interior of the home was a sanctuary for these cultured arts. The library to one side of the wide center hall on the first floor was made for fine editions of Scott and for the latest issues of *De Bow's Review* and the *Southern Literary Messenger.* "The beautiful Household Edition of the Waverley Novels" noted by the *Messenger* in 1857 might as well have been made for a place such as Castle Murray: "As the volumes multiply, their appearance on the shelves of the Library improves; and when the whole series shall have been issued, there can be no more desirable edition of the unrivaled novels of Sir Walter to be obtained anywhere."[21]

The Castle Murray library claimed a cultivation that could come only from enslaving others—one of the South's justifications for slavery. As a proslavery writer wrote in 1857, "A farmer or planter in the South, not rich, but in independent and comfortable circumstances, gives a portion of his time to social and mental preoccupation," whereas "a farmer in New York or Pennsylvania, in like moderate, but independent circumstances as to amount of property . . . , would be compelled to be one of his own continual laborers." Likewise, the Northern man's "wife would be the most unceasing drudge on the farm. His sons, and not less his daughters, would be brought up to continued labor in the lowest and most repulsive employments, and without any improving social intercourse, because its cost could not be afforded."[22] In these terms, Castle Murray was friendly to the discourse of books and letters.

Yet in another sense Murray's home, in its very thickness, seemed to acknowledge and fear an ever-greater sound of publication and other far-spreading words from without. The effect of this citadel is of a closing down, a shutting of ears: "You advise me to listen to no more of our demagogues," wrote the Fauquier County slaveholder Isham Keith in 1845, assuring his uncle that he did not listen to "those infernal abolition clans." Keith, who was of Scottish descent and lived in his own stately home called Greenbriar, also wrote to the Virginia state legislature, lamenting "that the time is not far distant" when free blacks in Fauquier County "will outnumber the slaves" and that their "idlings" will increasingly disturb the productivity and contentment of those slaves. Because this was "a state of affairs to be avoided I think by any or all means," Keith wrote, the time had come for the legislature to "take absolute control of" free blacks "and either send them to Africa or enslave them" in Fauquier and elsewhere in the state.[23]

Sheltering such writing within its walls, Castle Murray asserted the bluntness, crudeness, and even illiteracy of those on the outside. A keep of learning and culture, it made a wasteland all around it. The medieval here alludes, just as Hugo imagined, to a time before published writing, before the indiscriminate spread of opinion. The style of Murray's castle establishes—even exalts—an ideal of preliteracy or illiteracy: a time and a place when the world just *was,* when authority was established in a mountain to which all eyes turned. The little universe of Rock Hill, with slaves supporting the central house, surrounded a building that housed a privileged world of let-

Fig. 57. Timothy O'Sullivan, *Castle Murray, near Auburn, Va., November 1863*. From Alexander Gardner, *Gardner's Photographic Sketch Book of the War*, 1866 (plate 47). Library of Congress, Washington, D.C.

ters within and presented an unassailable blankness of obdurate stone to those outside its walls. These stone walls seemed to define all the words around the house—every spoken sentence—as so much futility, so much ephemera, meaningless and lost against a rock so indestructible and dumb.

This spatial scheme did not work, however. The house that was built to drown all outside communications began to trap and hold these outward sounds, letting them stroke and caress the walls built to fling them away. This shift began as soon as the war came to Fauquier County. Another of O'Sullivan's photographs of Castle Murray, from *Gardner's Photographic Sketch Book of the War* (1866), shows the Union occupation of the Rock Hill grounds in more detail (fig. 57). Gardner's accompanying caption describes Federal effects playing off the castle and its surroundings. Each creates a fleeting but somehow permanent impress of the Union forces on the Southern redoubt. One effect is aural: "The band of the Sixth U.S. Cavalry would make the stone walls ring to its martial music." The others are visual: "The slanting sun, beaming through the trees, gilded the General's banner, and tinged rosily the canvas homes" of General Pleasanton's camp in fall 1863, and "at night, the green lamps, that showed the position of the General's camp, would shine mysteriously over the trees."[24]

In one sense, these effects indicate a temporary presence on or in front of Castle Murray, like the canvas tents themselves. The inadvertent icon of this impermanence is the ghostly man standing at the lower left of O'Sullivan's photograph, who evidently grew tired of posing. Standing there, he augurs the eventual disappearance of all the tents, in contrast to the looming rock of Castle Murray itself, which stands to this day. The man and the tents represent only the buzz of ordinary life—here, just a day in camp—and by extrapolation the ephemeral quality of the phenomena Gardner describes: the martial music bouncing off the walls, the lanterns and sunlight in the trees.

Yet in another sense these everyday phenomena have an aura of permanence. The photograph is a temporary brushing up against the scene, a moment in time, that nonetheless gathers and captures the activities there, making a permanence akin to Castle Murray's own. Tents and castle are icons of a photographic gesture, both momentary and everlasting, that is itself both a tentlike inhabitation and an all-but-architectural solidity. Imagining the powers of his medium, O'Sullivan seemed to want to think of the two terms—ephemeral gesture and rocklike permanence—as not just opposed but interrelated, overlapped like the forms of the tents rising up to obscure the foundations of the castle.

The overlapping, relevant to all photographs, is especially pertinent here. The castle that was built as a citadel—meant to shed the life around it, to cast it as so much transience—is now patriotically framed as a place overrun by the daily life it had repelled, including the photographs that record it. Instead of being a definitive place in the surrounding emptiness—one that haughtily acknowledges and seems to dole out shocks of inconsequence to all its quotidian surroundings (you are just a tent, just a shack, just a soldier, just a slave)—Castle Murray has become a recorder of ephemeral effects. Perhaps its function all along had been to trap on its crenellated battlements and rusticated walls the shimmering, sliding world of passing presences it had hitherto defined as bits of demagogic meaninglessness.

The castle in O'Sullivan's photograph is vulnerable to Yankee ingenuity. The spread of tents indicates not only the hum and activity of the army—a productive legion surrounding the stately singular grace of the building—but also the rhetorical ingenuity that now turns the place that would silence all debate into a sounding board for the articulation of passing effects: light playing off trees, music playing off walls, a photograph capturing the scene. Occupied by the enemy, the castle must now play the tunes it had sought to silence. Having been a symbolic center that would repel the world, Castle Murray becomes in the photograph a place whose only significance now is to receive the chance impressions of that world, to let that world bounce off it or even glide to rest upon it.

Even the interior of the house could trap ephemeral sound. At the Fauquier Historical Society is an oak shelf board from Castle Murray. On it, written in pencil in cursive script, is a note from a Union officer, Lieutenant George W. Steele of the Twelfth Indiana Infantry, one of the occupying forces on the castle grounds. It is dated April 15, 1862: "Dear Sir, I think you would have saved the destruction of your beautiful house by remaining in it. I am much pained to see so fine a place destroyed. Yet I presume you think it none of my business either. Is it. My desire is that all good citizens shall enjoy their homes. Of course you do not fall under the above title."[25] Steele imposes his own echo on the house, taking the opportunity to write a partisan graffito on the home of an enemy that also identifies the home as now a mere site, a blank slate for expressions of daily life.

Castle Murray was not just any site, however. Its status as an isolated work of art made it an ideal ground to capture these ordinary impressions. That it was not destroyed during the war, as Steele had predicted, attested to the power of its newfound status—powerfully expressive—as a sounding board. At a time when many large homes in Fauquier and Prince William counties were destroyed by Union forces, Castle Murray was left standing, perhaps because it was such an enticing building for noting one's own passing presence—a backdrop for the graffito impressions of where and who one was (even *that* one was) in otherwise disquietingly empty surroundings. In a war-desolated area with few landmarks—it was near a nonplace called Three Mile Station, a spot with "no depot buildings," Gardner noted, that was still somehow "recognized as a stopping place"—Murray's residence was a rare monument.[26] By 1863, however, it did not so much make the world around it take shape as allow that world to come to it—to speak, pose, and write upon it, using its venerable power of place now as a way to confer a stony permanence on the vapor of ordinary life.

These Union echoes, moreover, allowed a hitherto-silenced sound of slavery to reverberate around Castle Murray. A closer look at *Castle Murray, near Auburn, Va., November, 1863* reveals that at least two of the figures in the foreground are black: the slightly blurry standing man in white sleeves

Fig. 58. Timothy O'Sullivan, *Castle Murray,* 1863. Stereograph (half). Library of Congress, Washington, D.C.

and farmer's hat and, more obscurely, the seated man in dark clothes who appears to wear a Union kepi. A stereograph that O'Sullivan took on the same day shows a black figure on the right among the foreground group (fig. 58). The presence of these black men not only allows us to see the contrabands of 1863 making their mark on the castle but also conjures the slaves of the property, reappearing at the place that aimed to make them vanish and be silent. The blur is the perfect figure for this quasi-appearance.

The blur extends also to the writings about slavery made within the walls of places like Castle Murray. By virtue of the transformation of 1862–63—in which a world silencing all outside echoes came now to record those sounds—the documents that might have been signs of the slaveholder's subjectivity begin to read more and more as impressions, blurs, of the slaves they described. For example, two other Murray brothers elsewhere in Fauquier County—no relation, apparently, to the Murray of the castle—

had differing views about the fate of some family slaves in 1860. Alfred Murray, in his will, announced that he wished to free his slaves and send them to the American Colonizing Society for passage to Liberia. His brother, James E. Murray, meanwhile, contested the act. Their disagreement brought into play the names, ages, and occupations of Alfred Murray's slaves, including Martin (a blacksmith), Benjamin (a farmhand), Burr, Peter, Mary, William, Dick, Susan, Kane, Adam, Lusinda, Robert, and Catharine.[27] Each registers as a blur, as clear as day, always gone.

We also have the case of Isham Keith, the man who fulminated against abolitionists and free blacks and who wrote in 1861 of whipping a slave named Mary Jane for burning his fence rails. The story invokes the edges of the plantation—a zone where the master's power starts to unravel—and the slave's personhood that, there all along, slowly glows into independent visibility in the very pages that would banish it. About Mary Jane, Keith writes, "I had reluctantly allowed in Oct. 1859, her mother to go into a cabin in a corner of my field in the woods and told her that she could burn as much wood as she might desire but my fence was not to be touched." But

> in a short time I found the rails from the fence disappearing. I had rails split and made them put up the fence telling them if the thing was repeated I would thrash them soundly because wood was at the door for the cutting. On the 17th inst. I found my neighbors cattle in my field among my calves. . . . They went out where the fence had been again burned by this family. Seeing this I flogged Mary Jane soundly.

Then comes retribution:

> On the 19th one of my calves died and though my suspicions were *excited* I did not examine it, but gave another free negro the hide if he would skin it, requesting him to let me know if he saw any reason or cause for its death; on the 24th another calf was found dead. I had that examined, it was black on the inside from the kidneys and its lips and hind legs were in the same condition. I suppose that mortification had taken place before its death. On the 25th I found another, the third one, not yet dead but much injured in the left shoulder. This died the next day and was found bruised from forward of the shoulder nearly to the hip, so much so that large clots of blood was found between the skin and flesh.[28]

This tale of revenge, violence, and blood makes Keith seem to wander in a ghost story of his own. As in a gothic plot, the slaves apparently leave mysterious brutal tokens for their master to find. Moreover, the story makes visible at the limits of his property—the places he can apparently least police, where murky things can happen—an alternative set of subjects. Who was this Mary Jane? Who was her mother? What about the free man? These people appear in Keith's memorandum like the figures before Castle Murray in O'Sullivan's photograph. War and emancipation give those who had seemed incidental, even invisible, a blurred presence perhaps more striking and hardy than the slaves of the abolitionist imagination—a glimpsed solidity of forgotten actions. The haunting power of these figures, to put it another way, achieves a reversal. Whereas in the previous order of things, all that was important gathered and solidified in the stone of the master's house, now the area *around* the house, the peripheral space of rails and railings, resounds with a life, echoing through the master's letters as much as upon his walls.

The ephemerality of this life is what makes it powerful. We do not see a biographical "Life" but one that is forever starting to appear. The life is held, as much by the letters and the walls as by any photograph, not in a present tense exactly but in a suspended ongoing happening. "The muffled shape stealing silently into the solemn scene has already written a hundred biographies in our imagination," Oliver Wendell Holmes, Sr., wrote in 1859, describing the fascination of blurred figures in stereographs. Of one such human blur he writes, "This is life; we seem to see her come and go. All the longings, passions, experiences, possibilities of womanhood animate that gliding shadow." For Holmes, this ghost is "nameless, dateless, featureless, yet more profoundly real than the sharpest of portraits traced by a human hand."[29] So it is with the shapes in Keith's letter and against the walls of Castle Murray.

Since those years Castle Murray has remained just a setting. But as the war receded it became *all* setting—a place that largely silenced the echoes that had begun to bounce off it in the 1860s. In 1908 the house was the location for a popular mystery novel, Mary Roberts Rinehart's *Circular Staircase,* "the story of how a middle-aged spinster lost her mind . . . and found herself involved in one of those mysterious crimes that keep our newspapers and detective agencies happy and prosperous," as the narrator describes it. In Rinehart's frivolous tale, the racial causes of the Civil War are forgotten. The death of the black butler, Thomas, offers only the slightest suggestion of Castle Murray's slaveholding past—"something fell partly forward in a heap on the floor. It was Thomas—Thomas without a mark or injury on him, and dead." But even this body—"without a mark or injury"—mystifies the violence of slavery on the site while calling attention to it.[30] Apart from the body and the titular staircase—an emblem maybe of the corkscrew distortions of a phenomenon as massively repressed in 1908 as the horrors of antebellum slavery—the book gives no meaningful blur.

In that sense Rinehart's novel is indebted to a process started during the war, one whose meaningfulness the novel nonetheless helped to end at Castle Murray. Its author inherited the Union practice of rendering the building as mere background, a setting for superimposed echoes, here her own. Yet she also effectively restored Castle Murray to its would-be antebellum simplicity. The house, as the setting for Rinehart's ghost story, loses all real echoes—all truly haunted blurs—and becomes just a generic backdrop for a popular tale whose point is to shut out these disquieting apparitions.

Back in 1863, however, Castle Murray was a place alive to crackling associations. In its then-new position as ground or echo board, it was set not only to receive messages but to become a center of life in Holmes's sense—a gathering point for trivial and accidental presences, shadows and shards, that required the notable solidity and artistic ambition of the building to confer a stony gravity of place upon them: on this spot.

Could *Macbeth* on October 17 have connected with this place? From one point of view, the play's misfortune that night was that it was too busy being whole—too busy configuring itself into a statement all of a piece, all of a purpose, that would close down all outside references, avoid all blurs, and never itself be a blur, graffito, or slanting lantern light. It was a fancy library edition, sitting beautifully on the shelf, the token of an art cut off from life. "What is the picture of a drum without the marks on its head where the beating of the sticks has darkened the parchment?" Holmes asked, extolling the realism of stereographs. Life was in the darkened parchment, carefully revealed in "the very thing which an artist would leave out, or render imperfectly."[31] The place where a white ground is developed into dark, the place where, in 1859, in 1863, white became black, is also the place where the blur of something impatient of representation, something too quick to see and excluded from representation, comes into view. The fingers turning the page, not the page itself, are the most meaningful. Yet *Macbeth* on October 17, as a perfected work of art, seemed to be only a drum without sticks, a closed book, unable to send meaningful reverberations.

Fatefully the play could accrue no lifelike superimpositions of its own. Nor could it spread its massive self outward, in monumental wholeness, to a world whose defining feature was the echo, the blur, the fragment. The play's sets, accordingly, presented only a ponderous allegorical backdrop, full of weighty significance and making a grand gesture of architectural closure somewhat like Castle Murray's antebellum one. Charlotte Cushman's script calls for the following castle settings: "Interior of the Palace at Fores," "A Room in Macbeth's Castle at Inverness," "Exterior of the Same," "Court within Macbeth's Castle," "Chamber in the Palace at Fores," "Banqueting Hall in the Palace," "Chamber within Macbeth's Castle, at Dunsinane," "Court of the Castle, "View near the Castle," "Outer Walls of the Castle."[32] As potential allusions to the gothic world outside, however, these props were silent and frozen, too big and portentous to move. As Cushman's imploring, importuning style of acting made clear, the performance searched for but seemed to lack the power to send itself out—or to receive—sudden, sensuous reverberations like the fluttering grooves of Nydia's dress, the bent echoes of a distant shot, the glimmered blur of a contact with life.

Even so, the play might still have sent forth such ghostly emanations and flighted shadows, flinging them to grounds newly ready to receive them. Each speech, for example, no matter how polished and how integral a part of the whole, might in that charged wartime environment have separated itself from the play and spun or spiraled outward into distant locations, thudding to earth the speaker knew not where. Henry Kyd Douglas suggests such a principle in his rumination on the chance effects of poetry, except in the play on October 17 it was spoken words, not published ones, that might have fancied themselves spreading out to find some right time, place, and circumstance where they could alight and be a meaningful blur. The play's words might have been a type of radio before radio, Beecher-like utterances so sonorous and urgent, so insistent on spreading across the nation, that they might have been impatient of not being broadcast like so many seeds strewn on the land. The principle of dissemination is at the heart of any story of the play's supposed allegorical relevance on October 17—for example, the tale of Lincoln staring into space after he heard certain lines of Malcolm and Macduff. Somewhere out there, these words apply; they stick.

The connection between *Macbeth* and Castle Murray is thus not allegorical. If an allegorical relation were to have occurred, it would have been only as two blank fronts simply and silently confronting one another—each a completed work of art impervious to daily life. Instead, the opportunity to hear or perceive something that resonates resides only in the momentary phantoms, the chance alightings, for which the blurred figures of O'Sullivan's photographs are our closest approximation. These figures are a sign of otherwise forgotten people, given lives worth a thousand biographies (in Holmes's sense), and, even more, embodiments of *all* resoundings, *all* happenstance impressions, that might gather, fall, and be forgotten at a site where they still leave a trace.

In this respect, maybe no words echoed more on October 17 than Lady Macbeth's "Out, damned spot." Her attempt to wash the blood from her hands may have been an allegorical sign of the slaveholder's guilt to those in the audience who wanted to construe it that way. But it may also have suggested the performance's own failure to eradicate all imperfections, all weird, unsettling allusions to life. Here the play might even have provided a gripping moment of self-reflexive drama as one of its characters contemplated the indelible stain, the mark, that would fatefully reintroduce life and therefore break the marble perfection of the museum-quality performance. Throwing from itself such an allusion, the play would comport momentarily with all such stains, spots, and blurs—all such drummings on a parchment otherwise white. The line acknowledges kinship with all stains that haunt a place, pronouncing that the play too, in ways it cannot be sure of, sends forth ghostly emanations, flighted shadows, landing and sticking who knows where but perhaps in some of the receptive places of Virginia—places newly fitted for the reception of these chance signals.

One object—a clear glass bottle—found on the grounds of Castle Murray crystallizes these relations between art and daily life in 1863 (fig. 59). Dated to 1860–80, it calls to mind Wallace Stevens's "Anecdote of the Jar," but with a key difference. In Stevens's poem, the jar is a work of art that defines the world around it, but the bottle is part of the "slovenly wilderness" that for Stevens could take shape only thanks to the ordering principle of an aesthetic gesture. Now the slovenly surroundings—the tent-strewn space of soldiers and former slaves—define Castle Murray rather than the other way around. A chance object like the bottle helps give the house historical texture, without which the building would be just a museum piece.

This idea goes beyond the notion that context shapes a work of art. It goes beyond the idea that the layers of historical association around Castle Murray make the house resonate. The bottle is an enigmatic sign. Empty and trivial, it is an incidental discovery. Yet it is also full, full of the emptiness its streamlined shape so carefully holds. This shaped emptiness of the incidental, as a historian's find, is neither meaningless nor portentously allegorical but instead a chance disruption of the artistic site where all would be whole, all complete, finished in walls of world-shunning stone. On the work of art's seamless backdrop, this disruption is manifest as a

Fig. 59. Bottle, ca. 1860–80. Fauquier Historical Society, Warrenton, Virginia. Photograph: Sonshine Pictures, Warrenton.

just-perceptible darkening, a blending of shadow and rock, without grand significance, except that it draws the eye again and again.

Macbeth on October 17 might have sent such random disruptions. It may also have been ready to receive them. Back at Grover's, the performance could have acknowledged that it was most whole when it presented itself as just a site ready to receive signals from elsewhere. Only then might it imagine itself as a setting for the chance superimpositions that could bring it to life. Those superimpositions might be invisible to the audience and to the participants but be felt nonetheless, as a shaped emptiness in the air. Indeed, perhaps the purpose of the play was to gather, as Charlotte Cushman hoped she might, some signal, some chance saying or presence from the world outside that it could *not* turn effortlessly into part of its broad exhortation of national purpose. The next chapter attends to one such trace within the walls of the theater.

SIX

Ghosts

The Death of Colonel Thomas Ruffin, October 17, 1863

ACROSS THE POTOMAC, in Alexandria, Virginia, the Confederate colonel Thomas Ruffin died the night *Macbeth* was performed. Wounded in a skirmish at Auburn, Virginia, near Castle Murray, early in the morning of October 14—at the start of the fighting that ended later that day at Bristoe Station—Ruffin had been taken to Alexandria as a prisoner of war and died there at Grace Church Hospital.[1]

Ruffin's death had no bearing on the performance on the other side of the river. Probably some people in attendance knew who he was, but few knew that he was a prisoner, and no one knew that he died or would die that night. But his death dramatizes a reality that the play could not put onstage even though it made allowance for it: the daily presence of death in the Washington area during the war.

"What may be the number of soldiers who, since the commencement of the war, have died in hospitals and camps, in and about Washington, out of the very many thousands who have come to the capital, there is probably no means of definitely ascertaining," a writer noted in the *Daily National Intelligencer* on October 17. Discussing the soldiers' graveyard near the Soldiers' Home, the site of Lincoln's summer cottage, the writer noted, "There have been over seven thousand interments of the remains of soldiers, of which about five thousand bodies still remain—the other two thousand having been disinterred by relatives."[2]

In Washington in 1863 the Civil War dead were starting to be the living presence that they fully became many years later, according to Drew Gilpin Faust, when their vast numbers demanded proper commemoration. Then, in the postwar reburial movement, they "gathered together in mass cemeteries with graves marshaled in ranks like soldiers on the field of battle," Faust writes, "a constituency of the slain, insistent in both its existence and its silence, men whose very absence from American life made them a presence that could not be ignored."[3] But even before they were a constituency, the dead might still have created a presence—equally insistent and silent—in wartime Washington and elsewhere.

If these dead haunted *Macbeth* on October 17, how might they have done so? Would they have inhabited the banquet scene, where the guilt-wracked Macbeth alone among the diners spots the ghost of Banquo, the close friend whom he has ordered killed? "Never shake / Thy gory locks at me," Lester Wallack's Macbeth would have screamed while his guests and wife look on, amazed:

> If charnel houses and our graves must send
> Those that we bury back, our monuments
> Shall be the maws of kites. (3.4.51–52, 72–74)
>
> Avaunt, and quit my sight! Let the earth hide thee!
> Thy bones are marrowless, thy blood is cold;
> Thou hast no speculation in those eyes
> Which thou dost glare with. (3.4.94–97)

Yet *Macbeth*'s dramatization of death might have generated little superstition that night. The reviews give little indication that the bloody, apparition-haunted play induced an especially eerie feeling in its audience. (One reviewer, in fact, noted the audience's "enthusiastic" response.) As an official utterance, the play had to quell real phantoms and replace them with theatrical conjurings such as Banquo's ghost. The moments of deathly fright, in other words, may have been the moments of exorcism—when the dim and the dead would lie all the more secure in their thickets and piles of dirt, *un*conjured, unseen, at the moment when the symbolic rites of particular words pushed rocks over their graves. The dead would actually vanish at the moment when a ghost appeared onstage, garbed in a symbolic raiment of blood smear and chalk. Even watching Banquo's spirit, the audience might have shared the incredulous reaction of Lady Macbeth and the banqueters, who cannot see what Macbeth sees. "What sights, my lord?" asks Ross (3.4.118).

Yet there is another way to envision the presence of death—Ruffin's death, for example—at the performance. We can think of the ubiquity of death then and there as a faint mortal smudge on the play's simple backdrops, the warrior signs of battlement and tower. Presumably those sets were made by D. A. Strong, the man who painted the proscenium and "all the scenic accessories" for the theater's opening-season performance of *Othello* on October 6. Maybe the *Macbeth* sets, like those for *Othello,* were "capitally done," as a newspaper reported.[4] D. A. Strong was maybe like Richard Thornton, the scene painter in Mary Braddon's novel *Eleanor's Victory,* advertised in *Harper's Weekly* on October 17, whose job was "to paint the best part of the scenery for a large theatre in which new pieces are brought out pretty frequently," and to give each set a well-studied "glue and pasteboard" plausibility, perfectly legible to the last row.[5] But on this legible heraldry, through no fault of Strong's, we must imagine a small spatial breakdown, a telltale smudge or spot where the illusionistic perspective becomes confused.

This spot would be a place where space simultaneously narrows and expands—where narrowing and expanding spaces combine, through and through, to produce a disturbance that is neither vast nor small but some hallucinated flexing of the two: a vista of contracted density. Mortality would be a disruption on the heraldic field of controlled accounts, a place where the clear scene sways and shimmers.

The spot would be lawless—a moment, a place, where something fails to keep ranks. At the soldiers' graveyard the life of the dead was efficient, a symbol of order: "These interments are systematically made," the *Daily National Intelligencer* noted, "with every grave marked, and a record accurately kept of the name, date, military organization . . . so that, as a general thing, the visitor may always find the tomb of any of the departed in whom he may be interested."[6] Against this coherence—a nascent part of the efforts described by Faust to manage the vast numbers of Civil War dead—the *moment* of death was something different. It was the buzzing of a fly, in Emily Dickinson's words, the moment when small things take on an unwonted strangeness:

> The last night that she lived,
> It was a common night,
> Except the dying; this to us
> Made nature different.
>
> We noticed smallest things,—
> Things overlooked before,

By this great light upon our minds
Italicized, as 'twere.[7]

The fate that night of Thomas Ruffin, had it been known, could have fit any of the allegories the play offered to audience members—the death of a traitor, the demise of a brave rebel—depending on their political inclinations. But the moment of death, whenever it occurred that night, represented one of those "italicized" instants, common in and around Washington during the war, that never quite resolved into stories set down on page and stone. "A pause, a hush" is how Walt Whitman describes "the murder of Abraham Lincoln" (the moment of the shot counting as a moment of death for the man who would not regain consciousness before he died the next morning). That pause in the theater was "a passing blur, a dream, a blotch," transpiring "with the quiet and simplicity of any commonest occurrence—the bursting of a bud or pod in the growth of vegetation, for instance." It was an unremarkable instant not unlike the fate of any soldier, "North or South, East or West," whose moment of death occurs in "some bush-clump, or ferny tuft," who soaks "roots, grass and soil" in his blood before dying on that "secluded spot."[8] The moment of death for Whitman is an unknown vegetal blur around which the arts of embalmer, eulogist, and political strategist spring up like concentric circles of ruddy-faced explanation. Above that death then rise monuments like pasteboard flats of national purpose, while still higher up adoring angels transport the soul to its place of rest. Yet all the while the moment of death remains hidden, saturated, an unreadable blotch at the center of things.

Could the play have represented some moment, some place, when all for once was not explained away? Could it have harbored some clearing where the ordinary flow of time was suspended, pushed away, so that, for just a moment, another world might be glimpsed? To ask this question is to be at once absurdly hypothetical and historically accurate. On the one hand, the answer is as unknowable as the evanescent discernments of individual members of the audience that night, passing reflections that were obscure perhaps even to them let alone to a latter-day interpreter. On the other hand, how could a play of bloody murder and civil war performed in wartime Washington fail to conjure the fate of the war's many dead, and not just the fate but the moment of death, the moment *before* the symbolic efficiencies and aggrandizements the play set out to exemplify, when the slanted strangeness of the blur might manifest itself in some anamorphosis cutting across the splendidly legible world? If that distortion was as fleeting as a single spoken line—indeed, more so, because it never cohered into a recognizable representation for the actors or for the audience—one phenomenon from that performance remains: the ability of the smudge to outlast the polite representation it has defaced.

And was the blur just itself? Did it contain only the unknowable mystery of bursting pod and ferny tuft, the hallucinated swim of a castle angle fogged into streaked grayness, a distortion without meaning? Or did the moment of death contain more than these dissolutions? Did it contain in fact a whole world that could be envisioned, if not "read," and that could be understood, within its waves and swirls, as holding not just a death but a life—a life's story—within it?

Think of the questions that must have coursed in Washington during the war, sometimes expressed in sad letters and diaries but extending well beyond these documents. Who was this person who just died? Who was the person I knew, the person my friend knew? What was his life? Arguably the deepest potential of the performance on October 17 was to attract these thoughts of life and death. Only nominally, in a puffed estimate of its own importance, was the play a work of remote and sacrosanct art, cut loose from life. Its greatest potential was to be a rough-sketched forceful backdrop on which audience members could project the wartime worries and haunted spots that preoccupied them. Adam Gurowski's "We are at *guessing,*" written on the night of October 17, suggests this ready atmosphere of surmise and speculation. In a time when theatergoing was becoming an increasingly private experience, as Bruce McConnachie has described—when each member of the audience was alone with his or her thoughts under the dimming lights—a play might readily conceive itself as a receiving ground for many points of view.

The audience might still lose itself in a perfected drama, set off in the realm of Art, without apparent reference to their own attitudes. But the play at its most powerful might have been an occasion for people to think. The thought would not be exactly of Shakespeare, Cushman, or other unapproachable grandiosities or sterling messages to humankind, but of other people and places—gathered by chance in mordant association—that might accrue to sturdy structures of art in a time of war. In fact, at its best the play would be a ready-painted set, inviting an audience's *lost* focus: an occasion for a person to wonder about that sight or thought over there—that disturbance, vague space, or daydream. What is that? What was that?

Only the most exalted of these associations would matter. The trifling ones would fall away. Who is to measure the layers of ordinary reverie and distraction that accumulated that night like dust on the play's venerable surface? Those meanderings—thoughts of work, thoughts of him, thoughts of her, glancing perceptions or preoccupations, a stare at the ceiling, at the floor, the steady contemplation of a crumpled paper—would be a more uneventful loss of focus. The inconsequence of a thousand social interactions, the ebb and flow of gossip and news sharing—the hum of conversation as the audience gathered for the performance—must have flowed across the space like a wave of insects. It would even be the purpose of the play to ceremonially cancel all that daily life. Shakespeare would not only transcend ordinary experience, as in Thomas De Quincey's definition, but steal it, evaporating each grain of sand, each ordinary moment, as the life's blood of its own immortality. The theater space meanwhile would be an impassive accomplice, trapping and canceling the vagaries of what went on there, recasting the breath and boredom of a million gestures and idle thoughts as only more of the luster glowing dully from the woodwork.

Yet the play would also have invited less random associations. Attuned to the actions onstage, these associations would gather before the play much as the men and tents stand before Castle Murray in O'Sullivan's images: tokens of a solemn awareness, a recognition that one is beholding a special work of art, a kind of *there,* built up for the purpose, for which one had better compose oneself into a rough-and-ready dignity befitting the opportunity. The tent is to the castle as the individual association is to *Macbeth*—a crude temporary structure, without pretense to grandiosity or permanence, that yet can enliven the grand building, *if* it recognizes the place, *if* it arrays itself in quiet ordinary dignity around it, even if the purpose of this temporary dwelling proves to be nothing less than a reversal or misreading of the grand structure before which it sits.

On October 17 the most solemn of the play's associations might have been thoughts of death, of fate, of last moments—of all that art could be a ground for. Such is the type of "horrible shadow" (3.4.107) the play readies itself to receive. When Malcolm says to Macduff, "Let us seek out some desolate shade and there / Weep our sad bosoms empty," starting the exchange about the costs of war that seemed to affect Lincoln, the audience had a similar reaction. It became "suddenly silent as the grave" in the theater, according to Frazar Kirkland. In that quietness, Macduff's reply was not only a commentary on the times—this was only its most basic and ritually exorcising feature—but a meditation on the way the implacable play, as a fixed structure of art, might yet reverberate and even cry out itself if it could attract enough lamentation, enough personal association, which on October 17 it might sometimes have done:

> Each new morn
> New widows howl, new orphans cry, new sorrows
> Strike heaven on the face, that it resounds
> As if it felt with Scotland and yelled out
> Like syllable of dolor. (4.3.4–8)

The play, like heaven, would receive the cry of widows and orphans until it too began to speak or cry. It would speak not in its own words, or in the actors' sentiments, or even as an echo of the audience's thoughts but rather, like water from a stone, as some autonomous emanation extracted, made palpable, only in response to a dense crush of forces at just the right moment—a geological release of some element that, on most nights, would go unexpressed. The perfection of a place beyond reach, beyond the earth, of a play that seemingly no mortal could have conceived, then would sound dolorously in response to private sorrows. On the glass case of the performance, as at the Patent Office hospital, reflections of souls would blur upon the transparency of polished display. Even if the performers themselves might have been blind to those personal investments—even if they could not possibly attend to every face among the twenty-five hundred in the audience that night—these actors and actresses must have known that their lines were opportunities to attract these chance smudges and miraculous distortions.

The silence of the theater and the sound of the performers' words would in fact exactly and ceremonially *reverse* the process the play really invited—for it was the audience, even in its quiet, that would have the most to say. At its best, the play would create a buzz of loud thinking, a hum of private thought, that would drown the boldest of its speeches into so much pantomime. The linear sharpness of Strong's sets and Cushman's words would only be wires to attract this melting haze of association. Perhaps such distortions might even have flown thickly that night, attracted by almost every line and every gesture, in a play still moving resolutely through its line-by-line motions. If a play were to be meaningful in wartime Washington, it would have to allow for these existential thoughts—accruing to itself in the chance reflections of spectators—of the experiences a morbid wartime play could stage but never fully explain: death, dying, the moment of death itself.

The play, in this sense, would enact another kind of biography than the kind springing up about Civil War figures, living and dead. The chance it gave to think—to be alone with one's thoughts—was an opportunity to wonder about lives. More precisely, it gave a different shape to those lives. The moment of death in wartime might be not just the expiration of a last breath but the container for a whole lifetime's experiences that now took a final shape.

A soldier's death shaped his life. The moment of death held his life within it, frozen in the glass of it, so that, tipping the glass this way and that, watching the shadows and reflections play, wondering if they are somehow inside the glass or only skittering along its surface, the beholder might find much to ponder, even a great weight to contemplate, in the empty container. The glass shape housing these phantasms would not be a tomb-closing epithet such as the Confederate soldier Henry Berkeley's pronouncement on the Union men his regiment had killed, "Such is War." Nor would it be the surgeon John Perry's sad addendum on Colonel Mallon: "He was just married."[9] It would be instead a commemoration made of the moment of death, where the glass shape *is* the gasped breath and the shining eye, hardened into a container for the mysteries they murkily reveal.

Let us look inside Thomas Ruffin's life, treating it as a smudge on the play. A far-from-random disturbance, the blur of his life opens up a whole other set of spaces—a life's story, expanding and contracting—on the surface of the performance. Let us visit the southern Missouri town of Bolivar, where Ruffin (born in 1820) went to practice law after graduating in 1841 from the University of North Carolina in his native state. The Polk County Court House in Bolivar symbolized the prospective spatial power of the law in this rural location (fig. 60). The county had been organized only a few years before, in 1835, with a range of fifty-four miles from east to west and thirty-one miles from north to south. It was a place of Osage Indians, abandoned flint and limestone mines, a few remaining panthers ruthlessly treed and killed by settlers, a bridge of barely submerged huge logs made from the remnants of a dam, fields of prairie grass with seed stems as tall as a man, and sod so unyielding that teams of four to eight oxen had to pull a beam fourteen feet across and cut ten inches deep to break it.[10] In the center of Bolivar, the county seat, the courthouse symbolically established law and order over this rough space. Ruffin registered as an attorney there on June 26, 1843.[11]

The courthouse neatly fronted all four directions, spreading dominion and seeming to aspire to make every blade of grass and shard of flint sit up under the impress of its four-square pretense to order. Around the fence enclosing it, the tied horses of residents indicated that they would come to

Fig. 60. Polk County Court House, Bolivar, Missouri, ca. 1850. Polk County Genealogical Society, Bolivar, Missouri.

this place of law just as surely as it would extend outward to them. An 1841 plan of Bolivar shows the neatly laid out town with the courthouse square at its center (fig. 61). Two blocks north of the courthouse, at square number 3 on the map, Ruffin owned lots 3 and 5, where he helped shape the region in which he was so near the center.[12]

For a white man in Polk County, bodily sovereignty was as important as spatial dominion. Indeed it was the same thing. In a case on September 29, 1845, Ruffin tried Absolem and Loretta Baker for their attack on a relative, a man they did "strike beat bruise and wound in and upon the head face and arms" with "certain large stones," so that he was "then and there greatly . . . wounded and disfigured and received great bodily harm." The crime was committed not only against this man but "against the peace and dignity of the State," as Ruffin wrote in a court statement.[13] As much as the trial itself, Ruffin's legal prose and neat handwriting asserted the power of the law to make a salient space around this man, to wrap him in a protection that would also protect the entire civilizing project of the state. This man's body was a representative of the state of Missouri which, in turn, inhered in his physical presence.

Owning slaves increased one's power of personal and spatial dominion.

Fig. 61. Plan of Bolivar, Missouri, 1841. Polk County Genealogical Society, Bolivar, Missouri.

Ruffin owned one slave valued at $300, according to the 1844 Tax Assessment Book for Polk County. Other than perhaps his real estate, the slave was by far Ruffin's most valuable possession, far surpassing his horse ($30) and watch ($10).[14] Possessing a slave was not unheard of in Polk County, which stood in proslavery country. "Many of the early settlers had come from the south, and . . . they and their sons were fully imbued with the southern idea of the defensibility of slavery," a late nineteenth-century report noted. Another resident of the county, for example, had brought three slaves with him from Virginia. Ruffin most likely would not have moved to the Ozark region if that part of Missouri did not largely support slavery. He had come from a significant slave-owning family in North Carolina: his father, Henry John Gray Ruffin, was "owner of a large number of negroes and large tracts of land."[15]

In Bolivar Ruffin's ownership of a slave gave him a further measure of prestige, an additional command of space, liberating him from daily chores and allowing him a greater chance to make his reputation and protect the sovereignty of other white persons. Several hundred miles away, in central and eastern Illinois, Abraham Lincoln was then busy practicing law in county-seat courthouses not unlike the one in Polk County, Missouri, but between Ruffin and Lincoln was the widest gulf. When Lincoln went to Congress, he gave his Spot Resolutions speech against President Polk's Mexican War to expand slavery, but Ruffin volunteered for that war, getting as far as Fort Leavenworth, Kansas, before his unit, the Third Regiment of Missouri Volunteers, was disbanded, on September 29, 1846.[16]

Ruffin's convictions led him to expand his domain further—into the realm of national politics, where he put forth views about the mutual unassailability of a white person (here himself) and a set of space-controlling political principles: those of the Democratic Party. Having returned to North Carolina by 1850, he ran for office, competing against the Whig incumbent, Edward Stanly, in a race for one of North Carolina's seats in the House of Representatives. Stanly was a "master of ridicule and sarcasm, and it is said that no man could stand before his brilliant sallies of sparkling wit and humor, and the remorseless darts of his withering invective," wrote a historian in the early twentieth century. But when Stanly began mocking his opponent in a debate, "Ruffin at once sprang from his seat and walked up in front of Stanly and pointing his finger at him and looking him squarely in the eye," threatened to kill him. Stanly desisted, ended up barely winning the vote, and left the state before the next election, which Ruffin won.[17] In those years when the opening of new territory, free or slave, was the crucial political issue, Ruffin went to Washington in 1853 as a Democrat intent on protecting and expanding the spaces of the slave owner, defending the South's right to secede, and fighting all those, such as Stanly, who would attempt to enforce "the unconstitutional acts and intolerable oppression" of the federal government and the abolitionists.[18]

In Washington, where he served until 1861, Ruffin affirmed the power of the slave owner to stand at the center of the world. In a speech before the House on February 27, 1855, he proclaimed slavery "one of the greatest moral, social and political blessings that was ever vouchsafed to man." By then he had inherited the Gulley Plantation in Johnson County, North Carolina, including fifty slaves. Ruffin's views were undoubtedly similar to those of Edmund Ruffin, a friend and relation who is widely remembered even now as the man who fired the first shot of the Civil War. Edmund (1794–1865), an educated planter, wrote proslavery tracts such as *The Political Economy of Slavery,* published in 1857, which Thomas Ruffin used his Senate privileges to frank for him. Edmund's opinions in that pamphlet might as well have been Thomas's: "Slavery has ever been the means, if it is not the only possible means, of civilizing barbarous tribes and regions, spreading the culture of the earth, and instructing the most ignorant and degraded races of men."[19]

The spatial power of the master was predominant—even when he was not present. Thomas Ruffin grew up in a North Carolina newly defined by a ruling that became nationally and even internationally famous—*State v. Mann* (1830), an opinion given by an older relative also named Thomas Ruffin (1787–1870), a member of the state's supreme court. The elder Ruffin ruled that John Mann, who had rented a slave from her master and beaten her, should not be charged with battery. Even though Mann was not the master, he had the master's rights: "the hirer of a slave succeeded for the duration of the term of hire to all the rights of owner." Though the elder Ruffin had personal misgivings about the ruling, he determined that in a time of abolitionist ferment, the greatest danger to the public welfare was the threat of slave revolt. Any court ruling favoring slaves, he reasoned, could cause the enslaved to denounce "the injustice of slavery itself, and, upon that pretext, band together to throw off their common bondage entirely."[20] As the younger Ruffin himself might well have believed, the master must be everywhere, even where he was not.

In Washington, Ruffin believed that the proslavery politician needed to carve a space around himself—to beat back, if necessary, those who assailed him. On August 2, 1856, speaking in Congress, he excoriated "the history of Black Republicanism in this House" and cited a specific example: the forced resignation of Preston Brooks, representative from South Carolina. Less than three months earlier, on May 22, Brooks had committed the most outrageous act of physical violence ever seen on the Senate floor, caning Massachusetts senator Charles Sumner in response to Sumner's antislavery speech a few days before.

Brooks subsequently resigned his position, and Ruffin's construction of the meaning of these events is extraordinary. "Representatives sent here by the people have been harassed, hunted down, and, in effect, driven from this Hall, for entertaining political principles antagonistic to those of a majority here," he told his fellow congressmen. "Yes, sir; members, pandering to the morbid appetite of northern fanaticism, have deprived South Carolina of two of her Representatives on this floor—Messrs. Brooks and Keitt."[21] Ruffin claimed that the grievous injustice was suffered not by the brutally beaten Sumner but by Brooks and his fellow South Carolinian Laurence Keitt. It was not escaped slaves but Brooks and Keitt who had been "hunted down." For Ruffin, the politician who had threatened to kill Edward Stanly if he impugned his dignity, Brooks was the gentleman forcefully protecting his space, beating Sumner as a master would his slave.

The Southern slaveholder stood tall, for Ruffin, by showing the stooped deformity of those outside his orbit. Horace Greeley, as Ruffin described him in his speech of 1856, was "a queer looking New York editor, an unfortunate specimen of nature's handicraft, a living libel on humanity, who, day after day, was to be seen lounging with apparent listlessness there, like a certain foul old bird on the bough of a dead tree."[22] To Ruffin the Know-Nothing Party member was "a little, scrawny, rickety scrofulous bantling, that had not strength to stand upon his legs."[23] The "agrarian mobs" of the North, "the very scum of the earth, parade the streets by thousands," representing "that section of the country where weak-minded men, crazy fanatics, meet in convention with strong-minded women clothed in boots and breeches, to discuss the important question of women's rights."[24] Hessian mercenaries in Washington, "reeling and staggering in drunken revelry," intruded upon the true man's space and affronted his dignified self-control. So did "the obsequious miscreants and crouching menials" of the Republican Party; likewise "the vitiated taste of the cross-roads demagogue and political charlatan of the tippling shop."[25]

In contrast, poetry shaped and freed the Southern white man. Ruffin's 1839 junior-class essay at the University of North Carolina answered the question "Is it probable that poetry will ever be brought to a high degree of excellency in the United States?" Ruffin thought yes, eventually, and he cited liberty as the reason: "For some of the most celebrated [poets] of any age or nation lived in free countries and almost seem to have caught inspiration from freedom."[26] He meant the liberty occasioned by slavery, his views according with those of Edmund Ruffin, who would note that "the extensive use and employment of African slaves" occurred in "the same remarkable epoch when the European mind, and European enterprise, received their greatest impulse, and made the greatest improvements."[27]

For Thomas Ruffin, greatness in poetry traveled around the world, thriving where the republics were. First it had "floated around the Grecian isles / And made melodious all the hills of Rome," he explained in the junior-class essay. Then the muse of poetry, which "does not seem to be content to live for a long time in one land," had gone to England, "distinguished above all other nations for the number and quality of her poets," including Milton, whose *Paradise Lost* was "perhaps the best poem ever written." Eventually the genius of poetry might come to America if the country could suppress its "love of wealth" and appreciate the arts of cultivation.

Ruffin's turns of phrase as a political speaker implied that, for him, the liberating spirit of poetry had alighted in the American South. His congressional allusions to *Macbeth*'s blood and omens were a part of this cultivation. The "slavery agitators in the North" had made Kansas a place "drenched in human gore," where "pro-slavery and anti-slavery men . . . lie in their cold and bloody graves in the wilderness, where the wolf of the forest howls their requiem, and the owl, the ill-boding bird of night, shrieks their death-dirge." When unqualified men replaced senior generals, "the eagle . . . [was] stricken from his eyre to put the mousing owl there."[28] The poetic flourish was finally the same as the partisan flag of the slaveholding party sweeping the land: "It floats proudly in the breeze that sweeps the Atlantic coast; and, in distant California, from the golden shores washed by the blue surges of the Pacific, its inspiring folds reflect the last departing rays of the setting sun, as, far westward, it sinks into the briny deep."[29] Each—the coast-to-coast vision and the poetic language used to describe it—expressed the freedom of the slaveholding man.

In the early morning of October 14, 1863, however, Ruffin's expansive world began to contract. He had resigned his position in Congress shortly after his last formal speech in the House in February 1861 and returned to his home state, where he joined the newly formed First North Carolina Cavalry as a captain. In late June 1862 he was captured during the Seven Days' Battles in Virginia, sent to a military prison near Boston, and returned to the South in a prisoner exchange in early August. The following year he was wounded at Gettysburg but returned to active service. In Auburn on the night of October 13, 1863, now with the rank of colonel, he was among the members of General J. E. B. Stuart's cavalry who were cut off by a movement of the Union Army's Second Corps, which did not know Stuart was there. Stuart and his men hid in the valley of Cedar Run, a wooded ravine within a short distance of Federal troops, as they awaited morning and a chance to escape.

What did Ruffin see and hear that night and the following morning? Each impression might have intensified sensuous experience, vivified and italicized it, because these were dangerous moments when each sight and sound mattered a great deal and because, as it happened, these hours were the last sentient ones he spent on earth. Hidden in the woods, Stuart and his men could see across a grassy field to a ridge about 150 yards away, where lines of Federal troops marched all night long. "Almost every man, it seemed, carried a lantern which gave the scene a very picturesque effect in the dark, still night," recalled Stuart's aide, William Willis Blackford. From their hidden position, Stuart's men could hear the Union soldiers' conversation even as they tried to keep their own camp silent. "It was necessary to place a man at the head of every mule in the ambulances to keep them from betraying our presence," Blackford wrote, "for the poor beasts needed food and water" and had to be quieted. Lying on a slope to watch the passing Union soldiers, amid the pine thickets and near the small creek of Cedar Run, Stuart fell asleep, his head on Blackford's stomach.[30] Ruffin was somewhere in those same thickets.

Early the next morning, Stuart ordered his artillery to open fire on Federal troops making camp nearby, and Ruffin was selected to spearhead a charge at the Union position, in the hope of allowing Stuart's command to escape. Riding directly into the ranks of the 125th and 126th New York Infantry Regiments, Ruffin was shot and fell from his horse, and then left behind as the cavalry retreated, the attack having failed. A Union cavalry officer came by and took his sword. Ruffin, still conscious, felt that his wound was mortal and gave a Union sergeant his money and his watch (probably the same one he had had since his days in Missouri), with instructions to send them back to his relatives in North Carolina.[31]

Then a new person appeared in front of him. The Union chaplain Thomas G. Grassie came over to Ruffin, who, trusting this new man more, asked him to retrieve the watch and money from the sergeant (the items were apparently never found). Grassie, born in Kildrummie, Aberdeenshire, Scotland, in 1831, a resident of Massachusetts from the age of ten, had been ordained at the South Church in Andover only six months before. In all his future service as a pastor—in Richmond, Maine; Methuen, Massachusetts;

Sycamore, Illinois; Keokuk, Iowa; and Appleton, Oshkosh, and Milwaukee, Wisconsin, until he died in 1898—he perhaps retained a portable impression of Ruffin.[32] But Ruffin's world was contracting. As others carried away his possessions—"Heir-looms were very transitory valuables to carry into battle," the historian of the 108th New York, Grassie's regiment, noted—and as others, like Grassie, took his image (the memory of him shedding in layers for anyone wanting a copy)—Ruffin began to diminish.

Transported back to Grace Church Hospital in Alexandria, in the care of a surgeon and attendants, Ruffin found himself in a small space as physically limited as his hold on life, a pocket of comatose quiet amid the surrounding chaos of the Virginia town. "Such a place as it was there—a perfect Bedlam; all confusion," recalled Septima M. Collis, who traveled to Alexandria in fall 1863 on her way to visit her wounded husband, a Union officer. "The muddy streets thronged with negroes and affrighted cattle; wounded soldiers staring with amazement at the young woman in civilized attire who seemed dropped among them from the clouds, I suppose; and drunken recruits and conscripts singing ribald songs." For the adventurous Collis, writing years later, nothing in the world compared with Alexandria:

> I have crossed the Atlantic a dozen times; have been in a collision in mid-ocean; and will carry to the grave the recollection of the agonizing cries of the drowning victims; have stood upon the crater of Vesuvius during an eruption; have lived in a railroad construction camp on the Rocky Mountains, with its ruffians, its gamblers, and its Chinamen; have made an ascent in a balloon; have seen a Cinnamon bear within fifty yards of me; have for nights slept upon the bare floor of an isolated log-hut amidst the geysers of the Yellowstone; had a volley of rifle-balls whistle around my ears; yet never in my experience did my heart throb as nervously as when I was alone in the streets of Alexandria.[33]

Maybe the tumult of Alexandria was part of the dreamy atmosphere sporting above Ruffin's head on October 17, as in an illustrator's vignette of a dying person's recollections: first, the swinging lanterns of the Union soldiers, the foggy morning of the charge, the face of Thomas Grassie; then, around these visions at a further radius, like outer stars or lesser dignitaries, the ribald soldiers and citizens of drunken, confused Alexandria. All these visions, whatever they were, came to rest where Ruffin was. The gods beaming from balconies of cloud were not kindly deities but a motley, quixotic array, the happenstance lords of a particular place and time, bearing inscrutable attributes of lantern, blood, and pine. And still more outward, beyond those

Fig. 62. Burial ground, Louisburg, North Carolina, including tomb of Thomas Ruffin. Photograph: Ray Strawbridge.

gods, the experiences of the life would also gather, even the places of that life—Missouri, North Carolina—and even the documents of the life, the written records summoned across the miles from their remote locations of dusty book and desk, the cabinets having opened, seemingly by themselves. They all would come to rest at that point, vanishing in an empty bottle that, shown to the light, still reveals the half-phantasm of a stain.

How was Ruffin's death commemorated? The space around the dead person might expand, it is true. Having narrowed to a single point, the dead man's world might now in death breathe again, spreading around the body an allegorical set of spirits attesting to the significance of the life. "No sparrow falls to the ground" without the knowledge of the Divine Power, resolved the noncommissioned officers and privates of Ruffin's Company H at a camp near Culpeper Court House on November 3, remembering their dead leader. The tiniest point is a node in a vast domain overseen by "the Ruler of all."[34]

Last words, last rites: these too conferred space on the dead person. On Sunday, October 18, Ruffin's body was placed in a vault in the Methodist Protestant burial ground in Alexandria. Unlike the vast majority of Civil War fatalities, dumped with little fanfare in common, unmarked, or simply

Fig. 63. Thomas Ruffin's tomb, Louisburg, North Carolina. Photograph: Ray Strawbridge.

designated graves, laid to rest beneath "row after row of identical markers," Ruffin received more elaborate and personal funerary services, not once but twice.[35] After the war his body was brought back to Louisburg, North Carolina, and reinterred in the family cemetery on the plantation grounds (fig. 62). His grave is the middle and most tilted one in the nearest row of three slabs, the one with the full play of shadows atop it in the photograph. The writing on that tomb gives some spatial legibility to the life, supplanting the blur of death (fig. 63). The inscription marks specific places, Alexandria,

Fig. 64. Ruffin's tomb, Louisburg, North Carolina. Photograph: Ray Strawbridge.

Bristoe Station (the latter technically incorrect), that helped shape the dead person's world, establishing a range of reference well beyond the cemetery's stone walls. Independent of what it says, the inscription itself—chiseled in the stone—establishes a principle of order, creating meaning on what would otherwise be only so much planar blankness.

Yet the inscription appears in the photograph only by virtue of a bit of magic. One day in 2005 a local man named Joseph Pearce took me to Ruffin's tomb, where not surprisingly we found the chiseled words to be so eroded as to be nearly unreadable. Only when Pearce dusted the slab with cornmeal did the inscription wondrously appear, as good as new (fig. 64). (The cornmeal is also visible as the light patches on the tomb in figure 62. The photographer, Ray Strawbridge, manipulated figure 63 to omit evidence of the cornmeal.) When Pearce made the letters on the tomb appear, the date of October 17, 1863, was especially stunning to me, and so was the equally clear metaphor for history. The past comes out of nowhere, emerging from moribund tilted blankness, suddenly and as clear as day to the person who happens upon it.

Yet the revelation hid a more important historical metaphor, one having to do with blankness. This blankness was much more than a sign of the toll of years, the melancholy effects of the passage of time dooming the historian to a latter-day effort to reconstruct what was once clear. It seemed to indicate an *original* inscrutability—not just of that day and that person but of his moment of death and of the life contained in that moment. The performance of *Macbeth* on October 17, no less than the inscription on Ruffin's tomb, was an epitaph giving meaning to unknowable blankness, bestowing breadth and legibility on the vanishing points where lives condensed and came to rest. The real trick of history, however, would be to understand such writing and speaking as only a ground for the revelation of blankness, rather than the other way around. The underlying ground, in turn, would not be exactly unimaginable but would contain all sorts of traces and other half-articulations. These smudges on the rock, abraded and mute, comprising all the world of the not-said, would be the emptiness that official declarations make visible. To glimpse that wordless ground is to touch the wartime questions—who was this person? what was his life?—that gathered to the performance of the play.

SEVEN

Sound and Fury

Nature in Virginia

THE PLAY THAT NIGHT SENT ITS SIGNALS into nature. As much as it hoped to affect the world around it—the city of Washington, the buildings and battlefields of Virginia—the play tried also, strange as that might seem, to imprint itself on the very leaves and streams of the natural world. To consider how it did this, and failed to do this, is to think of the work of art in the age of evolution, especially in a time of civil war. Under such pressures, nature would either be hospitable to human acts or would increasingly crowd around those acts, staring back with alien eyes. In the latter case the natural ground ready to receive the impress of human achievement would be blank. The performance at its most powerful would conspire to reproduce this blankness within itself, to acknowledge that it, too, meant nothing, and to acknowledge, in a final fit of glory, that the work of art could express this nothingness better than anything else in the world—in a petulant, forceful little act, stamped in one place, a mark made: I was here.

If nature *was* hospitable, however, then there would be no limit to the play's power to make a mark. Its marks would extend across all grounds and even out to the stars. At the time of the performance of *Macbeth* on October 17, 1863, people just might still find it possible to think in such improbable terms, as they had right before the war, just before the publication of Charles Darwin's *Origin of Species* in 1859. The performance came when science and religion could still combine to imagine an earth and even a cosmos receptive to human achievements, and when the telegraph and the photograph were conceived as wondrous technologies that could record such supernatural contact.

"Men fancy that the wave of oblivion passes over the greater part of their actions," Edward Hitchcock, a professor of theology and geology at Amherst College, wrote in *The Religion of Geology and Its Connected Sciences,* published in 1851. "But physical science shows us that those actions have been transfused into the very texture of the universe, so that no waters can wash them out, and no erosions, communication, or metamorphoses, can obliterate them." Thus, for Hitchcock, "Material creation receives an impression from all our words and actions that can never be effaced. *Our words, our actions, and even our thoughts, make an indelible impression on the universe.*"[1] Thrown into a poetic form, this principle converts creation

Into a vast sounding gallery
Into a vast picture gallery;
And into a universal telegraph.

This "telegraphic system of the universe," as Hitchcock called it, relies on the butterfly effect: "The word which is now going out of my mouth causes pulsations or waves in the air, and these, though invisible to human eyes, expand in every direction until they have passed around the whole globe, and produced a change in the atmosphere."[2]

More striking, the telegraphic system reproduces—on nature itself—a photograph of our every action, Hitchcock's "indelible impression on the universe." The chemical properties of sunlight not only impress human features on daguerreotype plates but also produce effects on vegetation, making leaves green, for example: "Indeed, a large part of the changes of color in nature depend upon these invisible rays." Hitchcock speculated on the sun's powers to record *all* human appearance and action: "We do not know but it may imprint upon the world around us our features, as they are modified by various passions, and thus fill nature with daguerreotype impressions of all our actions that are performed in daylight."[3]

Hitchcock extended this idea to impressions made in total darkness, and he even suggested that the moon, planets, and stars might contain pictures of happenings on earth, captured at a delay, allowing for the speed of light. Whereas the moon might hold pictures of events on earth a little more than one second ago, Jupiter's picture gallery would record impressions that took place fifty-two minutes earlier, Neptune would receive pictures from four hours and fifteen minutes ago, and "a star of the twelfth magnitude" would make its images from light four thousand years old. Absorbing all these images, the universe would then be "a vast panorama of the world's entire history." We cannot imagine these messages and pictures in the heavens or perceive them on earth, he wrote, only because of the "bluntness of mortal sensibilities." Let us be aware instead "of senses far more acute . . . senses that can trace out and feel the vibrations of the delicate web of organic influence that binds together the great and the small, the past, the present, and the future, throughout the universe."[4]

Hitchcock's views now are "almost comically dated," in the words of one literary historian. "Nearly every word he wrote," another scholar notes, "appears obsolete from our vantage point."[5] But from another perspective, we can credit Hitchcock for finding language for the end of an era—a few years before the publication and initial dissemination of *The Origin of Species*—when it was still possible to think of human beings and vaster worlds in harmonious relation. In that respect Hitchcock was not much different from Oliver Wendell Holmes, Sr., clearly a reader of *The Religion of Geology,* who in 1861 offered this Hitchcock-inspired definition of photography: "What if the sky is one great concave mirror, which reflects the picture of all our doings, and photographs every act on which it looks upon dead and living surfaces, so that to celestial eyes the stones on which we tread are written with our deeds, and the leaves of the forest are but undeveloped negatives where our summers stand self-recorded for transfer into the imperishable record?"[6]

But what if those stones and leaves were blank? What if the creatures out there were utterly uninterested in our presence? Then it would be much more difficult to exclaim, as Hitchcock did in 1851, "*What a centre of influence does man occupy!*" Then it would be much harder to write, as he did, that "each man had his foot upon the point where ten thousand telegraphic wires meet from every part of the universe," so that "he were able, with each volition, to send abroad an influence along these wires, so as to reach every created being in heaven and in earth." It would be hard indeed to say, as Hitchcock did, that "we had the more than Gorgon power of transmuting every object around us into forms beautiful or hideous," to feel as though "we were linked to every created being by a golden chain."[7] In place of these notions would be Darwin's "entangled bank," his intricate web of "action and reaction" among all organic beings competing for food or space, that whirs as a dumb, endless, mechanical environment for human actions.[8]

Where did *Macbeth* stand on October 17 in relation to this change? The fiction of George Eliot offers a useful gauge. "If we had a keen vision and feeling of all ordinary human life," Eliot wrote in the famous passage from *Middlemarch* (1872), "it would be like hearing the grass grow and the squirrel's heart beat, and we should die of that roar which lies on the other side of silence."[9] The natural world for Eliot teems: it runs riot. Her view parallels that of the Darwinian scientist Thomas H. Huxley, writing in 1869 and quoted by Gillian Beer in *Darwin's Plots:* "The wonderful noonday silence of a tropical forest is, after all, due only to the dullness of our hearing; and could our ears catch the murmur of those tiny Maelstroms, as they whirl in the innumerable myriads of living cells which constitute each tree, we should be stunned, as with the roar of a great city."[10] No wonder Eliot writes that "the quickest of us walk about well wadded with stupidity."[11] From this stupidity back to Hitchcock's "bluntness of mortal sensibilities" may not seem far, but for Eliot what lies on the other side of silence is not God but a deafening chaos.

In that environment an artistic act could no longer claim to explain the universe. It could no longer make the world around it take shape, made clear by a dazzling penetration. Dorothea Brooke's husband, the scholar Edward Casaubon, is only the best-known example in *Middlemarch* of a person embarked on a futile search for a totalizing explanation, a "key to all mythologies." Casaubon's quest is grim and pompous, a pedantic failure, but at other points Eliot speculates on the remnant power of at least an illusory wholeness manifest in art, as in this passage about a mirror:

> Your pier-glass or extensive surface of polished steel made to be rubbed by a housemaid will be minutely and multitudinously scratched in all directions; but place now against it a lighted candle as a centre of illumination, and lo, the scratches will seem to arrange themselves in a fine series of concentric circles round that little sun.

The random world gathering around the lighted candle is a false sensation: "It is demonstrable that the scratches are going everywhere impartially, and it is only your candle that produces the flattering illusion of a concentric arrangement, its light falling with an exclusive optical selection."[12]

But Eliot's is still a marvelous fantasy of aesthetic order, showing the power of such dreams at the moment they face an unprecedented challenge. One can even find a quasi-religious definition of artistic wholeness in *Middle-*

march, a God-discovering aesthetic act wherein the world, magically, still rings to a single tune if the musician but knows the right note to play, as in Eliot's poetic epigraph to chapter 31:

> How will you know the pitch of that great bell
> Too large for you to stir? Let but a flute
> Play 'neath the fine-mixed metal: listen close
> Till the right note flows forth, a silvery rill:
> Then shall the huge bell tremble—then the mass
> With myriad waves concurrent shall respond
> In low soft unison.[13]

Even so, the aesthetic act for Eliot ultimately can give order only to a very small space, a limited sphere that is itself a Darwinian slice of nature. Eliot conceives her task as a working out, in miniature, of the extraordinary "multiplicity of connections" among the human beings in a limited place—the village of Middlemarch is itself an entangled bank. If Henry Fielding and other earlier writers, as Eliot recounts, believed the entire world was at their command, she can attend only to the enormously intricate little space she has set herself to describe: "I at least have so much to do in unravelling certain human lots and seeing how they were woven and interwoven that all the light I can command must be concentrated on this particular web, and not dispersed over that tempting range of relevancies called the universe."[14] To try to record all those relevancies would be, in Beer's phrase, "artistically and existentially threatening."[15]

In 1863 that threatening sense of nature was still in the future for Eliot and, even more, for a performance of *Macbeth* in America. The evolutionary debate had hardly started in the United States, having been confined mostly to exchanges between certain intellectuals such as Asa Gray and Louis Agassiz of Harvard. Huxley's *Evidence as to Man's Place in Nature* was published in New York in 1863, but only in the early 1870s would American scientists begin to make their own contributions to evolutionary theory, and only much later, in, say, turn-of-the-century naturalist fiction, would evolutionary ideas take hold in the larger culture.[16]

In 1863 the old idea of unification and wholeness—of artistic acts and of a God-driven universe—would have been as plain to many Americans as to scientists such as Joseph Henry and Alexander Dallas Bache. Here again were dreams of a whole world administered, made to take shape and obligingly reflect, tree to tree and leaf to leaf, the blessed imprint of God and a people imagining themselves his chosen ones. Hitchcock's supernaturalism, though undoubtedly eccentric, matched the era's progressive instinct. His universal claims approximated those of Sanitary Commission president Henry Bellows or his emissary, Cushman, for example. Supernatural telegraphy and photography were simply additional examples of Bellows's "transmissive influences" that made possible the cabled spread of progressive American values.

Macbeth, however, may not have lent itself entirely to these beneficiary purposes. Perhaps a play about darkness, blood, and witches could never consent to sit so neatly within the dual space of museum perfection and universal expression, to be the far-spreading bell that made every blade of grass vibrate to its unifying tone. Instead it conjured the poisonous blankness of the world around it and the matching emptiness, the gurgled incoherence, of even the most eloquent attempts to explain that world. Macbeth's "sound and fury, / signifying nothing," his idea of life as "a walking shadow, a poor player / That struts and frets his hour upon the stage," of life as "a tale / Told by an idiot" (5.5.24–28) suggest an existential emptiness that even some Victorians might not have fully explained away—an emptiness, moreover, that may have been becoming more vivid for audiences in the 1860s.

The evolutionary era in Britain gave *Macbeth*'s emptiness a particular bang. The witches, the literary critic Edward Dowden would write in 1882, are manifestations of an "unknown somewhat that lies behind the entire universe," an unknown matching the phenomenon that theologians call "divine grace" and "Satanic temptation" but more mechanical; this elusive element enfolds the "large impersonal life of the world" and is increasingly mysterious and inscrutable, making it even more fruitless for artists to "enclose themselves in a little pinfold of demonstrable knowledge, and call it the universe."[17] This other life catches us in its sway, appearing only in tokens and signs as distant, curious, and imponderable as the comet and cliffs of William Dyce's *Pegwell Bay* (see fig. 33). We can express it, however eloquently, only as Dyce did: through careful brushstrokes that would match the dumbness of stones and the far-spreading pantomime of a comet in the sky. These strokes would carefully emulate the sound and fury of these signs of a world grown sinister and strange, as if the individualized articulation of, say, thousands of leaves blowing in the breeze were meant to capture and record not the glad face of nature but the sounds on "the other side of silence," where cacophony bursts through, suddenly the sole object of a serious representation, visible as a fragmentation where the wholeness was, an incoherence where the eloquence was, as even an eloquence *of* incoherence: "Sound and fury signifying nothing."

In America in 1863, however, it was not evolution but the war that made nature seem most strange, even haunted—like a blasted ruckus of the sinister unknown, seemingly forever baking in vistas of red clay and blank sky—and that made aesthetic gestures and claims of universal command unconvincing. If the natural world loomed around *Macbeth* on October 17, staring back at it instead of receiving, like a slate, the inscription of human action, the coexistence in wartime of two antithetical modes of nature description helps us see how this is so.

The first and more hopeful mode is the pathetic fallacy. In the Civil War, the immediate sense of the fallacy was gentle and friendly. It allowed a person-centered belief like Hitchcock's to continue even amid horrific conflict, making the natural world resound with a voice mirroring the writer's. The sadness of these personifications was an affirmation, a sentimental reassurance that nature really did sit up and respond with kindred emotion. For Fanny Seward, aboard a boat steaming down the Potomac in the last days of the war, the river's waves "seemed almost to speak the words" of the poem "Drifting" by Thomas Buchanan Read:

I care not if
My rippling skiff
Float swift or slow from cliff to cliff—
With dreamful eyes
My spirit lies
Under the walls of paradise

The waves call to Fanny "with gentle imperativeness, 'Come, Come, Come, Come.'" She begins to think of the soldiers the waves had borne throughout the war, wondering "what hearts had felt the throb of the waves, what ears had listened to their invitation." Then her meditation turns somber: "Some—the same waves bore them back too—but their hearts gave no answering thrill to the throb of the waves, their calm, closed eyes beheld no shores wrapt in the dreamy twilight haze, their ears were deaf to the sweet wave's call—as to the sobs at home." In 1856 John Ruskin condemned the pathetic fallacy, singling out ocean waves as among the natural phenomena foolishly impersonated, but for Fanny Seward the river's waves were a chance to imagine a benign nature lamenting almost like tearful mermaids as they transported bodies back to loved ones and souls "beyond the stream of time."[18] This sorrow of nature, moreover, was the occasion and the expression of Fanny's own, as if her sadness could not have been represented had she not recognized it, over there, away from herself in the water, as a flitting picture of her own voice.

Virginia was a notable place during and immediately after the war for establishing this sentimental contact. The James River running near the burial place of Stonewall Jackson in Lexington "sings an unceasing requiem to his memory," wrote Jedediah Hotchkiss and William Allan in 1867, and at the place where Jackson died "the proud mountains, like some vast chain of sentinels, stand keeping eternal watch over the dust of the honored dead":

> His spirit wraps yon dusky mountain,
> His memory sparkles o'er each fountain,
> The meanest rill, the mightiest river,
> Rolls, mingling with his fame for ever.[19]

As a landscape, the state of Virginia was made to resound with the voices of the mourners and the dead until it, too, became a universe, a pantheon or church in which even the most obscure place displayed human pictures.

The second mode describing nature rejected this personification. It concentrated on geographical coordinates, the reduction of all natural phenomena to so much information, to pave the way for efficient military action and, after the war, commercial development. This mode assumed that the natural world was brute material—dross to be shoved and plowed out of the way, churned for human benefit. Hotchkiss, a mapmaker for the Confederacy during the war (his map of Bristoe Station is a Confederate analogue to the precision of Gouverneur Kemble Warren), may have sentimentalized the site of Jackson's death, but a postwar book featuring his maps of Virginia is cold and clinical. "Portions of Fauquier and Fairfax, which are on the Triassic, or New Red sandstone formation, differ considerably in appearance from the rest of the middle country, which is on the Eozoic, or granite, gneiss, &c, rocks," is a representative passage from *Virginia: A Geographical and Political Summary,* published in 1876. "Virginia had more acres of cleared land than any of the States of the Union except Illinois, New York and Pennsylvania. . . . Swine are easily and cheaply raised in all portions of Virginia, especially in the portions abounding in forests, where they subsist much of the year on the nuts of the beech, oak, chestnut, and other trees."[20]

This dispassionate mode is striking, however, because it is haunted by the personified landscape it tries to banish. In these data-filled accounts, superstition or sentimental folklore returns with a sinister force lacking in direct uses of the pathetic fallacy such as Fanny Seward's or that of the poem about Jackson. The ominous quality is not present as a repressed force showing through the incessant recitations of information. No grimalkin lurks beneath the sentence "Tidewater has extensive amounts of yellow pine, oak, cypress, cedar, locust; sumac is an abundant shrub."[21] Instead, whether a Federal or a Confederate wrote them, these accounts are ominous in their steadfast aim to treat every detail of the natural world as subject to triumphant quantification. Such a rubric makes nature so inert and lifeless that it seems, paradoxically, to bear the haunted aspect of having *once been alive.*

One pictorial example of this quantification is a photograph, attributed to Alexander J. Russell, of Union soldiers standing at the site of a bridge on the Orange and Alexandria Railroad (fig. 65). Here the late autumn world is reduced to nothing more than a coordinate in place and time—a location on the railroad and a location to be photographed, divested of personifying qualities. The land is disenchanted, a mere setting for the soldiers who pose. Their mien suggests that for them the taking of their image is as far from being animistic as the unremarkable set of sticks and stones they stand among. They occupy this stream. They have perhaps used the surrounding woods to build the bunkhouse at background left and for other purposes of war. It is all a matter of fact.

Yet this very reduction of the landscape—the remorseless subjection of each detail to the same dispassionate, dutiful photographic scrutiny—gives the image a haunted look, as if a world so neatly, efficiently, and triumphantly emptied of animistic properties for that reason has never appeared more perfectly dead—that is, as once having had a life. That dead landscape would terrify more, in its blankness, than any quasi-human shape of contorted limb and hollow mouth. It would have, not a voice, not a ghostly echo of a requiem, but an absolute, opaque, and dreadful *silence.* This photograph tells a story not of environmental revenge, the land's punishment of those who have subjected it to the brutal efficiencies of wartime, but of the inevitable result of a vanquishing so strong, so industrially efficient, that rhetorically it produces the death—the sense of sticks and stones and water that were once alive—that it had dismissed scientifically as so much folklore.

Where did *Macbeth* stand on October 17 in relation to these two modes? On the one hand, it was an anthem whose soundings equaled the great organ's, a melodramatic declaration that human eloquence might symbolically

Fig. 65. Andrew Joseph Russell (attributed), *Orange and Alexandria R.R. Bridge near Union Mills, the burned block,* 1863. The Metropolitan Museum of Art, New York, Harris Brisbane Dick Fund, 1933 (33.65.271). Copy photograph © The Metropolitan Museum of Art.

stretch through the trees and across the streams and bring those sounds of nature reassuringly back through the words of individual persons, just as surely as Fanny Seward spoke on behalf of the waves that articulated her thoughts, or as Cushman, reciting Annie Fields's poem, spoke of the Boston Music Hall organ, which

> shall tell of mountain streams,
> Until we hear their quickly flowing dreams,
> Ringing to music for our waking hours;
> It shall rehearse the tale of pine-strewed woods,
> Until their pensive moods
> Shall haunt the common street with their weird powers.[22]

On the other hand, the play's existential emptiness—its sound and fury signifying nothing—might never have rebounded more eerily than from the blank mounds the war left in its wake.

A skeletal emptiness of battlefields surrounded the play. Nature on those battlefields was not a verdant sward of eternal rest—rustling with murmurs and other gentle haunted sounds—but a grim thicket with nothing to say, token of a world devastated into nullity. If Birnam Wood truly could come to Dunsinane, the silence of that haunted nature—whose animism was blank and whose terror consisted precisely in its *not* speaking from beyond the grave—would be the play's most vivid achievement.

This silence was a question of witchcraft. It was a question, in another sense, of the difference between Virginia in the 1780s and the 1860s, the difference between Thomas Jefferson and Abraham Lincoln, who admired Jefferson so much. Jefferson's Virginia, with Monticello at its symbolic center, was without sorcery. "Monticello would signify Enlightenment," cultural historian Mitchell Robert Breitwieser writes. The building would embody a "mental gaze at a world no longer mystified by the self-serving obscurities of priests, ministers, and despots." Situated on a hill, Monticello was "the clear prospect, a comprehending gaze, unvexed by perturbations of fear, desire, conformism, or ambition."[23]

Monticello shaped the surrounding world, in Breitwieser's words, "like Stevens's Tennessee jar." Jefferson admired Thomas Whately's *Observations on Modern Gardening* (1771), which noted that buildings "mark the spot where they are placed with so much strength, they attract the relation of all around with so much power." The world took shape around that building, moreover, while maintaining a strangeness, an otherness, that was not occult. Breitwieser writes that Jefferson enjoyed the tension between the designing mind and the mysterious physical facts of nature. The process of understanding was a constant give and take, a pleasurable back and forth, between the intellect and the surrounding world. In contrast to the artificial ordering of a land survey—which amounted to "a willful occlusion of the real terrain and of the animal and human life that occupies the terrain"—Jefferson's inductive mode would constantly test, and wonder at, the world gathering around the mind at work. The oddest phenomena would appear—the "looming" of a mountain forty miles from Monticello, for example, that Jefferson describes in *Notes on the State of Virginia* (1785) as appearing to change its shape in different atmospheric conditions—but no witchcraft lay in such apparitions; they were simply curious occurrences to ponder.[24]

What, then, must Jefferson have thought of *Macbeth* when he saw the play in London in June 1786? He attended a performance featuring Sarah Siddons as Lady Macbeth while on a visit to the city, during which he arranged for an English edition of *Notes on the State of Virginia* that would

Fig. 66. James Caldwall after Henry Fuseli, *A Heath: Macbeth, Banquo, and Three Witches.* In John Boydell, *Illustrations of the Dramatic Works of Shakespeare* (New York, 1852). Yale Center for British Art, Paul Mellon Collection.

be published the following year. Henry Fuseli's picture of the 1780s, reproduced in the American edition of John Boydell's *Illustrations of the Dramatic Works of Shakespeare,* published in 1852, gives some sense of the performance Jefferson saw (fig. 66). Macbeth and Banquo react with horror at the first appearance of the witches, but for Jefferson perhaps such an apparition was only so much stage-business chicanery, or, at best, a phantasmagoria flattering the enlightened viewer with an invitation to discern how the trick was done.

No matter how those weird sisters appeared, they were only illusions to be pondered, like the looming mountain to be seen from Monticello. The mountain "sometimes subsides almost totally in the horizon; sometimes it arises more acute and more elevated; sometimes it is hemispherical; and sometimes its sides are perpendicular, its top flat, and as broad as its base. . . . It assumes at times the most whimsical shapes, and all these perhaps successively in the same morning," but Jefferson views this shape-shifting as a subject only of scientific curiosity, beheld from the removed elevation of

Monticello, whereas Macbeth and Banquo shake with the sublimities that stun their medieval souls: "What seemed corporal melted / As breath into the wind" (1.3.81–82).[25]

Jefferson could therefore walk among the dead without resorting to so much as a graveyard stroller's nervous whistle. He describes in the *Notes* excavating an Indian burial mound near the Rivanna River, finding all sorts of bones "lying in the utmost confusion, some vertical, some oblique, some horizontal, and directed to every point of the compass, entangled, and held together in clusters by the earth. . . . sculls, jaw bones, teeth, the bones of the arms, thighs, legs, feet, and hands. . . . The sculls were so tender, that they generally fell to pieces on being touched." After making a cut through the barrow to investigate its interior in a cross section—a cut "wide enough for a man to walk through and examine its sides"—he remained dispassionate even amid these great masses of the dead. "I conjectured that in this barrow might have been a thousand skeletons."[26] It is inconceivable that he would have investigated a cemetery of white people in the same way, but Jefferson's cut through the burial mound tells us that, for him, Virginia had no ghosts.

Abraham Lincoln's Virginia, in contrast, was haunted. The witches, so to speak, were really there. The haunting was palpable in the sheer waste of the wartime landscape—the military emptying of space accomplished by a rational decimation of fields and farms. The administration of such large-scale warfare put to rest Jefferson's delicacies of induction, making Virginia no longer a site of careful investigation but a vast ground subject to the brute requirements of military operations on both sides. The lone trees Lincoln liked to contemplate were, in effect, the singular repositories of a natural world previously far more flowing and widespread, surrounded by the leveled spaces of a territory strategically administered and denuded, and bearing now the burden of holding within their branches an entire forest's worth of wisdom. (Lincoln made the most of this concentration of effect, finding in these single trees the snow and sun that must have once accumulated in a thousand oaks and pines.) The land, like the bodies lying on it, was as blank as any blade of straw or jumbled twig, attaining now the haunted power of a world perfectly divested of all life. Call it an animate blankness.

No wonder the Virginia landscape abounded in witches and other eerie signs. At the Spotsylvania battlefield in 1865, a scene of horrific fighting the year before, the Northern writer J. T. Trowbridge observed an old woman and two young girls "stooping among the bushes along by the breastworks." At first it appeared they were gathering nuts, but then Trowbridge noticed that the old woman and girls were reaching down to the ground itself. "The woman had a haversack slung by her side; one of the girls carried an open pail. They passed along the intrenchments, searching intently, and occasionally picking something out of the dirt." Trowbridge approached them, intent on learning more: "They scarcely deigned to look at me, but continued their strange occupation. I questioned them about the battle; but their answers were as vague and stupid as if they then heard of it for the first time. Meanwhile I obtained a glance at the open mouth of the heavily freighted haversack and the half-filled pail, and saw not chincapins [a type of nut], but several quarts of old bullets."[27]

The woman and girls are cryptic tokens of what Trowbridge discerns everywhere around him on the battlefield, the "sphinx-like lips of the earth . . . rigid and still." He writes, "Even the winds seem to hush their whispers about that scene of desolation." Amid this silence and a field of nearby graves he sees a conventional poetic utterance—a board nailed to a tree and featuring four lines about "Fame's eternal camping-ground"—but the poetry is less powerful than the "hacked and barkless trunk at the angle of the woods" where the board is hung.[28] The location of the poetic utterance—brought to an almost physical intensity by the repeated "*k*'s" of *hacked, barkless,* and *trunk*—stands out more than the utterance itself. The tree is as inscrutable and castrating a sign as the vague and stupid answers of the woman and girls or the open silent mouth of the haversack.

The blankness of that angle in the woods, however, is more than nothing. Warranting a description, it marks a spot and draws the eye, making vision gather at the place where an especially thick emptiness coalesces. The purpose of the poetic utterance, in this sense, is to call attention not to itself but to the physical location it occupies. The old woman and two young girls are emissaries of this eerie blankness, goddesses of sterility gathering the balls of dead men, nuts of a landscape serried with earthworks and graves. Sphinxlike, they appear to Trowbridge not to explain anything but to state the vague and stupid mystery, the hacked and barkless place, with greater intensity.

On October 17, 1863, the Virginia landscape already featured many of these weird signs. After the Battle of Bristoe Station, the Confederate army busied itself tearing up the tracks of the Orange and Alexandria Railroad, the line that ran from Alexandria through the battlefield to points south such as Union Mills, where the photograph attributed to Russell was taken. At Bristoe Station, the victorious Union army having left the field to them, the Confederates ripped up the rails, placed them on fires, and wrapped the melted metal around nearby trees, posts, and telegraph poles, calling the bent rails "iron neckties."[29] The process was a purely military procedure, but it made for a landscape of sinister omens.

Those signs on October 17 might have seemed like mysterious expressions, properly violent and unintelligible, of an entire landscape laid waste. The Confederate officer Walter Taylor wrote on October 25 about the area around Bristoe Station: "As far as the eye can reach on every side, there is one vast, barren wilderness; not a fence, not an acre cultivated, not a living object visible." Another officer wrote, "Not a living thing save a few partridges and other small birds! No horse or cow, no hog or sheep, no dog or cat,—of course, no man, woman, or child!"[30] In that landscape, the iron neckties were like the bullet gleaners Trowbridge would see at Spotsylvania: sphinxes of a wordless landscape whose landmarks did nothing more than give a crudely memorable form to the expressionless emptiness. Such a haunted space, generating iron and scrawled signs, could muster only these vivid declarations of the surrounding incoherence.

When actual monuments appeared in such a landscape, they had the effect of an exorcism. Trowbridge described the postwar memorial a few miles from Bristoe Station, a "pyramidal monument of rough red sand-stone" dedicated "In Memory of the Patriots Who Fell at Bull Run, July 21st, 1861." The monument, he wrote, is "a silent preacher, with its breast of stone, and its austere face of stone, preaching inaudible stern lessons." That masculine religious voice seemed destined not only for contemplators of the war but for the surrounding land, a "vast, neglected barren tract of country" in which the site of the house of the widow Judith Henry, killed during the battle, was now only "a small square space run up to tallest weeds" within a few yards of the monument.[31]

The widow Henry's house was the place of an uncanny feminine flowering every bit as eerie as any sign of sterility. The peaches of the widow's trees continued to ripen year after year after her death, causing Trowbridge to see "the haunting figure of the poor widow . . . with her apron full of the fruit" on a battlefield where now one finds "many a whitened bone scattered about or protruding." In that landscape, where Trowbridge enjoyed a luncheon "sauced with Widow Henry's peaches" among the bones, the monument's reverend solemnity did more than assert meaning, purpose, and spatial control over an otherwise weed-filled boneyard of bullet-nicked peach trees. It established a principle of stony masculine oratorical command over a land whose automatic flowering, year after year, peach after peach, was the fecund version of the gullies of bullets gathered in sack and pail.

Well might that landscape demand a preacher. The widow Henry, at age eighty-five, was killed by an artillery round as she lay in bed, having refused to leave the house (where she had lived since 1822) as the fight loomed. But from her, at this ground zero of the Civil War, a frosty birth took place. The grapeshot of the exploding round sprayed through Judith Henry's house, killing her instantly, but at this epicenter of the first major land battle of the war, she was the shriveled mother of war, strewing the fallow fields with a generation of dead men. The true testament of these soldiers was not monuments, or even the stones that went into the making of the monuments, but the leaves, the air, wherever the sounding otherness of nature was. That rustling sound was not an imitation, echo, or anticipation of human speech but something outside that speech. It was the rustle that twisted the skirts of the widow Henry and required an exorcism to vanquish, but it was also what fecundated the land and, sometimes, even after the exorcism, continued to sound in the mouths of men. Hearing a Southerner's enunciation of the word *Virginia*—"*V-i-r-g-i-n-i-a*"—is "as good as eating a peach," Trowbridge wrote.[32] An elixir and an incantation, the words savor of a cannibal sacrament: talk of the war still had a strange taste in 1865, a flavor of the earth and bones and the flowerings there, one that the official histories (yet to be written) and the solemn monument (just erected) had yet to banish.

Virginia during the war—the land *Macbeth* flowed into—had no such monuments. Then, the landscape of Virginia was all witchy. Blasted into perfected nothingness, it made a nice clear ground only for antimonuments reasserting and even memorably articulating a choked, hollow lack of meaning. An anonymous photograph taken after the war at the Wilderness Battlefield depicts such a ground (fig. 67). The photograph was exposed to sunlight, probably inadvertently, along with some twenty-seven other images of the famous Virginia site made presumably by the same photographer, giving it a strange night-for-day glow befitting its grim subject.[33]

The solarized photograph shows three skulls on the ground. The central one is most visible, inverted and darkened against the ground and staring back at us, whereas the half-buried skulls to either side stare straight up. The central skull grins upside down at us from atop a mound of dirt on which it has probably been placed for the purpose, becoming the sphinx of this little swath of wildness. It marks the dead area, forcing us to fix our eyes on it, even if it commemorates only an unidentifiable spot where anonymity and silence comport in a jumble of twigs, branches, and bones. In the photograph of the Orange and Alexandria Railroad bridge, the location is also hardly a place at all, the haunted blankness of the scene arising

Fig. 67. Unknown photographer, *The Wilderness Battlefield,* ca. 1865–67. The Metropolitan Museum of Art, New York, Gilman Collection, Purchase, The Horace Foundation Gift, through Joyce and Robert Menschel, 2005 (2005.100.94.1–21). Copy photograph © The Metropolitan Museum of Art.

because the spot is treated as a mere coordinate in space and time. But the anonymous Wilderness photograph does something slightly different. It pays greater attention to a no-place, not subjecting it to matter-of-fact treatment but trying to *bring out,* through concerted attention, the haunted emptiness of a particular ground.

In the contest between representation and such a slovenly no-place, moreover, the photograph acknowledges that the wildness wins. The photograph is well composed (the central skull beneath the dead tree, likely manipulated to create an effective composition, the bones repeating the branches), but it comes across less as a shaping of the forest than as an attempt to allow the forest to shape it. We see no grand patch of sky, no enunciation to the stars, no moralistic message that would make this bony place speak in any other way than as a grinning silence of roots and leaves.

The photograph says nothing at all. As devoted to a lack of commentary as the patch of wilderness it shows, it implies that this lack of utterance, this bubbling up of an incoherent space into only a silent sign here and there, is the only thing that can fix a place or mark a spot. Later, Alexander Gardner would include a photograph of the Bull Run monument as the one hundredth, and last, image in his *Photographic Sketch Book of the War* (1866), a capstone that aligns photography with the exorcising powers of official commemoration even as other photographs in that book famously fail to deliver that remedy. But the Wilderness photograph conceives a different purpose. It understands that a representation, to be meaningful about the war, must approach the wild emptiness and let it work, contour by contour, upon the image's will to clarity—let the wildness reduce the art, slowly but surely, to an inscrutable sign. This sign would be neither meaningless babble nor mysterious incantation but some wise combination of the two, a profound incoherence.

Macbeth on October 17, 1863, faced a comparable boneyard. As a representation, it faced the same pressures that would confront the Wilderness photographer, albeit at a greater remove. It could try to be a memorial, an exorcism; it could try to set itself up as a ceremonial stone or other becalming representation, something like the still-uncompleted Washington Monument a few blocks from Grover's Theatre or the later Bull Run memorial. Or it could feel the incoherent sway of the land it tried to shape around it. And in 1863, the land may well have exerted a greater magnetic pull on a would-be cultural monument than the monument did on it. If so, the play could feel itself being drawn, even dragged, toward the emptiness it would exorcise—spread into the thin air and fierce thickets where it too would go to die, as sure of oblivion as any man expiring in the woods. It might also feel the woods come to it, infusing each brave declaration—each stentorian phrase of stark consonants and throaty "O's," cutting the air and encompassing the world—as itself only a blur, a deathly incomprehensibility. The ravages of emptiness worked their effects on the clarifying statement, making it as worn and terrifyingly smooth as the moldering, moss-draped sharpness of a medieval lord carved atop his casket. Space dissolved place like an acid. What was left, however, was something like the play's most powerful form: the haunting loss of articulation, the smooth rounded crack of the stones beneath the legible statements, the spot where a certain especially intense *nothing* demands to be seen.

How did *Macbeth* on October 17 register that surrounding emptiness? Consider the opening words of the play, spoken by the first witch. "When shall we three meet again? / In thunder, lightning, or in rain?" (1.1.1–2). As an opening, these words shape emptiness like an artist's first line on a blank paper. They create a world where a moment before there had been nothing. In that sense they had the spatial power of the expression "O" as Bruce Smith describes it in *The Acoustic World of Early Modern England.* To say "O" is "an environmental gesture," he writes. "As a burst of energy from within," to say "O" "is an act of aggression, a projection of one's body into the world. It is, in the most basic sense of the word, an *environmental* gesture." In crying "O," Smith claims, "I extend my person into 'the about-me.' "[34] The witches do not use this declamation, but as the play's first articulation, their words similarly cut the air, aggressively shaping space.

Their utterance, however, establishes an even more important principle of vanishing. Like the words of the poor player, strutting and fretting his hour upon the stage, the witches' declarations pierce the air only to be "heard no more" (5.5.26; 5.5.20). Their words register the "petty pace" of time that swallows them as soon as they speak. The words also acknowledge that they flow into an equally voracious space. The witches say in unison, "Fair is foul, and foul is fair. / Hover through the fog and filthy air" (1.1. 12–13). Then they themselves disappear: "When I burned in desire to question them further, they made themselves air, into which they vanished" (1.5.3–4). When Cushman read these words in Macbeth's letter in her first scene, according to a critic commenting on her appearance in Philadelphia in September 1863, she did so with a "wonder that such things as witches should be. How strange that they should make themselves air."[35]

The witches describe the chanted spread of their words hovering and dissipating in the blasts and filth of consuming space. The floating disappearance of these words is therefore an invitation to imagine the spaces these words *do not affect*—to see a world going on just as it always had, unchanged by the flow of would-be transformative speech. It is an invitation to see deep into the most remote recesses of that unchanged world—to see into the most chaotic areas where the emptiness is thickest and where the need for clarity is most dire—and to see that these places too, especially these, remain unchanged. In that sense the witches' evaporating chant is like the thicketed blankness of the Wilderness photograph—a careful depiction of the space it is fated not to change.

The most self-aware representations would then be those that imagine their own invisibility at the very scene they wish to shape. Like the photograph and the witches' chant, these portrayals would arrive at the inchoate patch of woods—the horrible wilderness requiring only a bit of sturdy definition to cohere—and instead allow the chaos to portray *them.* Losing themselves in the caress of every stick and stone, they would leave the impression of a scene eerily unchanged. Any macabre adjustments to that outer world—the photographer's manipulation of a skull, for example—would only intensify the silence of a representation whose precise point is to cause you to fail to hear your own voice, to see the world as it exists right now, out there somewhere, without you. The chant of the photograph, as much as that of the witches, conjures an alien space.

Such space reverses all world-making acts. The solarized photographs of the Wilderness Battlefield, such as one of a looming forest, are a metaphor for this reversal (fig. 68). The photograph acts on the space, but then the sunlight acts on the photograph, reversing its tonalities and much else. James Russell Lowell, in "Columbus," had written in 1844 that the explorer finds that "A hand is stretched to him from out of the dark, / Which grasping without question, he is led / Where there is work that he must do for God." But by 1865, to judge by the solarized photograph, there is only a darkened thicket where the exploring person stretches a hand in search of God, or, rather, only an emptiness that *takes hold* of all affirmative gestures, all acts of faith, that closes and drapes an alien world around the proffered mortal hand until that hand starts to take on the burning patina of the space it ventured into, becoming, at last, the color of a land it does not know.

The photographer, whoever he was, journeyed into a space that made him unknown. "There it was, black under the darkening sky: no motion, no sound near," Eliot wrote in *Adam Bede* (1859), describing the hidden pool that Hetty Sorrel at last discovers on her lonely wanderings, the pool

Fig. 68. Unknown photographer, *The Wilderness Battlefield,* ca. 1865–67. The Metropolitan Museum of Art, New York, Gilman Collection, Purchase, The Horace W. Goldsmith Foundation Gift, through Joyce and Robert Menschel, 2005 (2005.100.944.1–21). Copy photograph © The Metropolitan Museum of Art.

she has long envisioned as the place to drown herself. In black contrast to the speckled mirror Hetty would stare into for hours at a time at home, the pool is the image of the world without her, a glass without reflection, akin to the Wilderness photographs. In this novel published the same year as *The Origin of Species,* Hetty dreams of this blank mirror with its "wintry depth" into which she would sink without a trace.[36] She seeks it, not just as a suicidal end to her sorrow but as the culmination of an existential quest that makes her, no less than the Wilderness photographer, a paragon of the times: seeking a place where she would disappear, where she would no longer be the center of a world, where even once the water got shallow—once they found her body—there would be no way to know who this skeleton was. In that place of death, the Wilderness Battlefield, the anonymous photographer perhaps did not go to get lost, but as his positive mission became negative, as the sunlight picked his images clean, he too merged with the faceless world.

The reversal of the photograph is like sleep to waking hours. As day turned to night, the gesture of reason became alien. That other world was not a "Dreeme" of aesthetic retirement and ennui, like that in Theodore Winthrop's novel *Cecil Dreeme* (1861), but a space of indifference. Such spaces did not cohere at the behest of a world-making fantasy. Instead, as the sign of their indifference, they drooped and drowsed, sleeping at all points, forms curving downward as though hung by moss, in a narcotic quietude enveloping all human affairs. When Winthrop was killed in Virginia in the first days of the war, perhaps a person, battlefield, and nation could cohere around the signal death of a man struck down while leading his troops. "For one moment that brave, inspiring form is plainly visible to his whole country," George William Curtis wrote of Winthrop's last seconds of life.[37] But as the war dragged on, eerie Virginia spaces like the Wilderness allowed no éclat of heroic visibility. A sleepwalker saw them best: as the inside-out of reason, a world drowsing to individual fates, nameless as the men who died there. In the drugged wooziness of those surroundings, a person might be as imperceptible as an insect blending into a leaf.

Macbeth's most famous reversal occurs when Birnam Wood comes to Dunsinane. "That will never be," says Macbeth. "Who can impress the forest, bid the tree / Unfix his earthbound root?" But the lie proves true (4.1.117–18; 5.6.44). When the ivy clings to the casement, when the trees envelop the castle—when the winds, let loose by the witches, "fight / Against the churches," and "the yeasty waves / Confound and swallow navigation up" (4.1.74–76)—the human act disappears. Amid the "scraggy oaks, bushy firs, cedars and junipers, all entangled with a thick, almost impenetrable undergrowth and criss-crossed with an abundance of wild vines," as a later account described the Battle of the Wilderness;[38] and amid a natural battleground, too, like the ones "in the Southern United States" that Darwin described in *The Origin of Species*—where trees, insects, birds, and beasts of prey "all striving to increase, and all feeding on each other or on the trees or their seeds and seedlings," have made a "struggle," a "war" lasting for centuries—the leader is lost, and the direct statement is consumed by the world it would shape. Person and voice alike drown in the speechless clamor existing on the other side of silence.[39]

Did that noise come into the theater on October 17, 1863? If encompassing space became visible and audible inside the charmed circle, no longer held at bay, then Cushman would have been turned inside out. The postures of clarity would have groped and carved the air as though entwined in tendrils and vines. If pagan Shakespeare made the world ring—if sound in the plays could symbolically push "beyond the theater's walls to the limits of the cosmos," as Bruce Smith writes—then in the 1860s those circular waves might have begun rebounding to haunt single points of emanation such as Cushman. Strangely, they would have sounded not as affirmative horizons of possibility and personal scope but as echoes of an alien world creeping to the stage's edge, and then on to the stage itself, to inhabit the actress-exorcist whose character summoned these demons.[40] Somewhere between the sharp locution and the animal cry, the incantation prophesies the impossible, forest to castle, so that what had been unseen and unheard would there suddenly find voice—in an actress whose words might betoken some other sound from elsewhere that hollowed out those words from within, a sound perhaps as startling and strange to the actress as to anyone else in the theater. At that moment the self-seclusion of some unknown spot in the great world would become apparent for a moment, and then vanish, cease.

Maybe, however, there was one way to make a statement, to leave a mark amid the emptiness. This mark would not redeem the blank surroundings, would not offer at the last moment a vision of plenitude that guaranteed purpose and meaning to an individual human gesture and to the surrounding world. Instead it would partake of the emptiness it displaces and yet be more than thin air, more than a cry, more than an entangled thicket. It would even offer an image of a life: in a little blot, a mesmerizing stain, a sign that someone had been there. That blot, too, would be more than the existential record of a person at a certain place and time, more than a happenstance document of one day or one night in that person's life. It would be the mark of an infinitely expansive world, a lifetime of experiences, condensed into this one opaque smear or scuff.

Cushman onstage held that power. Accustomed to playing witches and witchlike characters like Meg Merrilies, she knew the occult qualities of Lady Macbeth, that incantatory sister to the witches. Lady Macbeth's powers of gathering, echoing those of the witches who toss "eye of newt, and toe of frog" into their cauldron (4.1.6), summon from the ends of the earth a great many forces all to one place:

> Come, you spirits
> That tend on mortal thoughts, unsex me here,
> And fill me from the crown to the toe topful
> Of direst cruelty. Make thick my blood;
> Stop up th' access and passage to remorse,
> That no compunctious visitings of nature
> Shake my fell purpose nor keep peace between
> Th' effect and it. Come to my woman's breasts
> And take my milk for gall, you murd'ring ministers,
> Wherever in your sightless substances
> You wait on nature's mischief. Come, thick night,
> And pall thee in the dunnest smoke of hell,
> That my keen knife sees not the wound it makes,
> Nor heaven peep through the blanket of the dark
> To cry "Hold, hold." (1.5. 39–53)

In a good performance, this incomparable speech concentrates energy in the spot where the actress stands. Cushman, nothing if not intense, must have gathered these spirits until the air around her fairly vibrated with supernal powers brought to bear at a single place and time. Hers must have been a "tremendous concentrativeness," like that of Hollingsworth in her friend Hawthorne's *Blithedale Romance.*[41]

What forces gathered in Cushman's Lady Macbeth? The murdering ministers came as emissaries of a universe without meaning, the malevolent energies of an alien world. But these same energies, concentrating on her, marked her place, gathering there to stamp a ground that would otherwise leave no trace. They wrapped her in the blackness of an indelible image, a black hole where she stood. They made a space as wide as the spirit-summoned universe, condensed now as the cloak of a thick stain in one spot.

In making that mark did Cushman look up or down as she stood onstage? Fuseli showed Lady Macbeth looking up in his depiction of the speech for Boydell's Shakespeare gallery.[42] Had Cushman looked up on October 17 as she said "Come, you spirits," she probably would have seen something like what Fanny Seward described at Ford's Theater on their tour a few days earlier: standing on the empty stage, they tilted their heads and stared "up among the 'flys,'" where they saw "a curtain with flowers, spangles, etc., and a fairy painted on it. . . . Story upon story over our heads rose complicated pulley work all connected with stage machinery."[43] The actress, had she looked up at Grover's a few nights later, would have seen the theater's mechanical operations, which gave audiences backdrops for story on story of faraway places. Watching Cushman act, Fanny herself felt "uplifted into another region, breathing another air."[44] The glimpse of a distant region was itself stage machinery that could break the theater's pitiless limits, thanks to the pulleys of an elevating emotional manipulation. Maybe Cushman summoned the "murdering ministers" from up there, the better to fix her image indelibly onstage.

Or maybe she called them by looking down. A rough-walled basement was below the stage on which she stood. Back in 1863 a stream apparently ran through this basement. "In the 1800s," according to the staff of the current National Theatre, "the Tiber Creek flowed in an open raceway beneath the stage floor. That channel was not enclosed in a storm sewer until the 1950s." The clear running water, "which could be heard in the auditorium above only during the quietest scenes and after the heaviest of downpours," ran through a cavern that still makes "the acoustics on the stage . . . perfect," according to one recent theater manager.[45]

Who is to know if a waterway really did run below the stage in 1863? The present-day staff cannot confirm the report, though possibly a tributary of the nearby Tiber Creek did run under some city buildings back then. In an essay imagining a 1792 walking tour of present-day Washington, D.C., the landscape historian Don Alexander Hawkins describes how the waterway called Slash Run began in "the many small streams that flow down from the northern tier of surrounding hills," coalescing further on in a "strongly flowing" stream that was not "entirely enclosed in pipes" and buried until 1871.[46] Perhaps the Tiber Creek was similarly wild back then, maybe even running underneath the National Theatre. We cannot know for sure. What is certain, however, is that to this day a rough basement, a stony hollow or "cavernous opening," lies beneath the stage on the same spot as the Grover's stage.[47] The foundation, no less than the brick walls around the stage, appears to date to the Grover's era and probably before, back to the previous theaters on the spot, in the opinion of the current theater manager, Donn Murphy.[48] Cushman, like any performer on that stage, knew that she walked above that cavern.

It was the better part of performing to forget all that. Or was it? Lady Macbeth courts the abyss. She is more in touch with the ground beneath her feet than many a character. She knows "Hell is murky" (5.1.36). Cushman, playing the role of Nancy in *Oliver Twist,* "was able to descend into the depths of its abasement," Emma Stebbins wrote, and she must have given a similar depth to her Lady Macbeth.[49] The hollowness below Cushman must have given a peculiar resonance to her words, shaping them with vibrations drawn from underground. Playing the role, she might have agreed with tragic Miriam in Hawthorne's *Marble Faun,* who stands at the spot in Rome where a legendary chasm opened and gives her gloomy meditations: "The chasm was merely one of the orifices of that pit of blackness that lies beneath us, everywhere." Miriam, whose white hand, her companion Donatello tells her, "all the water in the ocean could not have washed clean," sees life propped over the abyss: "The firmest substance of human happiness is but a thin crust over it, with just reality enough to bear up the illusive stage scenery amid which we tread." In later years the ghost of John McClullough, the actor whose performance so impressed Lincoln, would be said to haunt the hollow beneath the National Theatre stage, providing an apt legend for a weird space. Performing was a matter of life and death, here today, gone tomorrow: "It needs no earthquake to open the chasm," Miriam says. "A footstep, a little heavier than ordinary, will serve."[50]

Cushman often thought of the space beneath her. Writing in 1861, she recalled how the death of her younger brother had made "the world . . . *liquefy* beneath my feet," so that "the waters went over my soul." Coming to the United States in 1863 from her home in Rome, "where the long-buried past rises up to confront the present," as Stebbins wrote, she knew as well as Hawthorne's Miriam about stepping "very daintily, not to break through the crust, at any moment." There she would ride on the Campagna, "in many places a vast rolling roof covering buried buildings, and honeycombed everywhere by hidden galleries and hollows . . . very dangerous to riders, the thin crust of earth often giving way under the weight of the horse. . . . There is no warning whatever of these hidden pitfalls; the turf looks as smiling over them as elsewhere, only fate lurks below and seizes one out of a hundred by the leg which happens to touch upon the small weak point." In the back garden of Cushman's home at 38 Via Gregoriana was a well: "if you looked down it, you beheld far below in the bowels of the earth the surface of the water, and, to your astonishment, women coming and going, drawing the water from its source, and you recognized that it was a large reservoir, to which the well-mouth above was only an opening or conductor," Stebbins wrote. "Underneath all this neighborhood existed numerous excavations, eerie underground passages, giving access to this well."[51]

In Washington Cushman thought of underground Rome. On Monday, October 12, she gave Fanny a copy of a ring found in the catacombs. "Miss Cushman . . . put out her hand and said there was a ring for me," Fanny wrote. Cushman took the ring, "which she had worn during the morning off her finger," and presented it to her: "The ring from which these are copied was found in the catacombs," explained Fanny, who died at the age of twenty-one in 1866. "These rings were worn as badges by the early Christian martyrs who wished some sign by which to be known to one another—but as it was not safe to have the ordinary cross in full sight they contrived it thus."[52]

Down beneath the stage, running on, without purpose, without meaning, that body of water—if there was one—might have given the right empty shape to Cushman's performance, the right quality of sound and fury, welling up to take a strange visible shape on the surface, where she stood. Her performance would not then be different from the natural world. It would not shape that world. It would not create a universe. Rather it would draw on heedless nature, deep down, to fashion the smallest cryptic mark, the dumbest little jewel, dirt still in the grooves, dropped back to earth so that one day it might be found.

ACKNOWLEDGMENTS

So many people have helped my research on this book. In Washington, I thank Yvonne Carignan and her staff at the Kiplinger Research Library; Dan Mattausch, independent scholar; Donn Murphy, of the National Theatre; Mari Nakahara, of the American Architectural Foundation; Richard Stamm, of the Smithsonian Institution; David Ward, of the National Portrait Gallery; and Barbara Wolanin and Jennifer Pullara, of the Architect of the Capitol.

In Virginia, I benefited from the help of Frances Allshouse, director of the Fauquier Historical Society in Warrenton; David Born and Heather Hembrey, of the Prince William County Historic Preservation Division in Dumfries; Jim Burgess, of the Manassas National Battlefield Park; Jane Butler, of the Afro-American Historical Association of Fauquier County in The Plains; Ted Hostetler, of Randolph College in Lynchburg; and E. Lee Shepard and William Rasmussen, of the Virginia Historical Society in Richmond.

In North Carolina, I received the extraordinary kindness and help of Joseph Pearce, of Louisburg. Others elsewhere helped me in crucial ways: in Missouri, Susan Sparks, of the Polk County Genealogical Society in Bolivar; in Tennessee, Scott Newstok, of Rhodes College in Memphis; and in New York State, Peter Wisbey and Jennifer Haines of the Seward House in Auburn.

In New Haven, I benefited from the encouragement and wisdom of Marc Robinson and Joseph Roach. George Miles and the staff at the Beinecke Rare Book and Manuscript Library helped me in many ways.

The readers of my manuscript have made it better. To these readers—Marcia Brennan, David Peters Corbett, David Lubin, Julia Lupton, and Kathleen Pyne—I offer my heartfelt thanks for their comments and questions. My editors, Stephanie Fay, Sue Heinemann, and Adrienne Harris, deserve great credit for their wisdom and care editing the text. Finally, I reserve special gratitude, as how could I not, for my family—my wife, Mary, and my daughters, Lucy and Anna.

NOTES

INTRODUCTION. A DROP THAT DYES THE SEAS

1. Wallace Stevens, "Anecdote of the Jar" and "The Idea of Order at Key West," *Wallace Stevens: Collected Poetry and Prose,* ed. Frank Kermode and Joan Richardson (New York: Library of America, 1997), 60, 105.

2. Text references here and throughout the book are to act, scene, and line(s) of William Shakespeare, *Macbeth,* ed. Stephen Orgel (London: Penguin, 2000).

3. Harold Bloom, *Shakespeare: The Invention of the Human* (New York: Riverhead, 1998), 525, 521–22; Sanders, quoted in Bloom, 522.

4. Nathaniel Hawthorne, *The Marble Faun* (New York: Penguin, 1990), 26–27. The book abounds in references to *Macbeth,* which especially gather around the tragic figures of Miriam and Donatello in descriptions of hand washing and indelible blood stains (97, 246).

5. Herman Melville, *Moby-Dick; or, The Whale* (Indianapolis: Bobbs-Merrill, 1964), 301, 220, 366.

6. Ibid., 527.

7. Ibid., 527, 530.

8. Ibid., 530.

9. Walt Whitman, "Song of Myself," *Leaves of Grass* (New York: Library of America, 1992), 219.

10. Nathaniel Hawthorne, *The Blithedale Romance* (New York: Modern Library, 2001), 207.

11. For an account of the Astor Place Riots, see, for example, Lawrence Levine,

Highbrow/Lowbrow: The Emergence of Cultural Hierarchy in America (Cambridge, Massachusetts: Harvard University Press, 1988), 63–68.

12. Abraham Lincoln to James Hackett, August 17, 1863, in *Abraham Lincoln: Speeches and Writings, 1859–1865,* ed. Don Edward Fehrenbacher (New York: Library of America, 1989), 493. For more on Lincoln's admiration of *Macbeth,* see James Stevenson, "Abraham Lincoln's Affinity for *Macbeth,*" *Midwest Quarterly* 31 (Winter 1990): 270–79; and especially Robert Berkelman, "Lincoln's Interest in Shakespeare," *Shakespeare Quarterly* 2 (1951): 303–12.

13. See, for example, *The Martyr of Liberty,* a lithograph of the assassination issued ca. 1865, bearing a caption adapted from *Macbeth:* "This Lincoln / Hath borne his faculties so meek; has been / So clear in his great office; that his virtues / Shall plead, trumpet-tongued, against / The deem damnation of his taking off." The lithograph is reproduced and discussed in Harold Holzer, Gabor Boritt, and Mark Neely, Jr., *The Lincoln Image: Abraham Lincoln and the Popular Print* (Urbana: University of Illinois Press, 1984), 152–53.

14. Martin Heidegger, "The Thing" and "The Origin of the Work of Art," *Poetry, Language, Thought,* trans. Albert Hofstadter (New York: Harper & Row, 1971), 172, 42–43, 53.

15. Marc Robinson, *The American Play* (New Haven, Connecticut: Yale University Press, 2009), 5.

ONE. A STONE'S THROW: CHARLOTTE CUSHMAN

1. Henry Bellows to Charlotte Cushman, November 7, 1863; quoted in Emma Stebbins, ed., *Charlotte Cushman: Her Letters and Memories of Her Life* (New York: Benjamin Blom, 1972 [1879]), 186.

2. Fanny Seward diary, typescript, October 9, 1863, pp. 821–23, Rare Books and Special Collections, Rush Rhees Library, University of Rochester, New York. The quotations in the following two paragraphs are also from this source.

3. "After luncheon Mr. Gutman brought Mr. Grover the manager to see Miss Cushman. He wishes her to play at his theater—had not invited her before because a friend of hers told she was not going to play in Washington. He makes her the same offer of everything as Mr. Ford—& has the advantage of being able to give her the support of Messrs. J. W. Wallack Jr. & E. L. Davenport, who are now playing for him" (Fanny Seward diary, typescript, October 12, 1863, p. 829). For the capacity of the theater, see "The Ovation and Benefit at Grover's Theatre . . . ," *Daily National Republican,* October 19, 1863, 2; "Opening of Grover's New Theatre," *Daily National Republican,* October 7, 1863, 2 ("The house will seat comfortably, in the permanent seats, 2500 persons, and with extra seats will accommodate over 3,000 persons with a view of the stage"). For the cast, see the satin souvenir playbill for the performance in the Charlotte Cushman Papers, Manuscript Division, at the Library of Congress, and the playbill pasted in the

diary of Benjamin Brown French, October 18, 1863, between pages 152 and 153, Benjamin Brown French Papers, Manuscript Division, Library of Congress.

4. "Ovation and Benefit at Grover's," 2.

5. Fanny Seward pocket diary, October 18, 1863, Seward House, Auburn, New York.

6. "Amusements," *New York Herald-Tribune,* October 23, 1863, 5.

7. Sermon delivered by the Reverend Dr. Bartol, quoted in Stebbins, *Charlotte Cushman,* 292.

8. William Winter, "Players: Past and Present—Great Actress and Great Woman Charlotte Cushman," *Saturday Evening Post,* September 29, 1906, 10.

9. Maud Howe Elliott, *This Was My Newport* (Cambridge, Massachusetts: A. M. Jones, 1944), 91.

10. Emma Crow Cushman, the actress's friend who married the actress's adopted son, Ned, described Cushman's mouth as like the "Arc de Triomphe" in "Charlotte Cushman: A Memory," 5; Bartol, quoted in Stebbins, *Charlotte Cushman,* 293.

11. Bartol, quoted in Stebbins, *Charlotte Cushman,* 293.

12. Charlotte Cushman, "The Actress," *Godey's Lady Book,* February 1837, 71.

13. "Dramatic and Musical," *Boston Daily Advertiser,* September 28, 1863, 1.

14. Benjamin Brown French diary, October 18, 1863, p. 153.

15. Fanny Seward diary, typescript, October 10, 1863, p. 827.

16. "Opening of Grover's New Theatre," *Daily National Republican,* October 7, 1863, 2. The ampitheatrical shape is mentioned in "Grand Opening of Grover's New Theatre," *Daily Morning Chronicle,* October 7, 1863, 2.

17. A. Dexter, "Plays and Play-Acting," *Atlantic Monthly,* September 1862, 288.

18. Bartol, quoted in Stebbins, *Charlotte Cushman,* 293; Winter, "Players: Past and Present," 10.

19. Martha J. Lamb, ed., *The Homes of America* (New York: Appleton, 1879), 202.

20. Mrs. Humphrey H. Swift to William Winter, October 4, 1906, Charlotte Cushman Papers. Swift wrote to Winter after reading his essay on Cushman in the *Saturday Evening Post* the week before, recalling a trip aboard a Cunard steamer to New York when the rumor of a Confederate victory was announced: As "Miss Cushman's little foot resounded on the deck, with a positive protest she said, 'I don't believe a word of it,' turned upon her heel and marched away."

21. Hosmer, quoted in Stebbins, *Charlotte Cushman,* 302–3.

22. Winter, "Players: Past and Present," 10.

23. For Willard's Hotel as the "centre of Washington," see Nathaniel Hawthorne, "Chiefly about War Matters," *Atlantic Monthly,* July 1862, 59. See also Richard Wallace and Marie Pinak Carr, *The Willard Hotel: An Illustrated History* (Washington, D.C.: Dicmar, 1986), 27–36. For Howe's writing of the "Battle Hymn" at the Willard, see Gary Williams, *Hungry Heart: The Literary Emer-*

gence of Julia Ward Howe (Amherst: University of Massachusetts Press, 1999), 208–9. See also chapter 3 here for an extended account of Howe's writing of the poem.

24. Walt Whitman, *Memoranda during the War,* ed. Peter Coviello (Oxford: Oxford University Press, 2004), 212.

25. Fanny Seward diary, typescript, October 11, 1863, p. 828.

26. William Warren to Gouverneur Kemble Warren, October 27, 1863, Gouverneur Kemble Warren Papers, New York State Library, Albany. On September 5, Cushman had written from Manhattan to that friend, Algernon Chase, Emily's father, "I had heard of Mr. Warren's promotion & rejoiced greatly thereat" (Cushman to Algernon Chase, September 5, 1863, Warren Papers). On August 16 Warren had been promoted to commander of the Second Corps after playing a key role in the victory at Gettysburg on July 1–3 (David M. Jordan, *"Happiness Is Not My Companion": The Life of General G. K. Warren* [Bloomington: Indiana University Press, 2001], 101).

27. Cushman's praise of "Massachusetts to Virginia" is described in Stebbins, *Charlotte Cushman,* 199; Cushman's handwritten copy of the poem is in the Charlotte Cushman Papers.

28. John Greenleaf Whittier, "Massachusetts to Virginia," *The Complete Poetical Works of John Greenleaf Whittier* (Boston: Houghton Mifflin, 1894), 286–88.

29. Giles, quoted in "Ovation and Benefit at Grover's," 2.

30. Ralph Waldo Emerson, "Shakespeare; or, the Poet," in *Ralph Waldo Emerson: Essays & Lectures* (New York: Library of America, 1983), 718.

31. U.S. Sanitary Commission, *Statement of the Object and Methods of the Sanitary Commission* (New York: William C. Bryant, 1863), 6–7.

32. Charles J. Stillé, *History of the United States Sanitary Commission* (Philadelphia: J. B. Lippincott, 1866), 252.

33. Henry W. Bellows, *A Sequel to 'The Suspense of Faith,' Addressed to His Own Congregation, Sunday, Sept. 25, 1859, on the Reopening of All Souls' Church, after the Summer Vacation* (New York: D. Appleton, 1859), 44, 46.

34. Bellows to James Miller McKim, August 18, 1865, quoted in Witold Rybczynski, *A Clearing in the Distance: Frederick Law Olmsted and America in the Nineteenth Century* (New York: Scribner, 1999), 199; Cushman to Bellows, October 31, 1863, quoted in Stebbins, *Charlotte Cushman,* 186.

35. David M. Henkin, *The Postal Age: The Emergence of Modern Communications in Nineteenth-Century America* (Chicago: University of Chicago Press, 2006), 2.

36. Fanny Seward diary, original, October 10, 1863, p. 63, Rush Rhees Library, University of Rochester, New York. Here and at other points in this book I cite Seward's original diary to discover the passages occasionally omitted by the typist-transcriber. Fanny's account of Cushman's letter writing and record keeping is one such passage.

37. Cushman to Frederick W. Seward, November 4, 1863, Charlotte Cushman Papers.

38. This desk is part of the Charlotte Cushman Collection, Lipscomb Library, Randolph College, Lynchburg, Virginia. More compact than I had imagined, the desk gives a more vivid sense of Cushman's physical presence—above all her size—than any other artifact I know. It must be seen in person for this to be clear.

39. Fanny Seward diary, typescript, October 13, 1863, pp. 831–32.

40. "Ford's Theatre—Benefit to the Sanitary Commission," *Daily National Republican,* October 13, 1863, 2.

41. Paul Gilmore, "Aesthetic Power: Electric Words and the Example of Frederick Douglass," *American Transcendental Quarterly* 16 (December 2002): 291. See also Gilmore, "Mechanical Means: Emersonian Aesthetic Transcendence and Antebellum Technology," *Modern Language Quarterly* 65 (June 2004): 245–68; Gilmore, "Romantic Electricity, or the Materiality of Aesthetics," *American Literature* 76 (September 2004): 467–94; Elizabeth Maddock Dillon, "Sentimental Aesthetics," *American Literature* 76 (September 2004): 495–523; Eliza Richards, "Lyric Telegraphy: Women Poets, Spiritualist Poetics, and the 'Phantom Voice' of Poe," *Yale Journal of Criticism* 12 (Fall 1999): 269–94; and Edmund Reiss, "Whitman's Debt to Animal Magnetism," *Proceedings of the Modern Language Association* 78 (March 1963): 80–88. See also Jennifer Roberts's discussion of the telegraph in *Transporting Visions: The Movement of Images in Early America* (forthcoming, University of California Press).

42. Menahem Blondheim, *News over the Wires: The Telegraph and the Flow of Public Information in America, 1844–1897* (Cambridge, Massachusetts: Harvard University Press, 1994), 130.

43. Oliver Wendell Holmes, "The Stereoscope and the Stereograph," *Atlantic Monthly,* June 1859, 739.

44. Nathaniel Hawthorne, *The Blithedale Romance* (New York: Modern Library, 2001), 184.

45. James Russell Lowell, "Columbus," *The Poetical Works of James R. Lowell,* vol. 2 (Boston: Ticknor and Fields, 1862), 132. For the story of "Columbus" being read to Cushman on the night of February 17, 1876, see Stebbins, *Charlotte Cushman,* 284–85.

46. Mrs. J. H. Hanaford, "An Interview with Charlotte Cushman," *Boston Daily Journal,* August 24, 1858, Charlotte Cushman Papers.

47. Fanny Seward diary, original, October 10, 1863, p. 67.

48. Fanny Seward diary, typescript, October 12, 1863, p. 831.

49. Holmes, "The Stereoscope and Stereograph," 738.

50. Lucretius, quoted in Alfred Gell, *Art and Agency: An Anthropological Theory* (Oxford: Clarendon Press, 1998), 105.

51. Fanny Seward diary, original, February 9, 1863.

52. Gell, *Art and Agency,* 104.

53. For Barton and the Sanitary Commission, see Elizabeth Brown Pryor, *Clara Barton: Professional Angel* (Philadelphia: University of Pennsylvania Press, 1987), 100–102. For the story of the dramatic rediscovery of Barton's lodging and office in 1997, when a worker during a building renovation found an attic full of papers and other personal effects from the Civil War era at the site, long since forgotten as the place where she worked, see Gary Scott, "Clara Barton's Civil War Apartments," *Washington History* (Spring/Summer 2001): 24–31. To me, the emptiness of the place as it was found suggests Barton's state of being missing—of being everywhere and nowhere—that had somehow always characterized the spot, even and maybe especially when she lived and worked there.

54. *The Poetical Works of James R. Lowell,* vol. 2, 159, 110. Fanny Seward's copy of these volumes, inscribed to her by Cushman, is in the collection of the Seward House, Auburn, New York, which preserves Fanny's library intact or nearly intact. The library is fascinating, as the historian Deirdre Stam points out, for what it reveals about the midcentury reading taste of a well-to-do American young woman (see Stam, "Growing up with Books: Fanny Seward's Book Collecting, Reading, and Writing in Mid-Nineteenth-Century New York State," *Libraries & Culture: A Journal of Library History* 41 [Spring 2006]: 189–218). Although the marginal notations in the Lowell volumes might be Fanny's, the more likely writer was Cushman, noting the particular favorites she wished Fanny to read after having talked with her about the poet ("Miss Cushman came to me in my room—told me about Lowell's poems" [Fanny Seward pocket diary, October 19, 1863]). Cushman's authorship of the marginal notations seems especially likely since one of the poems marked with an X is "Columbus," the poem that must have been among her favorites, since she requested that it be read to her on her deathbed on the night of February 17, 1876 (see, as noted, Stebbins, *Charlotte Cushman,* 284–85).

55. Peter Smith, *Explaining Chaos* (Cambridge: Cambridge University Press, 1998), 1.

56. Herbert Spencer, *A System of Synthetic Philosophy,* vol. 1 (New York: D. Appleton, 1873 [1864]), 189.

57. Peter Hall, interview with John Russell Brown, "Directing *Macbeth,*" in Brown, ed., *Focus on Macbeth* (London: Routledge, 1982), 248.

58. Cushman to Mr. Stewart, September 24, 1863, October 9, 1863, Gouverneur Kemble Warren Papers.

59. *The Poetical Works of James R. Lowell,* 160.

60. Elizabeth Barrett Browning, "Life," *Poems,* vol. 1 (London: Chapman & Hall, 1853), 355.

61. Browning, "Hiram Powers' Greek Slave," *Poems,* vol. 1, 354.

62. "Editor's Easy Chair," *Harper's Monthly,* January 1864, 275.

63. Annie Fields, "ODE. Recited by Miss Charlotte Cushman at the Inauguration of the Great Organ," *Boston Daily Courier,* November 3, 1863.

64. Mary Loeffelholz, "The Religion of Art in the City at War: Boston's Public Poetry and the Great Organ, 1863," *American Literary History* 13 (2001): 219, 220, 215; Hawthorne, *The Scarlet Letter* (New York: Signet, 1959), 65.

65. Ralph Waldo Emerson, "Voluntaries," *Atlantic Monthly,* October 1863, 505. For the link between Fields's "Ode" and "Voluntaries," see Loeffelholz, "Religion of Art," 227.

66. Loeffelholz, "Religion of Art," 223.

67. Howe, *Boston Daily Commonwealth,* November 13, 1863, quoted in ibid., 220.

68. The organ became obsolete unexpectedly quickly, dismantled in 1884 after a symphony orchestra replaced it as a sign of civic musical status. The instrument remained in storage until 1897, when it was purchased by Edward Francis Searles, of Methuen, Massachusetts, who moved it to that town. The organ still operates there, sounding out from the Methuen Memorial Music Hall built to house it. To hear it now, as I did in a performance on May 25, 2005, is to get a sense of how wondrous it must have been for its first American viewers (and auditors). Some five stories tall, the organ virtually grazes the ceiling of the building made to house it. For more on the organ, see Edward J. Sampson, Jr., *The Great Organ: Methuen Memorial Music Hall* (Methuen: Fish and Maria Design, n. d.).

69. John D. Stockton, "Charlotte Cushman," *Scribner's,* July 1876, 262.

70. Stebbins, *Charlotte Cushman,* 11–12.

71. Bellows, quoted in Stebbins, *Charlotte Cushman,* 187; Fanny Seward diary, typescript, October 12, 1863, pp. 830–31.

72. Augustus Waldauer, trans., *Fanchon, the Cricket; A Domestic Drama, in Five Acts, from a Tale of George Sand* (New York: Samuel French & Son, 1862), 29.

73. Joseph Leach, *Bright Particular Star: The Life & Times of Charlotte Cushman* (New Haven, Connecticut: Yale University Press, 1970), 323.

74. Noah Brooks, "Letter from Washington, October 9, 1863: Building at the Capitol," *Sacramento Daily Union,* November 4, 1863, 1.

75. Winter, "Players: Past and Present," 10.

76. Ibid.

77. The advertisement appears in *Harper's Weekly,* October 17, 1863, 671; Mary Braddon, *Aurora Floyd* (London: Virago, 1984), 11.

78. Emma Crow Cushman, "Charlotte Cushman: A Memory," 6.

79. Fanny Seward pocket diary, October 17, 1863.

80. Gabrielle Gopinath, "Harriet Hosmer and the Feminine Sublime," *Oxford Art Journal* 28 (2005): 61–81.

81. For Cushman as Romeo, see Lisa Merrill, *When Romeo Was a Woman: Charlotte Cushman and Her Circle of Female Spectators* (Ann Arbor: University of Michigan Press, 1999), 111–35.

82. Rainer Maria Rilke, "Auguste Rodin, First Part (1903)," in *Auguste Rodin* (Mineola, New York: Dover, 2006), 3, 12. Rilke likens antique sculpture's self-enclosure also to a walled city: "The plastic object is comparable to those cities of ancient times whose life was passed entirely within their walls; this does not mean that the citizens held their breath, nor did it cramp their life. But nothing passed beyond the limits of the circle enclosing them, nothing lay on the far side, nothing suggested a world outside, no hopes lay open towards the beyond. However great the movement in a piece of sculpture, whether it comes from infinite distances or from the depths of the heavens, it must return to the marble, the vast circle must be closed, that circle of solitude within which a work of art exists. This was the unwritten law alive in the sculpture of the past. Rodin recognized it" (13).

83. Thomas De Quincey, "On the Knocking on the Gate in *Macbeth,*" in John Wain, ed., *Shakespeare Macbeth: A Casebook* (London: Macmillan, 1968), 93.

84. Winter, "Players: Past and Present," 10.

85. "Her dark elf-locks shot out like the snakes of the gorgon" (Walter Scott, *Guy Mannering* [London: Penguin, 1999], 14).

86. "At the Haymarket," *Sunday Times,* February 12 [?], clipping, Charlotte Cushman Papers.

87. Adelaide Kemble Sartoris, *Medusa, and Other Tales* (London: Smith, Elder, 1868), 82, 84; Sallie Bridges, *Marble Isle: Legends of the Round Table and Other Poems* (Philadelphia: J. B. Lippincott, 1864), 256, 259, 247; Nathaniel Hawthorne, "The Gorgon's Head," in *A Wonder Book; and, Tanglewood Tales* (London: J. M. Dent, 1906), 34.

88. Marjorie Garber, "Macbeth: The Male Medusa," in Susanne L. Wofford, ed., *Shakespeare's Late Tragedies* (Upper Saddle River, New Jersey: Prentice-Hall, 1996), 74–103.

89. D. J. Palmer, " 'A New Gorgon': Visual Effects in *Macbeth,*" in Brown, ed., *Focus on Macbeth,* 65, 64, 63.

90. Holmes, "The Great Instrument," *Atlantic Monthly,* November 1863, 643, 641.

91. *Boston Daily Courier,* November 2, 1863, 2.

92. Enna Duval [Anne Hampton Brewster], *Spirit Sculpture; or, The Year before Confirmation* (Philadelphia: James Fullerton, 1849), viii; Anne Hampton Brewster diary, December 13, 1863, Library Company, Philadelphia.

93. "Tableaux Vivans," *Harper's Monthly,* October 1863, 701.

94. Karen Halttunen, *Confidence Men and Painted Women: A Study of Middle-Class Culture in America, 1830–1870* (New Haven, Connecticut: Yale University Press, 1982), 184.

95. Holmes, "Sun-Painting and Sun-Sculpture," *Atlantic Monthly,* July 1861, 17–18.

96. Ibid., 21, 27.

97. Henry Wadsworth Longfellow, *Tales of a Wayside Inn* (Boston: Ticknor and Fields, 1863), 16.

98. For the autographed copy of *The Scarlet Letter,* see Leach, *Bright Particular Star,* 288; the satin playbill is in the Charlotte Cushman Papers.

99. Stebbins, *Charlotte Cushman,* 152.

100. Clara Erskine Clement, *Charlotte Cushman* (Boston: James R. Osgood, 1882), 131.

101. Anne Hampton Brewster, "Miss Cushman," *Blackwood's,* August 1878, 173.

102. The photograph is reproduced in Elizabeth Milroy, "The Public Career of Emma Stebbins: Work in Marble," *Archives of American Art Journal* 33 (1993): 6.

103. "Great Men's Autographs: The Collection Made by the Late William H. Ferris. Names of Artists, Statesmen, Poets and Soldiers Written in the Little Morocco-Covered Album," *New York Times,* April 25, 1886, 6. My thanks to Jennifer Greenhill for calling this quotation to my attention.

104. Walter Benjamin, *The Arcades Project,* trans. Howard Eiland and Kevin McLaughlin (Cambridge, Massachusetts: Belknap Press of Harvard University Press, 1999), 14, 8.

105. Gaston Bachelard, *The Poetics of Space,* trans. Maria Jolas (Boston: Beacon Press, 1994), 136–47.

106. Hawthorne, "Chiefly about War-Matters," 43.

107. For embalming during the war, see Drew Gilpin Faust, *This Republic of Suffering: Death and the American Civil War* (New York: Alfred A. Knopf, 2008), 92–98. For a fascinating discussion of embalming during and after the war, and the connection of this technology to other methods of preservation (canning food, recording sound), see Jonathan Sterne, *The Audible Past: Cultural Origins of Sound Reproduction* (Durham, North Carolina: Duke University Press, 2003), 287–307; Bellows to his sister and brother-in-law, March 7, 1862, quoted in George M. Frederickson, *The Inner Civil War: Northern Intellectuals and the Crisis of the Union* (New York: Harper & Row, 1965), 103.

108. John Montgomery Gordon, *Several Letters to the Mayor and City Council of Washington on the Subject of the Public Theatres, Pennsylvania Avenue and the Canal* (Norfolk: Virginia Printers, 1870), 5, quoted in Roger Meersman and Robert Boyer, "The National Theatre in Washington: Buildings and Audiences, 1835–1972," *Records of the Columbia Historical Society of Washington, D.C. 1971–1972* (Washington, D.C.: Columbia Historical Society, 1972), 200.

109. Clement, *Charlotte Cushman,* 78.

110. Peter Brooks, *The Melodramatic Imagination: Balzac, Henry James, Melodrama, and the Mode of Excess* (New Haven, Connecticut: Yale University Press, 1976), 47, 77–78.

111. Elihu Vedder, *The Digressions of V* (Boston: Houghton Mifflin, 1910), 375.

112. For accounts of Rogers and the sculpture, see Lorado Taft, *The History of American Sculpture* (New York: Macmillan, 1903), 159–70; Joyce K. Schiller,

"Nydia: A Forgotten Icon of the Nineteenth Century," *Bulletin of the Detroit Institute of Arts* 67 (1993): 37–45; Theodore E. Stebbins, Jr., *The Lure of Italy: American Artists and the Italian Experience, 1760–1914* (Boston: Museum of Fine Arts, 1992), 264–66; and *American Sculpture in the Metropolitan Museum of Art,* vol. 1, ed. Thayer Tolles (New York: Metropolitan Museum of Art, 1999), 117–20.

113. Paul Mantz, quoted in Anne Middleton Wagner, *Jean-Baptiste Carpeaux* (New Haven, Connecticut: Yale University Press, 1986), 149.

114. Rilke, "Auguste Rodin, First Part (1903)," 21.

115. Ibid.

116. Holmes, "The Stereoscope and the Stereograph," 739.

117. John Jackson Jarves, *The Art-Idea* (Cambridge, Massachusetts: Belknap Press of Harvard University Press, 1960), 214, 219.

118. Emerson, "Art," from *Essays: First Series,* in *Ralph Waldo Emerson: Essays & Lectures* (New York: Library of America, 1983), 438–39.

119. "The towering chimneys and the peaked roofs, topped by cresting and finials, the high windows, the sharply hooded dormers, and the dramatically corbelled little balcony in the attic all contributed to the vertical thrust of the two-and-one-half-story structure" (Paul R. Baker, *Richard Morris Hunt* [Cambridge, Massachusetts: MIT Press, 1980], 238). For the later history of the Corners, up to the time of its destruction in 1938, see "Mrs. Mason D. Rector Buys the 'Corners,'" *Newport Daily News,* January 21, 1938, 7, Newport Historical Society, Newport, Rhode Island.

120. "The Grave of Charlotte Cushman," unidentified newspaper clipping, Charlotte Cushman Papers.

121. Georges Bataille, "The Obelisk," in *Visions of Excess: Selected Writings, 1927–1939,* ed. Allan Stoekl, trans. Allan Stoekl, Carl R. Lovitt, and Donald M. Leslie, Jr. (Minneapolis: University of Minnesota Press, 1985), 215, 216, 217.

122. Ibid., 219.

123. Brewster, "Miss Cushman," 174.

TWO. THE FLAME OF PLACE: ABRAHAM LINCOLN

1. Frazar Kirkland, *The Pictorial Book of Anecdotes and Incidents of the War of the Rebellion* (Hartford, Connecticut: Hartford Publishing Co., 1866), 134. My thanks to Jennifer Greenhill for alerting me to this source. For a similar version of this story, perhaps drawn from the same source, see Carl Sandburg, *Abraham Lincoln,* vol. 3: *The War Years* (New York: Harcourt, Brace, 1939), 443.

2. *Daily National Republican,* October 17, 1863, 2.

3. John G. Foster to Abraham Lincoln, telegram, October 17, 1863, Papers of Abraham Lincoln, Library of Congress.

4. On the Wright case, see John P. Gray, "The Case of Dr. David M. Wright,

for the Murder of Lieutenant Sanborn.—Plea, Insanity," *American Journal of Insanity* 20 (January 1864): 284–300; L. B. Anderson, "The Execution of Dr. David Minton Wright, by the Federal Authorities at Norfolk, Virginia, October 23, 1862 *[sic]*," *Southern Historical Society Papers* 21 (1893): 326–37; and Ervin Leon Jordan, Jr., "A Painful Case: The Wright-Sanborn Incident in Norfolk, Virginia, July–October 1863" (master's thesis, Old Dominion University, 1977).

5. Thomas Wertenbaker, *Norfolk: Historic Southern Port* (Durham, North Carolina: Duke University Press, 1931), 220.

6. Quoted in Jordan, "A Painful Case," 24–25.

7. Gray, "The Case of Dr. David M. Wright," 293–94.

8. Ibid., 286–88, 291–92.

9. Ibid., 291, 293, 299–300.

10. David Homer Bates, *Lincoln in the Telegraph Office* (New York: Century, 1907), 3, 7, 11.

11. Ibid., 257.

12. Ibid., 259.

13. For the time the play started, see Benjamin Brown French, October 18, 1863, p. 152, Benjamin Brown French Papers, Manuscript Division, Library of Congress.

14. Lincoln, "'Spot Resolutions' in the United States House of Representatives," December 22, 1847, in *The Collected Works of Abraham Lincoln,* vol. 3, ed. Roy Basler, 420–22 (New Brunswick, New Jersey: Rutgers University Press, 1953–55).

15. Ibid.

16. John Channing Briggs, *Lincoln's Speeches Reconsidered* (Baltimore: Johns Hopkins University Press, 2005), 104.

17. For the references to "spotty" Lincoln, see Stephen B. Oates, *With Malice Toward None: A Life of Abraham Lincoln* (New York: Harper & Row, 1994), 80; for the reprint of the speech in 1860, see William Dean Howells, *Life of Abraham Lincoln* (Springfield, Illinois: Abraham Lincoln Association, 1938), 58–59. Lincoln's melancholy imagination recurred to the spot. Returning in the 1840s to his childhood home, he found "every spot a grave" in a poem he wrote soon after ("My Childhood Home," *The Poems of Abraham Lincoln* [Bedford, Massachusetts: Applewood Books, 1991, 12]). At his request, a passerby once gave him the lyrics of a song he had heard her sing, "The Enquiry" (William H. Herndon and Jesse W. Weik, *Herndon's Lincoln,* ed. Douglas L. Wilson and Rodney O. Davis [Urbana: University of Illinois Press, 2006]). The lyrics return to the tragic spot:

> Do ye now know some spot
> Where mortals weep no more?. . . .
> Knows't thou some favored spot,

Some island far away. . . .
Hast thou not seen some spot
Where miserable man
Might find a happier lot?. . .
Is there no happy spot
Where mortals may be blessed . . . ? (200–202).

Recalling coming upon the bodies of men killed during the Black Hawk War of 1836, Lincoln remembered that "every man had a round, red spot on top of his head" and that the "red sunlight seemed to paint everything all over" (Oates, *With Malice Toward None,* 23).

18. William H. Emory, U.S. Department of War, Army Corps of Topographical Engineers, *Notes of a Military Reconnaissance from Fort Leavenworth, in Missouri, to San Diego, in California, including Parts of the Arkansas, Del Norte, and Gila Rivers,* 30th Cong., 1st sess., 1848, S. Doc. 7, serial 505, 88; quoted in Robin Kelsey, *Archive Style: Photographs & Illustrations for U.S. Surveys, 1850–1890* (Berkeley: University of California Press, 2007), 51.

19. Lincoln's first substantive study of the telegraph occurred in March 1857, according to the operative Charles A. Tinker, who explained the device to him then in Pekin, Illinois: "Lincoln asked him to explain the operation of the new and mysterious force. . . . Tinker says that Lincoln seemed to be greatly interested in his explanation, and asked pertinent questions showing an observing mind already well furnished with knowledge of collateral facts and natural phenomena; and that he comprehended quite readily the operation of the telegraph, which at that time was a comparatively new feature in business and social intercourse" (Bates, *Lincoln in the Telegraph Office,* 4–5).

20. Benjamin Thomas, *Abraham Lincoln* (New York: Alfred Knopf, 1952), 13.

21. Henry C. Whitney, *Life on the Circuit with Lincoln* (Boston: Estes and Lauriat, 1892), 46.

22. On looking into the coffin at the daguerreotypes there, and on Wright's remark, see Anderson, "The Execution of Dr. David Minton Wright," 334; on the coffin and on Minton Wright's fate, see George Holbert Tucker, *Norfolk Highlights, 1854–1881* (Norfolk, Virginia: Norfolk Historical Society, 1972), 97. Penelope, aged nineteen, was married on October 17 to a local farmer named William H. Talbot. On October 21, Penelope tried to help her father escape by bringing him women's clothing in his jail cell. Wright changed into the clothing while Penelope lay disguised in the prisoner's bunk, like Sydney Carton in *A Tale of Two Cities* (1861); Wright's disguise, however, was detected by the guards (Jordan, "A Painful Case," 46; "The Execution of Dr. David Minton Wright,"33). In contrast to the Southern accounts of Wright's execution, Eli Walter Osborn, a Connecticut officer stationed in Norfolk, wrote to his father on October 25 that he had not been able to be present at the execution but that he would have

gone if he could: "I have never had a desire to see a man hung, but I believe if I had been at liberty, I should have attended this one" (Osborn to his father, October 25, 1863, New Haven Museum & Historical Society, New Haven, Connecticut). For a detailed account of the execution, see "The Execution of Dr. Wright," *Washington Evening Star,* October 26, 1863, 1.

An interesting connection between Wright and Lincoln is their common use of the *Macbeth* word "malice." At the gallows, Wright said, "Gentlemen, the act which I committed was done without the slightest malice" (*Washington Evening Star,* October 26, 1863, 1). One of the October 17 petitions written on Wright's behalf asserts that he acted with "no malice aforethought." Writing to Hackett, who felt bad about revealing Lincoln's August 17, 1863, letter about Shakespeare (the press ridiculed the president), Lincoln eased Hackett's conscience: "These comments [of the journalists] constitute a fair specimen of what has occurred to me through life. I have endured a great deal of ridicule without much malice" (Lincoln to Hackett, November 2, 1863, in *Abraham Lincoln: Speeches and Writings, 1859–1865,* ed. Don Edward Fehrenbacher [New York: Library of America, 1989], 532). "With malice toward none" begins the final paragraph of Lincoln's Second Inaugural Address, of March 4, 1865 (*Abraham Lincoln: Speeches and Writings, 1859–1865,* 687).

23. Harold Holzer and Lloyd Ostendorf, "Sculptures of Abraham Lincoln from Life," *Antiques* 113 (February 1978): 393.

24. See for example the stories recounted in Oates, *With Malice Toward None,* 196. For one of the morbid dreams, see ibid., 425–26; for Lincoln's identification with Duncan, see, for example, Briggs, *Lincoln's Speeches Reconsidered,* 57.

25. Adolphe de Chambrun, *Impressions of Lincoln and the Civil War: A Foreigner's Account,* trans. Aldebert de Chambrun (New York: Random House, 1952), 83. Senator Charles Sumner also described the shipboard recitation in his eulogy of Lincoln on June 1, 1865. See Robert Berkelman, "Lincoln's Interest in Shakespeare," *Shakespeare Quarterly* 2 (1951): 306.

26. W. A. Murray, "Why Was Duncan's Blood Golden?" in *Shakespeare: Macbeth, A Case Book,* ed. John Wain (London: Macmillan, 1968), 288.

27. Garry Wills, *Lincoln at Gettysburg: The Words That Remade America* (New York: Simon and Schuster, 1992), 174.

28. Alan Trachtenberg, "Lincoln's Smile: Ambiguities of the Face of Photography," in *Lincoln's Smile and Other Enigmas* (New York: Hill & Wang, 2007), 75.

29. Strangely, the Lincoln mask seems to include the thoughts of the sculptor as much as Lincoln's, and in that additional and surprising way to show Lincoln's powers of concentrating the views of others. On March 23, 1865, the *Daily National Republican* ran a story about the sculptor Mills, stating that as Union troops searched the State House in Columbia, South Carolina, they found an 1861 letter from Mills to the state legislature offering for the sake of his "adopted

state" to "lay aside my favorite art and to engage in the manufacture of bronze cannon." The article, noting that Mills was still working from a studio in the U.S. Capitol, called for his imprisonment for treason ("Clark Mills, the Sculptor," *Daily National Republican,* March 23, 1865, 1). Understood through this information, the February 11, 1865, cast seems to portray not just Lincoln's but the sculptor's imagination of Lincoln's death. Mills's method—smothering, then breaking the dried plaster from Lincoln's face, and reassembling the broken pieces into a smooth and seamless whole—must have been, if not a ritual assassination, a remarkably fraught act. Striking the man's face into pieces in order to reveal the real face beneath—a real face that the broken pieces would yet perfectly come to represent—Mills commemorated a man whose death had not yet happened, a death to which the sleeping face acquiesced, as if it expressed not only the morbidity of the sitter but the wish of the man who smothered on the plaster. Lincoln, reading Macbeth's lines about Duncan en route back to Washington on April 9, simultaneously held the thought of victim and assassin in his mind.

30. William O. Stoddard, quoted in Berkelman, "Lincoln's Interest in Shakespeare," 309.

31. Noah Brooks, *Washington in Lincoln's Time* (New York: Century, 1896), 71–72. For the career of McCullough, see William Winter, *The Wallet of Time* (New York: Moffat, Yard, 1913), 240–77.

32. André Bazin, "Theater and Cinema: Part Two," in *What Is Cinema?* vol. 1, trans. Hugh Gray (Berkeley: University of California Press, 1967), 101.

33. Francis Carpenter, *Six Months at the White House* (New York: Hurd and Houghton, 1869), 224.

34. Thomas, *Abraham Lincoln,* 9.

35. Chambrun, *Impressions of Lincoln and the Civil War,* 81.

36. William Herndon, quoted in Edmund Wilson, *Patriotic Gore: Studies in the Literature of the American Civil War* (New York: Oxford University Press, 1962), 119.

37. Brooks, *Washington in Lincoln's Time,* 302–3.

38. M. Helen Palmes Moss, "Lincoln and Wilkes Booth As Seen on the Day of the Assassination," *Century,* April 1909, 951.

39. Many of these photographs (though not the ones reproduced here) appeared in David Plowden, *Lincoln and His America, 1809–1865, with the Words of Abraham Lincoln* (New York: Viking, 1970). Plowden's photographic archive is in the collection of the Beinecke Rare Book and Manuscript Library, Yale University.

40. Carpenter, *Six Months at the White House,* 52.

41. "Opening of Grover's New Theatre," *Daily National Republican,* October 7, 1863, 2.

42. Daniel Mattausch, e-mail to the author, March 10, 2008. For a detailed discussion of the lighting in nineteenth-century theaters, see Terence Rees, *The-*

atre Lighting in the Age of Gas (Cambridge: Entertainment Technology Press, 2004).

43. *Macbeth* (New York: Douglas, 1850), Charlotte Cushman Papers, Manuscript Division, Library of Congress.

44. For the fiery effects of *Macbeth,* see William A. Armstrong, "Torch, Cauldron and Taper: Light and Darkness in 'Macbeth,'" in *Poetry and Drama, 1570-1700: Essays in Honor of Harold F. Brooks,* ed. Antony Coleman and Antony Hammond, 47–59 (London: Methuen, 1981).

45. For the fires on the site, see Roger Meersman and Robert Boyer, "The National Theatre in Washington: Buildings and Audiences, 1835–1972," *Records of the Columbia Historical Society of Washington, D.C. 1971–1972,* ed. Francis Coleman Rosenberger (Washington, D.C.: Columbia Historical Society, 1972), 196–97, 200–201. For detailed accounts of the fiery destruction of Grover's National Theatre on January 28, 1873, see "Destructive Fire, National Theater Burned," *Washington Evening Star,* January 28, 1873, 2; "Reminiscences Theatrical," *Washington Evening Star,* January 29, 1873, 2; "The Last Act: The National Theater in Ruins," *Daily Morning Chronicle,* January 29, 1873, 4; and "Destruction of the National Theatre," *Daily National Republican,* January 29, 1873, 4.

46. "The Ovation and Benefit at Grover's Theatre . . . ," *Daily National Republican,* October 19, 1863, 2.

47. Bruce McConnachie, "American Theatre in Context, from the Beginnings to 1870," in *The Cambridge History of American Theatre,* vol. 1: *Beginnings to 1870,* ed. Don B. Wilmeth and Christopher Bigsby (Cambridge: Cambridge University Press, 1998), 174

48. Kirkland, *Pictorial Book of Anecdotes,* 134.

49. The Hartford Wide-Awakes, "the first of all Wide-Awake organizations," had the "post of honor" at the October 3 New York march ("New-York Wide Awake!" *New-York Daily Tribune,* October 4, 1860, 5).

50. Ibid., 8; "The Great Demonstration," *New-York Daily Tribune,* October 4, 1860, 4.

51. "The Jubilee Last Night," *Washington Evening Star,* April 5, 1865, 2.

52. Benjamin Brown French diary, April 6, 1865, p. 384 (emphasis French's).

53. "New-York Wide Awake!" 5.

54. Ibid., 8.

55. Oates, *With Malice Toward None,* 107. A more hopeful version of the solitary Lincoln and the fireplace is Eastman Johnson's painting *Boyhood of Lincoln* (1868, University of Michigan Museum of Art).

56. "Our Streets—Obstructions Left in Them Nights Without Beacons," *Daily National Republican,* October 19, 1863, 2.

57. Margaret Leech, *Reveille in Washington, 1860–1865* (New York: Harper & Brothers, 1941), 276.

58. For Melville's move back to New York, see Douglas Robillard, "Intro-

duction: Melville's Poems," in Robillard, ed., *The Poems of Herman Melville* (Kent, Ohio: Kent State University Press, 2000), 10. For an alternate reading of the poem, one that differentiates Melville from the housetop speaker, see Stanton Garner, *The Civil War World of Herman Melville* (Lawrence: University Press of Kansas, 1993), 255–57.

59. Herman Melville, "The House-top: A Night Piece (July, 1863)," from *Battle-Pieces* (1865) in Robillard, ed., *The Poems of Herman Melville,* 94.

60. These lone lights in the panorama of darkness are not redemptive, as they are in an earlier poem. In the 1850 *Prelude,* William Wordsworth recalls how as a young man he had gazed on the "spots" of the French Revolution (the Bastille, the King's Palace) and that now, with the passage of years, these had become "spots of time"

> That with distinct pre-eminence retain
> A renovating virtue (XII, 208–10)

because his mind can hold them jewel-like as precious stays against death. For Robert Duggan, who connects "The House-top" to this passage in Wordsworth, Melville's solitary fires are more complex. They demand action, not contemplation, the kind of draconian measures (like Lincoln's) that the observer endorses when, staring at the flames, he implores "wise Draco" (both the dragon constellation and the Federal army) to come "deep in the midnight roll / Of black artillery" to restore order as Lincoln did when he employed Union soldiers to quell the riots. But in another sense the flames are those of an extinguished Wordsworth, suggesting a romantic vivacity of perception equal to the earlier poet's that nonetheless finds within these spots of flame not restorative wholeness but lurid intensities of isolation (Duggan, " 'Sleep No More' Again: Melville's Rewriting of Book X of Wordsworth's Prelude," *Romanticism on the Net* 38–39, May–August 2005, www.ron.umontreal.cal [accessed August 2008]).

61. Bates, *Lincoln in the Telegraph Office,* 264–65.

62. Lincoln, "First Inaugural Address," March 4, 1861, in *Abraham Lincoln: Speeches and Writings, 1859–1865,* 224.

63. Lincoln, "Address to the Young Men's Lyceum of Springfield, Illinois: The Perpetuation of Our Political Institutions," in *Abraham Lincoln: Speeches and Writings, 1832–1858,* ed. Don Edward Fehrenbacher (New York: Library of America, 1989), 30.

64. Russ Castronovo, *Fathering the Nation: Genealogies of Slavery and Freedom* (Berkeley: University of California Press, 1995), 6.

65. Lincoln, "Address to the Young Men's Lyceum," 36. Lincoln maintained his sense of patchwork dispersion during the Civil War, even as he fought to preserve the Union. Addressing a delegation of Indian chiefs in Washington on March 27, 1863, he turned to a globe brought to him for the purpose, laid his hand on it, and told the delegation, "We have people now present from all parts

of the globe—here, and here, and here. There is a great difference between this pale-faced people and their red brethren, both as to numbers and the way in which we live." Dwelling on difference—"here, and here, and here"—Lincoln evoked a fragmented space akin to that of the Lyceum Address (Lincoln, "Speech to Indian Chiefs, Washington, D.C.," in *Abraham Lincoln: Speeches and Writings, 1859–1865,* 441).

66. J. Hillis Miller, *Illustration* (Cambridge, Massachusetts: Harvard University Press, 1992), 61.

67. "New-York Wide Awake!" 8.

68. For dark-lantern political societies, see Frank L. Klement, *Dark Lanterns: Secret Political Societies, Conspiracies, and Treason Trials in the Civil War* (Baton Rouge: Louisiana State University Press, 1984).

69. Marc Simpson, *Winslow Homer Paintings of the Civil War* (San Francisco: Fine Arts Museums of San Francisco, 1988), 131.

70. For more on Donati's Comet, see G. P. Bond, *Account of the Great Comet of 1858, Annals of the Astronomical Observatory of Harvard College,* vol. 3 (Cambridge: Welch, Bigelow, 1862). See also "The Comet," *Harper's Weekly,* October 9, 1858, 653.

71. William H. Herndon and Jesse W. Weik, *Abraham Lincoln: The True Story of a Great Life,* vol. 2 (London: Sampson Low Marston, 1893), 119.

72. George W. Smith, *When Lincoln Came to Egypt* (Herrin, Illinois: Trovillion Private Press, 1940), 121.

73. See Bond, *Account of the Great Comet of 1858,* xix. The book features many of Watts's engravings of Donati's Comet.

74. Melville, "The Portent," from *Battle-Pieces,* in *The Poems of Herman Melville,* 53.

75. For proslavery feeling in southern Illinois, see, for example, Mary A. Livermore, *My Story of the War: A Woman's Narrative of Four Years Personal Experience* (Williamstown, Massachusetts: Corner House, 1978), 359–63. Livermore, a relief worker for the Sanitary Commission, describes transporting a black boy from the South through Cairo and finally to Chicago, despite the "Black Laws" of Illinois that punished whites with fines and imprisonment for bringing a black person into the state. See also "From Cairo and Below: Hanging of Three Negroes for Murder," *New-York Daily Tribune,* October 16, 1863, 1.

76. Carl Sandburg, *Abraham Lincoln,* vols. 1 and 2, *The Prairie Years* (New York: Harcourt, Brace, 1926), 101–2.

77. Marcia Pointon, "The Representation of Time in Painting: A Study of William Dyce's *Pegwell Bay: A Recollection of October 5th, 1858,*" *Art History* 1 (March 1978): 101.

78. Walt Whitman, *Memoranda during the War,* ed. Peter Coviello (New York: Oxford University Press, 2004), 17–18; Emerson, "Abraham Lincoln," *Journal of Historical Studies* 1 (Spring 1968): 260; Hay, quoted in Berkelman, "Lincoln's In-

terest in Shakespeare," 305; on Duff Armstrong, see Oates, *With Malice Toward None,* 141; Edward Steers, *Blood on the Moon: The Assassination of Abraham Lincoln* (Lexington: University of Kentucky Press, 2001).

79. B. A. Gould, *Memoir of Lewis Morris Rutherfurd, 1816–1892,* in *National Academy of Sciences: Biographical Memoirs,* vol. 3 (Washington, D.C., 1895), 417–18.

80. Benjamin Brown French diary, April 15, 1865, p. 386.

81. William Owner diary, April 14, 1865, Manuscript Division, Library of Congress.

82. "Grover's Theatre—'Aladdin, or the Wonderful Lamp'; grand illumination and pyrotechnic display, and the recitation of several national poems. This superbly mounted play is having a great run at Grover's" (*Washington Evening Star,* April 1, 1865, 3).

83. Charles M. Harvey, "Seward, Empire-Builder and Seer," *Putnam's Monthly,* June 1907, 272; Seward, quoted in ibid., 272–73; Seward, "Mr. Seward's Speech in Salem, Oregon," in *Alaska. Speech of William H. Seward at Sitka, August 12, 1869* (Washington, D.C.: Philip and Solomons, 1869); Edward Everett Hale, *William H. Seward* (Philadelphia: George W. Jacobs, 1910), 367; Thomas Bulfinch, *Legends of Charlemagne; or, Romance of the Middle Ages* (Boston: J. E. Tilton and Co., 1864), xiii–xiv. "I sat by the side of the bed nearest the door, reading 'Legends of Charlemagne,'" Fanny wrote in her diary for April 14, 1865 (original, p. 183, Rare Books and Special Collections, Rush Rhees Library, University of Rochester, New York).

84. Fanny Seward diary, original, April 14, 1865, pp. 195, 187, 183. 187.

85. Mattausch, interview by the author, October 24, 2007; Mattausch, e-mail to the author, March 10, 2008.

THREE. THE GLASS CASE: INTERIOR LIFE IN WASHINGTON, D.C.

1. Bruce McConnachie, "American Theatre in Context, from the Beginnings to 1870," in *The Cambridge History of American Theatre,* vol. 1, *Beginnings to 1870,* ed. Don Wilmeth and Christopher Bigsby (Cambridge: Cambridge University Press, 1998), 174.

2. "The Ovation and Benefit at Grover's Theatre . . . ," *Daily National Republican,* October 19, 1863, 2.

3. Lawrence Levine, *Highbrow/Lowbrow: The Emergence of Cultural Hierarchy in America* (Cambridge, Massachusetts: Harvard University Press, 1988), 9, 63–65, 68. Artemus Ward, one of Lincoln's favorite comic authors, expressed the shift in "Wax Figures vs. Shakespeare," published in 1862. Ward, whose real name was Charles Farrar Browne, affected the errant voice of a self-important hick promoter comparing the value of his popular entertainments to the highbrow kind. "My show konsists of a serious of wax works, snakes, a paneramy kalled a Grand Movin Diarea of the War in the Crymear." Ward claims that his shows are more

edifying than high-culture productions, which by the 1860s increasingly came to mean Shakespeare. "I manetane that wax figgers is more elevatin' than awl the plays ever wroten. Take Shakespear for instunse. . . . There's Mrs. Macbeth—sheze a nise kind of wooman to have round aint she, a putting old Mack, her husband, up to slaying Dunkan with a cheeze knife, while heze payin a friendly visit to their house. O its hily moral, I spoze." Ward satirized the promoter's ignorance but also imagined a working man's resentment of middle-class cultural pretensions (Artemus Ward [Charles Farrar Browne], "Wax Figures vs. Shakespeare," in *Artemus Ward: His Book* [New York: Carleton, 1862], 82–84). A well-known story about Lincoln is that he read Ward's story "High-Handed Outrage at Utica" to his cabinet on September 22, 1862, prior to announcing his plans to issue the Emancipation Proclamation. See Stephen B. Oates, *With Malice Toward None: A Life of Abraham Lincoln* (New York: Harper & Row, 1994), 318–19. See also Michael Bristol, *Shakespeare's America, America's Shakespeare* (London: Routledge, 1990), for a discussion of the affirmative middle-class values that American audiences began to find in Shakespeare: "Shakespeare's originality is closely tied to the primary affirmative theme of much American, and also British, criticism: the analysis and celebration of individuality and of the values of expressive autonomy as these are revealed both in various characters and in the poetic textures of the plays" (123).

4. "Charlotte Cushman at Grover's Theatre—Go Early," *Daily National Republican,* October 17, 1863, 2.

5. "Grand Opening of Grover's New Theatre," *Daily Morning Chronicle,* October 7, 1863, 2.

6. Fanny Seward diary, typescript, October 10, 1863, p. 826, Rare Books and Special Collections, Rush Rhees Library, University of Rochester, New York.

7. "Opening Night of Grover's New Theatre," *Daily National Republican,* October 7, 1863, 2.

8. *Harper's Monthly,* December 1863, 133.

9. Benjamin Brown French diary, October 18, 1863, 152–53, Benjamin Brown French Papers, Manuscript Division, Library of Congress.

10. George Augustus Sala, *My Diary in America in the Midst of War,* vol. 2 (London: Tinsley Brothers, 1865), 72.

11. Leonard Grover, "Lincoln's Interest in the Theater," *Century,* April 1909, 946–47.

12. "Attempt at Suicide," *Washington Evening Star,* October 19, 1863, 3.

13. "Sleeping in Centre Market," *Daily National Republican,* October 17, 1863, 3.

14. "Suspicion of Horse-Stealing," *Washington Evening Star,* October 19, 1863, 3.

15. Charles Congdon, "The Decline of Tragedy," *Harper's Monthly,* November 1864, 747–48.

16. *Romola* was advertised in *Harper's Weekly,* October 17, 1863, 671; George Eliot, *Romola* (London: Penguin, 1996), 339, 341.

17. Ibid., 341, 342, 348–49, 354, 342.

18. For the relation of the Rucellai Gardens scene to *Macbeth,* see Dorothea Barrett's introduction to *Romola,* xx.

19. John Davis, "Eastman Johnson's *Negro Life at the South* and Urban Slavery in Washington, D.C.," *Art Bulletin* 80 (March 1998): 68–69.

20. Ibid., 75–76.

21. Peter Brooks, *Realist Vision* (New Haven, Connecticut: Yale University Press, 2005), 3.

22. Eliot, *Adam Bede* (London: Penguin, 1980), 72–73, 56.

23. Ibid., 179; Teresa Carbone and Patricia Hills, *Eastman Johnson: Painting America* (Brooklyn: Brooklyn Museum of Art, 1999), 21. The process in the 1850s could be cast as psychological and devious, too, especially in the hands of a darkly tempered novelist disinclined to trust the new realist mode. Hawthorne, in *The Scarlet Letter,* makes Roger Chillingworth an implacable realist searching out the innermost privacy of Arthur Dimmesdale, excavating his interior as though the hapless minister's body were a fourth wall to be penetrated. Chillingworth "now dug into the poor clergyman's heart like a miner searching for gold; or, rather like a sexton delving into a grave, possibly in quest of a jewel that had been buried on the dead man's bosom." Searching for Dimmesdale's secrets, Chillingworth "groped along as stealthily, with as cautious a tread, and as wary an outlook, as a thief entering a chamber where a man lies only half asleep—or, it may be, broad awake—with purpose to steal the very treasure which this man guards as the apple of his eye" (Hawthorne, *The Scarlet Letter* [New York: Signet, 1959], 127–28).

24. Fredric Jameson, "The Experiments of Time: Providence and Realism," in *The Novel,* vol. 2: *Forms and Themes,* ed. Franco Moretti (Princeton, New Jersey: Princeton University Press, 2006), 122–23.

25. Ibid., 123.

26. Here I am questioning two powerful accounts of the nineteenth-century bourgeois interior, those of Walter Benjamin and Theodor Adorno. Each saw a relation between the inwardness of middle-class subjects and the inwardness of their deep-sunk, fortresslike residences. Cut off so completely from the social world of the street, sequestered in gas-lit privacy, these subjects could invent a kind of interiority based on fantasy, dreams, and spirituality. See Benjamin, "[The Interior, the Trace]" in *The Arcades Project,* ed. Rolf Tiedemann, trans. Howard Eiland and Kevin McLaughlin (Cambridge, Massachusetts: Belknap Press of Harvard University Press, 1999), 212–27; Theodor Adorno, *Kierkegaard: Construction of the Aesthetic,* trans. Robert Hullot-Kentor (Minneapolis: University of Minnesota Press, 1989), for example, see 45–46, quoted in Michael Fried, *Menzel's Realism: Art and Embodiment in Nineteenth-Century Berlin* (New Haven, Connecticut: Yale University Press, 2002), 94.

27. Howe, quoted in Gary Williams, *Hungry Heart: The Literary Emergence of Julia Ward Howe* (Amherst: University of Massachusetts Press, 1999), 208; "Battle Hymn of the Republic," *Atlantic Monthly,* February 1862, 145.

28. Hawthorne, "Chiefly about War-Matters," *Atlantic Monthly,* July 1862, 59–60.

29. Sala, *My Diary in America,* 83–84.

30. Jeffrey J. Polizzotto, "Julia Ward Howe, John Brown's Body, and the Coming of the Lord," in *Worldmaking,* ed. William Pencak (New York: Peter Lang, 1996), 187.

31. Julia Ward Howe, *Reminiscences, 1819–1899* (Boston: Houghton, Mifflin, 1899), 270–71.

32. Ibid., 270.

33. Sarah Luria, *Capital Speculations: Writing and Building Washington, D.C.* (Durham: University of New Hampshire Press, 2006), 81–82.

34. Howe, *Reminiscences,* 238–40. The auspicious occasion came some years later, when Cushman and Edwin Booth, in Boston, offered to perform Howe's play, but the theater manager Edward Loomis Davenport, who went on to play Macduff on October 17, 1863, in Washington, declined to stage it.

35. Howe, "A New Sculptor," *Atlantic Monthly,* September 1862, 282–83.

36. Holmes, "The Great Instrument," *Atlantic Monthly,* November 1863, 638–39.

37. Quoted in Howe, *Reminiscences,* 228–29.

38. Ibid., 270.

39. "The United States Army," *New York Herald,* October 30, 1863; "The War," *New York Herald,* April 13, 1861; quoted in Mark M. Smith, *Listening to Nineteenth-Century America* (Chapel Hill: University of North Carolina Press, 2001), 212–13.

40. Howe, "How to Regard the Great Organ," *Boston Daily Commonwealth,* November 13, 1863, quoted in Mary Loeffelholz, "The Religion of Art in the City at War: Boston's Public Poetry and the Great Organ, 1863," *American Literary History* 13 (2001): 220.

41. S. Weir Mitchell, "The Case of George Dedlow," *Atlantic Monthly,* July 1866, 5. For Mitchell's experiences during the war, see Debra Journet, "Phantom Limbs and 'Body-Ego': S. Weir Mitchell's 'George Dedlow,'" *Mosaic* 23 (Winter 1990): 87–99.

42. Mitchell, "The Case of George Dedlow," 8. In the story, a New England hospital worker understands Dedlow's point: "Life," she tells him, "is the garnered condensation of objective impressions; and as the objective is the remote father of the subjective, so must individuality, which is but focused subjectivity, suffer and fade" when sensations are reduced (8).

43. Marshall McLuhan, *Understanding Media: The Extensions of Man* (New York: McGraw-Hill, 1964), 252.

44. See Mark Seltzer, *Bodies and Machines* (New York: Routledge, 1992), and Bill Brown, "Science Fiction, the World's Fair, and the Prosthetics of Empire, 1910–1915," in *Cultures of United States Imperialism,* ed. Donald Pease and Amy Kaplan, 129–63 (Durham, North Carolina: Duke University Press, 1993).

45. Brayton Harris, *Blue & Gray in Black & White* (Washington, D.C.: Brassey's, 1999), 137.

46. Edward Everett Hale, "The Man Without a Country," *Atlantic Monthly,* December 1863, 667.

47. Ibid., 677.

48. Ibid., 669.

49. Ibid., 673, 677.

50. Ibid., 669, 677.

51. William H. Gerdts connects Whittredge's painting to the German painter Adolph Menzel's *Room with a Balcony* (1845), a picture Whittredge could have known during his training in Germany (Gerdts, "The Empty Room," *Allen Memorial Art Museum Bulletin* 33 [1975–76]: 75–77). Whether the connection between the two paintings is coincidental or not, Michael Fried's phenomenological reading of *Room with a Balcony* intensifies the sense of Whittredge's picture as a concentration on sensuous effects (Fried, *Menzel's Realism,* 84–94). In a separate line of inquiry, Roberta Smith Favis notes a link between Whittredge's domestic and forest interiors, a rich topic for further study: "In his paintings of household interiors, Whittredge developed and personalized effects that he later transposed to a series of forest interiors [such as *The Old Hunting Grounds,* 1864], creating a landscape theme that would prove one of his most distinctive and successful artistic achievements" (Favis, "Home Again: Worthington Whittredge's Domestic Interiors," *American Art* [Spring 1995]: 20).

52. Adorno, quoted in Fried, *Menzel's Realism,* 94.

53. Hale, "The Man Without a Country," 665. My reading of Whittredge's painting differs from that of Gerdts, who argues that the painting shows the absence of persons away at the war: "It is not unlikely that the picture is a direct expression of the major historical event of the moment, the Civil War, for the picture *bespeaks* absence of those who might otherwise enjoy the simple comforts of a warm and cozy interior—those who were called away to serve their country" (Gerdts, "The Empty Room," 78).

54. Theodore Winthrop, *Cecil Dreeme* (Boston: Ticknor and Fields, 1861), 34, 56, 114–65.

55. George William Curtis, "Biographical Sketch of the Author," in Winthrop, *Cecil Dreeme,* 13, 11.

56. David Cody, "Blood in the Basin: The Civil War in Emily Dickinson's 'The name—of it—is 'Autumn,' " *Emily Dickinson Journal* 12 (2003): 25–52; Diana Fuss, *The Sense of an Interior: Four Writers and the Rooms That Shaped Them* (New York: Routledge, 2004), 47–48, 25, 57.

57. LeRoy H. Fischer, *Lincoln's Gadfly, Adam Gurowski* (Norman: University of Oklahoma Press, 1964), 75–76, 96.

58. Sumner, quoted in Robert Carter, "Gurowski," *Atlantic Monthly,* November 1866, 633.

59. Gurowski, August 2, 1863, *Diary,* vol. 2, *From November 18, 1862 to October 18, 1863* (New York: Carleton, 1864), 288.

60. Carter, "Gurowski," 628.

61. Ibid., 629.

62. Ibid., 633.

63. Gurowski, October 17, 1863, *Diary,* 347.

64. Ward Hill Lamon, *Recollections of Abraham Lincoln, 1847–1865,* ed. Dorothy Lamon (Chicago: A. C. McClurg, 1895), 268–69.

65. Fischer, *Lincoln's Gadfly,* 19, 19n32.

66. Ibid., 72.

67. Carter, "Gurowski," 628, 627–28, 629.

68. Gurowski, quoted in Fischer, *Lincoln's Gadfly,* 91.

69. Doris Kearns Goodwin, *Team of Rivals: The Political Genius of Abraham Lincoln* (New York: Simon and Schuster, 2005), 557.

70. See "A Chronological History of the United States Capitol," 93–98, file, Architect of the Capitol, Washington, D.C.

71. Walt Whitman to Louisa Van Velsor Whitman, October 20, 1863, in *Walt Whitman: The Correspondence,* vol. 1, *1842–1867,* ed. Edwin Haviland Miller (New York: New York University Press, 1961), 168–69.

72. Ibid.

73. Walt Whitman, *Memoranda during the War* (New York: Oxford University Press, 2004), 125.

74. Ibid., 17. See also my discussion of the word *case* in Alexander Nemerov, "Whitman's Moment," *PN Review* 33 (July–August 2007): 32. Subsequently I found that the literary historian James Dawes had already noted the double use of *case* in this passage, which he calls "uncanny figurative blending, or mutual substitution, of inorganic and organic matter" (Dawes, *The Language of War: Literature and Culture in the U.S. from the Civil War through World War II* [Cambridge, Massachusetts: Harvard University Press, 2002], 50).

75. Whitman, *Memoranda during the War,* 168, 95, 36.

76. Ibid., 47, 17–18.

77. Whitman, "Cavalry Crossing a Ford," *Leaves of Grass* (New York: Library of America, 1992), 435.

78. Whitman, "Bivouac on a Mountain Side" and "Sparkles from the Wheel," *Leaves of Grass,* 435, 514.

79. Whitman, "Vigil Strange I Kept on the Field One Night" and "When Lilacs Last in the Dooryard Bloom'd," *Leaves of Grass,* 438–39, 459–67.

80. Whitman, *Memoranda during the War,* 84–85.

81. Whitman, ibid., 27; "Come Up from the Fields Father," *Leaves of Grass,* 436–38.

82. Whitman, *Memoranda during the War,* 18.

83. Thornton Wilder, preface to *Three Plays: Our Town, The Skin of Our Teeth, The Matchmaker* (London: Longmans Green, 1957), x.

84. "Ovation and Benefit at Grover's," 2.

85. Joseph Henry, *Eulogy on Prof. Alexander Dallas Bache* (Washington, D.C.: Government Printing Office, 1872), 15; Merle M. Odgers, *Alexander Dallas Bache, Scientist and Educator, 1806–1867* (Philadelphia: University of Pennsylvania Press, 1947), 213.

86. Light-House Board memo, October 16, 1863, Alexander Dallas Bache Papers, Smithsonian Institution Archives, Washington, D.C.

87. Joseph Henry, "On Acoustics Applied to Public Buildings," in *Proceedings of the American Association for the Advancement of Science* (Washington, D.C.: American Association for the Advancement of Science, 1856), 120.

88. William J. Rhees, *An Account of the Smithsonian Institution, Its Founder, Building, Operations, etc.* (Washington, D.C.: Thomas McGill, 1857), 14.

89. Henry, *On Acoustics,* 126.

90. Rhees, *An Account of the Smithsonian Institution,* 15.

91. Henry, *On Acoustics,* 134.

92. For Smithson's will, see, for example, William H. Pierson, Jr.'s introduction to *The Castle: An Illustrated History of the Smithsonian Building,* ed. Cynthia R. Field, Richard E. Stamm, and Heather Ewing (Washington, D.C.: Smithsonian Institution Press, 1993), 1; on public lectures, see Rhees, *An Account of the Smithsonian Institution,* 35.

93. Edward N. Dickerson, *Joseph Henry and the Magnetic Telegraph: An Address Delivered at Princeton College, June 16, 1885* (New York: Charles Scribner's Sons, 1885), 32–33.

94. Albert E. Moyer, *Joseph Henry: The Rise of an American Scientist* (Washington, D.C.: Smithsonian Institution Press, 1997), 21, 68–69; William B. Taylor, "A Memoir of Joseph Henry: A Sketch of His Scientific Work," *Bulletin of the Philosophical Society of Washington,* vol. 2 (Philadelphia: Collins, 1879), 359.

95. Henry wrote to Asa Gray on November 7, 1863, "We reached home just three weeks ago today" (*The Papers of Joseph Henry,* vol. 10, ed. Marc Rothenberg [Washington, D.C.: Smithsonian Institution / Science History Publications, 2004], 345).

96. Odgers, *Alexander Dallas Bache,* 163, 185–86. Leonard Warren, *Joseph Leidy: The Last Man Who Knew Everything* (New Haven, Connecticut: Yale University Press, 1998).

97. "Extracts from correspondence between Lt. House Board and Major A. Bache relative to Lt. House for Pt. Lobos, Cal."; W. P. Trowbridge to Bache, May

28, 1855 [about the Farallon Islands lighthouse keeper's position]; "Lights on Delaware and Chesapeake Bays"; all in the Bache Papers.

98. Henry to Bache, October 3, 1863, *The Papers of Joseph Henry,* vol. 10, 338.

99. Richard Stamm, curator at the Smithsonian Castle, explains that some of the display cases came to the Smithsonian from the Patent Office "when the collections of the National Institute were transferred to the Smithsonian building beginning ca. 1857" (e-mail to the author, March 12, 2008).

100. Holmes, "Shakespeare, Tercentennial Celebration, April 23, 1864," *The Poetical Works of Oliver Wendell Holmes* (Boston: Houghton Mifflin, 1975), 211.

101. Henry, *Eulogy on Prof. Alexander Dallas Bach,* 20.

102. Henry, quoted in Moyer, *Joseph Henry,* 141.

103. For Peale and photography, see Kenneth Haltman, "Titian Ramsay Peale's Specimen Portraiture; or, Natural History as Family History," in *The Peale Family: Creation of a Legacy, 1770–1870,* ed. Lillian Miller (New York: Abbeville, 1997), 198–99.

104. Emerson, "Shakspeare; or, The Poet," from *Representative Men* (1850), in *Ralph Waldo Emerson: Essays & Lectures* (New York: Library of America, 1983), 720.

FOUR. ACOUSTIC SHADOWS: THE BATTLE OF BRISTOE STATION

1. William Owner diary, vol. 1, page facing first entry, December 20, 1860, and vol. 5, October 17, 1863, Manuscript Division, Library of Congress.

2. Charles D. Ross, *Civil War Acoustic Shadows* (Shippensburg, Pennsylvania: White Mane Books, 2001), 1–5.

3. William B. Taylor, "A Memoir of Joseph Henry: A Sketch of His Scientific Work," *Bulletin of the Philosophical Society of Washington,* vol. 2 (Philadelphia: Collins, 1879), 353; Ross, *Civil War Acoustic Shadows,* 32, 2.

4. Charles Longfellow to Henry Wadsworth Longfellow, October 17, 1863, Special Collections, Houghton Library, Harvard University.

5. Adam Gurowski, October 17, 1863, *Diary,* vol. 2, *From November 18, 1862 to October 18, 1863* (New York: Carleton, 1864), 347.

6. William Owner diary, October 19, 1863.

7. Noah Brooks, *Washington in Lincoln's Time* (New York: Century, 1896), 94.

8. Mary Livermore, *My Story of the War: A Woman's Narrative of Four Years Personal Experience as Nurse in the Union Army* (Hartford, Connecticut: A. D. Worthington, 1889), 141, quoted in David M. Henkin, *The Postal Age: The Emergence of Modern Communications in Nineteenth-Century America* (Chicago: University of Chicago Press, 2006), 138.

9. Thomas Claybrook Elder to Anna Fitzhugh Elder, October 17, 1863, Virginia Historical Society, Richmond; Charles Wellington Reed to his mother, October 17, 1863, Charles Wellington Reed Papers, Manuscript Division, Library

of Congress; Walter Herron Taylor to "my dear Bettie," October 17, 1863, in *Lee's Adjutant: The Wartime Letters of Colonel Walter Herron Taylor, 1862–1865,* ed. R. Lockwood Tower (Columbia: University of South Carolina Press, 1995), 75–78; Henkin, *The Postal Age,* x, 2.

10. William W. Chamberlain to Capt. Jno. M. Robinson, October 17, 1863, Virginia Historical Society.

11. For accounts of the battle, see William D. Henderson, *The Road to Bristoe Station: Campaigning with Lee and Meade, August 1–October 20, 1863* (Lynchburg, Virginia: H. E. Howard, 1987); Todd S. Berkoff, "Botched Battle at Bristoe," *America's Civil War* (September 2003): 22–29, 70–71; Shelby Foote, *The Civil War, A Narrative: Fredericksburg to Meridian* (New York: Vintage, 1963), 792–94. I am grateful to David Born, the historic programs coordinator at Bristoe, for conducting a tour of the battlefield for me in August 2006.

12. William A. Archer to Conway Robinson, October 19, 1863, Virginia Historical Society.

13. Ibid.

14. Henry Abbott to his father, October 17, 1863, in *Fallen Leaves: The Civil War Letters of Major Henry Livermore Abbott,* ed. Robert Garth Scott (Kent, Ohio: Kent State University Press, 1991), 223–24. Abbott, who was killed the following year, was idolized by his Twentieth Massachusetts comrade Oliver Wendell Holmes, Jr., as the epitome of the good soldier. See Louis Menand, *The Metaphysical Club* (New York: Farrar, Straus, and Giroux, 2001), 60–61. Holmes, convalescing from wounds back in Boston, was not at Bristoe Station.

15. John G. Perry, *Letters from a Surgeon of the Civil War* (Boston: Little, Brown, 1906), 113.

16. Henry Wadsworth Longfellow, "Killed at the Ford," *Atlantic Monthly,* April 1866, 479–80. See also Walt Whitman's "Come Up from the Fields Father," *Leaves of Grass* (New York: Library of America, 1992), where a letter ("here's a letter from our Pete") makes the receiver all but wish to "silent from life escape / and withdraw."

17. Thomas Wentworth Higginson, "Emily Dickinson's Letters," *Atlantic Monthly,* October 1891, 444–56, excerpted in *Selected Poems & Letters of Emily Dickinson,* ed. Robert N. Linscott (New York: Anchor, 1959), 19. Jerusha Hull McCormack has written about the telegraphic qualities of Dickinson's style—the way her dashes follow the telegraph operator's cryptic codes (McCormack, "Domesticating Delphi: Emily Dickinson and the Electro-Magnetic Telegraph," *American Quarterly* 55 [December 2003]: 569–601). Perhaps gunfire and telegraphy go together as metaphors for a poetry that hits hard and seemingly comes out of nowhere.

18. Herman Melville, "Shiloh," *The Poems of Herman Melville,* ed. Douglas Robillard (Kent, Ohio: Kent State University Press, 2000), 81. Dickinson, #986 (ca. 1865), in *The Complete Poems of Emily Dickinson,* ed. Thomas H. Johnson (Boston: Little, Brown, 1961), 460.

19. Charles Longfellow to Henry Wadsworth Longfellow, September 16, 1863, Houghton Library.

20. Arguably only by a feat of marksmanship could the poet overcome the developing anonymity and placelessness of publishing—of sending one's words out in books and magazines. In effect the poet would target an audience, aiming for a reader who might feel, in the midst of her devastation, grateful for having been so thunderstruck by a verse that appears to single her out: to have her name on it. Two decades earlier, when American publishing was not nearly as widespread—when periodicals such as the *Atlantic Monthly* did not exist—Longfellow could still put the problem succinctly, equating poetry and ammunition, as in "The Arrow and the Song": "I shot an arrow into the air, / It fell to earth, I knew not where. . . . "I breathed a song into the air, / It fell to earth, I knew not where." But back then, in 1845, it was possible to envision a specific landing place for the soft weapon of one's words—the poet finds the arrow, long afterward, "in the heart of a friend." "Killed at the Ford" also aims for the heart, but in a more impersonal publishing industry: the published poem, to be effective, must be like a letter mailed to a specific recipient, and the letter must strive for emotional directness (Longfellow, "The Arrow and the Song," *The Complete Poetical Works of Longfellow* [Boston: Houghton Mifflin, 1893], 68). A prefatory note to the poem explains that it was written on October 16, 1845.

21. "How I Saw an Explosion," *Frank Leslie's Illustrated Weekly,* October 17, 1863, 55.

22. *Macbeth* (New York: Douglas, n.d.), p. 16, Charlotte Cushman Papers, Manuscript Division, Library of Congress.

23. Fanny Seward diary, original, October 10, 1863, p. 65, Rare Books and Special Collections, Rush Rhees Library, University of Rochester, New York.

24. George Augustus Sala, *My Diary in America in the Midst of War,* vol. 2 (London: Tinsley Brothers, 1865), 86–88; Christian F. Eckloff, *Memoirs of a Senate Page (1855–1859),* ed. Percival G. Melbourne (New York: Broadway, 1909), 214; Brooks, *Washington in Lincoln's Time,* 105.

25. For the Union dead still on the battlefield on October 17, see Edward Bassett's diary entry of October 22 in M. H. Bassett, *From Bull Run to Bristow Station* (St. Paul, Minn.: North Central Publishing, 1962), 32: "Camped near Kittle Run Va. Oct. 22nd. . . . At Bristoe we found some of our men laying on top of the ground that had been killed the morning of the 14th. The Rebs did not bury them, guess they had enough of their own to take care of." For the Confederate burial on October 15, see, for example, Foote, *The Civil War, A Narrative,* 794.

26. David Born, e-mail to the author, June 18, 2007. Born surmises that the round was made at one of the foundries in the northeast, possibly the Ames Foundry in Chicopee, Massachusetts, which he believes manufactured Schenkl shells.

27. Henry Robinson Berkeley diary, October 14, 1863, Virginia Historical So-

ciety; Abner Crump Hawkins diary, October 16 and October 17, 1863, Virginia Historical Society; Watkins Kearns diary, October 17, 1863, Virginia Historical Society.

28. Richard Henry Watkins to Mary Watkins, October 15, 1863, Virginia Historical Society.

29. Edward Bassett, quoted in Bassett, *From Bull Run to Bristow Station,* 32, 111.

30. Bassett, *From Bull Run to Bristow Station,* 85, 83.

31. "The Battle of Bristoe Station," *Boston Post,* October 17, 1863, 1.

32. Carlo Rotella, *Cut Time: An Education at the Fights* (Boston: Houghton Mifflin, 2003), 116–17.

33. Seth Eastman, *Treatise on Topographical Drawing* (New York: Wiley and Putnam, 1837), 1. For the American survey tradition of picture making in which Warren operated, see two fine books on the subject: Kenneth Haltman, *Looking Close and Seeing Far: Samuel Seymour, Titian Ramsay Peale, and the Art of the Long Expedition, 1818–1823* (University Park: Penn State University Press, 2008) and Robin Kelsey, *Archive Style: Photographs & Illustrations for U.S. Surveys, 1850–1890* (Berkeley: University of California Press, 2007).

34. David M. Jordan, *"Happiness Is Not My Companion": The Life of General G. K. Warren* (Bloomington: Indiana University Press, 2001), 92. Warren's career ended in ignominy, however, when General Philip Sheridan relieved him of his command of the Fifth Corps after the Battle of White Oak Road in the closing days of the war (ibid., 224–34).

35. David McCullough, *The Great Bridge: The Epic Story of the Building of the Brooklyn Bridge* (New York: Touchstone Books, 1972), 158–59, 161. Roebling, who "had an almost uncanny gift for observation and could commit vast quantities of information to memory," had attended Rensselaer Polytechnic Institute and studied, among other subjects, "Analytical Geometry of Three Dimensions, Differential and Integral Calculus, Calculus of Variations, Qualitative and Quantitative Analysis, Determinative Mineralogy, [and] Higher Geodesy (the mathematical science of the size and shape of the earth)," making him a kindred spirit to the gifted engineer Warren, who pronounced him "a splendid young man" (ibid., 167, 154; Jordan, *"Happiness Is Not My Companion,"* 85).

36. For the sculpture, made by Karl Gerhardt, see *Unveiling of the Bronze Statue of Maj.-Gen. G. K. Warren, Gettysburg, Pa., August 8, 1888* (Brooklyn: Eagle Book Printing Department, 1888).

37. Gurowski, *Diary,* July 1, 1863, 257.

38. Jordan, *"Happiness Is Not My Companion,"* 108.

39. Henry Heth, report, October 25, 1863, Special Collections, Museum of the Confederacy, Richmond, Virginia.

40. Gurowski, *Diary,* October 17, 1863, 347.

41. Betsy Fahlman, *John Ferguson Weir: The Labor of Art* (Newark: University of Delaware Press, 1997), 65–69, 81.

42. Gouverneur Kemble Warren to Emily Chase Warren, October 17, 1863, Gouverneur Kemble Warren Papers, New York State Library, Albany.

43. Ibid., October 15, 1863. Even the obscurities in Warren's letters to Emily were clear signals. "I am quite ashamed of the blots and scratches on my paper," he wrote to her on October 6, "but they . . . will compare favorably with the facsimiles of Byron's verse in *Child Harolde* of the storm in the Alps in which his soul was in the sublimer tempest than the atmosphere he described." The blotches of ink spoke directly of a passionate romantic creativity, a blurring that was the opposite of Warren's careful topographic contours yet equally unmistakable: thin or smudged, the lines conveyed information directly. When disruptions occurred in these communications, they must have been only because of "some trouble with the mail," as he wrote to Emily on October 19, wondering why he had not received a letter from her responding to news of his victory. "You told me of Miss Cushman's visit to Washington and return and you had not then heard a word of what we had been doing here. I so much wished to hear you speak of it."

44. *Sappho: A Tragedy in Five Acts. After the German of Franz Grillparzer,* trans. by Edda Middleton (New York: D. Appleton, 1858), Gouverneur Kemble Warren Papers.

45. Ibid., 37, 34, 39.

46. Ch. Cocke, M.D., *An Account of the Alleghany Springs, in Montgomery County, Virginia with an Elaborate Analysis of the Water* (Lynchburg, Virginia: Virginian Job Office, 1861).

47. Lisa Merrill, *When Romeo Was a Woman: Charlotte Cushman and Her Circle of Female Spectators* (Ann Arbor: University of Michigan Press, 1999), 287.

48. "I feel so much that I have no one to talk to and like little Fanchon I go dance to my own shadow" (Warren to Emily Chase Warren, October 6, 1863, Gouverneur Kemble Warren Papers).

FIVE. CENTER OF ECHOES: CASTLE MURRAY, FAUQUIER COUNTY, VIRGINIA

1. Henry Kyd Douglas diary, January 4, 1863, quoted in Fletcher Melvin Green, *Democracy in the Old South and Other Essays,* ed. J. Isaac Copeland (Nashville, Tennessee: Vanderbilt University Press, 1969), 193.

2. Edmund Lind diary, typescript, January 7, 1856, pp. 54–55, Edmund Lind Papers, Manuscript Division, Library of Congress.

3. Ibid., November 18, 1855, p. 32; November 30, 1855, p. 38.

4. Ledger book, Edmund Lind Papers.

5. "I answered a phone call from a woman named Angie Moore. . . . She explained that she was interested [in Melrose Castle] because her ancestors were slaves there and her great-grandmother is buried there. . . . She did say that she

has been to Melrose Castle to try to find the grave. She says she remembers seeing it some time ago, but the building it, and other slave grave markers, were near is now gone and so are the tombstones? She feels sure the graves are still there, just unmarked. She agreed to sketch her memory of the building and grave locations in reference to the house and send the sketch to us for our records" ("Jeanna," to "Bea," memo, undated, Fauquier Historical Society, Warrenton, Virginia). The Fauquier Historical Society does not have such a sketch.

6. Charles E. Brownell, Calder Loth, William M. S. Rasmussen, and Richard Guy Wilson, *The Making of Virginia Architecture* (Richmond: Virginia Museum of Fine Arts, 1992), 290.

7. Ibid.

8. Mark Twain, *Life on the Mississippi* (New York: Harper's, 1917), 369ff, quoted in Grace Warren Landrum, "Sir Walter Scott and His Literary Rivals in the Old South," *American Literature* 2 (November 1930): 256. See also John Fraser, *America and the Patterns of Chivalry* (Cambridge: Cambridge University Press, 1982).

9. Landrum, "Sir Walter Scott and His Literary Rivals," 263. The tournament Landrum found a record of took place in 1845.

10. William M. S. Rasmussen and Robert S. Tilton, *Old Virginia: The Pursuit of a Pastoral Ideal* (Charlottesville, Virginia: Howell Press, 2003), 138–39; see also 102.

11. James Horrocks, *My Dear Parents: An Englishman's Letters Home to His Parents,* ed. A. S. Lewis (London: Gollancz, 1982), 37. "The English are very unpopular here and so are the Irish even more so (this is my impression) but the Scotch are a sort of go-between that the Yankees have no particular spite against, ergo—I become—Andrew Ross."

12. W. Mark McKnight, *Blue Bonnets O'er the Border: The 79th New York Cameron Highlanders* (Shippensburg, Pennsylvania: White Mane Books, 1998), xi, 3, 22.

13. "Statement of Significance," "National Register of Historic Places Inventory—Nomination Form," September 1981, www.dhr.virginia.gov/registers/counties/Fauquier/030_0070_melrose_1983_finalnomination.pdf (accessed January 2008).

14. Teresa A. Goddu, *Gothic America: Narrative, History, and Nation* (New York: Columbia University Press, 1997), 133; Andrea Henderson, "'An Embarrassing Subject': Problems of Value and Identity in the Early Gothic Novel," in *At the Limits of Romanticism: Essays in Cultural, Feminist, and Materialist Criticism,* ed. Mary A. Favret and Nicola J. Watson (Bloomington: Indiana University Press, 1994).

15. Ibid., 134, 137. "The gothic," Goddu writes, "is the fictional mode by which the factual horrors of slavery can be represented" (141). The scene of Aunt Hes-

ter's whipping is described in Frederick Douglass, *Narrative of the Life of Frederick Douglass, an American Slave* (New York: Signet, 1968), 26.

16. Eugene M. Scheel, *The Civil War in Fauquier County, Virginia* (Warrenton, Virginia: Fauquier National Bank, 1985), 1.

17. Thomas Ruffin, *The Constitution and the Union* (Washington, D.C.: Congressional Globe Office, 1856), 7, Library of Congress.

18. Victor Hugo, *Notre-Dame de Paris* (London: Penguin, 2004), 196, 200.

19. David McCullough, *The Great Bridge: The Epic Story of the Building of the Brooklyn Bridge* (New York: Touchstone Books, 1972), 109.

20. Henry Ward Beecher, "Street Cries and Orators' Voices," in *Eyes and Ears* (Boston: Ticknor and Fields, 1862), 280.

21. "Notice of New Works," *Southern Literary Messenger* 24 (June 1857): 480.

22. Edmund Ruffin, *The Political Economy of Slavery; or, The Institution Considered in regard to Its Influence on Public Wealth and the General Welfare* (Washington, D.C.: Lemuel Towers, 1857), 27.

23. Isham Keith to his uncle, February 21, 1845; Keith, statement to Virginia state legislature, n.d., Virginia Historical Society, Richmond. Keith's tombstone at the Warrenton Cemetery reads, "Isham / son of Thomas Keith / and grandson of Rev. / James Leith of Scotland, April 11, 1801 / Aug. 6, 1863 (Nancy Chappelear Baird, *Fauquier County, Virginia Tombstone Inscriptions* [Nancy Chappelear Baird, 1970], 185, Virginia Historical Society).

24. Alexander Gardner, "Plate 47: Castle Murray, Near Auburn, Va., November 1863," *Gardner's Sketch Book of the War* (New York: Dover 1979).

25. The board is in the collection of the Fauquier Historical Society in Warrenton, Virginia.

26. Gardner, "Plate 47."

27. Alfred Murray's will is in book 28, p. 13, at the Fauquier County Courthouse clerk's office; James E. Murray's contest of the will is in book 29, p. 13. The slaves' names appear in "A. Murray's Inventory of Appraisment," Fauquier County Court, August 29, 1860, p. 58. My thanks to Jane Butler of the Afro-American Historical Association of Fauquier County, The Plains, Virginia, for locating these documents.

28. Isham Keith, "Memorandum about the Death of My Calves," February 17, 1861, Virginia Historical Society.

29. Oliver Wendell Holmes, "The Stereoscope and the Stereograph," *Atlantic Monthly,* June 1859, 745.

30. Mary Roberts Rinehart, *The Circular Staircase* (Indianapolis: Bobbs-Merrill, 1908), 1, 202.

31. Holmes, "The Stereoscope and the Stereograph," 746.

32. "Programme of Scenery," *Macbeth,* Charlotte Cushman Papers, Folger Shakespeare Library, Washington, D.C.

SIX. GHOSTS: THE DEATH OF COLONEL THOMAS RUFFIN, OCTOBER 17, 1863

1. "Col. Thomas Ruffin, of N.C., of the Confederate Army, First N.C. Cavalry, who was severely wounded in the head, and taken prisoner at the battle of Bristoe's Station, on Wednesday, died on Saturday night, at the Grace church Hospital in this place. He received every attention from the surgeon in charge of the hospital and his attendants. His remains were yesterday afternoon deposited in a vault in the Methodist Protestant burial ground" (*Alexandria Gazette,* October 19, 1863, 1).

2. "Local Matters: The Soldiers' Cemetery," *National Daily Intelligencer,* October 17, 1863, 3.

3. Drew Gilpin Faust, *This Republic of Suffering: Death and the American Civil War* (New York: Alfred A. Knopf, 2008), 249.

4. "Opening of Grover's New Theatre," *Daily National Republican,* October 7, 1863, 2.

5. Mary Braddon, *Eleanor's Victory* (Gloucestershire: Alan Sutton, 1996), 49–50. Along with *Aurora Floyd* (another of her novels), *Eleanor's Victory* was advertised in *Harper's Weekly,* October 17, 1863, 671.

6. "Local Matters," *National Daily Intelligencer,* October 17, 1863, 3.

7. Emily Dickinson, #1100 (ca. 1866), *The Complete Poems of Emily Dickinson,* ed. Thomas H. Johnson (Boston: Little, Brown, 1961), 496–97.

8. Walt Whitman, *Memoranda during the War,* ed. Peter Coviello (New York: Oxford University Press, 2004), 84–85, 27.

9. Henry Robinson Berkeley diary, October 14, 1863, Virginia Historical Society, Richmond; John G. Perry, *Letters from a Surgeon of the Civil War* (Boston: Little, Brown, 1906), 113.

10. *Reminiscences of Early Polk Countians: Stories About Life When Polk County Was Young* (Bolivar, Missouri: Polk County Genealogical Society, n. d.), 2, 18, 6.

11. *History of Hickory, Polk, Cedar, Dade and Barton Counties, Missouri* (Chicago: Goodspeed, 1889), 297.

12. For Ruffin's purchase of these properties, see Polk County Deed Book B, 528–29, Deed Book C, 476–77, Polk County Genealogical Society. Bolivar, Missouri. My thanks to Susan Sparks of the Genealogical Society for locating these materials.

13. Case of Absolem Baker, September 29, 1845, Greene County, Missouri Circuit Court Cumulative Index, folder 175, Greene County Archives, Springfield, Missouri.

14. 1844 Tax Assessment Book for Polk County, Missouri, transcription by Maxine Dunaway, 1986, p. 59, Polk County Genealogical Society, Bolivar, Missouri.

15. *History of Hickory, Polk . . .*, 314; *Reminiscences of Early Polk Countians*, 19; "Life of Colonel Thomas Ruffin," *North Carolina Review*, January 5, 1913, 4.

16. Ruffin's notice of honorable discharge of September 29, 1846, is in the Missouri State Archives, Jefferson City. He was mustered into service on September 5, 1846.

17. "Life of Colonel Thomas Ruffin," 4. For more on the electoral contest between Stanly and Ruffin, see Norman D. Brown, *Edward Stanly: Whiggery's Tarheel "Conqueror"* (University: University of Alabama Press, 1974), 151–55.

18. *Goldsboro* [N.C.] *Republican and Patriot*, quoted in Joseph Carlyle Sitterson, *The Secession Movement in North Carolina*, James Sprunt Studies in History and Political Science 23 (Chapel Hill: University of North Carolina Press, 1939), 91. See Sitterson, 90–93, 126–27, 144–45, for more on Ruffin's political views.

19. Edmund Ruffin, *The Political Economy of Slavery; or, The Institution Considered in regard to Its Influence on Public Wealth and the General Welfare* (Washington, D.C.: Lemuel Towers, 1857), 30. "*April 23* [1858]. Began to cover & direct to names for the mail—Mr. Th. Ruffin of N. Ca. franking them" (*The Diary of Edmund Ruffin*, vol. 1, ed. William Kauffman Scarborough [Baton Rouge: Louisiana State University Press, 1972], 180).

20. Julius Yanuck, "Thomas Ruffin and North Carolina Slave Law," *Journal of Southern History* (1955): 461, 466.

21. Thomas, *The Constitution and the Union* (Washington, D.C.: Congressional Globe Office, 1856), 5, Library of Congress.

22. Ruffin, *The Constitution and the Union*, 4.

23. Ruffin, *The Constitution and the Union*, 6, Collection of North Caroliniana, Library of the University of North Carolina, Chapel Hill.

24. Thomas Ruffin, *Know-Nothingism, Speech of Hon. Thos. Ruffin, of N. Carolina, Delivered at the House of Representatives*, Feb. 27, 1855 (Washington, D.C.: 1855), 4, Collection of North Caroliniana.

25. Thomas Ruffin, *State Rights and State Equality, Speech of Hon. Thomas Ruffin of North Carolina, Delivered in the House of Representatives, February 20, 1861* (Washington, D.C.: H. Polkinhorn's Steam Job Press, 1861), 6–7.

26. Thomas Ruffin, junior composition, 1839, Special Collections, Library of the University of North Carolina.

27. Edmund Ruffin, *The Political Economy of Slavery*, 10.

28. Thomas Ruffin, *The Constitution and the Union*, 5; *State Rights and State Equality*, 9.

29. Thomas Ruffin, *The Constitution and the Union*, 6.

30. W. W. Blackford, *War Years with Jeb Stuart* (New York: Charles Scribner's Sons, 1945), 239; see also Carl R. Schmahl, "'Enemy Back of You!': J. E. B. Stuart's Close Call at Auburn in October 1863," *Fauquier* (Spring 1995): 34–41.

31. William D. Henderson, *The Road to Bristoe Station: Campaigning with*

Lee and Meade, August 1–October 20, 1863 (Lynchburg, Virginia: H. E. Howard, 1987), 157–59.

32. George H. Washburn, *A Complete Military History and Record of the 108th Regiment N.Y. Vols., from 1862 to 1894* (Rochester, New York: Press of E. R. Andrews, 1894), 59, 214; Rev. Frank N. Dexter, ed., *A Hundred Years of Congregational History in Wisconsin* (n.p.: Wisconsin Congregational Conference, 1933), 249–51.

33. Septima M. Collis, *A Woman's War Record, 1861–1865* (New York: Knickerbocker Press, 1889), 24–25.

34. "Tribute of Respect," *Biblical Recorder,* December 23, 1863, William and M. Emmet Robinson Collection, George Ragsdale Collection, Johnston County Heritage Center, Smithfield, North Carolina; file contributed for use in USGenWeb Archives, http://files.usgwarchives.org/nc/wayne/collections/robinson/ruffin.03.txt (accessed August 2008).

35. For a description of the typical burial practices for soldiers during the Civil War, see Faust, *This Republic of Suffering,* 249.

SEVEN. SOUND AND FURY: NATURE IN VIRGINIA

1. Edward Hitchcock, *The Religion of Geology and Its Connected Sciences* (Boston: Phillips, Sampson, 1851), 410.

2. Ibid., 410–11.

3. Ibid., 426.

4. Ibid., 416–18, 434.

5. Jerusha Hull McCormack, "Domesticating Delphi: Emily Dickinson and the Electro-Magnetic Telegraph," *American Quarterly* 55 (December 2003): 598; Nancy Pick, *Curious Footprints: Professor Hitchcock's Dinosaur Tracks & Other Natural History Treasures at Amherst College* (Amherst, Massachusetts: Amherst College Press, 2006), 4.

6. Oliver Wendell Holmes, "Sun-Painting and Sun-Sculpture," *Atlantic Monthly,* July 1861, 18.

7. Hitchcock, *The Religion of Geology,* 439, 433.

8. Charles Darwin, *The Origin of Species* (London: Penguin, 1968), 125–26.

9. George Eliot, *Middlemarch* (New York: Signet, 1964), 191.

10. T. H. Huxley, "The Physical Basis of Life," *Fortnightly Review* (February 1869), quoted in Gillian Beer, *Darwin's Plots: Evolutionary Narrative in Darwin, George Eliot, and Nineteenth-Century Fiction* (Cambridge: Cambridge University Press, 2000), 142.

11. Eliot, *Middlemarch,* 191.

12. Ibid., 257–58; quoted also in Beer, *Darwin's Plots,* 167.

13. Eliot, *Middlemarch,* 286.

14. Ibid., 140.

15. Beer, *Darwin's Plots,* 146.

16. Cynthia Eagle Russett, *Darwin in America: The Intellectual Response, 1865–1912* (San Francisco: W. H. Freeman, 1976), 1–4.

17. Edward Dowden, *Shakspere: A Critical Study of His Mind and Art* (London: Kegan Paul, Trench, 1882), 246–47, 249.

18. Fanny Seward diary, typescript, April 4, 1865, pp. 818–21, Rare Books and Special Collections, Rush Rhees Library, University of Rochester, New York. Charles Buchanan Read, "Drifting," *Atlantic Monthly,* April 1859, 452–53. John Ruskin, "Of the Pathetic Fallacy," in *Modern Painters,* vol. 3, ed. E. T. Cook and Alexander Wedderburn (London: George Allen, 1904), 206–20.

19. Jedediah Hotchkiss and William Allan, *The Battle-Fields of Virginia: Chancellorsville* (New York: D. Van Nostrand, 1867), 131.

20. *Virginia: A Geographical and Political Summary* (Richmond: R. F. Walker, 1876), 13, 70. For a persuasive and richly thoughtful account of a paradigm shift in mid-nineteenth-century American landscape paintings—a shift from knowledge to information as a basis for picturing the land—see Jennifer Raab, "Frederic Church and the Culture of Detail" (Ph.D. diss., Yale University, 2009).

21. Hotchkiss, *Virginia,* 90.

22. Annie Fields, "ODE. Recited by Miss Charlotte Cushman at Inauguration of the Great Organ," *Boston Daily Courier,* November 3, 1863, 1.

23. Mitchell Robert Breitwieser, "Jefferson's Prospect," *Prospects* 10 (1985): 316.

24. Ibid., 321, 327, 349.

25. Jefferson, *Notes on the State of Virginia,* ed. David Waldstreicher (Boston: Bedford / St. Martin's, 2002), 135–36.

26. Jefferson, *Notes on the State of Virginia,* 148–49.

27. J. T. Trowbridge, *The South: A Tour of Its Battle-fields and Ruined Cities* (New York: Arno Press / New York Times, 1969), 141.

28. Ibid.

29. "We go to tearing up R.R. track" (Abner Crump Hopkins diary, October 16, 1863, Virginia Historical Society, Richmond); "The brigade still down at the Rail Road" (Watkins Kearns diary, October 17, 1863, Virginia Historical Society). For an account of making the iron neckties, see Douglas Southall Freeman, in *R. E. Lee: A Biography* (New York: Charles Scribner's Sons, 1935), 185.

30. Walter Taylor and Pendleton, quoted in Freeman, *R. E. Lee,* 185–86.

31. Trowbridge, *The South,* 86, 85.

32. Ibid., 85, 87, 102. For an account of Judith Henry, see Mia T. Parsons and John W. Ravenhorst, eds., *Archeological Resource Study and Clearance for the Discovery Center Project at the Henry House, Manassas National Battlefield Park, Manassas, Virginia* (Archeology Program, Harpers Ferry National Historical Park, for Manassas National Battlefield Park, 2002).

33. Jeff L. Rosenheim, "135a, b, c. Anonymous [description of Wilderness Bat-

tlefield photographs]," *The Waking Dream: Photography's First Century: Selections from the Gilman Paper Company Collection* (New York: Metropolitan Museum of Art, 1993), 318. For the idea that the photographs were intentionally solarized—which both Jeff Rosenheim and Richard Benson (in conversations with the author) think is unlikely—see Pierre Apraxine, with plates by Richard Benson, *Photographs from the Collection of the Gilman Paper Company* (n.p.: White Oak Press, 1985), 446.

34. Bruce R. Smith, *The Acoustic World of Early Modern England: Attending to the O-Factor* (Chicago: University of Chicago Press, 1999), 14.

35. "Academy of Music—Charlotte Cushman and Edwin Booth—Macbeth," *Philadelphia Press,* September 14, 1863, 2, Rosenbach Museum and Library, Philadelphia.

36. George Eliot, *Adam Bede* (London: Penguin, 1985), 387.

37. George William Curtis, "Biographical Sketch of the Author," in *Cecil Dreeme* by Theodore Winthrop (Boston: Ticknor and Fields, 1861), 19.

38. Oliver O. Howard, "Jackson's Attack upon the Eleventh Corps," *Century* 32 (September 1886): 763. Howard's article reproduces three of the anonymous Wilderness photographs on p. 767.

39. Darwin, *The Origin of Species,* 126.

40. Smith, *The Acoustic World of Early Modern England,* 243.

41. Nathaniel Hawthorne, *The Blithedale Romance* (New York: Modern Library, 2001), 124. Cushman's "surpassing power of concentrativeness, which may be said to have been the keystone to the arch in her character, brought her at once, full, rounded, and complete, to the perfect possession of herself and the needs of the occasion. She seemed to cast off, with grand ease, every influence, every suggestion of any other life but the one she was for the time to interpret" (Emma Stebbins, ed., *Charlotte Cushman: Her Letters and Memories of Her Life* [1879; New York: Benjamin Blom, 1972]). Summoning the spirits that tend on mortal thoughts must have involved especially intense concentration.

42. Christian Schussele, in a watercolor of Lady Macbeth dated 1864 and presented to Cushman that year in thanks for her Sanitary Commission work (and perhaps depicting Cushman herself), shows the queen washing her hands in act 5, scene 1, while looking up. The Lady Macbeth in Schussele's watercolor does not look much like Cushman, but she does stand next to a lamp matching the drawing of a lamp in Cushman's script (*Macbeth* script, facing p. 49, Charlotte Cushman Papers, Manuscript Division, Library of Congress). Also, it seems unlikely that Schussele would agree to present a watercolor of this subject to Cushman without attempting to depict the actress herself. See Frederick Baekeland, *Roads Less Traveled: American Paintings, 1833–1935* (Ithaca, New York: Herbert F. Johnson Museum of Art, 1998), 106–7. My thanks to Graham Boettcher, William Cary Hulsey Curator of American Art at the Birmingham Museum of Art, for calling my attention to this picture.

43. Fanny Seward diary, original, October 10, 1863, p. 65.

44. Ibid., February 10, 1864, p. 841.

45. National Theatre home page, www.nationaltheatre.org/location/ghost.htm (accessed May 2009); Pamela Whitehead, "Who's That *Pale* Guy in the Crowd Scene?" *Washington Post,* October 27, 1978, 13.

46. Don Alexander Hawkins, "The Landscape of the Federal City: A 1792 Walking Tour," *Washington History* 3 (Spring/Summer 1991): 21.

47. Whitehead, "Who's That *Pale* Guy?"

48. Donn Murphy, interview by the author, February 26, 2008.

49. Stebbins, *Charlotte Cushman,* 154.

50. Nathaniel Hawthorne, *The Marble Faun* (New York: Penguin, 1990), 97, 161–62, 162. The chasm in Rome is the one into which Curtius and his steed plunged. On the haunting, see, for example, "Ghost of McCullough," *Washington Post,* October 4, 1896, 19.

51. Stebbins, *Charlotte Cushman,* 183, 138, 132, 115; Hawthorne, *The Marble Faun,* 162.

52. Fanny Seward diary, original, October 12, 1863, p. 68.

SELECTED BIBLIOGRAPHY

ARCHIVAL SOURCES

Architect of the Capitol, Washington, D.C.
Beinecke Rare Book and Manuscript Library, Yale University, New Haven, Connecticut
Bostonian Society Library and Special Collections, Boston, Massachusetts
Fauquier Historical Society, Warrenton, Virginia
Folger Shakespeare Library, Washington, D.C.
Greene County Archives, Springfield, Missouri
Houghton Library, Harvard University, Cambridge, Massachusetts
Kiplinger Research Library, Historical Society of Washington, D.C.
Library Company, Philadelphia
Library of Congress, Washington, D.C.

- Clara Barton Papers
- Charlotte Cushman Papers
- Benjamin Brown French Papers
- Edmund Lind Papers
- William Owner diary
- Charles Wellington Reed Papers
- Michael Shiner diary

Martin Luther King, Jr., Memorial Library, Washington, D.C.
Methuen Memorial Music Hall, Methuen, Massachusetts

Missouri State Archives, Jefferson City
Museum of the Confederacy, Richmond, Virginia
New Haven Museum & Historical Society, New Haven, Connecticut
Newport Historical Society, Newport, Rhode Island
New York State Library, Albany
Octagon Museum, Washington, D.C.
Polk County Genealogical Society, Bolivar, Missouri
Putnam County Historical Society, Cold Spring, New York
Randolph College, Lipscomb Library, Lynchburg, Virginia
Rosenbach Museum and Library, Philadelphia
Seward House, Auburn, New York
Smithsonian Institution Archives, Washington, D.C.
Sterling Memorial Library, Yale University, New Haven, Connecticut
University of North Carolina at Chapel Hill Library
University of Rochester, Rush Rhees Library, Rare Books and Special Collections
Virginia Historical Society, Richmond

NEWSPAPERS

Alexandria Gazette
Boston Daily Advertiser
Boston Daily Courier
Boston Daily Journal
Boston Post
Daily Morning Chronicle (Washington, D.C.)
Daily National Intelligencer (Washington, D.C.)
Daily National Republican (Washington, D.C.)
New-York Daily Republican
New York Herald-Tribune
North Carolina Review
Philadelphia Press
Sacramento Daily Union
Washington Evening Star
Washington Post

PRIMARY SOURCES

Anderson, L. B. "The Execution of Dr. David Minton Wright by the Federal Authorities, at Norfolk, Virginia." *Landmark* (December 31, 1892). Reprinted in *Southern Historical Papers* 21 (1893): 326–37.
Barrett, Lawrence. *Charlotte Cushman, a Lecture.* New York: Dunlap Society, 1889.
Bates, David Homer. *Lincoln in the Telegraph Office.* New York: Century, 1907.

Beecher, Henry Ward. *Eyes and Ears.* Boston: Ticknor and Fields, 1862.
Bellows, Henry W. *A Sequel to 'The Suspense of Faith,' Addressed to His Own Congregation, Sunday, Sept. 25, 1859, on the Reopening of All Souls' Church, after the Summer Vacation.* New York: D. Appleton, 1859.
Blackford, W. W. *War Years with Jeb Stuart.* New York: Charles Scribner's Sons, 1945.
Bond, G. P. *Account of the Great Comet of 1858, Annals of the Astronomical Observatory of Harvard College,* vol. 3. Cambridge: Welch, Bigelow, 1862.
Boydell, John. *Illustrations of the Dramatic Works of Shakespeare.* New York: 1852.
Braddon, Mary. *Aurora Floyd.* London: Virago, 1984 [1863].
———. *Eleanor's Victory.* Gloucestershire: Alan Sutton, 1996 [1863].
Brewster, Anne Hampton. "Miss Cushman." *Blackwood's* 124 (August 1878): 170–75.
———. [Enna Duval]. *Spirit Sculpture; or, The Year before Confirmation.* Philadelphia: James Fullerton, 1849.
Bridges, Sallie. *Marble Isle: Legends of the Round Table and Other Poems.* Philadelphia: J. B. Lippincott, 1864.
Brooks, Noah. "Letter from Washington, October 9, 1863: Building at the Capitol." *Sacramento Daily Union,* November 4, 1863, 1.
———. *Washington in Lincoln's Time.* New York: Century, 1896.
Browning, Elizabeth Barrett. *Poems,* vol. 1. London: Chapman & Hall, 1853.
Bulfinch, Thomas. *Legends of Charlemagne; or, Romance of the Middle Ages.* Boston: J. E. Tilton, 1864.
Campbell, Eric A., ed. *"A Grand Terrible Dramma": From Gettysburg to Petersburg: The Civil War Letters of Charles Wellington Reed.* New York: Fordham University Press, 2000.
Carpenter, Francis. *Six Months at the White House.* New York: Hurd and Houghton, 1869.
Carter, Robert. "Gurowski." *Atlantic Monthly,* November 1866, 625–33.
Chambrun, Adolphe de. *Impressions of Lincoln and the Civil War: A Foreigner's Account,* trans. Aldebert de Chambrun. New York: Random House, 1952.
Clement, Clara Erskine. *Charlotte Cushman.* Boston: Osgood, 1882.
Cocke, Charles. *An Account of the Alleghany Springs, in Montgomery County, Virginia with an Elaborate Analysis of the Water.* Lynchburg, Virginia: Virginian Job Office, 1861.
Collis, Septima M. *A Woman's War Record, 1861–1865.* New York: Knickerbocker Press, 1889.
Congdon, Charles. "The Decline of Tragedy." *Harper's Monthly,* November 1864, 745–48.
Covell, William King. *The Boston Music Hall Organ.* London: Musical Opinion, 1931.
Cushman, Charlotte. "The Actress." *Godey's Lady Book,* February 1837, 70–73.

Darwin, Charles. *The Origin of Species.* London: Penguin, 1968 [1859].
De Quincey, Thomas. "On the Knocking on the Gate in *Macbeth*" [1823]. In *Shakespeare: Macbeth, A Casebook,* ed. John Wain, 90–93. London: Macmillan, 1968.
Dexter, A. "Plays and Play-Acting." *Atlantic Monthly,* September 1862, 284–91.
Dexter, Rev. Frank N., ed. *A Hundred Years of Congregational History in Wisconsin.* N.p.: Wisconsin Congregational Conference, 1933.
Dickerson, Edward N. *Joseph Henry and the Magnetic Telegraph: An Address Delivered at Princeton College, June 16, 1885.* New York: Charles Scribner's Sons, 1885.
Dickinson, Emily. *The Complete Poems of Emily Dickinson,* ed. Thomas H. Johnson. Boston: Little, Brown, 1961.
———. *Selected Poems & Letters of Emily Dickinson,* ed. Robert N. Linscott. New York: Anchor, 1959.
Douglass, Frederick. *Narrative of the Life of Frederick Douglass, an American Slave.* New York: Signet, 1968 [1845].
Dowden, Edward. *Shakspere: A Critical Study of His Mind and Art.* London: Kegan Paul, Trench, 1882.
Eastman, Seth. *Treatise on Topographical Drawing.* New York: Wiley and Putnam, 1837.
Eckloff, Christian F. *Memoirs of a Senate Page (1855–1859),* ed. Percival G. Melbourne. New York: Broadway, 1909.
Eliot, George. *Adam Bede.* London: Penguin, 1985 [1859].
———. *Middlemarch.* New York: Signet, 1964 [1872].
———. *Romola.* London: Penguin, 1996 [1863].
Elliott, Maud Howe. *This Was My Newport.* Cambridge, Massachusetts: A. M. Jones, 1944.
Emerson, Ralph Waldo. "Abraham Lincoln" [1865]. *Journal of Historical Studies* 1 (Spring 1968): 355–59.
———. *Ralph Waldo Emerson: Essays & Lectures,* ed. Joel Porte. New York: Library of America, 1983.
———. "Voluntaries." *Atlantic Monthly,* October 1863, 504–6.
Gardner, Alexander. *Gardner's Sketch Book of the War.* New York: Dover, 1979 [1866].
Gould, B. A. *Memoir of Lewis Morris Rutherfurd, 1816–1892.* In *National Academy of Sciences: Biographical Memoirs,* vol.3. Washington, D.C.: National Academy of Sciences, 1895.
Gray, John P. "The Case of Dr. David M. Wright, for the Murder of Lieutenant Sanborn.—Plea, Insanity." *American Journal of Insanity* 20 (January 1864): 284–300.
Grover, Leonard. "Lincoln's Interest in the Theater." *Century,* April 1909, 942–50.

Gurowski, Adam. *Diary,* vol. 2, *From November 18, 1862 to October 18, 1863.* New York: Carleton, 1864.
Hale, Edward Everett. "The Man without a Country." *Atlantic Monthly,* December 1863, 665–79.
———. *William H. Seward.* Philadelphia: George W. Jacobs, 1910.
Hanaford, J. H. "An Interview with Charlotte Cushman." *Boston Daily Journal,* August 24, 1858.
Harvey, Charles M. "Seward, Empire-Builder and Seer." *Putnam's Monthly,* June 1907, 267–76.
Hawthorne, Nathaniel. *The Blithedale Romance.* New York: Modern Library, 2001 [1852].
———. "Chiefly about War Matters." *Atlantic Monthly,* July 1862, 43–61.
———. "The Gorgon's Head." In *A Wonder Book; and, Tanglewood Tales.* London: J. M. Dent, 1906 [1851].
———. *The Marble Faun.* New York: Penguin, 1990 [1860].
———. *The Scarlet Letter.* New York: Signet, 1959 [1850].
Henry, Joseph. *Eulogy on Prof. Alexander Dallas Bache.* Washington, D.C.: Government Printing Office, 1872.
———. "On Acoustics Applied to Public Buildings." In *Proceedings of the American Association for the Advancement of Science,* 119–35. Washington, D.C.: American Association for the Advancement of Science, 1856.
———. *The Papers of Joseph Henry,* vol. 10, ed. Marc Rothenberg. Washington, D.C.: Smithsonian Institution / Science History Publications, 2004.
Herndon, William H., and Jesse W. Weik. *Abraham Lincoln: The True Story of a Great Life,* vol. 2. London: Sampson Low Marston, 1893.
———. *Herndon's Lincoln,* ed. Douglas L. Wilson and Rodney O. Davis. Urbana: University of Illinois Press, 2006.
Higginson, Thomas Wentworth. "Emily Dickinson's Letters." *Atlantic Monthly,* October 1891, 441–56.
History of Hickory, Polk, Cedar, Dade and Barron Counties, Missouri. Chicago: Goodspeed, 1889.
Hitchcock, Edward. *The Religion of Geology and Its Connected Sciences.* Boston: Phillips, Sampson, 1851.
Holmes, Oliver Wendell. "Doings of the Sunbeam." *Atlantic Monthly,* July 1863, 1–15.
———. "The Great Instrument." *Atlantic Monthly,* November 1863, 637–47.
———. *The Poetical Works of Oliver Wendell Holmes.* Boston: Houghton Mifflin, 1975.
———. "The Stereoscope and the Stereograph." *Atlantic Monthly* , June 1859, 738–48.
———. "Sun-Painting and Sun-Sculpture." *Atlantic Monthly,* July 1861, 13–29.

Horrocks, James. *My Dear Parents: An Englishman's Letters Home to His Parents, by James Horrocks,* ed. A.S. Lewis. London: Gollancz, 1982.
Hotchkiss, Jedediah, and William Allan. *The Battle-Fields of Virginia: Chancellorsville.* New York: D. Van Nostrand, 1867.
"How I Saw an Explosion." *Frank Leslie's Illustrated Weekly,* October 17, 1863, 55.
Howard, Oliver O. "Jackson's Attack upon the Eleventh Corps." *Century,* September 1886, 761–70.
Howe, Julia Ward. "Battle Hymn of the Republic." *Atlantic Monthly,* February 1862, 145.
———. "A New Sculptor." *Atlantic Monthly,* September 1862, 282–83.
———. *Reminiscences, 1819–1899.* Boston: Houghton Mifflin, 1899.
Howells, William Dean. *Life of Abraham Lincoln.* Springfield, Illinois: Abraham Lincoln Association, 1938 [1860].
Hugo, Victor. *Notre-Dame de Paris.* London: Penguin, 2004 [1831].
Jarves, John Jackson. *The Art-Idea.* Cambridge, Massachusetts: Belknap Press of Harvard University Press, 1960 [1864].
Jefferson, Thomas. *Notes on the State of Virginia,* ed. David Waldstreicher. Boston: Bedford / St. Martin's, 2002 [1785].
Kirkland, Frazar. *The Pictorial Book of Anecdotes and Incidents of the War of the Rebellion.* Hartford, Connecticut: Hartford Publishing Co., 1866.
Lamb, Martha J., ed. *The Homes of America.* New York: Appleton, 1879.
Lamon, Ward Hill. *Recollections of Abraham Lincoln, 1847–1865,* ed. Dorothy Lamon. Chicago: A. C. McClurg, 1895.
"Life of Colonel Thomas Ruffin." *North Carolina Review.* January 5, 1913, 4, 13.
Lincoln, Abraham. *Abraham Lincoln: Speeches and Writings, 1832–1858,* ed. Don Edward Fehrenbacher. New York: Library of America, 1989.
———. *Abraham Lincoln: Speeches and Writings, 1859–1865,* ed. Don Edward Fehrenbacher. New York: Library of America, 1989.
———. *The Collected Works of Abraham Lincoln,* ed. Roy Basler. New Brunswick, New Jersey: Rutgers University Press, 1953–90.
———. *The Poems of Abraham Lincoln.* Bedford, Massachusetts: Applewood Books, 1991.
Livermore, Mary A. *My Story of the War: A Woman's Narrative of Four Years Personal Experience.* Williamstown, Massachusetts: Corner House, 1978 [1889].
Longfellow, Henry Wadsworth. *The Complete Poetical Works of Longfellow.* Boston: Houghton Mifflin, 1893.
———. "Killed at the Ford." *Atlantic Monthly,* April 1866.
———. *Tales of a Wayside Inn.* Boston: Ticknor and Fields, 1863.
Lowell, James Russell. *The Poetical Works of James R. Lowell,* 2 vols. Boston: Ticknor and Fields, 1862.
Melville, Herman. *Moby-Dick; or, The Whale.* Indianapolis: Bobbs-Merrill, 1964 [1851].

———. *The Poems of Herman Melville,* ed. Douglas Robillard. Kent, Ohio: Kent State University Press, 2000.
Middleton, Edda. *Sappho: A Tragedy in Five Acts. After the German of Franz Grillparzer.* New York: D. Appleton, 1858.
Miller, Edwin Haviland, ed. *Walt Whitman: The Correspondence,* vol. 1, *1842–1867.* New York: New York University Press, 1961.
Mitchell, S. Weir. "The Case of George Dedlow." *Atlantic Monthly,* July 1866, 1–11.
Moss, M. Helen Palmes. "Lincoln and Wilkes Booth as Seen on the Day of the Assassination." *Century,* April 1909, 951–53.
Perkins, Fred B. *The Picture and the Men.* New York: A. J. Johnson, 1867.
Perry, John G. *Letters from a Surgeon of the Civil War.* Boston: Little, Brown, 1906.
Rhees, William J. *An Account of the Smithsonian Institution, Its Founder, Building, Operations, etc.* Washington, D.C.: Thomas McGill, 1857.
Rinehart, Mary Roberts. *The Circular Staircase.* Indianapolis: Bobbs-Merrill, 1908.
Ruffin, Edmund. *The Diary of Edmund Ruffin,* vol. 1, ed. William Kauffman Scarborough. Baton Rouge: Louisiana State University Press, 1972.
———. *The Political Economy of Slavery; or, The Institution Considered in regard to Its Influence on Public Wealth and the General Welfare.* Washington, D.C.: Lemuel Towers, 1857.
Ruffin, Thomas. *The Constitution and the Union.* Washington, D.C.: Congressional Globe Office, 1856.
———. *Know-Nothingism, Speech of Hon. Thos. Ruffin, of N. Carolina, Delivered at the House of Representatives, Feb. 27, 1855.* Washington, D.C.: 1855.
———. *State Rights and State Equality, Speech of Hon. Thomas Ruffin of North Carolina, Delivered in the House of Representatives, February 20, 1861.* Washington, D.C.: H. Polkinhorn's Steam Job Press, 1861.
Ruskin, John. "Of the Pathetic Fallacy." In *Modern Painters,* vol. 3, ed. E. T. Cook and Alexander Wedderburn, 206-20. London: George Allen, 1904.
Sala, George Augustus. *My Diary in America in the Midst of War,* vol. 2. London: Tinsley Brothers, 1865.
Sartoris, Adelaide Kemble. *Medusa, and Other Tales.* London: Smith, Elder, 1868.
Scott, Robert Garth, ed. *Fallen Leaves: The Civil War Letters of Major Henry Livermore Abbott.* Kent, Ohio: Kent State University Press, 1991.
Scott, Walter. *Guy Mannering.* London: Penguin, 1999 [1815].
Seward, William H. *Alaska. Speech of William H. Seward at Sitka, August 12, 1869.* Washington, D.C.: Philip and Solomons, 1869.
Spencer, Herbert. *A System of Synthetic Philosophy,* vol. 1. New York: D. Appleton, 1873 [1864].
Stebbins, Emma, ed. *Charlotte Cushman: Her Letters and Memories of Her Life.* New York: Benjamin Blom, 1972 [1879].

Stillé, Charles J. *History of the United States Sanitary Commission.* Philadelphia: J. B. Lippincott, 1866.

Stockton, John D. "Charlotte Cushman." *Scribner's,* July 1876, 262–66.

"Tableaux Vivans." *Harper's Monthly,* October 1863, 698–704.

Taylor, Walter Herron. *Lee's Adjutant: The Wartime Letters of Colonel Walter Herron Taylor, 1862–1865,* ed. R. Lockwood Tower. Columbia: University of South Carolina Press, 1995.

Taylor, William B. "A Memoir of Joseph Henry: A Sketch of His Scientific Work." *Bulletin of the Philosophical Society of Washington,* vol. 2, 230–368. Philadelphia: Collins, 1879.

Trowbridge, J. T. *The South: A Tour of Its Battle-fields and Ruined Cities.* New York: Arno Press / New York Times, 1969.

Unveiling of the Bronze Statue of Maj.-Gen. G. K. Warren, Gettysburg, Pa., August 8, 1888. Brooklyn: Eagle Book Printing Department, 1888.

U.S. Sanitary Commission. *Statement of the Object and Methods of the Sanitary Commission.* New York: William C. Bryant, 1863.

Vedder, Elihu. *The Digressions of V.* Boston: Houghton Mifflin, 1910.

Virginia: A Geographical and Political Summary. Richmond: R. F. Walker, 1876.

Waldauer, Augustus, trans. *Fanchon, the Cricket; A Domestic Drama, in Five Acts, from a Tale of George Sand.* New York: Samuel French & Son, 1862.

The War of the Rebellion: A Compilation of the Official Records of the Union and Confederate Armies. Washington, D.C.: Government Printing Office, 1880–1901.

Ward, Artemus [Charles Farrar Browne]. *Artemus Ward: His Book.* New York: Carleton, 1862.

Washburn, George H. *A Complete Military History and Record of the 108th Regiment N. Y. Vols., from 1862 to 1894.* Rochester, New York, 1894.

Whitman, Walt. *Leaves of Grass.* New York: Library of America, 1992 [1855].

———. *Memoranda during the War,* ed. Peter Coviello. New York: Oxford University Press, 2004 [1876].

———. *Walt Whitman: The Correspondence,* vol. 1, *1842–1867,* ed. Edwin Haviland Miller. New York: New York University Press, 1961.

Whitney, Henry C. *Life on the Circuit with Lincoln.* Boston: Estes and Lauriat, 1892.

Whittier, John Greenleaf. *The Complete Poetical Works of John Greenleaf Whittier.* Boston: Houghton Mifflin, 1894.

Winter, William. "Players: Past and Present—Great Actress and Great Woman Charlotte Cushman." *Saturday Evening Post,* September 29, 1906, 10-11.

———. *The Wallet of Time.* New York: Moffat, Yard, 1913.

Winthrop, Theodore. *Cecil Dreeme.* Boston: Ticknor and Fields, 1861.

Wright, James A. *No More Gallant a Deed: A Civil War Memoir of the First Minnesota Volunteers,* ed. Steven J. Keillor. St. Paul: Minnesota Historical Society Press, 2001.

SECONDARY SOURCES

Apraxine, Pierre, with plates by Richard Benson. *Photographs from the Collection of the Gilman Paper Company.* N.p.: White Oak Press, 1985.

Armstrong, William A. "Torch, Cauldron and Taper: Light and Darkness in 'Macbeth.'" In *Poetry and Drama, 1570–1700: Essays in Honour of Harold F. Brooks,* ed. Antony Coleman and Antony Hammond, 47–59. London: Methuen, 1981.

Bachelard, Gaston. *The Poetics of Space,* trans. Maria Jolas. Boston: Beacon Press, 1994.

Baekeland, Frederick. *Roads Less Traveled: American Paintings, 1833–1935.* Ithaca, New York: Herbert F. Johnson Museum of Art, 1998.

Baird, Nancy Chappelear. *Fauquier County, Virginia Tombstone Inscriptions.* [N.p.: Nancy Chappelear Baird, 1970.]

Baker, Paul R. *Richard Morris Hunt.* Cambridge, Massachusetts: MIT Press, 1980.

Bassett, M. H. *From Bull Run to Bristow Station.* St. Paul, Minnesota: North Central Publishing, 1962.

Bataille, Georges. "The Obelisk." In *Visions of Excess: Selected Writings, 1927-1939,* ed. Allan Stoekl, trans. Allan Stoekl, Carl R. Lovitt, and Donald M. Leslie, Jr., 213–22. Minneapolis: University of Minnesota Press, 1985.

Bazin, André. "Theater and Cinema: Part Two." In *What Is Cinema?* trans. Hugh Gray, 95–124. Berkeley: University of California Press, 1967.

Beer, Gillian. *Darwin's Plots: Evolutionary Narrative in Darwin, George Eliot, and Nineteenth-Century Fiction.* Cambridge: Cambridge University Press, 2000.

Benjamin, Walter. *The Arcades Project,* ed. Rolf Tiedemann, trans. Howard Eiland and Kevin McLaughlin. Cambridge, Massachusetts: Belknap Press of Harvard University Press, 1999.

Berkelman, Robert. "Lincoln's Interest in Shakespeare." *Shakespeare Quarterly* 2 (1951): 303–12.

Berkoff, Todd S. "Botched Battle at Bristoe." *America's Civil War* (September 2003): 22–29, 70–71.

Blight, David W. *A Slave No More: Two Men Who Escaped to Freedom, Including Their Own Narratives of Emancipation.* New York: Harcourt, 2007.

Blondheim, Menahem. *News over the Wires: The Telegraph and the Flow of Public Information in America, 1844–1897.* Cambridge, Massachusetts: Harvard University Press, 1994.

Bloom, Harold. *Shakespeare: The Invention of the Human.* New York: Riverhead, 1998.

Breitwieser, Mitchell Robert. "Jefferson's Prospect." *Prospects* 10 (1985): 315–52.

Briggs, John Channing. *Lincoln's Speeches Reconsidered.* Baltimore: Johns Hopkins University Press, 2005.

Bristol, Michael. *Shakespeare's America, America's Shakespeare.* London: Routledge, 1990.

Brooks, Peter. *The Melodramatic Imagination: Balzac, Henry James, Melodrama, and the Mode of Excess.* New Haven, Connecticut: Yale University Press, 1976.

———. *Realist Vision.* New Haven, Connecticut: Yale University Press, 2005.

Brown, Norman D. *Edward Stanly: Whiggery's Tarheel "Conqueror."* University: University of Alabama Press, 1974.

Brownell, Charles E., Calder Loth, William M. S. Rasmussen, and Richard Guy Wilson. *The Making of Virginia Architecture.* Richmond: Virginia Museum of Fine Arts, 1992.

Carbone, Teresa, and Patricia Hills. *Eastman Johnson: Painting America.* Brooklyn: Brooklyn Museum of Art, 1999.

Castronovo, Russ. *Fathering the Nation: Genealogies of Slavery and Freedom.* Berkeley: University of California Press, 1995.

Cody, David. "Blood in the Basin: The Civil War in Emily Dickinson's 'The name—of It—is 'Autumn.'" *Emily Dickinson Journal* 12 (2003): 25–52.

Davis, John. "Eastman Johnson's *Negro Life at the South* and Urban Slavery in Washington, D.C." *Art Bulletin* 80 (March 1998): 67–92.

Dawes, James. *The Language of War: Literature and Culture in the U.S. from the Civil War through World War II.* Cambridge, Massachusetts: Harvard University Press, 2002.

Dillon, Elizabeth Maddock. "Sentimental Aesthetics." *American Literature* 76 (September 2004): 495–523.

Dudden, Faye E. *Women in the American Theatre: Actresses and Audiences, 1790–1870.* New Haven, Connecticut: Yale University Press, 1994.

Duggan, Robert. "'Sleep No More' Again: Melville's Rewriting of Book X of Wordsworth's *Prelude.*" *Romanticism on the Net* 38–39 (May–August 2005), www.ron.umontreal.cal (accessed August 2008).

Fahlman, Betsy. *John Ferguson Weir: The Labor of Art.* Newark: University of Delaware Press, 1997.

Faulkner, William. *Absalom, Absalom!* New York: Vintage, 1990 [1936].

———. *The Sound and the Fury.* New York: Vintage, 1956 [1929].

Faust, Drew Gilpin. *This Republic of Suffering: Death and the American Civil War.* New York: Alfred A. Knopf, 2008.

Favis, Roberta Smith. "Home Again: Worthington Whittredge's Domestic Interiors." *American Art* (Spring 1995).

Field, Cynthia R., Richard E. Stamm, and Heather Ewing. *The Castle: An Illustrated History of the Smithsonian Building.* Washington, D.C.: Smithsonian Institution Press, 1993.

Fischer, LeRoy H. *Lincoln's Gadfly, Adam Gurowski.* Norman: University of Oklahoma Press, 1964.

Foote, Shelby. *The Civil War, A Narrative: Fredericksburg to Meridian.* New York: Vintage, 1963.

Fraser, John. *America and the Patterns of Chivalry.* Cambridge: Cambridge University Press, 1982.
Frederickson, George M. *The Inner Civil War: Northern Intellectuals and the Crisis of the Union.* New York: Harper & Row, 1965.
Freeman, Douglas Southall. *R. E. Lee: A Biography.* New York: Charles Scribner's Sons, 1935.
Fried, Michael. *Menzel's Realism: Art and Embodiment in Nineteenth-Century Berlin.* New Haven, Connecticut: Yale University Press, 2002.
Furgurson, Ernest B. *Freedom Rising: Washington in the Civil War.* New York: Alfred A. Knopf, 2004.
Fuss, Diana. *The Sense of an Interior: Four Writers and the Rooms That Shaped Them.* New York: Routledge, 2004.
Garber, Marjorie. "Macbeth: The Male Medusa." In *Shakespeare's Late Tragedies,* ed. Susanne L. Wofford, 74–103. Upper Saddle River, New Jersey: Prentice-Hall, 1996.
Garner, Stanton. *The Civil War World of Herman Melville.* Lawrence: University Press of Kansas, 1993.
Gell, Alfred. *Art and Agency: An Anthropological Theory.* Oxford: Clarendon Press, 1998.
Gerdts, William. "The Empty Room." *Allen Memorial Art Museum Bulletin* 33 (1975–76): 72–88.
Gilmore, Paul. "Aesthetic Power: Electric Words and the Example of Frederick Douglass." *American Transcendental Quarterly* 16 (December 2002): 291–311.
———. "Mechanical Means: Emersonian Aesthetic Transcendence and Antebellum Technology." *Modern Language Quarterly* 65 (June 2004): 245–68.
———. "Romantic Electricity, or the Materiality of Aesthetics." *American Literature* 76 (September 2004): 467–94.
Goddu, Teresa A. *Gothic America: Narrative, History, and Nation.* New York: Columbia University Press, 1997.
Goodwin, Doris Kearns. *Team of Rivals: The Political Genius of Abraham Lincoln.* New York: Simon and Schuster, 2005.
Gopinath, Gabrielle. "Harriet Hosmer and the Feminine Sublime." *Oxford Art Journal* 28 (2005): 61–81.
Green, Constance McLaughlin. *Washington: Village and Capital, 1800–1878.* Princeton, New Jersey: Princeton University Press, 1962.
Green, Fletcher Melvin. *Democracy in the Old South and Other Essays,* ed. J. Isaac Copeland. Nashville, Tennessee: Vanderbilt University Press, 1969.
Grimsted, David. *Melodrama Unveiled: American Theater and Culture.* Chicago: University of Chicago Press, 1968.
Grob, Alan. "The Poetry of Pessimism: Arnold's 'Resignation.'" *Victorian Poetry* 26 (Spring–Summer 1988): 25–44.

Hall, Peter, interview with John Russell Brown. "Directing *Macbeth.*" In *Focus on Macbeth,* ed. Brown, 231–48. London: Routledge, 1982.
Haltman, Kenneth. *Looking Close and Seeing Far: Samuel Seymour, Titian Ramsay Peale, and the Art of the Long Expedition, 1818–1823.* University Park: Penn State University Press, 2008.
———. "Titian Ramsay Peale's Specimen Portraiture; or, Natural History as Family History." In *The Peale Family: Creation of a Legacy, 1770–1870,* ed. Lillian Miller, 87–101. New York: Abbeville, 1997.
Halttunen, Karen. *Confidence Men and Painted Women: A Study of Middle-Class Culture in America, 1830–1870.* New Haven, Connecticut: Yale University Press, 1982.
Hambourg, Maria Morris. *The Waking Dream: Photography's First Century—Selections from the Gilman Paper Company Collection.* New York: Metropolitan Museum of Art, 1993.
Harris, Brayton. *Blue & Gray in Black & White.* Washington, D.C.: Brassey's, 1999.
Hawkins, Don Alexander. "The Landscape of the Federal City: A 1792 Walking Tour." *Washington History* 3 (Spring/Summer 1991): 10–33.
Heidegger, Martin. *Poetry, Language, Thought,* trans. Albert Hofstadter. New York: Harper & Row, 1971.
Henderson, Andrea. " 'An Embarrassing Subject': Problems of Value and Identity in the Early Gothic Novel." In *At the Limits of Romanticism: Essays in Cultural, Feminist, and Materialist Criticism,* ed. Mary A. Favret and Nicola J. Watson, 225–45. Bloomington: Indiana University Press, 1994.
Henderson, William D. *The Road to Bristoe Station: Campaigning with Lee and Meade, August 1–October 20, 1863.* Lynchburg, Virginia: H. E. Howard, 1987.
Henkin, David M. *The Postal Age: The Emergence of Modern Communications in Nineteenth-Century America.* Chicago: University of Chicago Press, 2006.
Holzer, Harold, Gabor Boritt, and Mark Neely, Jr. *The Lincoln Image: Abraham Lincoln and the Popular Print.* Urbana: University of Illinois Press, 1984.
Holzer, Harold, and Lloyd Ostendorf. "Sculptures of Abraham Lincoln from Life." *Antiques* 113 (February 1978): 382–93.
Jameson, Fredric. "The Experiments of Time: Providence and Realism." In *The Novel,* vol. 2, *Forms and Themes,* ed. Franco Moretti, 95–127. Princeton, New Jersey: Princeton University Press, 2006.
Jordan, David M. *"Happiness Is Not My Companion": The Life of General G. K. Warren.* Bloomington: Indiana University Press, 2001.
Jordan, Ervin Leon, Jr. "A Painful Case: The Wright-Sanborn Incident in Norfolk, Virginia, July–October 1863." Master's thesis, Old Dominion University, 1977.
Journet, Debra. "Phantom Limbs and 'Body-Ego': S. Weir Mitchell's 'George Dedlow.' " *Mosaic* 23 (Winter 1990): 87–99.

Kauffman, Michael W. *American Brutus: John Wilkes Booth and the Lincoln Conspiracies.* New York: Random House, 2004.

Kelly, James C., and William M. S. Rasmussen. *The Virginia Landscape: A Cultural History.* Charlottesville, Virginia: Howell Press, 2000.

Kelsey, Robin. *Archive Style: Photographs & Illustrations for U.S. Surveys, 1850–1890.* Berkeley: University of California Press, 2007.

Klement, Frank L. *Dark Lanterns: Secret Political Societies, Conspiracies, and Treason Trials in the Civil War.* Baton Rouge: Louisiana State University Press, 1984.

Landrum, Grace Warren. "Sir Walter Scott and His Literary Rivals in the Old South." *American Literature* 2 (November 1930): 256–76.

Leach, Joseph. *Bright Particular Star: The Life & Times of Charlotte Cushman.* New Haven, Connecticut: Yale University Press, 1970.

Lee, Anthony W., and Elizabeth Young. *On Alexander Gardner's* Photographic Sketch Book *of the Civil War.* Berkeley: University of California Press, 2007.

Leech, Margaret. *Reveille in Washington, 1860–1865.* New York: Harper & Brothers, 1941.

Leuchtenburg, William E, ed. *American Places: Encounters with History, A Celebration of Sheldon Meyer.* Oxford: Oxford University Press, 2000.

Levine, Lawrence. *Highbrow/Lowbrow: The Emergence of Cultural Hierarchy in America.* Cambridge, Massachusetts: Harvard University Press, 1988.

Loeffelholz, Mary. "The Religion of Art in the City at War: Boston's Public Poetry and the Great Organ, 1863." *American Literary History* 13 (2001): 212–41.

Luria, Sarah. *Capital Speculations: Writing and Building Washington, D.C.* Durham: University of New Hampshire Press, 2006.

McConnachie, Bruce. "American Theatre in Context, from the Beginnings to 1870." In *The Cambridge History of American Theatre,* vol. 1, *Beginnings to 1870,* ed. Don B. Wilmeth and Christopher Bigsby. Cambridge: Cambridge University Press, 1998.

McCormack, Jerusha Hull. "Domesticating Delphi: Emily Dickinson and the Electro-Magnetic Telegraph." *American Quarterly* 55 (December 2003): 569–601.

McCullough, David. *The Great Bridge: The Epic Story of the Building of the Brooklyn Bridge.* New York: Touchstone Books, 1972.

McKnight, W. Mark. *Blue Bonnets O'er the Border: The 79th New York Cameron Highlanders.* Shippensburg, Pennsylvania: White Mane Books, 1998.

McLuhan, Marshall. *Understanding Media: The Extensions of Man.* New York: McGraw-Hill, 1964.

Meersman, Roger, and Robert Boyer. "The National Theatre in Washington: Buildings and Audiences, 1835–1972." *Records of the Columbia Historical Society of Washington, D.C. 1971–1972,* ed. Francis Coleman Rosenberger, 190–242. Washington, D.C.: Columbia Historical Society, 1972.

Menand, Louis. *The Metaphysical Club.* New York: Farrar, Straus, and Giroux, 2001.

Merrill, Lisa. *When Romeo Was a Woman: Charlotte Cushman and Her Circle of Female Spectators.* Ann Arbor: University of Michigan Press, 1999.

Miller, J. Hillis. *Illustration.* Cambridge, Massachusetts: Harvard University Press, 1992.

Milroy, Elizabeth. "The Public Career of Emma Stebbins: Work in Marble." *Archives of American Art Journal* 33 (1993): 2–12.

Moe, Richard. *The Last Full Measure: The Life and Death of the First Minnesota Volunteers.* New York: Henry Holt, 1993.

Moyer, Albert E. *Joseph Henry: The Rise of an American Scientist.* Washington, D.C.: Smithsonian Institution Press, 1997.

Murray, W. A. "Why Was Duncan's Blood Golden?" In *Shakespeare: Macbeth, A Case Book,* ed. John Wain, 276–91. London: Macmillan, 1968.

Naisawald, L. VanLoan. *Cannon Blasts: Civil War Artillery in the Eastern Armies.* Shippensburg, Pennsylvania: White Mane Books, 2004.

Nemerov, Alexander. "Whitman's Moment." *PN Review* 33 (July–August 2007): 30–34.

Oates, Stephen B. *With Malice Toward None: A Life of Abraham Lincoln.* New York: Harper & Row, 1994.

Odgers, Merle M. *Alexander Dallas Bache, Scientist and Educator, 1806–1867.* Philadelphia: University of Pennsylvania Press, 1947.

Olivier, Laurence. *Confessions of an Actor: An Autobiography.* New York: Penguin, 1982.

Palmer, D. J. "A New Gorgon: Visual Effects in *Macbeth.*" In *Focus on Macbeth,* ed. John Russell Brown, 54–69. London: Routledge, 1992.

Parrott, Sara Foose. "Networking in Italy: Charlotte Cushman and 'The White Marmorean Flock.'" *Women's Studies* 14 (1988): 305–38.

Parsons, Mia T., and John W. Ravenhorst, eds. *Archeological Resource Study and Clearance for the Discovery Center Project at the Henry House, Manassas National Battlefield Park, Manassas, Virginia.* Archeology Program, Harpers Ferry National Historical Park, for Manassas National Battlefield Park, 2002.

Pick, Nancy. *Curious Footprints: Professor Hitchcock's Dinosaur Tracks & Other Natural History Treasures at Amherst College.* Amherst, Massachusetts: Amherst College Press, 2006.

Pointon, Marcia. "The Representation of Time in Painting: A Study of William Dyce's *Pegwell Bay: A Recollection of October 5th, 1858.*" *Art History* 1 (March 1978): 99–103.

Polizzotto, Jeffrey J. "Julia Ward Howe, John Brown's Body, and the Coming of the Lord." In *Worldmaking,* ed. William Pencak, 185–91. New York: Peter Lang, 1996.

Pryor, Elizabeth Brown. *Clara Barton: Professional Angel.* Philadelphia: University of Pennsylvania Press, 1987.

Raab, Jennifer. "Frederic Church and the Culture of Detail." Ph.D. diss., Yale University, 2009.

Rasmussen, William M. S., and Robert S. Tilton. *Old Virginia: The Pursuit of the Pastoral Ideal.* Charlottesville, Virginia: Howell Press, 2003.

Ray, Frederic E. *Alfred R. Waud, Civil War Artist.* New York: Viking, 1974.

Rees, Terence. *Theatre Lighting in the Age of Gas.* Cambridge: Entertainment Technology Press, 2004.

Reiss, Edmund. "Whitman's Debt to Animal Magnetism." *Proceedings of the Modern Language Association* 78 (March 1963): 80–88.

Reminiscences of Early Polk Countians: Stories About Life When Polk County Was Young. Bolivar, Missouri: Polk County Genealogical Society, n.d.

Rilke, Rainer Maria. *Auguste Rodin.* Mineola, New York: Dover, 2006 [1903, 1907].

Robinson, Marc. *The American Play.* New Haven, Connecticut: Yale University Press, 2009.

Rosenheim, Jeff L. "135a, b, c. Anonymous [description of Wilderness Battlefield photographs]." *The Waking Dream: Photography's First Century: Selections from the Gilman Paper Company Collection.* New York: Metropolitan Museum of Art, 1993.

Ross, Charles D. *Civil War Acoustic Shadows.* Shippensburg, Pennsylvania: White Mane Books, 2001.

Rotella, Carlo. *Cut Time: An Education at the Fights.* Boston: Houghton Mifflin, 2003.

Russett, Cynthia Eagle. *Darwin in America: The Intellectual Response, 1865–1912.* San Francisco: W. H. Freeman, 1976.

Sampson, Edward J., Jr. *The Great Organ: Methuen Memorial Music Hall.* Methuen, Massachusetts: Fish and Maria Design, n.d.

Sandburg, Carl. *Abraham Lincoln,* vols. 1 and 2, *The Prairie Years.* New York: Harcourt, Brace, 1926.

———. *Abraham Lincoln,* vol. 3, *The War Years.* New York: Harcourt, Brace, 1939.

Scheel, Eugene M. *The Civil War in Fauquier County, Virginia.* Warrenton, Virginia: Fauquier National Bank, 1985.

Schiller, Joyce K. "Nydia: A Forgotten Icon of the Nineteenth Century." *Bulletin of the Detroit Institute of Arts* 67 (1993): 37–45.

Schmahl, Carl R. "'Enemy Back of You!': J. E. B. Stuart's Close Call at Auburn in October 1863." *Fauquier* (Spring 1995): 34–41.

Scott, Gary. "Clara Barton's Civil War Apartments." *Washington History* 13 (Spring/Summer 2001): 24–31.

Shumway, Floyd M., and Richard Hegel. "On the Campaign Trail: Abraham Lincoln's Visit to New Haven." *Journal of the New Haven Colony Historical Society* 39 (Fall 1992): 13–24.

Simpson, Marc. *Winslow Homer Paintings of the Civil War.* San Francisco: Fine Arts Museums of San Francisco, 1988.

Sitterson, Joseph Carlyle. *The Secession Movement in North Carolina.* James Sprunt Studies in History and Political Science 23. Chapel Hill: University of North Carolina Press, 1939.
Slater, Ann Pasternak. "Macbeth and the Terrors of the Night." *Essays in Criticism* 28 (1978): 112–28.
Smith, Bruce R. *The Acoustic World of Early Modern England: Attending to the O-Factor.* Chicago: University of Chicago Press, 1999.
Smith, George W. *When Lincoln Came to Egypt.* Herrin, Illinois: Trovillion Private Press, 1940.
Smith, Mark M. *Listening to Nineteenth-Century America.* Chapel Hill: University of North Carolina Press, 2001.
Smith, Peter. *Explaining Chaos.* Cambridge: Cambridge University Press, 1998.
Stam, Deirdre. "Growing Up with Books: Fanny Seward's Book Collecting, Reading, and Writing in Mid-Nineteenth-Century New York State." *Libraries & Culture: A Journal of Library History* 41 (Spring 2006): 189–218.
Stebbins, Theodore E., Jr. *The Lure of Italy: American Artists and the Italian Experience, 1760–1914.* Boston: Museum of Fine Arts, 1992.
Sterne, Jonathan. *The Audible Past: Cultural Origins of Sound Reproduction.* Durham, North Carolina: Duke University Press, 2003.
Stevens, Wallace. *Collected Poetry and Prose.* New York: Library of America, 1997.
Stevenson, James. "Abraham Lincoln's Affinity for *Macbeth. Midwest Quarterly* 31 (Winter 1990): 270–79.
Taft, Lorado. *The History of American Sculpture.* New York: Macmillan, 1903.
Taylor, Joshua C. *William Page, the American Titian.* Chicago: University of Chicago Press, 1957.
Teague, Frances. *Shakespeare and the American Popular Stage.* Cambridge: Cambridge University Press, 2006.
Thomas, Benjamin. *Abraham Lincoln.* New York: Alfred Knopf, 1952.
Tolles, Thayer, ed. *American Sculpture in the Metropolitan Museum of Art,* vol. 1. New York: Metropolitan Museum of Art, 1999.
Trachtenberg, Alan. "Lincoln's Smile: Ambiguities of the Face of Photography." In *Lincoln's Smile and Other Enigmas.* New York: Hill & Wang, 2007.
Tucker, George Holbert. *Norfolk Highlights, 1854–1881.* Norfolk, Virginia: Norfolk Historical Society, 1972.
Wagner, Anne Middleton. *Jean-Baptiste Carpeaux.* New Haven, Connecticut: Yale University Press, 1986.
Wallace, Richard, and Marie Pinak Carr. *The Willard Hotel: An Illustrated History.* Washington, D.C.: Dicmar, 1986.
Wertenbaker, Thomas. *Norfolk: Historic Southern Port.* Durham, North Carolina: Duke University Press, 1931.
Wilder, Thornton. Preface to *Three Plays: Our Town, The Skin of Our Teeth, The Matchmaker.* London: Longmans Green, 1957.

Williams, Gary. *Hungry Heart: The Literary Emergence of Julia Ward Howe.* Amherst: University of Massachusetts Press, 1999.

Wills, Garry. *Lincoln at Gettysburg: The Words That Remade America.* New York: Simon and Schuster, 1992.

———. *Witches and Jesuits: Shakespeare's* Macbeth. New York: Oxford University Press, 1995.

Wilson, Edmund. *Patriotic Gore: Studies in the Literature of the American Civil War.* New York: Oxford University Press, 1962.

Yanuck, Julius. "Thomas Ruffin and North Carolina Slave Law." *Journal of Southern History* (1955): 456–75.

ILLUSTRATIONS

1. Mathew Brady, *Charlotte Cushman,* 1857 / 9
2. Grover's National Theater, 1868 / 10
3. *Miss Charlotte Cushman as Lady Macbeth,* ca. 1850s / 11
4. John Bachmann, *Bird's Eye View of the City of Washington, D.C., and the Seat of War in Virginia,* 1862 / 14
5. Organ, Music Hall, Boston, ca. 1863–84 / 26
6. Interior of Music Hall, Boston, 1876 / 27
7. Thomas Crawford, *Freedom,* 1863 (atop Capitol) / 30
8. Thomas Crawford, *Freedom* / 32
9. Charlotte Cushman as Lady Macbeth / 33
10. Harriet Hosmer, *Zenobia in Chains,* 1859 / 34
11. Unknown artist, *Charlotte Cushman's Eye,* n.d. / 37
12. Cushman as Meg Merrilies in *Guy Mannering* / 38
13. Harriet Hosmer, *Medusa,* 1854 / 39
14. Boston Music Hall organ, with Thomas Crawford's *Beethoven,* ca. 1863–84 / 41
15. Broadway on a rainy day, ca. 1860 / 42
16. Giorgio Sommer, *Plaster Cast of Pompeii Victims, February 5, 1863* / 44
17. Giorgio Sommer, *Plaster Cast of Pompeii Victims, February 5, 1863* / 44

18. Randolph Rogers, *Nydia, the Blind Flower Girl of Pompeii,* ca. 1854–55 / 48
19. Detail of Randolph Rogers, *Nydia* / 51
20. Detail of Randolph Rogers, *Nydia* / 51
21. Charlotte Cushman's home, ca. 1875 / 52
22. Richard Morris Hunt, *Charlotte Cushman House: Details of Finials,* ca. 1870 / 54
23. Charlotte Cushman's obelisk, Mount Auburn Cemetery, 1876 / 55
24. Clark Mills, *Life Mask of Abraham Lincoln,* ca. 1917 / 66
25. Henry Fonda as Abraham Lincoln in John Ford's *The Young Mr. Lincoln,* 1939 / 71
26. David Plowden, *Tree near Relay, Maryland,* 1964 / 72
27. David Plowden, *Antietam,* ca. 1965 / 73
28. David Plowden, *Aquia Creek,* ca. 1965 / 73
29. *Grand Procession of Wide-Awakes at New York on the Evening of October 3, 1860,* in *Harper's Weekly,* 1860 / 75
30. Winslow Homer, *Rebels Outside Their Works at Yorktown Reconnoitering with Dark Lanterns,* in *Harper's Weekly,* 1862 / 81
31. Winslow Homer, *In Front of Yorktown,* ca. 1862–63 / 83
32. James W. Watts, *Comet of Donati 1858, September 16th* / 85
33. William Dyce, *Pegwell Bay, Kent—A Recollection of October 5th, 1858,* ca. 1858–60 / 86
34. Lewis Rutherfurd, *Moon, March 4, 1865* / 88
35. Globe from William Seward's house, ca. 1860 / 90
36. Emanuel Leutze, *Signing of the Alaska Treaty,* 1869 / 91
37. Eastman Johnson, *Negro Life at the South,* 1859 / 99
38. "Plan of the organ of hearing as an architect might describe it," in Oliver Wendell Holmes, "The Great Instrument," 1863 / 107
39. Thomas Eakins, *Perspective Drawing for the "Pair-Oared Shell,"* 1872 / 110
40. Worthington Whittredge, *Interior of the Bedroom of Thomas Whitredge, Tiverton, Rhode Island,* ca. 1863 / 113
41. Thomas Crawford, *The Progress of Civilization,* ca. 1854–63 / 120
42. Plaster cast of Thomas Crawford's seated Indian from *The Progress of Civilization* / 121
43. The Lecture Room at the Smithsonian Institution / 131
44. Joseph Henry, drawing of new Lecture Room, 1849 / 132

45. Titian Ramsay Peale, *Interior of Joseph Henry's Apartments at the Smithsonian Building,* 1862 / 135
46. Meteorite from Coahuila, Mexico / / 136
47. Charles Wellington Reed, sketch of figures in tents, 1863 / 141
48. J. F. Hillers, *The War in Georgia—Battle of Chickamauga, Sept. 19 and 20,* in *Frank Leslie's Illustrated Newspaper,* 1863 / 146
49. Schenkl shell fragment, 1863 / 149
50. Alfred Waud, *Battle of Bristoe Station,* 1863 / 152
51. Gouverneur Kemble Warren, *Uniontown, Karo River,* ca. 1850s / 155
52. Gouverneur Kemble Warren, *Spanish Peaks . . . Aug. 6,* ca. 1850s / 155
53. *Sappho,* in Edda Middleton, *Sappho: A Tragedy in Five Acts,* 1858 / 158
54. Timothy O'Sullivan, *Castle Murray,* 1863 / 162
55. *Melrose,* presentation drawing, ca. 1857–58 / 164
56. *Our Chief, Lochiel* (tobacco label), 1876 / 165
57. Timothy O'Sullivan, *Castle Murray, near Auburn, Va., November 1863* / 169
58. Timothy O'Sullivan, *Castle Murray,* 1863 / 172
59. Bottle, ca. 1860–80 / 178
60. Polk County Court House, Bolivar, Missouri, ca. 1850 / 188
61. Plan of Bolivar, Missouri, 1841 / 189
62. Burial ground, Louisburg, North Carolina, with tomb of Thomas Ruffin / 196
63. Thomas Ruffin's tomb, Louisburg, North Carolina / 197
64. Close-up of Ruffin's tomb, Louisburg, North Carolina / 198
65. Andrew Joseph Russell (attributed), *Orange and Alexandria R.R. Bridge near Union Mills, the burned block,* 1863 / 209
66. James Caldwall after Henry Fuseli, *A Heath: Macbeth, Banquo, and Three Witches* / 211
67. Unknown photographer, *The Wilderness Battlefield,* ca. 1865–67 / 216
68. Unknown photographer, *The Wilderness Battlefield,* ca. 1865–67 / 220

INDEX

Page numbers in italics refer to illustrations.

Abbott, Major Henry, 143, 254n14
abolitionists, 15, 24, 103, 159, 163, 166, 173–74, 191
Academy of Music (New York), 9
acoustics, 129–30, 132, 218, 224
acoustic shadows, 138–39, 141, 147, 148, 154, 160
Adorno, Theodor, 114, 248n36
Agassiz, Louis, 119, 204
Aladdin; or, The Wonderful Lamp (play), 89, 246n82
Allan, William, 207
All Souls' Church (New York), 16
American Colonization Society, 172
American Journal of Insanity, 61
Amherst College, 201
amputations, 108
Antietam, Battle of, 115
Archer, Robert L., 142
architecture, 39–40, 101, 162–64, 166–69; of stage sets, 129, 176
Armory Square Hospital (Washington, D.C.), 125
Armstrong, Duff, 87
army. *See* Confederate army; Union army
artifacts, 129, *136,* 143, 148, 233n38; glass cases for, 134–35
Associated Press, 18–19
Astor Place Riots (New York, 1849), 4, 95
Athenaeum Club (New York), 119
Atlantic Monthly, 27, 105, *107,* 108–11, 144, 255n20

Bache, Alexander Dallas, 129–30, 132–35, 204; "Notice of Earthquake Waves on the Western Coast of the United States," 133
Bachelard, Gaston, *The Poetics of Space,* 46
Bachmann, John, *Bird's Eye View of the City of Washington, D.C., and the Seat of War in Virginia,* 13, *14,* 22, 35
Baker, Absolem, 188
Baker, Loretta, 188
Baker, Paul R., 53, 238n119
Balzac, Honoré de, 100
Barnum's Museum (New York), 117
Barton, Clara, 21, 22, 234n53
Bassett, Edward, 150, 151, 153

Bataille, Georges, 56
Bates, David Homer, 62, 63, 78
Bazin, André, 69, 88–89
Beckford, William, 166
Beecher, Henry Ward, 163, 167
Beer, Gillian, *Darwin's Plots,* 203, 204
Beethoven, Ludwig van, Crawford's statue of, 36, 40, *41*
Bell, Rosa, 96–97
Bellows, Henry W., 16–17, 29, 46, 205
Benjamin, Walter, 45, 248n26
Berkeley, Henry, 187
Bible, the, 142, 144; Romans, 163
billiards, 23
Birch-Pfeiffer, Charlotte, *Fanchon, the Cricket,* 20, 29, 159
Blackford, William Willis, 194
Black Hawk War, 240n17
Black Laws, 245n75
Blondheim, Menahem, 19
Bloom, Harold, 2
Bond, G. P., 84, 86
Booth, Edwin, 9, 104, 249n34
Booth, John Wilkes, 22–23, 119
Born, David, 148–49, 255n26
Boston Daily Courier, 40
Boston Music Hall, 25–28, *26, 27,* 36, 39–40, 102, 106, 209
Boston Post, 153
Boston Theatre, 12, 15
Boydell, John, *Illustrations of the Dramatic Works of Shakespeare,* 211, *211,* 224
Braddon, Mary: *Aurora Floyd,* 31–32; *Eleanor's Victory,* 182
Brady, Mathew, *Charlotte Cushman, 9*
Brahms, Johannes, 106
Breitwieser, Mitchell Robert, 210
Brewster, Anne Hampton, *Spirit Sculpture,* 40, 45
Bridges, Sallie, *Marble Isle,* 37–38, 40
Briggs, John Channing, *Lincoln's Speeches Reconsidered,* 64
Bristoe Station, Battle of, 14–15, 139–46, 148–51, *152,* 154–56, 161, 180, 198, 207, 213, 214, 255n25, 260n1
Bristol, Michael, 247n3
Broadway (New York, photograph), *42*
Brooke, Dorothea, 203
Brooklyn Bridge (New York), 154
Brooks, Noah, 31, 69, 70, 140
Brooks, Peter, 46–47, 100
Brooks, Preston, 192
Brown, Bill, 109
Brown, John, 84, 106
Browne, Charles Farrar, 246–47n3
Browning, Elizabeth Barrett: "Hiram Powers' Greek Slave," 24; "Life," 23–24
Bull Run, Battle of, 46, 137, 139, 214, 217; memorial to, 217
Bulwer-Lytton, Edward, *The Last Days of Pompeii,* 47
butterfly effect, 22–25
Byron, George Gordon, Lord, *Child Harolde,* 266n43

Caldwell, James, *A Heath: Macbeth, Banquo, and Three Witches,* 211
Cameron, William, and Brothers, *Our Chief Lochiel* tobacco label, 164, *165*
Canterbury Hall (Washington, D.C.), 77
Capitol Building (Washington, D.C.), *30,* 30–31, *120,* 120–22, 130
Carpeaux, Jean-Baptiste, *Young Fisherboy with a Shell,* 47
Carpenter, Francis, 71
Carrie Martin (ship), 14
Carter, Robert, 117–19
cartes de visite, 20–21, 29, 45, 83, 159
Casaubon, Edward, 203
Castle Murray (Auburn, Virginia), *161,* 161–64, *164,* 166–72, *172,* 174–77, 180, 185, 257n5
Chamberlain, William W., 141
Chambrun, Marquis Adolphe de, 66–67, 69
Channing, William Henry, 103
Charlemagne, 91–92
Chase, Algernon, 232n26
Chickamauga, Battle of, 145
Civil War, 4, 5, 25, 65, 112, 118, 144, 200, 206, 215, 244n65; acoustic shadows in, 138–39; aestheticism in context

of, 113; dead of, 180–82, 187, 194–98; outbreak of, 191; philanthropy during, 21; racial causes of, 174; telegraphy in, 18, 62–63, 65; Whitman's poetry of, 127; *see also specific battles*
Coast Survey, U.S., 133
Cocke, Charles L., 157, 159; *An Account of the Allegheny Spring, in Montgomery County, Virginia,* 159
Cole, C. M., 142
Collis, Septima M., 195
comets, 84–86, 205
commemorative objects. *See* souvenirs
Confederate army, 82, *83,* 84, 102, 163, 187; at Bristoe Station, 140–43, 148, 154, 161, 180, 213–14; First North Carolina Cavalry, 193; Sixth Virginia Infantry, 142; Third Army Corps, 141
Congdon, Charles, 97
Congress, U.S., 63, 110, 190–03
Cooke, General John R., 142, 149
Cooper Union (New York), 83
Copperheads, 111
Crawford, Thomas, 30–31, 36; *Beethoven,* 36, 40, *41; Freedom, 30,* 31, *32; The Progress of Civilization,* 30, *120,* 120–21; seated Indian in *The Progress of Civilization,* 120–23, *121*
Curtis, George William, 20–21, 115, 221
Cushman, Charlotte, 7–40, *11, 37, 38,* 58, 76, 89, 123, 124, 179, 184, 186, 205, 222, 231n10, 249n34; "The Actress," 12; arrival in Washington D.C. of, 7–8; audience command of, 36–40; at Boston Music Hall organ dedication, 25–27, 36, 102, 209; death of, 10, 19, 53; at Ford's Theater, 12, 20, 29, 95 147, 159, 224; gifts to Fanny Seward from, 22, 226, 234n54; Grover's Theatre chosen for performance by, 8, 230n3; in Italy, 18, 29–30, 165, 225–26; as Lady Macbeth, 7, 9–13, *11,* 18, 20–21, 28–29, 31, *33,* 35–36, 38–39, 43, 45, 47, 52, 71, 94, 147, 165, 177, 223–25, 264n42; letter writing of, 17–18, 22, 232n36; Newport, Rhode Island, mansion of, 13, *52,* 52–53, *54;* newspaper coverage of, 18–19; photographs of, *9,* 19–21, *33, 38;* physical presence of, 8, 10, 12–13, 15–16, 233n38; poetry recitals of, 49–50; preparation for performances by, 31, 32; reviews of acting of, 9–10, 12, 218; script notes of, 74, 176; souvenir hunting of, 45–46; tomb of, 53, *55,* 56–57; vocal power of, 10, 12, 13, 80, 132, 147, 148, 231n10; Warren and, 14–15, 154, 156, 232n26, 257n43
Cushman, Emma Crow, 8, 20, 32, 231n10
Cushman, Ned, 231n10

daguerreotypes, 20, 40, 65, 143, 201
Daily National Intelligencer, 180, 182
Daily National Republican, 15, 17, 23, 60, 94, 97, 241n29
Darwin, Charles, 203, 204; *The Origin of Species,* 200, 202, 221, 222
Davenport, Edward Loomis, 8, 59, 123, 147, 230n3, 249n34
Davis, John, 98
Dawes, James, 21, 251n74
De Bow's Review, 167
Deery, John, 23
Deery and Simpson Billiard Saloon (Washington, D.C.), 96
Democratic Party, 76, 190–91
De Quincey, Thomas, 36, 185
Dickens, Charles, 100; *Oliver Twist,* 56, 225
Dickinson, Anna, 103, 147
Dickinson, Emily, 115–16, 144, 182–83, 254n17; "The name—of it—is Autumn," 115; "Zero at the Bone," 144
Donati, Giovanni Battista, 84
Donati's Comet, 84–85, *85,* 245n73
Douglas, Henry Kyd, 161, 176
Douglas, Stephen, 84
Douglass, Alex, 96
Douglass, Frederick, 104, 166
Dowden, Edward, 205
Draft Riots (New York, 1863), 77, 150, 244n60
Duggan, Robert, 244n60

Dyce, William, *Pegwell Bay, Kent—A Recollection of October 5th, 1858,* 85, *86,* 205

Eakins, Thomas, 111; *The Pair-Oared Shell,* 109, *110*
Eames, Charles, 117
Eames, Fanny, 117
Eckert, Major Thomas, 78
Elder, Anna, 140
Elder, Thomas Claybrook, 140
Eliot, George: *Adam Bede,* 100, 219–21; *Middlemarch,* 100, 203–4; *Romola,* 97–98
Ellsworth, Elmer, 46
Emancipation Proclamation (1863), 96, 247n3
Emerson, Ralph Waldo, 16, 50, 87, 135–36; "Voluntaries," 27
Emory, Major William H., 64
Empire City (steamboat), 150
Enlightenment, 210
"Enquiry, The" (song), 248n17
evolution, theory of, 200, 204–6
exuviae, ancient theory of, 20

Fauquier Historical Society, 163, 171; bottle from collection of, *178*
Faust, Drew Gilpin, 181
Fielding, Henry, 204
Fields, Annie, 94; "Dedication Ode," 25–27, 209
Fiorelli, Giovanni, 43, 46
Flaubert, Gustave, *Madame Bovary,* 49
Fonda, Henry, 70–71, *71*
Ford, John (movie director), 70–71, *71*
Ford, John (theater owner), 8, 230n3
Ford's Theater (Washington, D.C.), 8, 18, 20, 69, 92, 159; assassination of Lincoln at, 4–5, 22–23, 70, 89, 127; Cushman and Fanny Seward's tour of, 12, 95, 147, 224
Forrest, Edwin, 4
Foster, General John, 60
Frank Leslie's Illustrated Weekly, 79, 83, 144–45, *146,* 151
Franklin, John, 37
Fredericksburg, Battle of, 143
French, Benjamin Brown, 29, 45, 76, 89, 95–96
French Revolution, 244n60
Fried, Michael, 250n51
frozenness, 39–40, 45, 124, 187; in performance, 28, 31, 36, 38–39, 43, 71, 124, 128, 176; in photography, 29, 40, 125; in poetry, 125–26
Fugitive Slave Act (1850), 119
Fuseli, Henry, 224; *A Heath: Macbeth, Banquo, and Three Witches,* 211, *211*
Fuss, Diana, 115

Gaines's Mill, Battle of, 138
Garber, Marjorie, 38
Gardner, Alexander, 87; *Gardner's Photographic Sketch Book of the War,* 169, *169–71,* 217
gaslight, 72, 76, 79, 83, 87, 133
Gell, Alfred, 21
Gerdts, William H., 250n51, n53
gestures, 2–4, 6, 28, 29, 56, 58, 185, 222; affirmative, 219; architectural, 176; environmental, 218; in film, 70; hierarchic, of ancient religions, 35; literary, 100, 177, 206; melodramatic, 10, 46–47, 49, 56; outsized, 34–35; in paintings, 101; photographic, 170, 221
Gettysburg, Battle of, 43, 61, 65, 143, 154, 194, 232n26
Gettysburg Address, 68
Giles, Henry, 15–16
Goddu, Teresa, 166
Gopinath, Gabrielle, 33
Gothic Revival architecture, 164
Grace Church Hospital (Alexandria, Virginia), 180, 195, 260n1
Grant, General Ulysses S., 16
Grassie, Thomas G., 194–95
Gray, Asa, 204
Gray, John P., 61–62
Greeley, Horace, 118, 192
Grillparzer, Franz, 157
Grover, Leonard, 8, 18, 28, 57, 95, 96, 230n3
Grover's National Theatre (Washington,

D.C.), 12, 18, 39, 70, 117, 123, 179, 217, 246n82; acoustics in, 132; backdrops at, 182, 224; façade of, *10*, 23, 57; frozenness of performance at, 40, 128, 129; genteel behavior of audience at, 94–97, 107; interior design of, 22, 46; legend of haunting of, 225; lighting in, 77, 89, 92, 246n82; Lincoln at, 4, 8, 28, 59–60, 62, 63, 71–72, 74–76, 79–80, 94, 185; neighborhood around, 96–99, 100; press row near, 13; rehearsals at, 32; stock company at, 58
Guadalcanal, Battle of, 127
Gulley Plantation (Johnson County, North Carolina), 191
Gurowski, Adam, 116–20, 122, 139, 146, 154–55, 184
Gutenberg Revolution, 166

Hackett, James, 69, 241n22
Hale, Edward Everett, "The Man Without a Country," 111–15
Hall, Peter, 23
Halttunen, Karen, 40
Hamlin, Hannibal, 76
Hanaford, Mrs. J. H., 19–21
Harper's Monthly, 13, 40, 95, 97
Harper's Weekly, 31, 63, *75*, 79, 80, *81*, 83, 97, 151, 182
Harvard University, 84, 119, 204
Haskell, Erastus, 125
Hawkins, Don Alexander, 224
Hawthorne, Nathaniel, 2–4, 19, 46, 102–3; *The Blithedale Romance*, 4, 19, 223; "The Gorgon's Head," 38; *The Marble Faun*, 2, 225; *The Scarlet Letter*, 26, 45, 248n23
Hay, John, 86, 87, 122
Heidegger, Martin, 14
Henderson, Andrea, 166
Henkin, David, *The Postal Age*, 17, 140–41
Henry, Joseph, 130–35, 138–39, 204; apartments at Smithsonian Building of, 134, *135;* drawing of new Lecture Room, *132*
Henry, Judith, 214, 215
hereness, sense of, 68, 69, 71
Herndon, William, 70, 86
Heth, Henry, 154
Higginson, Thomas Wentworth, 144
Hiller, J. F., *The War in Georgia—Battle of Chickamauga, Sept. 19 and 20, 146*
Hitchcock, Edward, 203, 205, 206; *The Religion of Geology and Its Connected Sciences*, 201–2
Hollywood Cemetery (Richmond), 164
Holmes, Oliver Wendell, Sr., 134, 175, 202; on Boston Music Hall organ, 39–40, 106, *107;* on photography, 20, 40, 42, 174, 177; on telegraphy, 19, 50
Holmes, Oliver Wendell, Jr., 254n14
Homer, Winslow, 80, 82–83; *A Bivouac Fire on the Potomac*, 82; *In Front of Yorktown*, 82, *83; Rebels Outside Their Works at Yorktown Reconnoitering with Dark Lanterns*, 80, *81*, 82; *Winter Quarters of a Camp—The Inside of a Hut*, 82
Horrocks, James, 164
Hosmer, Harriet Goodhue, 13, 30; *Medusa*, 37, *39; Zenobia in Chains*, 33–34, *34*
Hotchkiss, Jedediah, 207
House of Representatives, U.S., 63, 130, 147, 190–93
Howe, Julia Ward, 10, 28, 101–8, 114, 124, 134, 249n34; "The Battle Hymn of the Republic," 13, 101–3, 105, 106, 108; "A New Sculptor," 104–5; *Passion-Flowers*, 106
Howe, Maud, 10, 43
Howe, Samuel Gridley, 102, 106
Howells, William Dean, 64
Hugo, Victor, 167; *Notre-Dame de Paris*, 166
Hunt, Richard Morris, 52; *Charlotte Cushman House: Details of Finials*, 53, *54*
Huxley, Thomas H., 203; *Evidence as to Man's Place in Nature*, 204

illuminations, universal, *75*, 75–76
illustration, 79–80, *81*, 82, 151, *152*, 153–54
Indians, 244n65
isolation: literary 108–12, 114–16; in painting, 112–15

Jackson, Thomas J. "Stonewall," 164, 207, 208
Jameson, Fredric, 100, 101
Jarves, John Jackson, 50
Jefferson, Thomas, 210–12; *Notes on the State of Virginia,* 210, 212
"John Brown's Body" (marching song), 102
Johnson, Eastman: *Boyhood of Lincoln,* 243n55; *Negro Life at the South,* 98–101, *99*
Jones, James, 127
Jones, R. J., 74
journalism, 144–45; *see also* newspapers

Kean, Robert Garlick Hill, 138, 139
Keith, Isham, 168, 173–74, 259n23
Keitt, Laurence M., 192
Kingsley, Charles, "The Sands of Dee," 43
Kirkland, Frazar, 59–60, 185
Kirkland, General William W., 142
Know Nothing Party, 192
Kossuth, Lajos, 119

Lamon, Ward, 119
Lee, Robert E., 89, 118, 139, 140, 145–46, 148, 164
Leidy, Joseph, 132
letter writing, 156, 160; by Cushman, 17–18, 22, 232n36; by soldiers, 139–44, 149–50
Leutze, Emmanuel, *Signing of the Alaska Treaty,* 91, *91*
Levine, Lawrence, 95
Lewis, Monk, 166
Library of Congress, 76, 153
light, 71–93; of comets, 84–86; of flames, 77–80, 82–83; for glass-cased artifacts, 134–35; and Lincoln's death, 89; of moon, 87–88, 134–35, 128; in paintings, 82, *83,* 101, 112–14, *113;* in photography, 170, 171, 201, 215, 219, 221; in poetry, 77–78, 102–6, 114, 126–28, 244n60; stage, 71–72, 74, 92, 123, 128, 133; universal illuminations, *75,* 75–76
Light-House Board, U.S., 129, 133, 138
limelights, 74, 123, 128, 134
Lincoln, Abraham, 5, 6, 59–80, 83–89, 93, 96, 116, 120, 225, 243n55, 244n60, n65; assassination of, 4–5, 22–23, 66, 67, 70, 87, 89, 119, 127, 144, 183, 230n13; centennial of death of, 71; childhood home visited by, 239n17; in Congress, 190; Cooper Union speech of, 83; Dickinson's speech criticizing, 147; and Donati's Comet, 84–86; Emancipation Proclamation issued by, 247n3; Gettysburg Address delivered by, 68; in House of Representatives, 63–64; Illinois law practice of, 190; interest in Shakespeare, 4, 67, 241n22, n25; Jefferson and, 210; life mask of, 65–68, *66,* 87; Lyceum Address of, 78–79, 245n65; at *Macbeth* performance, 4, 8, 28, 59–60, 62, 63, 71–72, 74–76, 79–80, 94, 185; Mills's life mask of, 65–68, *66,* 87, 241n25; Second Inaugural, 87; summer cottage of, 69, 78, 180; and telegraphy, 18–19, 60, 62–63, 65, 68, 122, 240n19; trees admired by, 69–71; and Wright case, 60–63, 241n22
Lincoln, Mary Todd, 74, 96
Lincoln, Tad, 74
Lind, Edmund, 162–63
Livermore, Mary, 140, 245n75
Loeffelholz, Mary, 25–27
Longfellow, Charles, 139, 144
Longfellow, Henry Wadsworth, 139; "The Arrow and the Song," 255n20; "Killed at the Ford," 144, 255n20; *Tales of a Wayside Inn,* 43
Lowell, James Russell, 18; "Columbus," 19, 219, 234n43; "The Present Crisis," 22–24
Lucretius, 20, 21
Luria, Sarah, 104
Lyell, Charles, 85
lynching, 78–79
Lyons, Lord, 14

Macbeth, 10–11, 92, 101, 104, 107, 108, 116, 132, 150, 151, 156, 179, 200, 215; and

acoustic shadows, 138, 160; Banquo's ghost in, 57, 98; Castle Murray and, 161, 175–76; Cushman in, *see* Cushman, Charlotte, as Lady Macbeth; emptiness in, 217–18; and evolutionary theory, 200, 203–5; flame imagery in, 74, 77–78, 92, 133; Hawthorne and, 2–4, 229n4; illustration and, 79–80, 83; Jefferson and, 210–12; Lincoln and, 4, 60, 63–68, 71, 80, 83, 119–20, 122–23, 230n13, 241n22, 242n29; Melville and, 2–3, 77; and modes of nature description, 206, 208–9; as patriotic utterance, 145–46; power of heroines and artistry of, 159; randomness in, 23; remorse in, 61; reversals in, 221; riots over rival performances of, 95; Ruffin and, 193, 199; Scottishness of, 165; sets for, 182; vastness of, 15–16; war dead and, 180, 181; Whitman and, 128, 129
Macready, William, 4, 31, 32
Madison, James, 164
Mallon, Colonel James, 143–44, 187
Manassas. *See* Bull Run
Mann, John, 191
Marxism, 114
Mattausch, Dan, 72, 92
McClellan, General George, 117
McConnachie, Bruce, 75, 94, 184
McCormack, Jerusha Hull, 254n17
McCullough, John, 69, 87–88, 225
McLuhan, Marshall, 122; *Understanding Media,* 109
Meade, General George, 139, 154, 161
medievalism, Southern, 163–68
Medieval Revival architecture, 162, 167
Meigs, Captain Montgomery, 130
melodrama, 10, 46–47, 50, 57, 209
Melrose Castle. *See* Castle Murray
Melville, Herman, 2, 144, 244n60; *Battle-Pieces and Aspects of the War,* 144; "The House-top," 77–78; *Moby Dick,* 2–3; "The Portent," 84; "Shiloh," 144
Mendelssohn, Felix, 106
Menzel, Adolph, *Room with a Balcony,* 250n51
Mexican War, 63, 190
Middleton, Edda, *Sappho: A Tragedy in Five Acts,* 157, *158,* 159–60
Military Telegraph Corps, U.S., 62
Miller, J. Hillis, 79
Mills, Clark, *30,* 31, 241n29; *Life Mask of Abraham Lincoln,* 65–68, *66,* 87
Milton, John, *Paradise Lost,* 193
Mitchell, Maggie, 20, 29, 159
Mitchell, S. Weir, "The Case of George Dedlow," 108–11, 115, 249n42
Monte Cassino, Battle of, 127
Monticello, 210–12
Moore, Angie, 266n5
Morawski, Teodor, 119
Morse, Samuel, 18
Mott, Lucretia, 21
Mount Auburn Cemetery (Cambridge), 53, *55*
Murdoch, William Turnbull, 163
Murphy, Donn, 225
Murray, Alfred, 172–73
Murray, James D., 161, 163; *see also* Castle Murray
Murray, James E., 172–73
Murray, W. A., 67

National Institute, 253n99
National Register of Historic Places, 165
nature description, modes of, 206–9
neurasthenia, 110
newspapers, 8, 13, 18, 40, 131, 166, 174; accounts of battles in, 138; Lincoln's call for volunteers in, 60; *see also specific papers*
Newton, Isaac, 50
New-York Daily Tribune, 76, 80
New Yorker, 35
New York Herald, 114
New York State Lunatic Asylum, 61
New York Times, 80
Niblo's Garden (New York), 95

obelisks, 53, *55,* 56–57
Olmsted, Frederick Law, 17
Orange and Alexandria Railroad, 154, 208, 213, 215

Osage Indians, 187
Osborn, Eli Walter, 240n22
O'Sullivan, Timothy, 43; *Castle Murray,* 161, *162, 169,* 170–72, *172,* 174, 176–77, 185
Owner, William, 89, 137

Palmer, D. J., 38
Parrott, Robert Parker, 156
Patent Office, U.S., 125, 128, 134, 186, 253n99
pathetic fallacy, 206–8
Peale, Titian Ramsay, 134; *Interior of Joseph Henry's Apartments at the Smithsonian Building, 135*
Pearce, Joseph, 198–99
Pembroke, Earl of, 50
Perry, John, 143, 187
phantom limb, 108
Phelan and Collender billiards company, 23
photography, 56, 86, 201–2, 205, 208; architectural, 8, *10,* 31, *52,* 52–53, 55, 57, 161, *169,* 169–71, 174, 176; battlefield, 215, 217, 219–21; Cushman and, 19–20, 29, 31, 43, 45; freezing of images by, 40, 42, 125; of moon, 87–89, *88;* of trees, for centennial of Lincoln's death, 71, *72, 73;* war dead and, 143–44; *see also* daguerreotypes; stereographs
Pleasanton, General Alfred, 170
Plowden, David, 71; *Antietam, 73; Aquia Creek, 73; Tree near Relay, Maryland, 72*
Plymouth Church (Brooklyn, New York), 163
poetry, 153, 160, 161, 222, 254n17; chance effects of, 176; Southern white men and, 192–93; *see also specific poets*
Pointon, Marcia, 85
Polizzotto, Jeffrey, 103
Polk, James, 63–64, 190
Polk County Court House (Bolivar, Missouri), 187–88, *188*
Pompeii, stereographs of, 43, *44*
postal service, 17–18, 141–43
Powell, Lewis, 89–90
Prentiss, William S., 125
press. *See* journalism; newspapers
Princeton University, 134
Prince William County Historic Preservation Division, 148
Puritans, 26
Pyle, Ernie, 127

railroads, 17, 50, 208, 215; at Bristoe Station, 143, 154, 160, 213
Randolph, George Wythe, 138
Read, Thomas Buchanan, "Drifting," 206
Reed, Charles Wellington, 140–41, 144; sketch of figures in tents, *141*
Rensselaer Polytechnic Institute, 256n35
Republican Party, 64, 76, 84, 191, 192
Rhees, William J., *An Account of the Smithsonian Institution, 131, 136*
Rilke, Rainer Maria, 35, 47, 49, 236n82
Rinehart, Mary Roberts, *The Circular Staircase,* 174–75
River Queen (boat), 66–67
Robinson, Marc, 6
Robinson, Willie, 141–42
Rodin, Auguste, 47, 49, 236n82; *The Burghers of Calais,* 47; *Eternal Idol,* 35
Roebling, John, 154
Roebling, Washington, 154, 256n35
Rogers, Randolph, 30, 49–50; *Nydia, the Blind Flower Girl of Pompeii,* 47, *48,* 49, 50, *51,* 52, 159
Romantic movement, 165
Rosencrans, General William S., 16
Ross, Charles, 138
Rotella, Carlo, *Cut Time,* 153
Ruffin, Edmund, 191, 193; *The Political Economy of Slavery,* 191
Ruffin, Henry John Gray, 190
Ruffin, Thomas, 180, 182, 183, 187–88, 190–99, 260n1, 261n16; tomb of, 196–99, *196–98*
Ruskin, John, 206
Russell, Alexander J., 208; *Orange and Alexandria R.R. Bridge near Union Mills, 209*
Russia, 63

Rutherfurd, Lewis, *Moon, March 4, 1865,* 87–89, *88*

Sala, George Augustus, 96, 103, 147
Sanborn, Lieutenant Anson, 60, 62
Sandburg, Carl, 84–85
Sanders, Wilbur, 2
Sanitary Commission, U.S., 7, 16–17, 102, 129, 140, 205, 245n75, 264n42
Sartoris, Adelaide Kemble, *Medusa, and Other Tales,* 37, 38
Saturday Evening Post, 231n20
Schussele, Christian, 264n42
Scott, Walter, 163, 167; *Guy Mannering,* 36, *38,* 165; *Ivanhoe,* 164; Waverley novels, 167–68
Scottish immigrants, 164–65
sculpture, 29–51, 57, 98, 105, 120–23, 236n82
Searles, Edward Francis, 235n68
Seltzer, Mark, 109
Senate, U.S., 84, 120, 147–48, 191, 192
Seven Days' Battles, 193
Seward, Anna, 7, 8, 20, 92
Seward, Fanny, 7–9, 17, 18, 32, 91–92, 232n36; *cartes de visite* collection of, 20–21; *Fanchon* performance attended by, 29, 159; on Ford's Theater tour, 12, 95, 147, 224; gifts from Cushman to, 22, 226, 234n54; personification of waves by, 206–9
Seward, Frederick, 7, 18, 20, 30
Seward, William, 7, 8, 14, 87, 89–92, 119; globe in home of, *90*
Shakespeare, William, 15, 28, 67, 71, 133, 146, 184, 246n3; Boydell's gallery of illustrations for, 211, *211,* 223; Emerson on, 135–36; Holmes's poem for tercentennial of birth of, 134; influence on actors of ambient genius of, 123; Lincoln's interest in, 4, 67, 241n22; sound in plays of, 222; transcendence of ordinary experience in, 185; Wilder on Victorian performances of, 129
—WORKS: *Henry IV, Part I,* 69; *King Lear,* 69; *Othello,* 95, 182; *Richard III,* 71; *Romeo and Juliet,* 35, 159; see also *Macbeth*
Sheridan, General Philip, 256n34
Sherman, General William Tecumseh, 21–22
Siddons, Sarah, 210
Simmons, A. B., 142
slaves, 25, 61–62, 84, 99, 165, 258n15; Castle Murray and, 166–68, 170–75, 177, 257n5; fugitive, return of, 15, 119; Greek, sculpture of, 24; Johnson's painting of, 99, *99;* Middleton's play about, 157, 159–60; power and prestige of owners of, 188, 190–193; treatment of, in Baltimore, 162–63
Smith, Bruce, 222; *The Acoustic World of Early Modern England,* 218
Smith, Mark, *Listening to Nineteenth-Century America,* 107
Smith, Peter, 22
Smith, Roberta, 250n51
Smithson, James, 131
Smithsonian Institution, 78, 129–35, 138, 253n99; Board of Regents of, 129; Henry's apartments at, 134, *135;* lecture hall in, 130–32, *131, 132*
Soldier's Home (Washington, D.C.), 69, 78, 180
Sommer, Giorgio, *Plaster Casts of Pompeii Victims,* 43, *44*
sound, 129–33; architecture and, 162, 163, 167–69, 171; of battle, 137–41; in poetry, 106–8; of slavery, 171–72; *see also* acoustic shadows
South Church (Andover, Massachusetts), 194
Southern Literary Messenger, 167
souvenirs, 43, 45–46, 50
Spencer, Herbert, 22
Spot Resolutions (1847), 63, 65, 190
Spotsylvania, Battle of, 212, 214
Staël, Germaine de, 39
stage lighting, 71–72, 74, 123, 128, 133
Stam, Deirdre, 234n54
Stamm, Richard, 253n99
Stanly, Edward, 191, 192
State v. Mann (1830), 191

Stebbins, Emma, 30, 45, 226
Steele, Lieutenant George W., 171
Steers, Edward, *Blood on the Moon,* 87
stereographs, 42–43, 172, 174, 175
Stevens, Wallace, 1–2; "Anecdote of the Jar," 1, 5, 177, 210; "The Idea of Order at Key West," 1
Stillé, Charles J., *History of the United States Sanitary Commission,* 16
Stoddard, William O., 69, 74
Stowe, Harriet Beecher, 166; *Uncle Tom's Cabin,* 167
Strawbridge, Ray, *196, 197, 198,* 199
Strong, D. A., 182, 186
Stuart, J. E. B., 194
Sumner, Charles, 117, 192, 241n25
Sumter, Fort, 115
supernaturalism, 29, 108; telegraphy and photography and, 201, 205
Swift, Mrs. Humphrey H., 231n20

tableaux vivants, 40
Talbot, Penelope, 240n22
Talbot, William H., 240n22
Taylor, Tom, *Our American Cousin,* 14, 22
Taylor, Colonel Walter Herron, 140, 214
Taylor, William, 139
telegraphy, 17, 23, 43, 50, 65, 78, 109, 114, 131, 160, 202; invention of, 18; Lincoln and, 18–19, 60, 62–63, 65, 68, 122, 240n19; as metaphor, 201, 254n17; press use of, 13, 111
Tinker, Charles A., 240n19
Toombs, Robert, 148
Topographical Survey, U.S., 154
Trachtenberg, Alan, 68
transmissive influences, 17, 205
Tremont House (Boston), 19–20
Trowbridge, J. T., 212–15
Turner, Nat, 166
Twain, Mark, 163–64
Tyndall, John, 138–39

Union army, 13, 20, 45, 61, 64, 103, 115, 187, 194–95, 208, 241n29, 244n60; at Bristoe Station, 14, 139, 141, 143, 151, 154, 213; at Bull Run, 46, 139; call for volunteers for, 60; Castle Murray encampment of, 161, *162,* 169, 171–72, *172;* at Chickamauga, 145; medical and humanitarian supplies for, 16; Norfolk occupied by, 60, 62; sanitary conditions of camps of, 102; statistical account at end of war of, 21–22
—UNITS OF: Army of Northern Virginia, 118; Army of the Potomac, 16, 139, 161; First Minnesota Volunteers, 150; First Rhode Island Artillery, 151; Second Corps, 194; Third Missouri Volunteers Regiment, 190; Fifth Corps, 256n34; Sixth Cavalry Regiment, 169; Eighth Michigan Infantry Regiment, 164; Ninth Massachusetts Light Artillery Battery, 140; Twelfth Indiana Infantry Regiment, 171; Twentieth Massachusetts Volunteer Infantry, 143, 254n14; Forty-second New York Infantry Regiment, 143; Seventy-ninth New York Infantry Regiment, 164–65; 108th New York Infantry Regiment, 195; 125th New York Infantry Regiment, 194; 126th New York Infantry Regiment, 194; 154th New York Infantry, 125
Union Hotel (Jonesboro, Illinois), 84, 86
Unitarians, 103
University of North Carolina, 187, 192
Usher, John P., 30

Vallandigham, Clement, 111
Varieties Theatre (Washington, D.C.), 77

Walcker, E. F., 25
Wallack, Lester, Jr., 8, 95–96, 123, 147, 181, 230n3
Ward, Artemis, "Wax Figures vs. Shakespeare," 246–47n3
War Department, U.S., 62
Warren, Emily Chase, 14–15, 156, 159, 232n26, 257n43
Warren, General Gouverneur Kemble, 14, 154–57, 159, 161, 207, 232n26, 256n34, n35, 257n43; *Spanish Peaks . . . Aug. 6, 155; Uniontown, Karo River, 155*

Warren, Leonard, *The Last Man Who Knew Everything,* 132–33
Washington Evening Star, 76
Washington Monument, 217
Watkins, Richard Henry, 150
Watts, James W., 84, 245n73; comet of Donati, *85*
Waud, Alfred, 151, 153; *Battle of Bristoe Station, 152*
Webster, Daniel, 20, 119
Weir, John Ferguson, *The Gun Foundry,* 156
Westminster Abbey (London), 42
West Point, U.S. Military Academy at, 154
West Point Iron and Cannon Foundry, 156
Whately, Thomas, *Observations on Modern Gardening,* 210
Whig Party, 61, 64, 190
Whistler, James McNeill, 112
White, Horace, 84
White House (Washington, D.C.), 13, 62, 69, 70, 87, 92, 126, 128
White Oak Road, Battle of, 256n34
Whitman, Walt, 3, 6, 13, 87, 123–29, 183; "Bivouac on a Mountain-Side," 126; "Cavalry Crossing a Ford," 126; "Come Up from the Fields Father," 128; *Drum-Taps,* 126–27; "Vigil Strange I Kept on the Field One Night," 127; "When Lilacs Last in the Dooryard Bloom'd," 127
Whitney, Henry C., 65
Whittier, John Greenleaf, "Massachusetts to Virginia," 15, 166
Whittredge, Worthington: *Interior of the Bedroom of Thomas Whitredge,* 112–15, *113,* 124, 134, 250n51, n53; *The Old Hunting Ground,* 250n51
Wide Awakes, *75,* 75–76, 80, 82
Wilber, Oscar F., 125
Wilder, Thornton, 129
Wilderness Battlefield, 215, *216,* 217, 219–21, *220*
Willard's Hotel (Washington, D.C.), 13, 101–7
Wills, Garry, 68
Winter, William, 10, 31, 35, 36, 231n20
Winthrop, Theodore, 115; *Cecil Dreeme,* 114–15, 221
Wordsworth, William, *Prelude,* 244n60
World War II, 92, 127
Wright, David, 60–63, 65, 240n22
Wright, Minton, 61, 65

Young Mr. Lincoln (movie), 70–71, *71*

Text: 11.25/13.5 Adobe Garamond
Display: Adobe Garamond
Compositor: Integrated Composition Systems
Printer: Thomson-Shore